The Economic Crisis Reader

The
Economic Crisis
Reader

UNDERSTANDING DEPRESSION,
INFLATION, UNEMPLOYMENT, ENERGY,
FOOD, WAGE-PRICE CONTROLS,
AND OTHER DISORDERS OF AMERICAN
AND WORLD CAPITALISM

Edited by David Mermelstein

VINTAGE BOOKS

A Division of Random House, New York

VINTAGE BOOKS EDITION May 1975
FIRST EDITION

Library of Congress Cataloging in Publication Data
Main entry under title:

The Economic crisis reader.

  Bibliography: p.
  1. Economic history—1945–   —Addresses, essays, lectures. I. Mermelstein, David, 1933–
HC59.E363   330.9′047   75–11983
ISBN 0–394–71614–0

Grateful acknowledgment is made to the following for permission to reprint previously published material:

American Association for the Advancement of Slavic Studies: "A Soviet View of the Crisis," by N. Inozemtsev, excerpted from "Capitalism's Current Crisis Analyzed," reprinted with extensive deletions from Vol. XXVI:33, *The Current Digest of the Soviet Press,* published weekly at The Ohio State University. Translation copyright © 1974 by *The Current Digest of the Soviet Press.*

Beacon Press: "The Soviet Union, China, and the Capitalist Crisis," excerpted from pages 150–51, 152, 153–54, 155–56, 158, 159–60, 161, 172–73, 174–75, and 176–77, originally titled "The Soviet Bloc, China, and the Capitalist Crisis," reprinted from *America and the Crisis of World Capitalism,* by Joyce Kolko. Copyright © 1974 by Joyce Kolko.

Business Week: "The Debt Economy and the Options Ahead," by the editorial staff of *Business Week* and John Carson-Parker, reprinted from pages 45–50 and 120–123 of the October 12, 1974, issue. Copyright © 1974 by McGraw-Hill, Inc. Also for "A Japanese Giant in Trou-

from "Solidarity on the Embarcadero," reprinted from *Labor's Untold Story*, by Richard Boyer and Herbert Morais.

United Front Press: "The 'Energy Crisis' and the Real Crisis Behind It," excerpted from a booklet by the same title by Dave Pugh and Mitch Zimmerman.

The Wall Street Journal: "Wages, Productivity and Profits," by Alfred Malabre, excerpted from his article "A Day's Work" (October 31, 1974); "How a World Depression Just Might Happen," by Lindley M. Clark, excerpted from his article "World Depression?" (November 7, 1974); "Chaos Italian Style," by Ray Vicker, excerpted from his article by the same title (November 25, 1974); "The Meat Market: Free or Rigged?," by Jonathan Kwitny, excerpted from his article "Keeping Score" (December 6, 1974); "The Sugar Saga of '74," from an article originally titled "The Sugar Saga: Price Surge Is Running Out of Steam as Users Cut Back Consumption" (November 26, 1974). All articles Copyright © 1974 by Dow Jones & Company, Inc.

The Washington Monthly: "Why Price Controls Stopped Working," excerpted from an article by Robert Samuelson. Copyright © 1974 by The Washington Monthly Company, 1028 Conn. Ave., N.W. Washington, D.C.

The editor wishes to thank the following individuals for their selections which are being published in this volume for the first time:

Mr. Roger Alcaly for "The Relevance of Marxian Crisis Theory"

Mr. Richard C. Edwards for "The Impact of Industrial Concentration on the Economic Crisis"

Mr. David Gold for "James O'Connor's *The Fiscal Crisis of the State:* An Overview"

Mr. David M. Gordon for "Capital vs. Labor—The Current Crisis in the Sphere of Production"

Mr. Richard H. Levy for "The Crisis as Transformation"

Mr. Arthur MacEwan for "Changes in World Capitalism and the Current Crisis of the U.S. Economy"

Mr. William K. Tabb for "Capitalist State Planning Is Not Socialism"

Mr. Stephen W. Welch for " 'Zapping' Labor: A Radical Perspective on Wage-Price Controls"

Mr. Robert Zevin for "The Political Economy of the American Empire, December 1974"

Preface

MOST AMERICANS DO NOT READ the business press, such as the *Wall Street Journal* and *Business Week,* or even the financial pages of the *New York Times.* Were they to do so, they would be even more frightened than they already are. These journals soberly assess the possibilities of war, depression and the eradication of democratic institutions. There can be no mistake about it: we are in the early stages of a world crisis of historic dimensions. All we know for sure is that hard times loom ahead for the vast majority of the American people. The latter can no longer expect to enjoy yearly increases in their standard of living. To the contrary, families will consider themselves lucky if they avoid falling behind. Secondly, we can be certain that vast changes will occur in the way capitalism works, assuming it will survive at all the shocks to which it will be subject. If a precedent for social upheaval exists, it is the decade which followed 1929. Who expected then the development of the CIO and the sit-down strikes at Flint; the innumerable alphabet agencies—NRA, WPA, TVA —associated with Roosevelt's New Deal; the ravages of the dust bowl and the migrations of Okies looking for work (immortalized in Steinbeck's *Grapes of Wrath*); 25% unemployment, unprecedented peacetime government deficits, vast numbers of bank failures and farm foreclosures; and so much more? Nor can *we* know now—any more than *they* could then—*the specifics* of what is in store for us. The immediate picture is bleak indeed.

They *were* warnings that all was not right but most people, lulled by what they assumed was an endless prosperity, chose to shut their ears to the Cassandras of the 1960's. This book is an attempt to explain the economic crisis to a distressed public, one that has been falsely reassured year after year that our economy was basically sound. Unfortunately, there are no pat answers to the crisis that besets us, no equivalent of Dr. Reuben's book on sex that supposedly tells us all we need to know, even when we are not afraid to ask. It is not that there is a dearth of data. Facts bounce at us daily from our television sets, and the written press is replete with statistics, descriptive commentary and official pronouncements. But "facts" standing alone mean nothing. Unless organized in a meaningful framework, disparate facts simply add to our sense of foreboding. Nor are we reassured by those considered to be experts. The recent summit circuses show that professional economists have little to offer. One is sadly reminded of a parallel, the total irrelevance in the depths of the Great Depression of orthodox economic theory, whose central message was that depressions were a theoretical impossibility!

This is not the place to explore at length the considerable shortcomings—oh, why not say it, bankruptcy—of orthodox economics. Suffice it to say that the Samuelsons, Burnses, Mc-Crackens, Hellers, Friedmans and Tobins were totally unprepared for the bursting of the postwar boom. Since clearly they do not lack in IQ, their failures—and those of orthodox economics in general—must ultimately lie in the inappropriateness of their coordinating framework, or if you prefer, in the irrelevance of their economic paradigm. In short, orthodox economics, built as it is on a competitive model which assumes harmonious class interests and which has a national focus, is ill suited for the real capitalist world of monopoly, multinational corporations, and political manipulation of national and world economies.

But if it is one thing to say that there are no pat answers, it is wrong to say that there are no answers at all. This book attempts to bring to the reader's attention the relevant facts and it does so within a framework that differs completely from what one is likely to read in the popular press. These facts are analyzed from the point of view that the problem is *capitalism,* roughly defined as a socioeconomic system in which a relative handful own and control the means of production and operate them in the interests of profit. Along with ownership comes the power to make key decisions that affect our fate. Can there be any doubt that the Mellons, DuPonts, and the biggest enchiladas of them all, the Rockefellers, use their power to serve their individual and class interests which seldom coincide with the interests of the rest of us?

This is not to say that this is a book about alternatives to capitalism. It is not. It is a compendium of descriptive and analytical articles that attempt to explain how we got into this mess and what lies ahead. In the long run, however, assuming our survival, lasting solutions to the crisis are not to be found in more honest capitalist governments or in the never-never world of laissez-faire or in "nuking" the Arabs or even in a reconstituted world capitalist order organized by powerful multinational corporations. Call it what you will, and socialism seems the most appropriate term, the answer lies in a system of production in which our resources and factories, our mines and our land—in a word, our productive capacity—are owned by all collectively and used to enhance our well-being. Until such time, individuals may seek *personal* solutions—an economic equivalent of a fall-out shelter where, rifle in hand, one preserves one's own life at the expense of one's neighbor's. But only a *political* solution of the kind just alluded to, involving the vast majority, which has no real stake in the perpetuation of an irrational system of boom and bust, can create the social institutions that bring out the best that resides in the human spirit and not our most perverse instincts.

Two brief additional comments. First, events being as unexpected as they sometimes are, we are often forced to modify our analysis in the light of what has happened. At the end of the book is a short bibliography. It lists among other entries a number of sources where current critiques are often available. I would also recommend that groups in need of a speaker contact the Union for Radical Political Economics (URPE). Under its auspices, a large number of teach-ins and teach-outs have been held during the fall of 1974 and the spring of '75. Finally, some readers may be disappointed that there is no appended list of meaningful actions that people can engage in. Unfortunately, no such list exists. I am convinced, though, that as the crisis unfolds, there will be no shortage of proposals for actions. But I am also convinced that without a better understanding of the crisis, protests will ultimately come to naught. Even worse, a desperate but misguided people may be manipulated into disastrous "solutions" of a fascistic nature. For this reason, learning, I would assert, *is* an action, a vital first step on the road to a successful counter to a system of production in which economic crises are inevitable.

David Mermelstein
Polytechnic Institute of New York
January 1975

Acknowledgments

IT WOULD BE DIFFICULT to list everyone who offered aid in the preparation of this book. At a recent URPE conference in Amherst, Massachusetts, I fear I may have pestered legions of participants in an effort to solicit suggestions. I thank one and all. I am especially grateful to Jim Crotty, Ray Franklin, Louis Menashe, Leonard Rodberg and Bill Tabb for helping in various ways, and most of all to Roger Alcaly.

I also want to thank each of the following: Cindy Hounsell, Ruth Indeck, Julie Mermelstein, Neil Mullen, Wendy Siegal, Lila Waldman and Batya Weinbaum, but especially Jules Lobel. His aid in putting together Part I was invaluable. None of the above is to be held responsible for any errors or shortcomings that are to be found. Finally, my deep and growing love to Cindy, to whom this book is dedicated, whose lavish unselfish assistance was far exceeded by the value of her good cheer, loving affection, and rare and extraordinary thoughtfulness and consideration.

Contents

Part II. An Analysis of the Crisis

Part III. Corporate-Government Intervention and the Future of Capitalism

I
BACKGROUND TO
THE ECONOMIC CRISIS
OF THE 1970's

Introduction

WITH THE PRESS expanding its sales by publicizing one grim statistic after another, it is unlikely that the average American will mistake the prime rate for a choice cut at his or her favorite butcher. But more informed or not, it is also true that most people are gun-shy about the field of economics and approach it with a good deal of trepidation. In part, professional economists have preferred it that way and have developed an esoteric terminology that puts off all but the bravest. Then, too, those who have been to college have had to wrestle with endless geometric diagrams and the complex and typically irrelevant abstractions found in postwar texts. But there is also an authentic reason for uneasiness and confusion. Economics *is* complicated. Everything appears to depend on everything else and "answers" invariably have an ephemeral or tentative quality to them.

Nonetheless, there is no reason why a basic understanding of the crisis must elude anyone who really wants to know what is going on. One aim of this book is to avoid the pitfalls which have caused so many to throw up their hands and leave economics to the so-called experts. For this reason, the opening section attempts to ease one gently into a discussion of the issues. There is first of all a chronology of the major economic developments since 1929. A number of uncomplicated graphs follow, each throwing rays of light on one or another of the dark corners of the troubled world economy. Some show events or relationships that are discussed in later sections, while others are more in the nature of interesting miscellanea which round out one's understanding.

Most people are acutely aware of the consumer price index and the rate of unemployment. How in this age could one *not* know of these key indicators of economic distress! But it is

3

doubtful that many know where these figures come from or what to make of their reliability. Section C is devoted to these and other related questions. Finally, since lurking about in the minds of many is the fearful question of depression—indeed, the media have almost made the Great Depression into a commodity—a final section presents material contrasting the 1930's with today. None of the foregoing is meant to be more than an introductory overview to the contemporary crisis. But it is hoped that it will put the reader of this volume more at ease as he or she goes on to tackle the more analytical material in the sections which follow.

A.
The Crisis in Historical Perspective: An Economic Chronology

Sept. 1929—One month before the stock market crash, in a period of prosperity, 60% of Americans have incomes of less than $2,000, then estimated to be the bare minimum needed to supply the basic necessities of life.

Oct. 1929—Panic on Wall Street as 16 million shares are dumped on the market on October 29, 1929, by desperate stockholders. Almost $30 billion in paper value is wiped out by November 13.

June 17, 1930—President Hoover signs the Hawley-Smoot Tariff Act, raising duties prohibitively on 890 articles. This tariff helps set off a wave of economic nationalism leading to a breakdown in international trade.

Dec. 11, 1930—Bank of U.S. in New York folds; 400,000 depositors left stranded. During 1932 alone, more than 1,400 banks failed, an average of 4 a day.

June 20, 1931—Hoover proposes an international moratorium on war reparations and debts.

May 1931—Failure of Austria's most powerful bank, Credit Anstalt, sets off a crisis in Austria and Germany.

Sept. 1931—England goes off the gold standard.

Feb. 2, 1932—Reconstruction Finance Corp. established with more than $2 billion at its disposal to advance loans to fail-

ing banks, farm mortgage associations, building and loan societies, railroads and insurance companies.

1933—Unemployment reaches 13 million with 25% of the labor force out of work. Wages are 40% less than in 1929.
Production stands at half the maximum 1929 volume.

March 4, 1933—Franklin Roosevelt takes office. Start of the
famous first "100 days," when in rapid succession measures
such as the National Bank Holiday, the Gold Repeal Joint
Resolution (abandoning the gold standard), the Agricultural
Adjustment Act (AAA), Tennessee Valley Authority (TVA),
Civilian Conservation Corps (CCC), Federal Deposit Insur-
ance Corp. (FDIC) and the National Industrial Recovery
Act (NIRA) are enacted to try to alleviate the Depression.

1934—Severest drought in seventy-five years hits the Great
Plains, reducing crops by as much as a third.

1934—Unemployment starts to drop, reaching a low of 14%
in 1937.

July 16, 1934—General strike takes place in San Francisco.

1935—Roosevelt signs the Wagner Act, giving the workers the
right of self-organization, and the Social Security Act.

Nov. 9, 1935—Congress of Industrial Organizations (CIO) is
formed. In January 1937 CIO auto workers engage in a sit-
down strike against GM in Flint, Michigan. On February 3,
GM agrees to recognize the UAW and to negotiate a union
contract. By May 1937, the government estimates that half
a million workers had engaged in sit-down strikes since 1936.

1936—John Maynard Keynes's *The General Theory of Employment, Interest and Money* is published. It provides the
theoretical underpinnings for postwar monetary and fiscal
policies.

Aug. 1937—A new business recession sets in. By 1938, 19%
of the labor force is unemployed, despite New Deal measures.

Dec. 8, 1941—United States enters World War II. Federal expenditures rise from $12.8 billion in fiscal 1941 to about
$100 billion in 1945. Federal debt rises from $49 billion in
1941 to $259 billion in 1945. Unemployment drops from
16.5% in 1939 to 1.2% in 1944.

1942—Wage and price controls and rent ceilings are put into
effect. Nationwide gas rationing starts in September 1942.

Shoes, meats, fats, cheese and canned goods are among the items rationed. AFL and CIO agree not to strike during the war.

July 1–22, 1944—Conference held in Bretton Woods, New Hampshire, setting up the postwar international monetary system, which survives until 1971.

1945–1960

Feb. 20, 1946—President Truman signs the Employment Act of 1946, the objectives of which are "to promote maximum employment, production and purchasing power."

Nov. 9, 1946—All World War II wage and price controls end, except on rents, sugar and rice.

1946—Inflation runs rampant. Consumer price index rises 23% from mid-1946 to mid-1947, paced by a 40% rise in retail food prices.

1946—Highest strike wave in the postwar period. Number of man-days lost through strikes soars from 38 million in 1945 to 116 million in 1946.

June 5, 1947—U.S. Secretary of State, George C. Marshall, proposes a plan for economic aid to Europe. The "Marshall Plan," enacted the following year, provides a first-year sum of $5.3 billion for European recovery.

June 23, 1947—Taft-Hartley Act passed over President Truman's veto. It reduces or eliminates many labor-union advantages provided by the Wagner Act.

1948–1949—First postwar recession. Unemployment rises from a low of 3.4% in 1948 to a peak of over 6% early in 1950. Consumer prices fall 1.6% from December 1945 to November 1949. The federal budget falls to a post–World War II low of $33 billion in 1948, down from almost $100 billion in 1945.

Jan. 24, 1950—Minimum wage is raised to 75 cents an hour.

June 25, 1950—Korean War begins. Business on upswing. Military spending increases from $13 billion in 1950 to $44 billion in 1952. Unemployment falls to a low of 2.9% in 1953.

Jan. 26, 1951—Wage and price freeze announced. In February, organized labor withdraws from Wage and Price Control Boards in protest of pro-business bias. Consumer prices rise 11% between June 1950 and November 1951.

March 17, 1953—Price controls officially ended (wage controls having already been lifted the previous month).

1953–1954—Mild economic recession lasting thirteen months. GNP drops 4% between the second quarter of 1953 and 1954. Unemployment rises to a peak of 5.8%. Consumer prices remain stable, while interest rates fall.

Dec. 5, 1955—AFL and CIO merge, ending twenty years of conflict.

1954–1957—Period of economic expansion. GNP grows to exceed $400 billion in 1956. In 1957, Federal Reserve Board discount rate reaches 3½%, which at the time represents a postwar peak. Also, that same year there are fewer strikes than in any year since World War II.

Mid-1957–1958—Severest postwar recession. Unemployment reaches a seasonally adjusted peak of 7.5% in April 1958. Total industrial production drops 13%. Consumer price index, however, continues to rise slowly.

Oct. 4, 1957—Soviet Union launches Sputnik I, the first earth satellite.

1958—Balance-of-payments problems begin to attract attention as U.S. deficit exceeds $3 billion.

July 15, 1959—116-day steel strike begins, longest in U.S. history.

1960–1961—Expansion of economic activity that had begun in 1958 ended in the first half of 1960. Fourth postwar recession gets under way. By December 1960, unemployment rate shoots back up to 6.8%.

1961–1970

Feb. 1961—Recession "bottoms out" and economic recovery proceeds steadily, fueled by easy fiscal and monetary policy of Kennedy Administration. The longest post–World War II period without a recession follows, lasting from 1961 to 1970.

Feb 6–7, 1961—GE and Westinghouse found guilty of price fixing and bid rigging by U.S. District Judge Ganey. Penalties exacted included thirty jail sentences (twenty-three of which were suspended) and nearly $23 million in fines.

1962—Rachel Carson writes best-selling book, *Silent Spring,* anticipating the growing concern over environmental problems.

March 1, 1962—Biggest antitrust case in history. Du Pont ordered to divest itself of 63 million shares of GM stock.

April 10, 1962—Major steel companies, including U.S. Steel, announce big price hike in spite of "responsible" union settlement. Kennedy reacts angrily, forcing temporary rescinding of increase. Prices are raised again in 1963.

May 25, 1962—George Meany, president of AFL-CIO, announces nationwide campaign to cut workweek to 35 hours to counter loss of jobs through automation.

Aug. 28, 1962—Congress passes 7% investment credit, a tax cut for business.

Oct. 4, 1962—In a move to increase the world market for U.S. goods, Congress passes the Trade-Expansion Act, giving the President more authority to reduce tariffs. Competition from Germany and Japan becoming a major worry.

June 10, 1963—Rapidly growing employment of women reaches 23 million. Kennedy signs a bill for equal pay for equal work for women.

July 18, 1963—Special presidential message to Congress on the growing balance-of-payments problem. Treasury to raise short-term interest rates to slow capital outflow.

Aug. 5, 1963—Test-ban treaty signed, indicating a receding of the cold war, foreshadowing the era of détente.

Aug. 28, 1963—Martin Luther King, Jr., leads 200,000 people on a March on Washington demanding jobs and freedom for blacks.

Oct. 16, 1963—AT&T completes its third and longest trans-Atlantic cable, future expansion to be by use of satellite. By early 1964, U.S. foreign investments have quadrupled since 1950.

Feb. 26, 1964—Massive tax cut passed. Designed to stimulate the economy. Considered to be Keynesian economics' finest hour.

March 16, 1964—President Johnson calls for full-scale "War on Poverty."

June 14, 1964—U.S. Steel workers and eleven companies sign pact to encourage equal opportunity in steel industry. In spite of the pact, ten years later, black leaders are to denounce discriminatory policies in the steel industry.

July 1, 1964—California becomes the most populous state in

the United States, surpassing New York. Reflection of rapid industrial development.

Aug. 11, 1964—Economic Opportunity Act passed, creates Domestic Peace Corps, work training, etc.

Jan. 4, 1965—President Johnson, in State of Union address, promises a "Great Society."

Feb. 7, 1965—Prolonged U.S. air strikes begin against North Vietnam. First acknowledged U.S. ground troops are sent to Vietnam in March. U.S. troop build-up in Vietnam to reach a peak of 550,000. Total government spending increases rapidly, going over $100 billion by 1966. Total U.S. cost of Vietnam war from 1965 to 1971 alone is estimated at $120 billion.

March 4, 1965—25% gold backing of bank reserves at Fed eliminated as U.S. gold supply continues to fall.

April 28, 1965—Approximately 25,000 U.S. marines sent to the Dominican Republic to "stop Communism."

Aug. 14–16, 1965—$200 million in property damaged and thirty-five killed in Watts riot.

Nov. 9–10, 1965—Massive power failure blacks out most of the Northeast.

Jan. 24, 1966—In proposing a record budget, President Johnson admits that the necessity of appropriating funds for "our increased commitments in Vietnam" has hindered the advancement of the "Great Society."

Feb. 5, 1966—U.S. announces it will sell 200 tanks to Israel. It has already supplied similar tanks to Jordan.

April 27, 1966—After four years of hearings, ICC approves merger of NY Central and Pennsylvania RR, to form Penn Central Railroad, which will haul ⅛ of total U.S. rail freight. Biggest merger in U.S. history. In 1960's there is a wave of business mergers, many creating giant conglomerates.

Aug. 1966—Crunch puts money markets in near crisis.

Aug. 22, 1966—Consumer price index hits record high; 1966 is the most inflationary year since 1957. From 1961 to 1965, prices rose 1–2% a year; in 1966, 3.3%. Unemployment falls below 4% for the first time since 1953.

Sept. 9, 1966—Congress passes Traffic Safety and Highway Safety Acts. Former a result of a Ralph Nader book, *Unsafe at Any Speed*. By 1966 there are 78 million cars, which travel

10 billion miles a year. The number of auto deaths since 1900 is three times as great as all deaths in U.S. wars.

Sept. 23, 1966—President Johnson signs bill extending to farm workers the protection of the minimum wage. Minimum wage for industry is raised to $1.60.

Oct. 7, 1966—Congress approves $55 billion defense budget.

1967—Major strikes in auto and copper industries send work time lost due to strikes to highest levels since 1959.

May 11, 1967—100-millionth telephone installed in the United States, approximately one half of all the phones in the world.

June–Sept. 1967—Ghetto riots occur in more than a hundred cities. Over $200 million in property damage and forty-three people killed in Detroit riot alone.

June 1967—Six-day Mideast war. Suez Canal is closed.

June 30, 1967—United States and forty-five nations sign GATT (General Agreements on Trade and Tariff) in Kennedy Round talks.

Sept. 29, 1967—IMF and World Bank approve a plan to increase the world money supply by creating an international monetary reserve, later to be known as SDRs or Special Drawing Rights. Reflection of growing economic troubles and growing instability in the international money markets.

Nov. 20, 1967—U.S. population reaches 200 million.

1968—Highest federal budget deficit since 1945.

Jan. 1, 1968—President Johnson imposes mandatory restrictions on most direct investments overseas in order to curb outflow of dollars.

Jan. 18, 1968—President Johnson asks for legislation eliminating the requirement that 25% of U.S. currency be backed by gold.

March 19, 1968—London gold market closed at the request of the United States to halt heavy trading in gold. International financial crisis is intensified.

May 17, 1968—United States and European countries work out two-price system of gold, whereby gold transactions between governments are held at $35/ounce, while those in the private market are allowed to fluctuate. The United States hopes this will slow gold drain out of the country.

July 1968—Congress enacts President Johnson's 10% income-tax surcharge.

Sept. 1968—Three-week New York teacher strike. A sign of the growing militancy of state and municipal employees.

Nov. 20, 1968—Seventy-eight coal miners killed in Farmingham, West Virginia, as a result of a mine explosion. Sets off a call for increased mine-safety legislation.

Jan. 21, 1969—Government report issued showing hunger and malnutrition widespread in the United States.

Feb. 8, 1969—Oil spill off Santa Barbara. Over forty miles of beaches destroyed.

June 1969—Prime interest rate rises to 8½%.

Sept. 10, 1969—Alaska receives bids of more than $100 million for North Slope oil leases.

Sept. 23, 1969—Secretary of Labor George Shultz orders Philadelphia Plan put into effect setting up guidelines for minority hiring in the construction industry.

Oct. 27, 1969—150,000 GE workers strike.

Dec. 1969—Inflation growing rapidly. CPI up 6.1%, highest increase since 1947.

Dec. 22, 1969—Tax surcharge reduced to 5%. Liberals push through a reduction of the oil-depletion allowance from 27½% to 22%.

Late 1969—Recession. Unemployment rises to just over 6% by the end of 1970. Interest rates are falling from high of 8½% in February to 6¾% by December. Rate of inflation decreases slightly.

1970—Congress passes legislation authorizing the President to freeze wages and prices. Nixon signs bill but says he will not use it.

March 1970—Postal workers strike for first time in U.S. history.

May 1970—Invasion of Cambodia touches off massive and sustained antiwar protests.

May 1970—Arthur Burns, chairman of Federal Reserve Board, breaks with Nixon Administration and calls for wage and price controls.

May 1970—Dow-Jones falls to 631.16, its lowest point in seven years.

June 1970—Penn-Central files for bankruptcy, as fears of increasing corporate bankruptcies mount.

Sept. 1970—GM auto workers walk out, beginning a sixty-seven-day strike.

Sept. 1970—Wall Street brokerage houses in financial crisis. President of Stock Exchange predicts fifty brokerage houses will disappear in next six months.

1971–1974

1971—Balance-of-payments problem mounts. In 1949 the United States held $23.4 billion in gold; by 1971 it holds only $10.1 billion in gold.

1971—The U.S. economy remains stagnant. Unemployment is hovering around 6%.

1971—U.S. imports of goods exceed exports for the first time since 1888.

March 1971—Interest rates continue to fall, reaching a low in March. Falling interest rates, relative to Europe, increase dollar outflow and help deepen balance-of-payments problems.

June 10, 1971—Nixon announces end of twenty-one-year embargo on trade with China.

July 1971—Budget shows a near-record $23 billion deficit.

Aug. 2, 1971—Legislation providing a $250 million loan to Lockheed narrowly passed by Congress.

Aug. 15, 1971—President Nixon announces a New Economic Program, including a ninety-day wage and price freeze, budget cuts and a temporary 10% surcharge on imports. Furthermore, he announces that the United States would no longer convert foreign-held dollars into gold, essentially terminating the world monetary system created at Bretton Woods.

Sept. 30, 1971—Treasury Secretary John Connally tells the IMF annual meeting that the United States would remove the import surcharge if other countries would relieve barriers to trade and allow their currencies to float freely.

Oct. 13, 1971—Pay Board created. Contains five industry, five labor and five public spokesmen.

Nov. 14, 1971—Phase II goes into effect. Limits wage increases to 5.5% and price increases to 2.5%.

Dec. 11, 1971—EEC Council of Ministers says it will not negotiate trade concessions until after the U.S. dollar has been devalued and currencies realigned.

Dec. 18, 1971—Dollar is devalued by 8.57%. First dollar devaluation since 1934. Two days later, as part of the devaluation agreement, the United States rescinds the 10% import surcharge.

Jan. 1972—Nixon's 1972 budget has deficit of $25 billion, unprecedented except during World War II.

Feb. 1972—Gold price rises to almost $50/ounce in London and Zurich markets. European central banks intervene to support the dollar.

Feb. 21, 1972—Nixon visits China.

March 1972—Four Labor representatives walk out of Pay Board saying it offers "no hope for fairness, equality or justice." Only Fitzsimmons, Teamsters leader, remains on Board. Nixon reorganizes the Pay Board.

May 6, 1972—Japanese and European steel producers agree to limit exports to the United States for three years.

June 1, 1972—Iraq nationalizes Western-owned Iraq Petroleum Co., an indication of future events.

June 23, 1972—Britain floats pound.

July 1972—England enters Common Market.

July 8, 1972—President Nixon announces historic Soviet wheat deal, whereby USSR would purchase $750 million worth of wheat.

July 1972—GM reports highest three-month profit ever reported by a U.S. company.

Aug. 1972—Gold reaches a new high of $70/ounce.

Sept. 11, 1972—China buys ten Boeing 707 jets for $150 million.

Nov. 6, 1972—England announces ninety-day freeze on wages and prices.

Jan. 11, 1973—Phase III begins—providing for "self-administrating" wage-price guidelines.

Jan. 11, 1973—Dow-Jones average hits record high at 1051.70.

Jan. 1973—Iran tells Western oil consortium that it will not renew its contract under the existing terms.

Feb. 1973—Dollar is devalued by more than 10%, the second devaluation in fourteen months, raising the price of gold from $38 to $42.22/ounce.

March 1973—Six Common Market countries jointly float their currencies.

March 2, 1973—Foreign exchange markets close in London,

Brussels, Frankfurt, Amsterdam, Vienna and Tokyo, in the face of a new international monetary crisis.

April 7, 1973—Consumers hold a one-week meat boycott.

April 1973—Steelworkers' union signs a no-strike agreement to 1977.

June 7, 1973—U.S. Labor Department announces that the wholesale price index rose 2% seasonally adjusted in May, a peacetime high.

June 13, 1973—Phase III½, a sixty-day freeze of all prices except unprocessed agricultural products and rents, at June levels.

July 18, 1973—Price restrictions lifted on all foods, except beef.

Aug. 14, 1973—Phase IV goes into effect.

Aug. 1973—Wheat prices rise to over $5/bushel from the low of $1.60/bushel that existed before Soviet wheat deal.

Sept. 1973—Libya takes over 51% of major oil companies operating in Libya, raises its price from $1/barrel to $6 and threatens shutdown of oil fields if Western oil companies boycott Libyan oil.

Sept. 1973—A record 11.8 million '73-model cars sold. Prices raised on '74 models.

Oct. 16, 1973—New Mideast war breaks out. Saudi Arabia cuts production 10%. Arab states cut all oil shipments to the United States. Persian Gulf oil producers announce largest price hike in history & boycott of Europe.

Oct. 18, 1973—U.S. National Bank of San Diego collapses.

Nov. 1973—Airline flights cut and employees laid off due to energy crisis.

Nov. 1973—Nixon signs Alaska Pipeline Bill.

Nov. 19, 1973—Senate passes Emergency Energy Act, which includes a provision enacting year-round daylight saving time.

Nov. 25, 1973—President Nixon orders a 15% nationwide reduction in gas deliveries to wholesalers and retailers, and a speed limit reduction to 50 m.p.h.

Dec. 1, 1973—Federal Energy Office created. William Simon, its head, asks for voluntary ten-gallons-a-week rationing. GM lays off workers in order to convert to small cars.

Dec. 4–7, 1973—Truckdrivers blockade highway in protest of rising fuel prices.

Dec. 15, 1973—EEC summit ends in a nine-nation agreement to face the oil crisis together and a call for Israel to withdraw from Arab territories held since '67 war.

Dec. 19, 1973—Cost of Living Council allows oil industry to raise prices.

Dec. 22, 1973—Japanese declare Economic Emergency and Tanaka puts an "austerity" budget into effect for 1974.

Dec. 25, 1973—Arab oil producers announce 10% increase in production instead of a 5% cut. More oil to be shipped to Europe and Japan. Embargo on the United States continues. Persian Gulf producers raise prices from $5.11 to $11.65 a barrel.

Jan. 1, 1974—England goes on three-day workweek. Coal miners are on strike protesting government's refusal to grant a wage increase. Strike combined with energy crisis forces British government to enforce an emergency three-day week.

Jan. 19, 1974—French float franc in an effort to protect French gold reserve.

Jan. 23, 1974—Oil corporations report huge profits. Exxon announces profits were up 57% over the same period in 1972.

Jan. 23, 1974—Nixon issues Energy message that includes more stringent taxation on foreign profits of oil companies.

Feb. 13, 1974—Oil-consuming nations confer at Washington, D.C., on measures to combat the world energy crisis. French Foreign Minister Jobet accuses the United States of using energy matters as a "pretext" to strengthen its influence in Europe.

Feb. 1974—Libya nationalizes subsidiaries of Texaco, Standard of California and Atlantic Richfield.

Feb. 22, 1974—Sugar prices rise rapidly, 32 cents a pound in one day on London futures market.

March 18, 1974—Arabs lift oil embargo on the United States.

April 1974—Wage-price controls expire.

May 1974—With lifting of price controls, many corporations start raising prices. Copper rises 12 cents a pound. Steel corporations raise prices 5.7–9%.

May 1974—Treasury offers $300 million in bonds paying 8½%, the highest rate since the Civil War.

May 12, 1974—Franklin National Bank announces it had lost

$39 million in foreign currency. Federal Reserve begins to pump in funds to keep the bank solvent.

June 1974—Major banks raise prime rates to 11¾% from March rate of 8½%.

June 26, 1974—Big West German Herstatt bank liquidated, setting off reaction in Western banking circles.

July 17, 1974—Iran acquires 25% interest in Krupp enterprises in West Germany. Big purchase sets off Western concern over Arab use of petrodollars and spurs interest in recycling plans.

Aug. 14, 1974—Bill enacted allowing Americans to buy gold starting December 31.

Aug. 31, 1974—West German Chancellor Helmut Schmidt announces a $2 billion grant to Italy to bail her out of financial crisis.

Aug. 21, 1974—GM agrees to roll back price increases under "jawboning" pressure from President Ford. Its 9.5% increase in prices for '75 models reduced to 8.5%.

Sept. 1974—Unemployment begins sharp rise to 5.8%, up from 5.4% in August.

Sept. 1974—Chase Manhattan Bank reports that profits of largest international oil companies rose 73% in first six months of 1974.

Sept. 20, 1974—August consumer price index rose 1.3%, the largest monthly increase since 1947, with the exception of periods immediately following lifting of price freezes.

Sept. 23, 1974—President Ford and Secretary of State Kissinger in separate speeches issue warnings that continued high oil prices, set by oil-producing nations, imperil the world economy and could lead to a "breakdown of world order and safety."

Oct. 8, 1974—President Ford delivers economic plan for a one-year 5% tax surcharge.

Oct. 8, 1974—Franklin National Bank declared insolvent and sold to the European-American Bank & Trust Co.

Nov. 1974—Unemployment rises steeply, up to 6.5% from 6.0% in October.

Dec. 1974—Layoffs hit auto industry. By January an estimated 300,000 out of 700,000 blue-collar auto workers will be out of work. Unemployment rises to 7.1%.

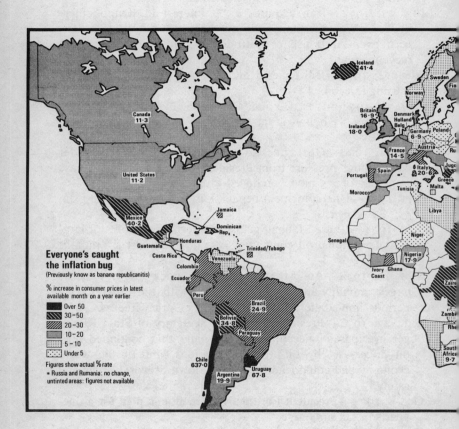

Everyone's caught
the inflation bug
(Previously know as banana republicanitis)

% increase in consumer prices in latest
available month on a year earlier

Over 50
30 – 50
20 – 30
10 – 20
5 – 10
Under 5

Figures show actual % rate
∗ Russia and Rumania: no change,
untinted areas: figures not available

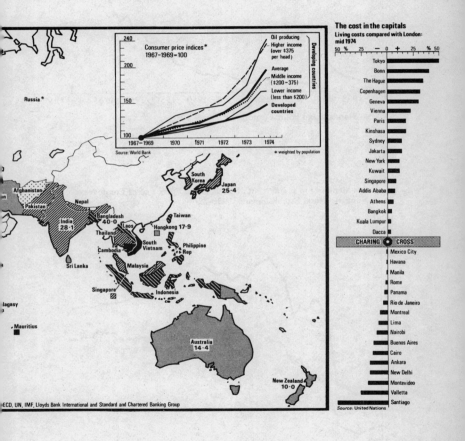

Index of Common Stock Prices (1941-43 = 10)

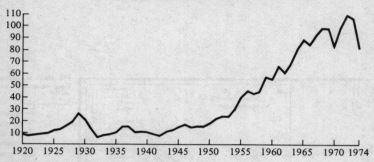

SOURCE: Standard and Poors Corporation

Union Membership as a Percent of Total Labor Force and of Employees in Nonagricultural Establishments, 1930-72[1]

[1]Excludes Canadian membership

SOURCE: U.S. Bureau of Labor Statistics

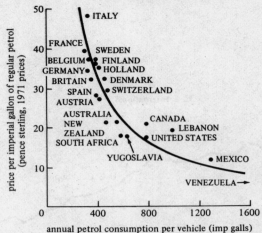

Petrol-pricing works

SOURCE: *Economist*, Nov. 16, 1974

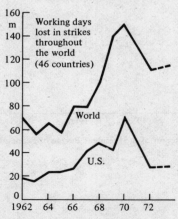

The stormy seventies

SOURCE: *Economist*, Sept. 21, 1974

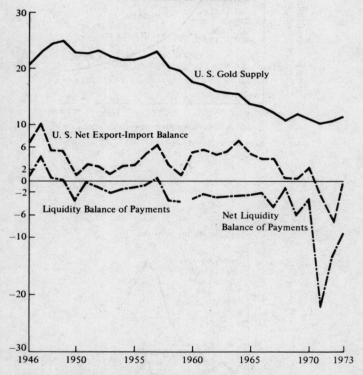

U. S. International Transactions

U. S. Gold Supply

U. S. Net Export-Import Balance

Liquidity Balance of Payments

Net Liquidity
Balance of Payments

SOURCE: Economic Report of the President Bureau of Economic Analysis

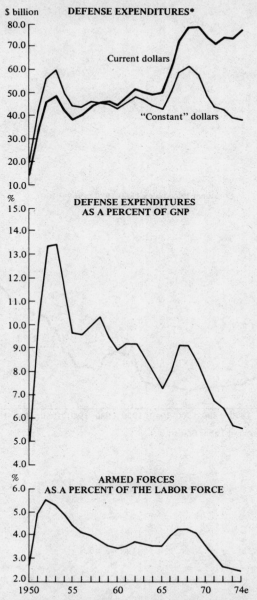

$ billion

DEFENSE EXPENDITURES*

Current dollars

"Constant" dollars

%

**DEFENSE EXPENDITURES
AS A PERCENT OF GNP**

%

**ARMED FORCES
AS A PERCENT OF THE LABOR FORCE**

1950   55   60   65   70   74e

*These are "national defense" expenditures for calendar years as
tabulated in the Commerce Department's national income accounts.
"Constant" dollar defense expenditures are expressed in 1958 dollars.

SOURCE: Morgan-Guaranty Survey

Consumer Price Index 1860-1970 (1967 = 100)

SOURCE: Bureau of Labor Statistics

Unemployment Rates

Unemployment: All Workers

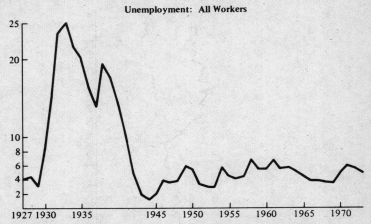

SOURCE: Historical statistics of the U.S. to 1957–Census Bureau Employment and Earnings

Unemployment Rate Up

Unemployment rose in December to a seasonally adjusted rate of 7.1% of the labor force from 6.5% the preceding month, the Labor Department reports.

SOURCE: *Wall Street Journal*, Jan. 6, 1975

26

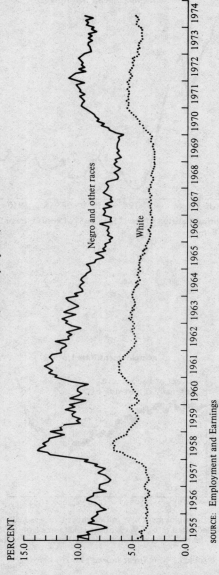

Unemployment rates by color
(Seasonally adjusted)

PERCENT

15.0

10.0

5.0

0.0

Negro and other races

White

1955 1956 1957 1958 1959 1960 1961 1962 1963 1964 1965 1966 1967 1968 1969 1970 1971 1972 1973 1974

SOURCE: Employment and Earnings

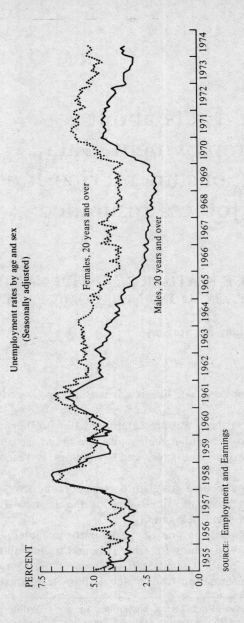

Unemployment rates by age and sex
(Seasonally adjusted)

Females, 20 years and over

Males, 20 years and over

PERCENT

7.5

5.0

2.5

0.0

1955 1956 1957 1958 1959 1960 1961 1962 1963 1964 1965 1966 1967 1968 1969 1970 1971 1972 1973 1974

SOURCE: Employment and Earnings

C.
Basic Facts about Unemployment Data, the Consumer Price Index and Jobless Insurance

1. THOSE STATISTICS ON THE NATION'S UNEMPLOYED DO NOT COME EASILY

by William K. Stevens

Some people do not like it when Billie Jo Tweedy knocks on the door.

To them she is a representative of Big Brother, the long arm of the Government reaching into the house, so she sometimes gets cussed at, she says, and sometimes is "escorted off the property."

But most people are glad to greet her, she says, especially in worsening economic times such as these when they feel they can in some way help out.

Mrs. Tweedy is one of 1,100 part-time interviewers across the country searching for what is bound to add up to bad news. Working for the United States Bureau of the Census, they collect the information from which Labor Department analysts in

From the *New York Times*, November 24, 1974. William K. Stevens is a member of the reporting staff of the *Times*.

Washington will calculate the national unemployment rate for November.

The figure is instrumental in the setting of national policy. It affects the responses of the Government, industry and labor to the economy's behavior. It helps alter the very mood of the country. This month's rate, to be announced on Dec. 6, is sure to be higher than October's 6.0 per cent, and December's figure may well be higher than November's.

The operation involved in deriving the figure, and the subcategories of employment information that accompany it, is said to constitute the largest social-science survey of its type in the world. Gradually developed and refined since it first was performed in the late nineteen-thirties, it is viewed as highly reliable.

It is part of the Census Bureau's routine monthly "current population surveys," or series of interim reports on a wide variety of topics. It costs more than $5-million a year, and makes use of the latest in computer technology.

Unlike the decennial census, the monthly surveys involve interviews with only a scientifically selected sample of the population.

The framework of the sample is what the Census Bureau calls "primary sampling units." These are 461 geographical areas across the country. The largest 170 metropolitan areas are included in it automatically. The remainder are counties or clusters of counties selected because their social and economic make-up is representative of an over-all group of similar areas across the country. Together, the 461 areas contain 75 per cent of the United States population.

Within each area, a sample of households is selected for interview by people like Mrs. Tweedy. Nationally, the sampling rate is roughly one in every 1,400 households for a total sample of about 60,000.

Each month, the groups of households from which the samples are drawn are updated. Because houses are sometimes torn down and new ones built, Census Bureau interviewers visit Building Permit offices and tour the land to see what has changed. New addresses are added and old ones deleted.

The houses to be included in the sample are selected from the updated list in the Census Bureau headquarters at Suitland,

Md. Working from lists of addresses, a selector picks an address randomly. That address and three neighboring households are included in the sample. Then the selector moves 6,400 places down the list and selects four more, and so on until the list is exhausted.

Each address selected is the site of an employment interview four times a year for two years. Each month, one-eighth of the sample is dropped and a one-eighth portion of new households is added.

The selected addresses are conveyed to the 12 regional Census Bureau offices around the country. One is in Detroit, whose region, basically Michigan and Ohio, includes 50 primary sampling units.

That is where people like Mrs. Tweedy come in. Usually housewives who want part-time work, they are given special training in interviewing and recording techniques, then sent out for their first two months of work under the eye of a supervisor.

Mrs. Tweedy's area includes some of the northeastern suburbs of Detroit—Roseville, where she lives, East Detroit, Saint Clair Shores and part of Warren.

The Census Bureau is careful to protect the privacy and identity of its sources.

"We're interviewing households, not people," Mrs. Tweedy explains.

No name appears on the detailed form with its uniform questions that Mrs. Tweedy and the other interviewers use to record findings about employment.

Once the interview starts, the questions are clipped, basic and simple: "What was the head of the household doing most of last week? Working? With a job but not at work? Looking for work?" And so on through about 35 questions or less, depending on the subject's situation.

Halfway through Mrs. Tweedy's list of households this week there emerged one tiny indication of the news that is in store for the public next month. She found one person unemployed in November who had been working in October. Nationwide, that one person would represent about 1,400 workers.

Each day Mrs. Tweedy mails completed questionnaire forms to the regional Census office in downtown Detroit. There they are checked and shipped daily by air to a processing plant at

Jeffersonville, Ind., just outside Louisville, Ky. At Jeffersonville, the questionnaires are coded clerically and reduced to one-word microfilm images smaller than a postage stamp.

The film is shipped, again by air, to Washington. It is picked up at the airport and driven to Census headquarters in Suitland, where a special device called FOSDIC (Film Optical Sensing Device for Input to Computers) scans the film and transfers the information contained there to computer tapes. Census computers separate and classify the information by dozens of categories useful to employment analysts—age, sex, race, schooling, income, occupation.

This month, all the questionnaires must be in Jeffersonville by Tuesday evening and all the microfilm in Suitland by Nov. 29. The completed tabulations will arrive in two large boxes at the Bureau of Labor Statistics on Dec. 2.

Then for four days, bureau analysts will adjust the figures for seasonal influences and prepare the tables to be released to the public.

In the end, they divide the number of unemployed by the total labor force to get the over-all unemployment rate. This is done on a sample basis, not a total one, and therefore provides not an exact figure but an estimate with a built-in error of plus-or-minus two-tenths of 1 per cent.

"That is far, far less an error than you would have on the public-opinion polls," said John Bregger, who supervises the Bureau of Labor Statistics' part of the operation. "It's an incredibly accurate survey."

At 10 A.M., Dec. 6, at the bureau's offices at 441 G Street, N.W., in Washington, the news for November—presumably bad —will be disclosed. Ten days later Mrs. Tweedy and her colleagues will swing into action again.

2. REAL UNEMPLOYMENT IS MUCH HIGHER THAN THEY SAY

by Bertram Gross and Stanley Moss

The concepts of real labor force and labor potential refer to those who would be potentially employable in conditions of peacetime full employment. We are not talking about the potential labor force that may exist during conditions of national mobilization, when all people who are capable of accomplishing any sort of work would be encouraged or compelled to take jobs. The real labor force differs from the national mobilization potential in that it considers only the official labor force plus the millions of others who have tried to get work and are no longer seeking it because they have become discouraged, and also those who could be encouraged to become available if suitable opportunities were presented.

We have been deliberately somewhat conservative in many of our estimates. Both in the literature of labor economics and in the survey and reporting work of the Department of Labor there has always been a recognition and admission of the limitations of the labor force concept and the fact that it understates the dimensions of real unemployment. In fact considerable work has been done to clarify some of the gray areas of understatement—especially as regards to the concept of underemployment and discour-

From *Public Service Employment: An Analysis of Its History, Problems, and Prospects,* edited by Alan Gartner et al. (New York, Praeger, 1973), pp. 30–36. Bertram M. Gross, Distinguished Professor of Urban Affairs and Planning at Hunter College, was the chief draftsman of the Employment Act of 1946 and first executive-secretary of the President's Council of Economic Advisors. Stanley Moss is employed by the Department of Urban Affairs and Planning at Hunter College.

aged workers. We have built upon the research done in both of these areas and have considered them as an example of unemployment that is "officially disclosed but set aside." To this group of 7.1 million we have added our estimates of what percentage of the millions of other persons not in the labor force would desire jobs if suitable opportunities were available. We have divided this group of "hidden and ignored" employables into six major groups—unemployables, housewives, men (25–54), older people (55 and over), students, and enrollees in manpower programs.

Table 3.3 presents a detailed listing and explanation of the various components that are included in our concept of real labor force and real unemployment.

A usual response to data such as presented in Table 3.3 takes the form of the "all right, but so what? What difference does it make?" Here the argument is pursued that we have enough information about the nature of existing inadequacies so as to enable us to focus our attention. It is foolhardy to introduce additional inadequacies, which, in addition to not being the most grievous, are also not addressable in the current political context.

Our response to such a line is twofold. If social reformers do not call attention to and call to account the fraudulence of government assertions, then to whom shall we look for such criticism? Also it must be considered that attention to the needs of the poor, given our current calculus of pressure and power, must result in inadequate attention. To the extent that full employment is enacted as a goal of public policy, but only for the poor who receive welfare, we can be sure that the nature of employment will be undesirable and unsuitable. To the extent that a full employment policy becomes identified with the question of "how many jobs for whom," and is discussed and understood as a question of responding to the needs and abilities of people of all sexes, ages and colors, we may witness the beginning of a political coalition that will be able to mobilize energy and power to attain the types of policies that will meet the needs of all the unemployed—of both the official and real of the poor and other groups in the population.

TABLE 3.3
Real Unemployment in the United States, 1971
(Preliminary Estimates)

CATEGORY	NUMBER (MILLIONS)
Official labor force (incl. armed forces)[a]	85.8
Gainfully employed (incl. armed forces)[b]	81.1
Official unemployment[c]	
Number	4.7
(As percent of civilian labor force)	(5.7%)
Unofficial unemployment[d]	
Disclosed but set aside	
Underemployed[e]	2.7
Job wanters[f]	
Discouraged	0.8
Encourageables	3.6
Hidden and ignored[g]	
Unemployables[h]	1.0
Housewives[i]	5.0
Men (25-54)[j]	0.5
Older people (55 and over)[k]	4.0
Students[l]	3.0
Enrollees in manpower programs[m]	0.3
Subtotal	20.9
Real labor force (official labor force plus unofficial unemployed, excluding underemployed)[n]	104
Real unemployment[o]	
Number	25.6
(As percent of real labor force)	(24.6%)

[a] *Official labor force:* armed forces are included in order to provide perspective on relationships and shifts from military to civilian employment. The institutional population, about two million, is excluded—a questionable omission considering the many jobs held at very low rates of pay by resident population. (*Source: Statistical Abstract of the United States 1971,* Table 327, p. 210.)

[b] *Gainfully employed:* refers solely to jobs involving direct cash payment. It does not include the unpaid work performed either by about 35.4 million persons, mostly women, who are not in the labor force and engaged in "keeping house" or by the millions more who hold paid jobs and also keep house. (*Source: Ibid.*)

[c] *Official unemployment:* based upon official Department of Labor categories, which consider only those persons who do not have a job at the current time, but who are available for work and have conducted an active search for a job

during the four-week period preceding the Current Population Survey. (*Source: Ibid.*)

ᵈ *Unofficial unemployment:* refers to those people who are able and willing to work and would be seeking jobs, either full- or part-time, if suitable opportunities were available. Suitability is a complex matter involving the nature of the work, pay, status, working conditions, and opportunities for personal growth and advancement. The emphasis on part-time relates to the fact that millions of people, especially older people and housewives, who would not be available for full-time jobs would be very available and most eager for part-time employment. Another aspect of suitability relates to the provision of services that would facilitate job holding, such as adequate day care arrangements.

In our consideration of unofficial unemployment, we build upon knowledge and evidence provided by the Department of Labor—knowledge that has been "disclosed but set aside"—and supplement this with our own estimates of additional hidden and ignored unemployment. What follows is a discussion and explanation of each of these eight elements, along with the basis upon which we arrive at our estimates. We have not considered in these eight categories all of the people not in the labor force who could be considered as likely to be unofficially unemployed; for example, young people not attending school who are also not in the labor force, disabled people not on public assistance who are not in the labor force, etc. There also exists overlap and double counting between some of the groups—for example, job wanters, unemployables, and housewives. Nevertheless we present these groups in the following manner because they represent a clear delineation of the nonlabor force population according to the major activities pursued. Other classifications are possible, and indeed we have developed some—for example, according to age and sex. We present the following, despite the lack of consistency and overlapping, because we believe it leads to a clearer delineation of areas for public policy focus and political action.

ᵉ *Underemployed:* the national figure of 2.7 million refers to the more limited underemployment concept of those who are working part-time and desire full-time jobs. *Source: Manpower Report of the President* (Washington, D.C., 1972), Table 825, p. 190.

These people are included in official labor force data and are counted as employed. This figure, based on quarterly survey by the Labor Department, does not include the many millions more who are underutilized in jobs below the level for which they are trained or capable. We are also not considering the concept of subemployment, which is a special form of labor force analysis applied to urban areas with high percentages of the poor and minority groups. Subemployment subsumes underemployment and also consists of unemployment, 50 percent of male nonlabor force participants in the area, numbers of males not reflected in the census undercount, and those earning substandard incomes. Recent studies indicate that the rate of subemployment in 60 poverty areas located in 51 cities is about 61 percent.

ᶠ *Job wanters:* the national figure of 4.4 million appears in Table A-8 of the *Manpower Report of the President,* p. 167. This category has been applied by the Department of Labor since 1967, and has been part of research on "persons not in the labor force, by desire for jobs and reason for non participation." The group was divided into those who stated they were not seeking because they "think they cannot get a job"—"discouraged" workers, and those who cited a variety of other reasons for not seeking (school, home responsibility, ill health)—"encourageable workers." We consider both the discouraged and encourageables to be those who would most likely be seeking jobs if suitable opportunities were available. Together with the underemployed they total 7.1 million people who are disclosed as a result of official surveys but are set aside and not included in the statistics on official unemployment.

ᵍ *Hidden and ignored:* this refers to the millions of other persons who have been excluded from the official labor force and therefore do not appear in the official figures on unemployment.

ʰ *Unemployables:* refers to recipients of public assistance, most of whom have been classified as unemployable in order to meet legal eligibility requirements. Of course we have always known that this was not a true description of the population. Many are now being compelled to admit the duplicity of our statistical categorization—both liberals and conservatives who cooperated in this fiction out of a marriage of political convenience. The *Statistical Abstract of the United States 1971*, Table 463, p. 291, reports a figure of 3.2 million adult recipients of ADC and General Assistance. This figure does not include the old, blind, or permanently disabled, who number 3.1 million more. We are conservatively estimating that one million members of the former group would desire employment if suitable opportunities were presented.

ⁱ *Housewives:* 35.4 million persons were reported as not in the labor force and keeping house (*Statistical Abstract of the United States 1971*, Table 327, p. 210). We conservatively estimate that about one in seven of this group would desire jobs if suitable employment were available. Labor force participation rates have been increasing for women at all ages. Of late the increase has been greatest for younger women in their twenties. There exists some overlap between this group and the ADC mothers who are included under unemployables.

ʲ *Men (25-54):* there are about 1.6 million men between the ages of 25 and 54 who do not participate in the labor force. (*Manpower Report of the President.*) About 100,000 have already been referred to under the heading of job wanters. We conservatively estimate that about one in three, 0.5 million, would enter the labor force if suitable opportunities were presented.

ᵏ *Older people:* 7.2 million persons between the ages of 55 and 64 were nonparticipants in the labor force in 1971; of these, 1.6 million were males. There were also 16.2 million aged 65 and over who were nonparticipants (*Manpower Report of the President*, Table A-7, p. 166). The push out and drop out rates are higher among the 55-64 age group than among younger workers. Here workers are encouraged to retire early, and are also discouraged from seeking employment at a time of job loss. Enforced retirement and leisure serve a function that schooling does for the young. We are making a *very* conservative estimate that about one in five of the 55-64 group would seek a job if suitable opportunities were available, resulting in an increase of 1.5 million in unofficial unemployment.

ˡ *Students:* 9.2 million persons over the age of 16 were reported as being enrolled in school and not in the labor force (*Statistical Abstract of the United States 1971*, Table 327, p. 210). We are estimating that about a third of this group would desire a job if suitable opportunities were presented. The schooling system has been developed as an alternative and substitute to labor market participation for the young. This has resulted in higher participation rates for each age cohort group, a lengthening of the educational careers of the young, and often the undesired extension of adolescence. The last of these is especially a result of the fact that there are not sufficient job opportunities available; many of the young are marking time in school and would prefer a job.

ᵐ *Enrollees in manpower programs:* about 500,000 were enrolled in these programs in 1972 (*Manpower Report of the President,* Table F-1, p. 261). This does not include the 700,000 who are involved in various aspects of the Neighborhood Youth Corps, many of whom are in school and therefore are considered under the heading of students. We conservatively estimate that 60 percent of this group would prefer a suitable job over participation in a training program, resulting in an increase of 0.3 million to the real unemployment figures. Manpower programs represent a new system of schooling designed to make people employable. While it may often not accomplish that purpose, it certainly does achieve the goal of keeping people out of the labor market and official unemployment calculation by developing another schooling system.

ⁿ *Real labor force:* our concept of real labor force differs from the concept of work potential. The work potential of a society refers to the fact that all people are capable of performing some kind of work and could in fact be mobilized to do so during periods of national crisis or emergency. Our estimates for real labor force and real unemployment extend traditional concepts and categories to include those groups who do not participate in the labor force but who do have a strong propensity for job seeking. They are not in the labor force because they have been pushed out, dropped out, or discouraged, and would be those most likely to be available and seeking work if suitable opportunities were presented.

º *Real unemployment:* this is the total of those disclosed by official unemployment data plus those who have been disclosed but set aside and those who have been hidden and ignored. We have deliberately presented conservative estimates, especially as regards to our not projecting a figure for older workers over 65. We believe that our figures reflect a truer picture of the extent to which the current economic system has failed to generate an adequate number of jobs to meet the needs and desires of people.

3. CONTROVERSY OVER THE CONSUMER PRICE INDEX

Dollars & Sense

Each month, a small army of federal investigators visits more than 15,000 places of business in 56 cities. They record the current prices of almost 400 different items, representing the entire

From *Dollars & Sense* (December 1974). This is a monthly bulletin of economic affairs, sponsored by the Union for Radical Political Economics (URPE). See Suggested Readings.

range of purchases made by urban blue collar and clerical workers. After processing their voluminous reports through its computers, the Bureau of Labor Statistics (BLS) releases its monthly price data—and we are told yet again that the Consumer Price Index (CPI) has reached record heights.

In spite of the massive scope and scientific precision of the procedures that produce the CPI, however, it should not be uncritically accepted as an accurate, neutral indicator of the rate of inflation facing American consumers.

One reason for this is that the CPI not only reports the rate of price increases, but it also plays a role in determining who gets what in the American economy. So it is not surprising that the statistic itself has been the subject of struggles between working people and business interests.

The federal government first compiled a price index in response to shipbuilding workers' militant demands for an accurate measure of cost-of-living increases to use in wage negotiations during the inflationary years of World War I.

Today a growing number of Americans receive incomes that are dependent in part on the CPI. "Escalator clauses" in collective bargaining agreements cover over 5 million workers, or about 6% of the labor force. Social security payments to 29 million persons, food stamps and some other similar arrangements are pegged to the CPI.

According to the Labor Department's chief statistician, "A one percent change in the index triggers at least a one billion dollar increase in income under escalation provisions."

In April 1974, the BLS announced plans to revise the CPI to reflect the spending habits of all urban dwellers rather than just blue collar and clerical workers (about 55% of the total urban population). Both business and labor responses showed that they knew more was involved than a simple statistical improvement. Because 1973 data showed the new index would register a lower level of inflation, business supported the proposed change while organized labor fought vigorously against it. As a result, the BLS agreed to publish both indexes beginning in 1977.

Labor's principal argument was not so much that tying wages to the more broadly-based index would regularly result in lower wage adjustments. Rather, they argue that cost-of-living adjustments for any group ought to correspond to the price changes facing *that* group, instead of an average for the whole economy. Averages are useful, but it is important to understand that all averages, by their very nature, conceal underlying differences.

The formula for calculating the CPI is based on an extensive study of the buying habits of urban blue collar and clerical workers. This determines the items to be priced, the types of retail outlets visited, and the relative importance (or "weight") attached to various groups of products. All of these factors are different for other groups: retired people spend a greater proportion of their incomes on medical care, those in rural areas buy more through mail-order catalogues, poor people buy cheaper cuts of meat—when they are able to afford meat at all—and professional people spend relatively more on recreation.

Because different prices increase at different rates, an average based on the spending patterns of urban blue collar and clerical workers will not accurately reflect how inflation affects groups excluded from the survey—nor will it necessarily be accurate in measuring the impact of inflation on different *sub-groups* of the workers surveyed.

Labor representatives argued that the BLS should prepare a whole "family" of indexes—for example, the present index, one for retired people, one for the very poor, one for salaried and professional workers. The BLS rejected this proposal as too expensive.

One dramatic instance of how the CPI can understate the impact of inflation on a particular group occurred in 1973. During the first eight months of that year, food prices rose a whopping 18.6% while all other prices rose only 2.6%. Because the very poor spend as much as one-third of their budgets on food, while the average proportion for the workers covered by the CPI is less than one-fourth, the overall price increase faced by the poor during this period was 7.9%, while the CPI registered an increase of only 6.6%.

4. JOBLESS INSURANCE BASICS

Economic Notes

Originally passed in 1935, the unemployment insurance program in the United States has changed little in the past 40 years. Recently, workers in small firms and non-profit institutions and some public employees have come under its coverage, but the failings of the system overshadow any positive changes.

Only 4 out of every 10 unemployed workers receive unemployment insurance. The rest, over half of the total, are denied insurance under various pretexts. Thus, in August 1974, of 5 million unemployed, only 2 million received any benefits. (The Federationist, 4/74).

Eighteen million workers, or almost 20% of the civilian labor force, are not even covered by the program. (News from the AFL-CIO, 11/13). In accordance with racist and anti-youth practices farm and domestic workers, as well as first-time job seekers, are denied coverage. In addition, most public employees are excluded.

Many workers' benefits are exhausted before they find new jobs—especially during bad times. During 1971, when the unemployment rate averaged 5.9%, over 30% of those who managed to qualify for unemployment insurance exhausted their benefits! (Social Security Bulletin, 9/74). By comparison, 19% exhausted their benefits during the peak year, 1969, when unemployment averaged 3.5%.

In most states, jobless payments stop after a maximum of 26 weeks, or 6 months. When unemployment rates rise above 6%

From *Economic Notes* (December 1974). This is published monthly by the Labor Research Association. See Suggested Readings.

(approximately), federal and/or state programs trigger payments for an additional 13 weeks.

The trigger mechanism is based upon the seasonally-adjusted insured unemployment rate (IUR), which drastically understates the actual unemployment rate. Lately, the gap between the two has widened. During the first five months of 1974, the IUR was 3.3% and the unemployment rate averaged 5.1%—a difference of 1.8%. From June through September, the IUR remained at 3.3% while the unemployment rate rose to 5.4%, or a gap of 2.1%. The gap exists because the IUR counts as unemployed only those actually collecting unemployment benefits. It excludes those whose benefits have run out, those who have been disqualified, those who work in industries not covered by the program, and first-time job seekers. In addition, the IUR does not use the total civilian labor force as the pool of potential workers. Instead it excludes those industries not covered by the program. Since these tend to have high unemployment rates, the ratio of unemployed to potentially employable is additionally reduced.

The national program to extend benefits is triggered when the national IUR reaches 4.5% for three consecutive months. The state programs require state IUR rates of 4% but also require them to rise continuously. If they level off, the programs stop. The program to benefit the long-term unemployed "has failed every test to which it has been exposed at both the state and national level. It depends upon complex and unresponsive trigger mechanisms." (The Federationist, 4/74).

Many workers are disqualified because they either quit or were fired from their last jobs. Originally, in 1935, short waiting penalties of up to 6 weeks were applied to those who quit or were fired (for good cause). Now many states totally disqualify such persons. In California in 1969, the claims of 44% of those applying for benefits were denied because they quit (30%), were fired (11%), or left for marital or domestic duties (3%), (Double affirmation, 4/71). In 1972, "harsh and unreasonable disqualifications" caused 2.5 million workers to fail to receive benefits. (The Federationist, 4/74).

Still other workers are denied benefits because they either have earned too little money or have not worked long enough. Thus, those needing the benefits most are denied them.

In 31 states, the maximum weekly benefit is below the Dept.

of Labor's 1973 poverty level for a non-farm family of four: $4,300 annually or $82.69 weekly. A majority of those who receive unemployment benefits in 20 states are eligible for these maximum payments. The many workers who receive less than the maximum suffer even more. For the U.S. as a whole, in March 1974 the average weekly benefit was only $63.85. Workers in Puerto Rico averaged only $36.43, and Miss. was not far ahead: $41.82. New York ($62.99), California ($63.10), and Michigan ($64.63) were average. Penn. ($73.41), Mass. ($70.77), and Ohio ($75.52) were among the highest. Only the District of Columbia ($85.53) had an average weekly payment above the poverty level.

Reforms are urgently needed. The AFL-CIO in the Federationist article quoted above, suggests that Congress immediately: (1) Extend coverage to all workers. (2) Establish federal standards to increase payments to at least ⅔ of former weekly earnings, up to a maximum not less than ⅔ of the average weekly wage in the state. (This would replace the current 50% mark). (3) Establish a federal duration standard for all covered workers with 20 weeks of work, or its equivalent, of 26 weeks. (4) Establish a new extended unemployment compensation program with 100% federal financing. The program "should entitle every jobless worker to an additional 26-week federal benefit period" and should include job training and counselling, relocation assistance, and job placement.

The Federationist also calls for "unemployment insurance payments at some minimum level" for young people who have never held a job. The financing should be borne by additional taxation of employers.

U.S. workers and their friends could take a tip from the French. Before 1975 begins, a new unemployment insurance plan will go into effect which will assure laid-off workers continued receipt of "the net take-home pay for 12 months, providing alternative employment at equivalent levels has not been found." (N.Y. Times, 10/15).

D.
Then and Now:
The Great Depression
of the 1930's
and the Current Crisis

5. CLASS WAR IN SAN FRANCISCO, 1934

by Richard Boyer and Herbert Morais

San Francisco is a busy city of 600,000, its heart the waterfront, the chief source of its life. And yet the men who kept the city alive, who did its most important work, the longshoremen who loaded and unloaded the vessels that made the city prosperous with trade, the seamen who manned the ships, received in 1933 little more than $10 a week.

And yet even more important was the fact that the maritime workers were voiceless serfs in an industrial autocracy, powerless employees of a shipping industry which received millions on millions of dollars, according to the Black Senatorial Investigation, in subsidies from the federal government. A few seamen belonged to a corrupt, sell-out organization, the International Seamen's Union, and still fewer to the militant Marine Workers Industrial Union (TUUL), but to all practical purposes they were unorganized. The longshoremen, since 1919, had been

Abridged from section entitled "Solidarity on the Embarcadero," in *Labor's Untold Story*, by Richard Boyer and Herbert Morais (New York, Cameron Associates, 1955), pp. 282–83.

dragooned into a creature of the shipping industry known as the Blue Book Union, an employers' organization controlled by gangsters who forced the underpaid longshoremen to bribe them for jobs.

The shape-up, that is, a crowd of longshoremen packing around a foreman on the street, each one hoping that he would be chosen for work, was the common method of hiring.

In 1933, under the impetus of NIRA and Section 7(A) as well as the spur of intolerable conditions, longshoremen in San Francisco and up and down the Pacific coast began flocking into the International Longshoremen's Association, AFL. Knowing something of Joseph P. Ryan, its president, they were determined on rank-and-file control. One of their leaders was a sharp-featured, sharp-witted longshoreman by the name of Harry Bridges. A tough and rugged character, his assets were an impregnable honesty and a stout belief in the ability and right of the rank-and-file to govern themselves.

Although federal law made it mandatory that the shipping magnates negotiate in collective bargaining with any union that their employees chose, they unhesitatingly broke the law by refusing to so negotiate. Instead, in September, 1933, they discharged four rank-and-file leaders of the union. When the regional labor board ordered their reinstatement, the longshoremen surged into the ILA with such unanimity that the Blue Book Union "became a little more than an office with a telephone number."

After the employers had refused to negotiate or recognize the union over a period of months 12,000 longshoremen went out on strike at 8 P.M. on May 9, 1934, in San Francisco, Seattle, Tacoma, Portland, San Pedro, San Diego, Stockton, Bellingham, Aberdeen, Grays Harbor, Astoria, and all other Pacific coast ports. The Marine Workers Industrial Union followed suit and by May 23 eight maritime unions and 35,000 workers were out on strike up and down the coast.

It was primarily unprecedented police brutality that turned the seamen's strike into a general strike of 127,000 San Francisco workers that in an instant transformed the city into a ghost town in which there was no movement. The police took their line from the Industrial Association, the combination of San Francisco's most powerful tycoons, organized in 1919 as a Law and Order

Committee to break a waterfront strike and developing until it was the real ruler of San Francisco. The slightest utterance of its officials became newspaper headlines. The employer organization was almost decisive in the election of mayors, governors, Congressmen. It maintained a powerful lobby in Washington. It was the Pacific coast's most powerful group, its members owning shipping companies, piers, warehouses, railroads, banks, utility companies, trust companies, land, insurance corporations, and public officials.

The longshoremen had drawn up a list of demands, pay of $1 an hour, a six-hour day, a thirty-hour week, a union hiring hall, but officials of the Industrial Association declared there was no issue at stake but the suppression of a Red Revolt. Press, pulpit, and radio combined with tireless unanimity to whip up hysteria against workers striving to better their lives. Not unusual was the first-page story of the *Chronicle*, "Red Army Marching on City." The story read in part:

> "The reports stated the communist army planned the destruction of railroad and highway facilities to paralyze transportation and later, communication, while San Francisco and the Bay Area were made a focal point in a red struggle for control of government.
>
> "First warning communist forces were nearing the Northern California border was relayed from J. R. Given, Southern Pacific superintendent at Dunsmuir, to District State Highway Engineer Fred W. Hazelwood who immediately reported to State Director of Public Works Earl Lee Kelly."

With the stage set and the police eager, the employers announced that they would smash the picket lines before the piers on the Embarcadero on July 3, 1934. At 1:27 P.M., with thousands of pickets massed before the piers, the steel rolling doors on Pier 38 went up and five trucks loaded with cargo, preceded by eight police radio patrol cars, moved out. Mike Quin in his history of the strike tells what happened:

> "A deafening roar went up from the pickets. Standing on the running board of a patrol car at the head of the caravan, Police Captain Thomas M. Hoertkorn flourished a revolver and shouted, 'The port is open!'

"With single accord the great mass of pickets surged forward. The Embarcadero became a vast tangle of fighting men. Bricks flew and clubs battered skulls. The police opened fire with revolvers and riot guns. Clouds of tear gas swept the picket lines and sent the men choking in defeat. Mounted police were dragged from their saddles and beaten to the pavement.

"The cobblestones of the Embarcadero were littered with fallen men, bright puddles of blood colored the gray expanse.

"Squads of police who looked like Martian monsters in their special helmets and gas masks led the way, flinging gas bombs ahead of them. . . ."

The next day, after the initial attack of the police, was July 4, and by common consent there was a one-day truce before the battle resumed on Thursday, July 5. Quin writes:

"There were no preliminaries this time. They just took up where they left off. . . . Teeming thousands covered the hillsides. Many high school and college boys, unknown to their parents, had put on old clothes and gone down to fight with the union men. Hundreds of working men started for work, then changed their minds and went down to the picket lines."

At 8 A.M. police went into action. One newspaper reported:

"Vomiting gas was used in many cases, instead of the comparatively innocuous tear gas, and scores of dreadfully nauseated strikers and civilians were incapacitated. There was no sham about the battles yesterday. Police ran into action with drawn revolvers. Scores of rounds of ammunition were fired, and riot guns were barking throughout the day."

But the strikers and their thousands of sympathizers fought on with their bare hands against bullets and bombs. Their only weapons were bricks and stones. Hundreds were badly wounded. Two, Nick Bordoise and Howard Sperry, were killed. Sperry was a longshoreman; Bordoise was a culinary worker, a member of the Cooks' Union and of the Communist Party. A reporter for the *Chronicle* in describing the bloodshed wrote:

"Don't think of this as a riot. It was a hundred riots big and little. Don't think of it as one battle, but a dozen battles."

All day the battle raged and all day reinforcements from other unions poured into the riddled picket lines, workers declaring, "If they win this, there'll never be another union in Frisco!" The police, clubbing and injuring literally hundreds of passersby and bystanders, charged into the union headquarters of the longshoremen and wrecked it. At the close of the day Governor Merriam ordered in the National Guard, two thousand of them with full equipment, and Harry Bridges said, "We cannot stand up against police, machine guns, and National Guard bayonets."

6. AKRON COLLAPSED IN THE SPRING OF '33

by Irving Bernstein

The rubber workers needed no prodding from the AFL to organize. This work force—largely native white from the Midwest and the South and heavily concentrated in and about Akron, Ohio—flocked into the union. "Indeed," Ruth McKenney wrote, "the first weeks of the new rubber union were something like a cross between a big picnic and a religious revival, except that under the surface ran the current of hunger and despair and poverty."

The rubber industry was an essay in concentration. Much the most important part of its business consisted of automobile tires and tubes, which was dominated by the Big Four—Goodyear Tire and Rubber Company, B. F. Goodrich Tire and Rubber Company, Firestone Tire and Rubber Company, and United States Rubber Company. Goodyear, Goodrich, and Firestone had their principal operations in Akron; the main U.S. factory was in Detroit; all four had big plants in Los Angeles. Each of these communities was notoriously open shop, and the rubber industry, with occasional lapses by U.S., strove to preserve their reputations.

From *Turbulent Years: A History of the American Worker, 1933–1941*, by Irving Bernstein (Boston, Houghton Mifflin, 1970), pp. 98–99.

Akron was a one-industry town, living on and smelling of rubber. Thus it was exceptionally vulnerable to the depression. In the years following the stock market crash the community gradually disintegrated. Employment fell by more than one half; homes were foreclosed; one out of four citizens was on relief. Akron collapsed in the spring of 1933. Firestone, Sieberling Rubber Company, and half a dozen small firms shut down; Goodyear was on a two-day week. The leading bank, First-Central Trust Company, failed, thereby freezing city, county, and relief funds along with the accounts of 100,000 depositors. The secretary of the Akron Savings and Loan Company was caught defacing school children's passbooks. In back alleys sleazy manipulators bought for cash First-Central accounts at discounts up to 80 per cent. The city went broke. Half the police force was laid off; all but three firehouses were closed; garbage collection stopped; street maintenance ceased; the city declared itself unable to support the airport; the school system staggered. Symbolically, on April 4 the U.S.S. *Akron,* the largest airship in the world, built at Goodyear and the city's pride, crashed in flames off the New Jersey coast with all but three of her crew dead.

7. WPA, PWA, CCC:
JOBS IN THE GREAT DEPRESSION

by Julius Duscha

To most Americans who are old enough to recall the Depression, nothing else about the Roosevelt New Deal is etched in their minds as sharply as the W.P.A. [Works Progress Administration]

Abridged from the *New York Times* (December 22, 1974), p. 1 of Business and Finance section. Julius Duscha is a member of the reporting staff of the *Times.*

—the butt of a thousand jokes, the epitome of wasteful Government spending. W.P.A., "We Poke Along." Shovel leaners!

Despite the jokes, the Republican opposition, the Congressional suspicion, the Hopkins-Ickes feud, the use of some money for political purposes and the construction of some roads that buckled with the first frost, the W.P.A. worked. Its monuments can still be seen everywhere in the United States.

Among the W.P.A. projects were the construction of what is now La Guardia Airport in New York City, the building of San Francisco's Aquatic Park, the renovation of the St. Louis waterfront, the restoration of the Dock Street theater in Charleston, S. C., and the construction of the magnificent Ski Lodge on Mount Hood in Oregon.

Hardly a city in the United States does not still have a school or hospital or playground built by the unemployed who worked on W.P.A. projects for $50 a month.

Not only did the W.P.A. change much of the physical face of the nation during the mid and late nineteen-thirties, but also it concerned itself with esthetic and intellectual needs of Americans through its theater, art and writers' projects. All of these were even more controversial than its construction work.

The playwright Elmer Rice, the actor Charles Coburn and the critic Hiram Motherwell were among the regional directors of the W.P.A.'s Federal Theater Project, which one night presented the premiere of Sinclair Lewis's "It Can't Happen Here" on 21 stages in 16 cities. In New York Mr. Lewis himself played his hero, Doremus Jessup.

Orson Welles, Marc Blitzstein, Rex Ingram, Canada Lee and Howard Da Silva were other theatrical figures who survived the Depression in part because of W.P.A. theater projects.

And who can forget the W.P.A.'s "Swing Mikado," its "Living Newspaper" or Representative Joe Starnes of Alabama asking the Federal Theater director, Hattie Flannagan, about Christopher Marlowe: "Now this Marlowe—is he a Communist type, too?"

Among artists who survived the Depression on the payroll of the W.P.A.'s Federal Art Project were Ben Shahn, Jackson Pollock and Willem DeKooning. The art project revived interest in murals, and post offices and other Federal buildings throughout the country still sparkle with the heroic figures of the W.P.A. muralists.

The Federal Writers' Project employed such men as John Cheever, Richard Wright, Maxwell Bodenheim, Edward Dahlberg, John Steinbeck and Vardis Fisher.

Averaging two million workers a year, the W.P.A. had 5 per cent of the nation's labor force on its rolls at its peak. Few persons stayed on a W.P.A. payroll as long as a year because Mr. Hopkins wanted to spread the work among as many of the unemployed as possible.

Mr. Hopkins's W.P.A. was often reviled and was sometimes confused with Mr. Ickes's Public Works Administration, which annoyed Mr. Ickes. The P.W.A., following normal Government contracting procedures, dealt with private contractors who paid prevailing wages. Its emphasis was on helping the established construction industry, not on creating jobs for the unskilled unemployed.

Nevertheless, the P.W.A. accounted for 225,000 jobs a year during the nineteen-thirties and spent $1.7-billion. Its projects included construction of the Triborough Bridge in New York City, completion of Boulder Dam on the Colorado River and building of two aircraft carriers, the Yorktown and the Enterprise.

Another Depression make-work program was the Civilian Conservation Corps, which enrolled a total of 2.5 million men from 17 to 23 years old at a cost of $3-billion. These men cleared forests, built forest roads and planted a 200-mile-wide "shelter belt" of trees stretching from North Dakota to the Texas Panhandle to hold the prairie soil after the devastating dust storms of the early thirties.

8. NO GREAT DEPRESSION AHEAD: DIFFERENCES NOW AND THEN AS SEEN BY A LEADING BANK

Monthly Economic Letter

It's not surprising that the current downturn is evoking comparisons with the Great Depression, even though some two-thirds of the people are too young to remember it. As this recession deepens—as the real output of goods and services falls and unemployment rises—the most spurious parallels with the 1930s will command great attention if only because it's easier to peddle fear than reason. But to see this slump as automatically degenerating into anything as severe and prolonged as the Great Depression is to overreact to what is happening now, and understate what happened then.

Those who lived and suffered through the Great Depression remember homeless men selling 5-cent apples on street corners, the soup kitchens, homes where milk was a luxury, and homes and farms that were lost when mortgages were foreclosed. Vast numbers of wage earners—almost one in four—were unemployed; thousands of people who had once given to charity now found themselves soliciting it. The phrase "jumped or fell" occurred with sickening regularity in the obituaries of the formerly wealthy. And many who lost their money also found they had

Excerpts combined from two articles, "The Great Depression: History Never Really Explains Itself" and "Depression Scare, or Lot's Wife Revisited," in the *Monthly Economic Letter* (September and December 1974), put out by the First National City Bank (of New York).

lost many of the intangibles that money can buy—security, freedom and self-esteem.

All segments of the economy were caught in the vise of economic contraction. The real gross national product fell more than 30% in the 1929–33 period. By 1933, real per-capita GNP had fallen almost all the way back to the 1909 level, and it did not exceed its 1929 peak until 1940.

In true domino fashion, the whole financial system was brought to the brink of collapse by policies that caused the money stock—currency plus checking-account deposits—to shrink by more than 25% in the 1929–33 period. More than one out of every five banks failed in the 1929–32 interval, as did many other financial intermediaries, including savings-and-loan associations, mutual savings banks, and insurance and mortgage companies. As the deflation of incomes and prices intensified, the burden of debt increased, bringing widespread defaults and bankruptcies that threatened not only industry but many state-and-local governments as well.

The chief point to grasp is that in the 1930s a U.S. recession, induced by monetary restraint, was allowed to get out of hand. When a gust of panic touched off a stampede of withdrawals from U.S. banks, the Federal Reserve clung to its tight-money policy, letting hundreds of banks go to the wall. This intensified the monetary contraction, and its devastating effects were transmitted far beyond U.S. borders by the rigid machinery of a world monetary system based on the gold-exchange standard. The deflationary impact was particularly severe in Germany, which had relied heavily on an inflow of U.S. capital to support its currency.

No central bank today would—or politically could—repeat the Fed's dismal 1928–32 performance. With this crucial element missing, a catastrophe of the 1930s type is not likely to recur.

And at other key points, the analogy between then and now breaks down. In the early 1930s, the value of currencies was expressed in fixed exchange rates tied to gold. To defend its gold parity, a central bank applied stiff monetary restraints even in the depths of a recession. But in 1974 exchange rates are floating, eliminating a need for excessive restraint.

Moreover, in 1974 every central bank is alert to its role as a lender of last resort, ready to assist its country's commercial banks. In the 1930s, central banks did not assume this role. In these and many other ways, 1974 is nothing like 1931.

Then, the banking system collapsed under the weight of disastrously wrong-headed monetary policies. Now, depositors are insured against loss, and bank failures, despite financial pressures, have been few.

At the onset of the Depression, there was very little by way of governmental machinery to provide income for the unemployed, the aged, the disabled, and the dependent young. Now, income-maintenance programs, while far from ideal, mitigate suffering. In 1929 the typical home mortgage was not amortized and fell due in about 7.5 years; now almost all home mortgages are amortized and the average maturity is over 20 years. These recession-braking changes in large part explain why, while real GNP fell by 9.9% in 1929–30, it fell at an average annual rate of only 3.6% between the fourth quarter of 1973 and the third quarter of this year.

None of the foregoing counsels complacency. The country is now gripped by a recession that will surely be longer and probably deeper than any experienced since the 1930s. But to say that is not to invite a perspective-bending analogy to the Great Depression. This recession will bottom out soon, probably by mid-1975. Such a turning point, however, while it will be duly recorded by business-cycle analysts and statisticians, will not bring an end to the pain. The recovery is likely to be sluggish, and that would imply that unemployment will remain uncomfortably high for some time. So the problem will be one of devising policies that encourage the expansion of real output without touching off still another inflationary explosion. The challenge is to avoid repeating the errors of the past. Looking backward in fear and trembling hardly sets the stage for achieving that goal.

9. THE CRASH WORSE THAN '29

by David Fromkin

In October of 1929 a golden era leaped to its death from a Wall Street window-ledge. America has been haunted ever since by the fear that the nightmare that began that month might one day recur. Now it has.

Of course there are differences. There always are, for no two historical episodes are identical. But in scale, intensity and duration today's continuing disintegration of the Wall Street capital market is of a magnitude comparable to that of the Great Crash. In some respects it has been, if anything, a greater crash.

For one thing it has lasted longer. Indeed the present market plunge is already the longest of the century. It began more or less simultaneously with the inauguration of Richard Nixon and his policy of high interest rates. We are therefore in the sixth year of this market, and the end is not in sight. In 1929 it was only about three years from the top of the market to its bottom. And even those three years were felt to be unbearably long. A common characteristic of earlier Wall Street troubles, Mr. Galbraith has written, "was that having happened they were over. The worst was reasonably recognizable as such. The singular feature of the great crash of 1929 was that the worst continued to worsen. What looked one day like the end proved on the next day to have been only the beginning." That is true of what has happened to us too—but more so. The search for the bottom of

Abridged from the *New Republic* (November 2, 1974). David Fromkin, a New York lawyer specializing in international finance, is the author of *The Question of Government* (1975).

this market has become a hopeless affair, as it sinks lower and lower.

As in 1929 even the concentrated power of great money has proved unable to stem the erosion of prices. Under the leadership of Morgan's Thomas Lamont, the New York bankers tried it and failed in the five days between October 24 and October 29, 1929. They made a better job of it this time around. They had learned their lesson; they realized that not even they could support a whole market. In 1970–1972, between phase one and phase two of the present bear market, the Morgan Guaranty Trust Company, a descendant of the earlier Morgan bank, followed by many of the other large institutions here and abroad, concentrated almost all of its investment funds in support of only a handful of selected stocks. It was a two-tier market in which the few stocks on the Morgan short list were given the financial backing to perform well while the rest of the market was left to flounder. This strategy proved to be successful for only a brief time. Circumstances were favorable, for the government suspended for a while its punishing economic and monetary policies under the pragmatic influences of John Connally, Arthur Burns and the upcoming presidential elections. Fueled by the money of the major banks and financial institutions, the big stocks of the Morgan list drove the market up to what appeared to be new highs, even though the stocks that most other people owned did not share in the benefits. Then Richard Nixon, liberated by his 1972 election victory, went back to being a Republican. The removal of guidelines and controls and the reimposition of high interest rates took everything in the market back down again; and even the Morgan list collapsed under the selling pressure of the Nixon market.

Thus the market collapse continues, heading downward toward its seventh year and the creation of ever more dismal records. More people have been losing more money than ever before. For one thing there are about six times more investors now than there were in 1929: then there were five million, now there are more than 30 million. For another the dollar value of investments is roughly 10 times greater: the aggregate value of New York Stock Exchange securities, which was $89 billion on September 1, 1929, was $871 billion at the end of 1972. From the autumn of 1929 to the summer of 1932, New York Stock Exchange stocks lost a record $74 billion in aggregate paper value. That covered a period of roughly three years. From the outset of President Nixon's first administration it was clear that his market was going to break that record: the *Guinness Book of World Records* (1973 edition) listed 1969 as the year in which price levels of New York Stock Exchange stocks fell more sharply than ever before in history, creating (according to the *Guinness* figures) $62.88 billion of paper losses in a single year. That record, too, now has been broken. The aggregate value of New York Stock Exchange securities fell by more than $170 billion in 1973, and by another $250 billion in the first nine months of 1974. Even this staggering loss of more than $420 billion in a period of merely 21 months does not tell the whole story, for it only includes the drop in value of the select list of stocks traded on the New York Stock Exchange. Most stocks are traded elsewhere: some on the American Stock Exchange or on regional exchanges, but the majority of them, over the counter. According to the National Quotation Bureau, between 7,500 and 9,000 stock issues are actively traded over the counter—roughly four times more issues than are traded on the New York Exchange. If the losses in all of these stocks were added to the figures for the New York Stock Exchange alone, the total loss in prices would be seen to be even greater. At the beginning of 1973 prices were so low that they bore no relation to reality. Now they bear no relation even to fantasy. The price of common stocks has lost its meaning in terms of value. All that prices now show is that sellers are dumping, while buyers for the most part aren't buying.

In the 1929–1932 crash unweighted market averages dropped by 89 percent. That record still stands for the moment, although the gap is rapidly closing. In terms of the same unweighted averages, an analysis in a recent *Barron's* showed us currently to be down more than 70 percent from the 1968 highs and still sliding. Some individual issues have been less battered than in the earlier crash, but many have fared far worse; a recent *Wall Street Journal* article listed Woolworth (down 79 percent then and 82 percent now), Addressograph (down 87 percent then and 95 percent now), W. T. Grant (down 81 percent then and 96 percent now), and a number of others.

Yet this terrible collapse of stock prices has not had the dramatic impact of 1929. Many people remain unaware that the

1969–1974 crash has been happening, and most people are unaware of its dimensions. It is because, happily, they have been spared some of the more dreadful consequences of previous market cataclysms; and for that we owe thanks to the young New Dealers who created the securities laws of the 1930s and who restricted the right to speculate with borrowed money. They restrained the over-leveraging of corporate financial structures that made the markets of the 1920s so wildly volatile and led them toward their fall. The pyramided investment trusts, structured so as to zoom from here to infinity on the flicker of an up-point—and to zoom back downward every bit as quickly—are a thing of the past; and not even the gaudiest structures of the 1960s were anywhere near so fragile. Moreover individual investors have been obliged to work mainly with their own money. In 1929 people lost money that was not their own and that they could never afford to repay; so that the crash meant they were ruined. Today people lose some or even most of their money, but can walk away with whatever is left. The New Deal has made it possible for us to conduct this, the greatest financial liquidation in the history of the world, with relative aplomb.

II
AN ANALYSIS
OF THE CRISIS

Introduction

WHEN AN ECONOMY turns sour, it is not surprising that people
look for villains and scapegoats. They are encouraged to do so
by the way in which the crisis is popularly presented. The press
focuses on glamorous personalities like Kissinger and the Shah
of Iran or dramatizes fragments of the crisis out of context.
Even worse, it trivializes the pain of unemployment or the despair of inflation by asking the man or woman in the street to
comment in fifteen seconds or less on what the crisis means to
them. What the press does *not* do—and this is crucial—is explain that we are talking about a crisis of the *system* of production. In this sense, specific villains are unimportant. What is
taking place today is no more than what has always taken place
in the past: periodic or recurring depressions are part and parcel
of the capitalist way of life. Not to present the crisis as an out-
growth of the natural workings of a capitalist economy is to engage in a fundamental distortion.

That the media present news this way is hardly surprising. It
is not that most news reporters, or even editors, consciously
fashion half-truths in order to preserve the status quo. The
process is considerably more subtle. Nonetheless, a selection
process *does* exist. Moreover, it is one that presents issues in
forms that do not challenge the hegemony of corporate capitalism. Partly it reflects the censorship (or editing) that news per-
sonnel at all levels must impose on themselves in order to avoid
making waves that would get them in Dutch or even cost them
their jobs. Perhaps more important is the fact that the news pre-
sentations of the men and women of the media simply reflect
their acceptance of the capitalist values of middle-class America.
Still, in the last analysis, these are only partial explanations of
why the popular press has little tolerance or room for the likes
of mavericks and critics like Ralph Nader, not to speak of those

more radical. Newspapers and TV are, after all, big business. Moreover, they are dependent on advertising revenue from other big businesses. Were there to be daily TV discussions on the nature of capitalism, it would raise serious "unthinkable" questions about the legitimacy of private property and the nature of our institutions. By having the news presented in the way that it is, our anger and resentments do not focus on the real source of our discontent. Thus are we being prepared for war, belt-tightening, scapegoats and the entire gamut of authoritarian rule.

Section A presents an overview of the crisis, and section B examines many of its particulars. Together they convincingly show that the economic mess is not an accident, that it is the culmination of long-standing forces which inevitably take place as a result of the institutions and incentives that the capitalist system creates. The postwar patchwork known as Keynesian economics has merely postponed the day of reckoning. Moreover, capitalism being a world system, the crisis must necessarily be world-wide. (We exclude, of course, the socialist world, which, though affected in various ways, presumably will escape the ravages of the contemporary depression, much as Russia escaped the catastrophe of the 1930's.) Section C explores the situation in Western Europe and Japan. It is after this framework is presented that the specific and most dramatic manifestations of the crisis, those that appeared in energy and food, are examined in more detail, sections D and E, respectively.

There is, admittedly, a degree of overlap between what is being said in the various sections, reflecting the fact that reality cannot be neatly pigeonholed. I submit that this repetition is beneficial, enabling one to see the same complex of events from a number of different angles.

One final warning: not all authors are in total agreement with one another. While the readings have been selected so as to present a coherent central thrust reflecting a viewpoint that I and others who consider themselves socialist share, friendly differences about details often exist. As stated in the preface, there are no pat answers and it would be dishonest to suggest that there are. Readers will have to make up their own minds about alternative radical formulations, just as they will have to decide whether a radical interpretation at all makes more sense than the alternatives offered by orthodox economists.

A.
An Economic Overview
of the Crisis

WITH NIXON'S RESIGNATION, public focus turned to the state of the economy. Its steady deterioration has made it a conversation piece everywhere. But as the distinguished historian Geoffrey Barraclough has noted:

> The trouble for the ordinary man and woman—for you, in fact, and for me—is that the gathering crisis has so many facets, so many interlocking ramifications, each reacting upon the other, until in the end we seem to be trapped in a deteriorating situaion with no obvious solution in sight. (The *New York Review of Books*, January 23, 1975, p. 20.)

Unfortunately, there *are* "solutions" or resolutions in sight but they are quite unappealing. The *last* section of this book examines the visible trend toward authoritarian rule and a fascist economy. (Nor should we rule out a positive solution resulting from a re-awakened socialist consciousness, although admittedly it is not yet "in sight." For more on the nature of socialism as an alternative, see the final paragraphs of the introduction to Part III.)

What *this* section attempts to do is pull together these "interlocking ramifications" and present a coherent account of the disintegrating capitalist economies. Since the United States is the cornerstone of the capitalist world, our overview will largely focus on what has happened in this country. In reading #10, sociologist Albert Syzmanski shows that by every significant measure, the economic position of the United States, relative to other capitalist powers, has declined drastically over the postwar era. As Syzmanski puts it, "the United States is rapidly becoming just another country in a multicentered world." In the concluding section of his essay (not reprinted in this book), he demonstrates the existence of a similar *moral* decay, as illustrated by a host of social indicators such as mental illness, crime rates, divorce, etc. In short, the loss in *external* hegemony has been accompanied by a serious process of *internal* decay which is increasingly reflected in a growing feeling among many that the system has lost its legitimacy. In effect, the major sources of working-class support for capitalism—gratitude for the highest living standard in the world and a strong, emotional belief in the system's moral right to exist—is eroding rapidly. It remains, of course, an open question whether this erosion will lead to a working-class reappraisal of socialism as an alternative.

This first reading is mainly in the nature of a sociological overview of the American economy, while those which follow (readings ##11, 12, 13 and 14, by Arthur MacEwan, James Crotty and Raford Boddy, Dick Roberts and Sidney Lens, respectively) are attempts to probe the inner economic workings of a capitalist economy. In doing so, they analyze the sequence of events which have produced the current crisis, one distinguished by the unique simultaneity of runaway inflation and massive unemployment.

A central point of reading #12 is that "recessions are inevitable in the unplanned economy of the United States because they perform an essential function for which no adequate substitute has thus far been available." This function is to "correct the imbalances of the previous expansion," especially the problem (from the capitalist point of view) of rising labor costs. In short, periodic unemployment (and inflation, should we postpone the unemployment) is the price we must pay for preserving the capitalist system. For most people, high as that price occasionally is, the ability of capitalism to eventually deliver the goods (never mind that they are often of dubious usefulness) keeps people loyal to the system—they are neurotic, perhaps, and insecure, but pacified by the adult equivalent of their childhood teddy bears. What is of crucial importance in the current context is that apparently the system can no longer deliver these goods, that the living standard in America, as elsewhere, is threatened by a sharp decline. If true, we enter a new era, fraught with dangers but with enormous transformational possibilities, both negative and positive. Sidney Lens's article (#14) is particularly addressed to these developments and their implications.

Other readings in this section place these developments in their international context. Arthur MacEwan (#11) surveys the post-war history of U.S. foreign investment, trade and the hegemonic position of the dollar, while Dick Roberts (#13) emphasizes the role of the two U.S. devaluations in creating double-digit inflation. Finally, it is interesting to look at a capitalist crisis through Soviet eyes (reading #15, by academician N. Inozemtsev).

Unfortunately, not all of the "interlocking ramifications" of the crisis are covered in these overviews—no such overview (or even "extended view") exists. Nonetheless, these readings provide a useful antidote to the confusing and distorted analysis one typically finds in the popular media. In combination with the sections which follow, it redirects our attention away from scapegoats and false formulations, and properly ascribes the causes of the crisis to corporate capitalism and the way it works. In essence, a wealthy handful direct our economy to suit *their* needs, not ours, and unemployment, inflation and hardship are the results.

10. THE DECLINE AND FALL
OF THE U.S. EAGLE

by Albert Syzmanski

Trends in the U.S. Relative Economic Position

In the years immediately after World War II, the gross domestic product (GDP) of the United States was approximately equal to

Excerpts from *Social Policy* (March-April 1974). Albert Syzmanski, Assistant Professor in the Department of Sociology at the University of Oregon, is on the editorial board of the *Insurgent Sociologist*.

that of the rest of the nations of the world combined. In 1950 it was about eight times greater than that of any other capitalist country. The combined GDP of the other five leading capitalist countries was less than 40 percent that of the United States. But since 1950 the relative position of the United States compared to other leading capitalist countries has declined steadily and significantly. (See Table 1.) In 1972 the combined GDPs of the other five leading capitalist countries almost equaled that of the United States.

The figures for GDP per capita are even more striking. (See Table 2.)

The gap in per-capita wealth among the leading capitalist countries is rapidly diminishing. Again, projections of current trends suggest that by the turn of the century there should be little significant difference among the leading capitalist countries in per-capita wealth. The era of extraordinary living standards for the American people seems to be ending.

The figures on GDP per capita are supported by those for wage levels in manufacturing. (See Table 3.) In most cases the increase in wages relative to U.S. wages is not as sharp as the rise in GDP per capita. This indicates either that capital is accumulating at a higher rate, or the share of profits in the GDP is increasing more rapidly in the other capitalist countries, or both.

The trends in wages generally parallel those for productivity. (See Table 4.) The most spectacular increase of all occurred in Japan where in this fifteen-year period productivity more than quadrupled. Again we see that the predominant United States

TABLE I

GDP as a Percentage of U.S. Gross Domestic Product

	1950	1955	1960	1965	1969	1972
France	9.7	12.3	12.0	14.3	15.1	16.5
West Germany	8.1	10.7	14.1	16.7	16.5	22.2
Italy	4.9	5.6	6.8	8.5	8.8	10.1
Japan	3.8	5.7	8.5	12.8	18.0	23.9
United Kingdom	12.6	13.5	14.0	14.3	11.7	13.6
All five	39.1	47.8	55.4	66.6	70.1	86.3

SOURCE: United Nations, *Yearbook of National Statistics,* various years; and *International Monetary Fund,* International Financial Statistics, April 1973.

TABLE 2

GDP Per Capita as a Percentage of U.S. GDP Per Capita

	1950	1955	1960	1965	1969	1972
France	35.3	47.2	47.4	57.1	60.8	66.6
West Germany	25.8	35.5	46.1	55.0	55.0	76.5
Italy	15.8	19.1	24.9	31.9	33.6	38.6
Japan	7.0	10.1	16.4	25.4	35.7	47.2
United Kingdom	38.0	43.9	48.4	51.2	42.7	50.7

SOURCE: United Nations, *Yearbook of National Account Statistics,* various years; and International Monetary Fund, *International Financial Statistics,* April 1973.

TABLE 3

Wages in Manufacturing as a Percentage of U.S. Wages in Manufacturing (Per Week)

	1950	1955	1960	1965	1970
France	17.6	24.1	21.5	26.0	29.0
West Germany	24.7	26.3	31.5	42.1	53.5
Italy	17.4	17.4	18.5	25.9	32.7
Japan	9.8	13.9	15.9	21.4	34.3
United Kingdom	31.6	35.7	39.2	43.9	43.3

SOURCE: United Nations, *U.N. Statistical Yearbook,* various years.

TABLE 4

Trends in Productivity as Output Per Man-hour (1963 = 100)

	1955	1960	1965	1970
France	78	87	112	155
West Germany	72	89	112	145
Italy	62	81	109	153
Japan	52	81	116	229
United Kingdom	83	94	110	127
USSR	69	86	108	142
USA	82	88	111	118

SOURCE: United Nations, *U.N. Statistical Yearbook,* various years.

TABLE 5

Production of Passenger Vehicles (Percentage of World Total)

	1950	1955	1960	1965	1970
France	3.1	5.1	8.7	7.2	11.0
West Germany	2.6	6.5	14.2	14.3	15.7
Italy	1.2	2.1	4.7	5.8	7.7
Japan	.02	.1	1.3	3.6	14.2
United Kingdom	6.4	8.2	10.6	9.0	7.3
USA	81.6	72.5	52.2	48.7	29.2

SOURCE: United Nations, *U.N. Statistical Yearbook,* various years.

economic position in the world is being undermined rapidly. Technological advance is occurring much more rapidly in most of the other leading countries, and this is reflected in their much more rapidly increasing wealth and standard of living.

The process of the relative economic decline of the United States is also illustrated by production statistics for such basic industrial goods as passenger cars and steel. (See Tables 5 and 6.)

The trend so prominent in the above series is present but less striking in the series on energy consumption. (See Table 7.) The fact that the U.S. share has not declined as rapidly as has its share of other measures suggests that the United States is increasingly consuming beyond its productive base.

The trends observable in most of the statistics reflecting the changing productive position of the United States are magnified in the series on its external economic position. In the postwar period the United States overwhelmingly dominated world export trade. Today it is barely managing to hold on to first place. All the other major capitalist countries except the United Kingdom have very rapidly been closing the gap in their share of world exports. (See Table 8.)

It appears that in a relatively few years the United States will rank third in total exports in the world.

A similar pattern can be observed in the trends in overseas investments in Third World countries (Table 9) for three of the five other major capitalist countries. In the period 1959 to 1970, West Germany, Japan, and Italy all demonstrated a considerable increase in their overseas private investments compared to the United States. On the other hand, France kept its share more or less constant at about 41 percent of new United States investment, while the United Kingdom, again revealing its stagnation, decreased its share relative to the United States.

These data together with the data on exports demonstrate that the United States overseas economic position is much weaker compared to the other capitalist powers than its relative productive position would necessitate.

TABLE 6

Steel Production as a Percentage of U.S. Steel Production

	1950	1955	1960	1965	1970
France	9.9	11.9	19.2	16.4	19.9
West Germany	15.9	23.2	37.8	30.8	37.7
Italy	2.6	5.1	9.1	10.6	14.5
Japan	5.5	8.9	24.5	34.5	78.2
United Kingdom	18.9	18.9	27.4	23.0	23.7
USSR	30.5	42.7	72.5	76.3	97.2
USA/World	54.5	39.4	26.1	26.0	20.1

SOURCE: United Nations, *U.N. Statistical Yearbook*, various years.

TABLE 7

Energy Consumption as a Percentage of U.S. Energy Consumption

	1950	1955	1960	1965	1970
France	7.5	7.2	7.7	8.0	8.5
West Germany	11.8	13.9	14.0	14.0	13.8
Italy	2.6	2.7	4.1	5.1	6.3
Japan	5.6	5.1	7.5	9.8	14.5
United Kingdom	19.6	19.8	17.8	15.8	13.1
Western Europe	68.5	56.5	57.7	58.4	59.1
USSR	—	34.3	42.3	46.5	47.3
Centrally Planned Economies	—	60.5	93.7	86.2	85.9
USA/World	50.0	39.9	34.2	34.2	33.3

SOURCE: United Nations, *U.N. Statistical Yearbook*, various years.

TABLE 8

Exports as a Percentage of U.S. Exports

	1948	1953	1959	1965	1969	1972
France	16.8	25.7	32.4	37.0	39.7	53.8
West Germany	6.2	30.3	57.1	65.8	77.6	95.1
Italy	8.6	9.6	16.7	26.5	31.3	37.8
Japan	2.1	8.1	19.8	31.1	42.7	58.4
United Kingdom	50.2	45.7	54.9	48.7	45.1	49.6
EEC (Original 6)	53.2	93.7	146	176	202	254
Centrally Planned Economies	29.5	50.4	81.3	79.8	79.3	—

SOURCE: *Yearbook of International Trade Statistics,* various years; and International Monetary Fund, *International Financial Statistics,* April 1973.

TABLE 9

Net Outflow of Long-Term Private Capital, Export Credits, and Portfolio Investments to Developing Countries and Multilateral Organizations (as a Percentage of U.S.)

	1959–61	1962–64	1965–67	1968–70
France	41.2	44.2	31.6	41.4
West Germany	31.9	20.2	22.1	46.5
Italy	14.1	23.8	15.9	28.6
Japan	11.6	9.6	9.7	26.1
United Kingdom	44.7	34.9	25.1	29.7

SOURCE: International Monetary Fund, *Balance of Payments Yearbook,* various years; and United Nations, *U.N. Statistical Yearbook,* 1972.

11. CHANGES IN WORLD CAPITALISM AND THE CURRENT CRISIS OF THE U.S. ECONOMY

by Arthur MacEwan

The period since World War II has been characterized by a continuous increase in the integration of the world capitalist system. However, throughout the period, forces have been building toward the destruction of the stability in that system. By the beginning of the 1970's, those forces had come into their own, and the basis for stability—U.S. hegemony—had been eliminated.

The simultaneous *integration* and destabilization of the world capitalist system constitute an important contradiction that has far-reaching implications. In particular, the operation of this contradiction has put the U.S. economy of the 1970's in a precarious position.

In this essay, I intend to describe some central features of the operation of world capitalism during the post–World War II period and to explain how the very success of those years was creating the conditions for the disruption of the system. I will then be in a position to relate the current crisis of the U.S. economy to the important changes in world capitalism and show how international affairs have played a central role in the development, precipitation and continuation of the crisis.

Creation of U.S. Hegemony

At the end of World War II, the United States was in a particularly fortunate position. While the economies of the other

Unpublished paper. Arthur MacEwan teaches economics at Harvard University and is a member of the staff of *Dollars & Sense*.

advanced nations—victors and vanquished alike—had been devastated by the war, the U.S. economy had flourished. Consequently, in 1945, the United States held a position of unique and unchallenged political-military and economic power among capitalist nations.

An era of U.S. hegemony had begun. The U.S. government was able to dictate economic and political policies within the world capitalist system.[1] Accordingly, it was possible to reestablish an international order which had been lacking for over half a century—since the time when other nations had begun to seriously challenge Britain's pre-eminence.

The new era of U.S. hegemony expressed itself in several new institutional arrangements. Most frequently noted are the set of monetary arrangements imposed on the other capitalist nations in 1944 at the Bretton Woods Conference. In the earlier periods of colonial expansion, each colonial power had imposed its currency—pound, franc, mark—within its empire. Now, after World War II, the United States established the dollar as the principal reserve currency throughout the capitalist world.

The role of the dollar was closely connected to the rapid international growth of U.S. business. The expansion of U.S. banking abroad highlights the general picture. In Europe, for example, U.S. banks had only 20 to 30 branches in the 1920's, and during the 1930's and the war, most of these were closed down. The 1950's and 1960's saw a steady advance to the point where by 1968 U.S. banks had 326 branches in Europe.

The largest industrial corporations were central actors in the postwar overseas expansion. In 1950 General Motors was annually producing fewer than 200,000 vehicles abroad. By 1952 it had expanded production to approximately 600,000 units. In another year, with European production being supplemented by Australian and Brazilian expansion, GM was producing over one million vehicles in its foreign plants. And the boom con-

[1] The ability of the U.S. government to dictate was, of course, limited in the ways that the power of any dictator is limited. A dictator must compromise sometimes, must cajole reluctant followers, and must smash rebellions. But as long as he is successful in maintaining the foundation of his power, the dictator remains a dictator.

tinued on into the 1960's: between 1963 and 1964 GM's overseas production grew by a quarter of a million.

Aggregate data show the same general picture of rapid growth of U.S. foreign investment in the 1950's and 1960's. The value of all U.S. direct investment abroad stood at roughly $11 billion in 1950; by 1960 the total had risen to over $30 billion; and in 1970 the figure was over $70 billion.

The absolute growth of U.S. business interests abroad is impressive, but it should be seen in the context of the establishment of overwhelming U.S. dominance in the international capitalist economy. In Latin America, for example, just prior to World War I, only 18% of foreign private investment and less than 5% of public debt was held by U.S. interests. British interests held 47% of private investment and 70% of public debt. In the early 1950's, direct investment in Latin America from sources other than the United States was negligible, and in the early 1960's the United States still accounted for roughly 70% of new foreign investment in Latin America. As to foreign public debt, the United States was supplying about 70% in the early 1950's and still more than 50% in the early 1960's.

Not only has the United States replaced the European nations as the leading economic power operating in the Third World, but the postwar years saw a substantial penetration of the European economies by U.S. business. The value of direct U.S. investment in Europe tripled between 1950 and 1959 (from $1.7 billion to $5.3 billion), then quadrupled (to $21.6 billion) by 1969, and will have roughly doubled again by the end of 1974.

On the political and military level, U.S. expansion kept pace with economic interests. Economic aid, military aid, and the establishment of overseas military bases helped provide a political environment conducive to corporate penetration. Throughout the European colonial world, the U.S. ambassadors began to replace the European colonial administrators as the dominant political figures. And in line with the new world order, European colonies were transformed to independent nations under the aegis of U.S. neocolonialism. More and more, the British and French military networks were replaced by U.S. centered "alliances" such as SEATO and CENTO.

The United States took on the role of maintaining an international police force to keep "law and order" throughout the capitalist world. Moreover, it became the organizer and chief participant in the general effort of capitalist nations to contain and harass the socialist bloc.

Benefits of Hegemony

This hegemony had its distinct advantages for U.S. business. To begin with, foreign activity has been a significant and growing source of direct profits. As a proportion of after-tax profits of U.S. corporations, profits from abroad rose steadily from about 10% at the beginning of the 1950's to about 20% at the beginning of the 1970's. Moreover, these profits accrue disproportionately to the very large firms in the U.S. economy. Gillette, Woolworth, Pfizer, Mobil, IBM and Coca Cola, for example, all earn more than 50% of their profits overseas. In 1972 the First National City Bank, the world's first bank to earn over $200 million in a single year, earned $109 million abroad. In 1965 thirteen industrial corporations, all ranking among the top twenty-five on the *Fortune* 500, accounted for 41.2% of foreign earnings.

In addition to these direct benefits of international activity, the maintenance of an open and stable international capitalist system under U.S. hegemony has provided important elements in the structural foundations of the post–World War II expansion of the U.S. economy.

It has been generally recognized that having the dollar as the central currency of world capitalism assured U.S. businesses of always having ample funds to undertake foreign activity. With the dollar-based monetary system, businesses in other nations had an increasing need for dollars in order to carry out their own international transactions. In the 1960's, for example, the growth of dollars held outside the United States averaged about $2 billion a year. As a result, U.S. business could make purchases abroad with dollars without having all of those dollars redeemed by equivalent purchases by foreigners in the United States. The rest of the world was effectively extending credit, to the tune of $2 billion more each year of the 1960's, to U.S. business.

Monetary matters are, however, only the beginning of the story. The story continues with the impact of international activity on domestic power relations and with the importance of access to and control over resources and markets.

Manufacturing has been the most rapidly growing sector of U.S. foreign investment. Foreign expansion of manufacturing has been motivated by the dual goals of obtaining a foothold in foreign markets and exploiting cheaper labor. The process has a structural impact on power relations that goes far beyond its direct impact on corporate profits. The ability of capital to move abroad greatly strengthens its hand in disputes with labor. Labor, whether demanding higher wages or better working conditions, is threatened by the possibility that management will choose to close shop and relocate abroad (or simply cease domestic expansion). The effectiveness of the threat has been demonstrated by the extensive expansion of overseas operations of U.S. manufacturers. And that extensive expansion has been greatly facilitated by U.S. hegemony.

Consequently, we may say that one of the elements establishing labor discipline in the domestic economy is the international mobility of manufacturing capital. The labor discipline—or the power relations between capital and labor which it represents—has been a central element upon which the successful domestic expansion of the U.S. economy has been based.[2]

[2] The argument here should be distinguished from another argument sometimes put forth by opponents of the runaway shop; to wit, that capital mobility means a slower overall growth of jobs in the U.S. economy. It is not at all clear that in aggregate and over time, capital mobility means less jobs. Of course, workers immediately affected by a runaway shop are thrown out of work. But overall, the effect of foreign investment is clearly to increase the surplus available for investment within the United States. In any given year, profits returned from former foreign investment exceed the outflow of new foreign investment and, accordingly, contribute to the expansion of the U.S. economy, including the aggregate expansion of jobs. And if the aggregate of jobs is increased, wages are likely to increase also. However, regardless of the aggregate, long-run impact of foreign investment, at any point in time the existence of options for capital weakens labor; or, which amounts to the same thing, the threat of joblessness for a particular group of workers at a particular time means it is less able to make effective demands on capital. Moreover, the sector of labor most immediately affected tends to be the most thoroughly organized, for it is in those cases relatively more advantageous for capital to move abroad. In other words, the argument here is that (aside from groups immediately involved) capital mobility hurts labor in terms of income distribution and in terms of power; the question of economic growth and of growth of jobs and earnings is another matter.

Another structural basis for economic growth has been provided by foreign investment based on natural resources. While not as rapidly growing as manufacturing investment, resource-based foreign investment has by no means been stagnant. The central issue in assessing the importance of natural-resource-based investment is *control*. In the first place, as the past year's experience with oil makes clear, natural-resource prices—of copper, bauxite, and so forth, as well as oil—are determined within a fairly wide range by power relationships. The low prices of certain resources which have been important to the postwar growth of the U.S. economy can now be seen to have rested on the combined economic and political power of U.S. corporations in the context of U.S. hegemony.

A second factor explaining the importance of natural-resource control is that control provides a basis for security, for both the nations and the companies involved. The U.S. military apparatus is dependent on several imported strategic raw materials, e.g., nickel and chromium. Thus, the position of the military and all that it implies is tied to the control of certain natural resources. From the point of view of the corporations, control of resource supplies provides security for their monopoly positions, both domestically and internationally. In oil, in aluminum, in copper, the major companies have used "vertical integration" —i.e., involvement in all phases of the industry from crude material production to sales of final products—as a basis for their power.

In numerous other types of industries as well, international activity is bound up with monopoly power. Domestic monopoly power provides the basis for successful international expansion, and the international expansion further enhances size and power which secure the original monopoly position. A description of the drug industry's activities has been provided by no less a source than Senator Russell Long, speaking in 1966: "For more than a dozen years, American drug companies have been involved in a world-wide cartel to fix the prices of 'wonder drugs' . . . the conspirators have embarked on an extensive campaign to destroy their competitors."

All of these benefits that have been obtained by U.S. business during the era of U.S. hegemony in world capitalism have not, of course, been theirs alone. Other advanced capitalist nations have participated in and their businesses have gained from the international stability. The United States may have led, but the followers have done well for themselves. And therein lies one of the problems.

Contradictions in the System

The good times for U.S. business could not last, because the successful operation of the system was, from the outset, leading toward its own destruction. Simply insofar as the U.S. used its power to maintain stability, it allowed the reconstruction of the other capitalist nations. Success for the United States meant stability, but stability would allow its competitors to reestablish themselves.

In fact, the United States did far more than simply maintain stability. For both economic and political reasons, the success of the United States required that it take an active role in rebuilding the war-torn areas of the capitalist system. Economically, U.S. business needed the strong trading partners and investment opportunities that only reconstruction could provide. Politically, the United States needed strong allies in its developing confrontations with the Soviet Union and China.

Consequently, throughout the post–World War II period, the other capitalist nations were able to move toward a position where they could challenge the United States, both economically and politically. As early as the late 1950's and early 1960's, it was becoming clear that Japanese and European goods were beginning to compete effectively with U.S. products. And other nations began to grumble about the costs of supporting a world monetary system based on the dollar. It was only a matter of time before the economic challenge would become serious, and the other nations would no longer allow the United States to dictate the rules and policies for the operation of international capitalism.

Still, "a matter of time" can be a long time or a short time. If the only challenge had been that from the expansion of other advanced capitalist nations, the United States might have maintained its position of hegemony for many more years. That was not, however, the only challenge.

The successful extension of capitalism into new geographic areas is—especially in the era of the rise of socialism—a process involving considerable conflict. In providing the police force for world capitalism, the U.S. government has been obliged to engage in numerous direct and indirect military encounters. Greece, Iran, Guatemala, Lebanon, the Dominican Republic only begin the list of nations that have felt the effect of U.S. coercion. In many cases the overwhelming military capacity of the United States was sufficient to prevent serious military conflict from developing.

Indochina, however, presented a different story. The liberation forces in Vietnam were not so easily contained, and the United States became more and more deeply involved. A particular dialectic was thus created which had far-reaching implications. On the one hand, unable to win in Vietnam, the United States was forced to act in a way that undermined its economic strength. On the other hand, as its economic position deteriorated, the U.S. government was less able to pursue a successful military policy in Vietnam.

This dialectic process combined the contradiction between the United States and other advanced capitalist nations with the contradiction between the United States (as the central power among the advanced nations) and the periphery of the system (i.e., the Third World). The combined operation of these contradictions has ended the era of U.S. hegemony.

First, however, it should be pointed out that the operation of these two contradictions established the foundation for the operation of still another contradiction. Success in the era of U.S. hegemony meant the integration of world capitalism, the creation of a system in which business was less and less constrained by national boundaries, a system in which capital could move freely. Consequently, a general interdependence has developed within world capitalism. The continued operation of a system of interdependence requires stability and coordination. Without U.S. hegemony the basis for stability and coordination no longer exists. The resulting contradiction between an integrated capitalist system and a capitalist system that has destroyed its basis for stability plays a central role in the crisis of the 1970's.

[At this point MacEwan discusses many of the issues that are examined in reading #12, by James Crotty and Raford Boddy, and also the questions of oil and food, both analyzed extensively in sections II D and II E, respectively.]

In conclusion, it is useful to take particular note of the complications that international instability, combined with integration, creates for the formulation of government monetary and fiscal policy. Quite simply, under the present circumstances the implications of any particular policy are at best unclear.

Most obvious are the difficulties in formulating monetary policy. When in 1971 the United States lowered its interest rates relative to those in Europe, a huge, unprecedented outflow of capital took place. That experience showed the degree to which capital markets have become integrated and the speed at which money managers respond to interest rate variations. The situation would seem at least as sensitive today with the large amount of "oil money" moving around the system. Accordingly, it makes little sense for the United States or any other major nation to formulate monetary policy and adjust interest rates on its own. In 1974 all of the major nations did, in fact, act in the same manner, maintaining high interest rates and tight money policies. There is, however, no reason to believe that in the absence of coordination they will continue to choose the same policies; different governments will face different circumstances and will act differently. Yet it is not clear how any coordinated policy would be developed.

The problems for fiscal policy are only slightly less immediate. It is at least a possibility that in carrying out expansionary programs designed to encourage investment, the U.S. government will find itself competing with the other advanced nations to see which can provide the most favorable investment climate. The result could be a substantial expansion of overseas investment, lacking any substantial direct and immediate impact on the U.S. economy.

Moreover, under conditions of international integration and instability, the impact of any policy is difficult to predict. When the time comes again for counter-inflationary actions, a deceleration of the economy could lead to a much greater cutback of investment than the government would be aiming for. If other governments were not following similar deflationary policies, overseas options might attract an unexpectedly large amount of U.S. capital. The results of the U.S. action could then be inflation-exacerbating shortages and the development of another round of recession.

The list of uncertainties and possible problems could be continued. Different nations may attempt to solve their own problems by raising tariffs; other nations might follow suit and a serious disruption of trade patterns could occur. Alternatively, a series of competitive devaluations may take place, or some nations might impose more stringent foreign exchange controls. Each such action would present new problems for the U.S. economy.

The governments of the leading capitalist nations are not unaware of the dangers in the current situation, but awareness and ability to cope are not the same thing. In his much publicized *Business Week* interview, Kissinger put the problem simply: "One interesting feature of our recent discussions with both the Europeans and Japanese has been the emphasis on the need for economic coordination . . . How you, in fact, coordinate policies is yet an unresolved problem."

Thus, international instability of an integrated world capitalism will continue to plague the U.S. economy for some time to come. Policy problems, trade and monetary instability, price shocks, and other unforeseeables will all be part of the new agenda.

12. WHO WILL PLAN THE PLANNED ECONOMY?

by James Crotty and Raford Boddy

Four months have passed since President Ford announced his ten-point economic program to a joint session of Congress. The

Reprinted from *The Progressive* magazine (February 1975). James Crotty teaches economics at the University of Massachusetts (Amherst), and Raford Boddy at American University (Washington, D.C.). Both are members of URPE.

program was dismissed at the time by most commentators as unimaginative, inconsistent and ineffectual. The *Wall Street Journal* characterized the program as "biting the marshmallow."

This was hardly an appropriate characterization for the *real* program chosen by the Ford Administration to deal with the crisis—a long, deep and potentially disastrous recession. While Ford was unveiling his marshmallow before Congress, the government monetary authorities were continuing the severe restriction of money and credit begun in the spring, while on the fiscal side, the federal high employment budget would have been in surplus for more than a year if high employment had prevailed.

The *real* Ford program is working—with a vengeance. The take-home pay of the average worker, adjusted for inflation, is more than 5% lower than a year ago. The unemployment rate has been rising since October 1973, and recently began a dizzying ascent. It is now generally agreed that it will top 8% sometime this year. The inflation-adjusted value of the gross national product has been declining for over a year. There is no hard evidence of an upturn in sight.

The Administration has made it clear that it intends to take any steps necessary to restore order to the economy. If the recessionary policy does not work, even stronger means are available, as we will note later in this article. What may not be as clear is our understanding of how we got into this mess. What is the nature of the crisis which has brought us to this chaotic and dangerous juncture in American and world history?

The Roots of the Crisis: Instability and Imperialism

The roots of the current crisis cannot be found in poor world grain harvests, nor in the diabolical machinations of some Harvard-trained sheiks, nor in the profligacy with which Arthur Burns has handled the money supply, though food, oil and money problems have had their effect. Rather, the crisis has evolved out of the basic institutions of American capitalism and the changing position of the United States in the world capitalist system during the past quarter century. That is, the roots of the current crisis lie in the fundamentally unstable nature of the capitalist growth process—instability which, though relatively dormant at the height of American imperialist power, resurfaced during the past decade when the United States fought to maintain its declining international hegemony.

By its very nature, a capitalist market economy develops through sporadic phases of hectic expansion followed by periods of recession or even depression. The contradictions in our system are such that balanced, full employment growth cannot be sustained. When an economic expansion reaches the stage of relatively full employment, a whole series of distortions and imbalances develop which destroy the basis for the continuation of that expansion. For example, increased worker militance at full employment results in an increase in wage rates and a reduction in the rate of growth of productivity. Inflation accelerates, but not by enough to prevent profit margins from starting to decline. Corporations are forced to turn increasingly to external sources in order to finance investment in plant and equipment and inventories. Debt thus accumulates just at the time when interest rates are highest. Moreover, serious balance-of-trade problems develop as the rising price of U.S. products retards exports, and, aided by strong aggregate U.S. demand, stimulates imports.

Eventually, of course, lower profits lead to cutbacks in production and investment and thus, before long, to the end of the expansion. The government also reacts to these developments, particularly to the decline in profits and the problems in the international sector. With the critical exception of the late 1960s, the government has reinforced the recessionary pressures developing in the private sector by restricting the supply of money and credit, and tightening its own budget. Thus, the expansion turns into its opposite—recession.

It is the economic function of the recession to correct the imbalances of the previous expansion and thereby create the preconditions for a new one. By robbing millions of people of their jobs, and threatening the jobs of millions of others, recessions erode worker militancy and end the rise of labor costs. They eventually rebuild profit margins and stabilize prices. During recessions, inventories are cut, loans are repaid, corporate liquidity positions improve, and the deterioration in the balance-of-payments position turns around. All the statements of Keynesian economists to the contrary notwithstanding, *recessions are inevitable in the unplanned economy of the United States* because they perform an essential function for which no adequate substitute has *thus far* been available.

The adoption in the postwar period of Keynesian approaches to managing the economy has not changed this basic characteristic of the system, nor has the continued monopolization and concentration of market power in the hands of the major corporations lessened the potential for economic instability. Until recently, Keynesian policies did moderate the fluctuations of the business cycle, but they managed to do so under what now appear to have been a set of unusually favorable conditions which are no longer operative.

From the end of World War II until the early 1960s, the United States was the unchallenged leader of world capitalism, and the dominant world military, political and economic power. The economic strength of China and the Soviet Union could not compare with that of the United States, and American foreign policy was built on this fact. Western Europe and Japan, on the other hand, began the period with devastated economies; they were almost completely dependent upon the United States for imports, particularly capital goods.

In the world of the 1950s, the United States could pour hundreds of billions of dollars into its military machine, waste countless billions on consumer gadgetry and planned obsolescence, and still dominate world trade, accumulate a vast corporate empire in the developed world, and maintain control of the vast natural resources of the underdeveloped world.

The world of the 1950s is gone forever. The United States' political power is now constrained by a strong Soviet Union; its economic supremacy has been challenged by Western Europe and Japan; and its assured supply of cheap raw materials has disappeared. The economic chaos we are now witnessing is the re-emergence of the basic instability of our economic system, a re-emergence triggered by the desperate attempts of the United States to maintain its status as the unchallenged leader of world capitalism in the face of the erosion of its power monopoly.

The Decline of the Empire and the Emergence of the Crisis

The changing status of American imperialism has had its greatest effect on the economy through the Indochina War, though its impact would eventually have been felt even if that war had not occurred. The outpouring of military expenditures on Vietnam between 1965 and 1968 came on top of an economic expansion which had about run its course.

But American imperialism demanded the pursuit of victory in Vietnam, so the Johnson Administration chose to overheat the economy through 1968 by accelerating military spending while taking no effective steps to reduce private spending. The prolongation of the U.S. expansion in turn created an environment in which the export-oriented economies of Japan and West Germany could sustain expansions.

In other words, in order to protect the world-wide empire of the multinational corporations, the U.S. government, by extending the expansion many years beyond its "natural life," created a situation wherein the distortions, pressures and imbalances in the capitalist economies were magnified to proportions which could only be eliminated by an unusually long and severe recession.

The incoming Nixon Administration did engineer a recession by the end of 1969, but it only lasted five or six quarters—clearly not long enough to restore balance to the economy. The Administration was forced to abandon restrictive policies in 1970 because their continuation would have resulted in an unemployment rate too high to be reduced to a politically acceptable level for the 1972 election; because corporate profits, squeezed first by five years of full-employment wage pressure and then by the initial impact of the recession, were in need of immediate relief; and because the debt and liquidity problems of many corporations and banks were too severe to respond to the usual medicine.

By 1971 the economy was clearly in crisis. Falling U.S. interest rates had triggered huge short-term capital outflows, and our trade surplus had completely eroded, leading to an explosion in the U.S. payments deficit. The international monetary system was drowning in a flood of U.S. dollars. These dollars in turn were bloating the money supplies of Japan and Europe, causing both inflation and demand-induced economic expansions.

The attempt to shore up the failing U.S. empire through the war in Vietnam can thus be said to have had several important repercussions. First, by prolonging the American economic expansion for three or four years, it left the system vulnerable to its fundamental instability. Second, by laying the foundation for a decade-long expansion in the world capitalist system, it led to a world-wide commodity or raw-material inflation. Third, by accelerating the relative decline in U.S. power, it created the preconditions for the political and economic revolt of the Third World raw-material suppliers, most significantly the actions of the exporters of oil, and it hastened the erosion of our balance of trade surplus and share of world markets. Fourth, it led to the introduction of government economic controls through Nixon's New Economic Policy, thus signaling the end of the postwar "miracle" of the Keynesian revolution.

The Role of Food and Oil Prices

The rise in oil and food prices is of relatively recent origin and cannot be held responsible for either secular inflation or the international financial crisis. But it has seriously exacerbated the existing crisis, and clearly must be taken into account.

The most important cause of the food crisis is the accelerated, world-wide growth in the demand for food which evolved from the sustained world economic boom of the last decade. The food crisis cannot be understood in isolation from the entire set of world economics forces under analysis. There were bad harvests in 1972 but these were more than compensated for by the good harvests of 1973. The average rate of growth of the world's food supply has not declined over this period. It is the growth of demand which has accelerated, leading to higher prices.

The staggering increase in food prices in the United States has the peculiar characteristic of being deliberately supported by the U.S. government. In an attempt to protect its international financial strength, the government embarked on a "great agricultural export drive." One reason the dollar was devalued was to make U.S. food exports more competitive in world markets. Further, the wage-price controls of 1971–1974 fostered the export of agricultural commodities. Raw agricultural products were exempt from controls, as were food exports. Profit margins on exported food products were thus higher than profit margins on food sold domestically. And wage controls in the face of skyrocketing food prices meant that American workers could not afford their historic share of agricultural production.

The export drive succeeded. Agricultural exports rose from an average of $5 billion per year in the late 1960s to $9.4 billion in 1972, and $17.5 billion in 1973.

Even in the case of oil prices, the declining world power of the United States has played a role. As long as this country enjoyed a virtual monopoly on economic, political, and military power, it could depend on a supply of cheap raw materials. Because of our weakened international position, however, it was impossible to prevent the oil-producing countries from quadrupling the price of crude oil in the fall of 1973. Despite the saber-rattling rhetoric from Washington recently, the U.S. government has been forced to exercise caution in its attempts to discipline the oil-producing nations and reduce the price of imported crude.

Will It Take a Depression to Stop Inflation?

What are the likely prospects for the future? There is no easy way out of the current crisis of inflation and falling real wages. In the twisted logic of capitalist development, the current crisis requires a prolonged recession as well as the possible imposition of wage and price controls.

The price of dampening world-wide inflationary pressure will be high, but no one really knows how much unemployment, idle capacity, and other waste it will take to win the fight against inflation. Unfortunately, there is little reason for optimism. The recession of 1969–70 was too short, and thus failed to restore balance to the economy. The Ford Administration certainly does not intend to repeat that mistake. The White House noted recently in a fact sheet distributed with Ford's October 8 speech that "twice within the past decade, in 1967 and in 1971–72, we let an opportunity to regain price stability slip through our grasp." Apparently, then, the present recession will have to be deeper and more widespread than any previous postwar recession if it is to overcome the forces of inflation.

But can the recession be contained within reasonable bounds

without deteriorating into a major economic depression? Several considerations indicate that the current crisis is easily the most serious of the post–World War II period. The relative prosperity of the entire postwar era in America has been built on the foundation of U.S. imperialism, and the long expansion of the 1960s and early 1970s was dependent on an incredible accumulation of corporate and family debt.

The declining international position of the United States has received much comment, and now the debt and liquidity position of the U.S. economy is in the spotlight. As *Business Week* put it in their special issue on the Debt Economy:

> The U.S. is leveraged as never before. There is nearly $8 of debt per $1 of money supply, more than double the figure of 20 years ago. Corporate debt amounts to more than 15 times after-tax profits, compared with under 8 times in 1955. Household debt amounts to 93% of disposable income, compared with 65% in 1955. U.S. banks have lent billions overseas through Euro-currency markets that did not even exist in 1955. (October 12, 1974)

Faced with profit levels which have probably peaked and will surely decline as the recession rolls into high gear, debt-ridden corporations will find it increasingly difficult to meet their fixed-interest obligations. A snowballing of bankruptcies could follow the failure of a few giant corporations. The inability of unemployed workers to maintain payment on their debt would only exacerbate the problem.

Astounding as it may seem, even some *countries* appear to be in danger of bankruptcy under the tremendous pressure of mounting bills for oil imports. At the moment, Italy is the most likely candidate. In addition to its debt to the International Monetary Fund and the central banks of other countries, Italy has borrowed $10 billion in the past few years from private international sources. Default on these massive debts would reverberate throughout the capitalist system—to what eventual effect no one is sure. Nor is it possible to forecast with any accuracy the political, economic, and financial impact of the massive accumulation of petrodollars by the oil-producing countries.

Moreover, Western Europe and Japan can no longer serve as a buffer to mitigate the impacts of a U.S. recession. They too are experiencing rising unemployment and falling output, bringing pressure on U.S. export markets just as our recession is pressuring their exports. To make matters worse, this recession-induced decline in world exports is occurring at a time when most capitalist countries have huge balance-of-payments deficits toward the oil-producing countries. These deficits, coupled with declining exports, might lead to export-import controls, controls on long-term capital movements, or competitive devaluations.

With the weakening of U.S. hegemony, it is no longer certain that the United States can organize and discipline their competitors in order to generate an orderly treatment of the deficit problem. The American defeat in Vietnam and the breakdown of international monetary arrangements in August of 1971 have had serious consequences for the world capitalist economic order. And the political strains emerging in Greece, Great Britain, Italy, Portugal, Japan, and France—not to mention the United States—make it even more difficult to count on economic cooperation as opposed to competition in dealing with mounting economic and political dislocations. This growing economic instability is fostering political instability which threatens capitalist governments throughout the Western world.

Because American capitalists no longer have the political and economic strength to control their allies, they may turn to a strategy of exploiting the existing economic and political instability. Although the decline in the power of the United States and the coming of age of Germany and Japan were the factors that permitted the oil-producing nations to impose dramatic price increases, the most damaging effects of higher oil prices have not been felt by the United States. Rather, the economies of Japan and Western Europe were, at least temporarily, most severely pummeled. Furthermore, since Japan and Western Europe are much more immediately dependent on their export sectors than the United States, the prospect of severe worldwide recession poses a more direct threat to them than it does to the United States.

Paradoxically, then, the combination of high oil prices and world recession constitute the situation in which the strength of the United States relative to its allies is greatest, because of their dependence on oil imports and world markets. It has become possible for a U.S. recession needed for domestic purposes to be turned into a weapon to be used against both the oil producers and our economic rivals.

If, as recent statements by high-level American officials seem to indicate, the U.S. oil strategy is to "break" OPEC and eventually reduce energy prices, then a huge reduction in the world demand for oil is essential. One way to guarantee such a decline in world oil demand is to have a long, deep, world-wide recession. Indeed, the mere threat of such an event may be enough to pressure Germany, Japan, and even France into participating in a subservient way in U.S.-designed and -dominated international economic and political tactics in the oil conflict. Maximizing the threat of world recession may therefore be attractive to those concerned with the maintenance of the American empire.

But this would be a dangerous gambit because the American corporate elite clearly has fewer means at its disposal for controlling the dynamics of a world-wide recession than it has with respect to a domestic one. And the political implications of an out-of-control world depression must be sobering indeed to corporate and government leaders.

Planning on the Horizon

All of these strains and uncertainties make it increasingly likely that the managers of the American system will seek new tools and policies for coping with their economic and political crisis. The contradictions inherent in the attempt to "solve" the current multidimensional economic crisis through the exclusive use of orthodox monetary and fiscal tools seem overwhelming.

If the government is unwilling to risk a depression, it could choose to postpone the day of reckoning by imposing mandatory wage and price controls. Although wage-price controls are generally thought of as a mechanism used to control inflation during an economic expansion, they have attracted increased interest in the face of projections of an 8% unemployment rate *and* a 10% rise in the hourly wage rate this year. Wage controls might handle part of the job of the recession by reducing the rate of wage increase.

But these controls are themselves contradictory. The experience in Western Europe and the United States with temporary or on-off aggregate wage-price controls indicates that a repetition of such controls as Nixon's Phases I through IV can only promote increased instability in the system. For one thing, wage and price decisions are themselves affected by the removal of controls or the anticipation of their introduction. Under these conditions, temporary controls simply reallocate inflation over time, they do not eliminate it. Moreover, controls eventually lead to surpluses and shortages because they suppress market forces which, however socially irrational, have their own internal coherence in our system. This is perhaps best seen in the confused decision to freeze the price of meat and poultry in the summer of 1973, a decision that led to the withdrawal of these foods from the market, followed by a mammoth increase in food prices in August of 1973.

In light of these considerations, more permanent and extensive controls than we had in 1971–74 appear to be required. The Democratic party at its mini-convention in Kansas City in December called for "an across-the-board system of economic controls, including prices, wages, executive compensation, profits and rents." Leonard Silk reported in the *New York Times* that some leading Democrats were "moving to support a program that would put far more stress on economic planning as a means of directing industrial investment to meet critical needs . . ." We assume that there has been serious private discussion among the corporate elite on the same topic. And since it is recognized that the use of planning by Japan, Germany, Sweden, and France contributed heavily to their superior economic performance in the 1960s and early 1970s, there are long-run as well as short-run forces pressuring the United States toward a planning imperative.

A move toward planning, it should be clear, would have profound economic and political implications. Government policy will directly determine the share of total income going to capital as opposed to labor, and perhaps the distribution of labor income among workers as well. This alone might produce considerable conflict because organized labor could be expected to fight for its share of production. But there would be more to permanent controls than the setting of wages and prices. They could require government-directed allocation of raw materials and credit, a detailed system of tax credits and subsidies, anti-strike or even anti-collective-bargaining legislation, and administratively coordinated investment strategies among firms and industries.

The planning process eventually will require detailed management of the economy and of people. This can obviously lead to serious political conflict. In short, controls may not deliver us from our current crisis, but may instead create a new one, overtly political in nature.

The development of detailed economic planning within the present array of political forces in the United States will undoubtedly mean corporate control of the planning process, just as the introduction of federal regulatory agencies has historically meant control by and for the regulated industries. It is therefore more important now than ever before that the present political balance of power be changed, and the power of the corporate elite broken. What we need now is a democratic, socialist, national political organization to defend the interests of the majority of the American people against the fundamentally antagonistic interests of the corporations and the super-rich who own and control them.

Because the problems we face are derivatives of our capitalist institutions, neither the Republican nor the Democratic parties offer real hope to the working people of this country. These parties are committed to existing power relations, and dominated by corporate money and capitalist ideology. Democratic party reformers may wish to return to the corporate liberalism of the 1950s and 1960s, but if the arguments presented here are correct, there can be no turning back.

It seems clear that over the long run the only permanent solution to the economic instability and insecurity which derive from the monopoly, inequality, and imperialism of modern capitalism is to build a democratic, socialist society. A nationwide socialist organization will be necessary to defend ourselves in the short run and to aid us in the task of developing an egalitarian society wherein production is for use rather than profit, and decisions are collectively made by workers, not bosses.

13. THE RIPENING CONDITIONS FOR WORLDWIDE DEPRESSION

by Dick Roberts

The capitalist world is undergoing its worst inflation in history. Stock markets are down in most major capitalist countries. Despite decades of claiming that the 1930s "can never happen again," today a number of experts believe that precisely this possibility once again faces world capitalism.

Real wages are declining across the globe; in many underdeveloped countries with large populations, food shortages—exacerbated by spiraling feed grain and fertilizer prices—have reached crisis proportions.

"Plainly . . . every country faces a time limit," says *Business Week*. "Inflation must be brought under control fairly quickly or the very fabric of European society will begin to unravel. The signs of strain are most visible in Italy where still another governmental failure could bring the Communists closer to power than they have come in any Western European government. The worry in France is that workers and students will stage a repetition of their 1968 uprising."

Background

Since World War II, U.S. industry has sent tens of billions of dollars abroad to build the foreign subsidiary corporations

---

Excerpts from a two-part article entitled "The Explosive Inflation They Failed to Foresee" and "The Ripening Conditions for Worldwide Depression," in *Intercontinental Press* (July 29 and August 5, 1974). Dick Roberts is an associate editor of the *International Socialist Review*.

of U.S. multinationals. Many of the U.S. giants do more foreign business than they do domestic business. Exxon sells more oil in Europe than in the United States—and given the recent energy squeeze, it need hardly be added, at much greater monopoly profits. *The overseas sales of U.S. corporations constitute a "Gross National Product" that is the third largest in the world after the United States and Soviet Union.*

Furthermore, it is precisely in the arena of international competition that we must locate the conditions that force world capitalism to its inflationary-recessionary crisis.

The markets that were opened up to U.S. (and foreign) goods and capital following World War II were not unlimited. The most significant factor was the rebuilding of Europe and Japan from the ashes of destruction. While the United States suffered frequent recessions following the war (it is now in its sixth postwar recession), for roughly fifteen years, into the mid-1960s, Europe and Japan sustained almost uninterrupted economic growth. These rising overseas economies cushioned the downturns in the United States.

A point was inevitably reached at which the rate of industrial expansion slowed down. Among the advanced capitalist countries, this was seen first in Europe and then in Japan.

President Nixon's declaration of a "New Economic Policy," August 15, 1971, marked a "turning point within a turning point" of world capitalist development. The signs of stagnation and deepening crisis were already on the horizon.

In 1964–65 the British Labour party, under Harold Wilson's leadership, imposed an "austerity" program on the workers, and by November 1967, the devaluation of the pound further signaled that the once mighty British imperialism would be among the first casualties of a new world capitalist crisis. Massive workers' struggles in France in 1968, in Italy since 1969, and on a broad scale in Britain since 1971, all reflected the stagnating standard of living in Europe, the beginning of the erosion of real wages, and the fact that the working class would not willingly accept the costs of a new round of capitalist contradictions.

In the United States real wages were essentially frozen beginning in 1965 under the impact of war-primed inflation. (They turned upward briefly in 1971–72, only to be hit all the harder by the food-price inflation that erupted in the spring of 1973.)

As inflation racked the United States in the late 1960s, billions of dollars worth of foreign goods poured into the American market; higher-priced U.S. goods found it increasingly difficult to meet competition in foreign markets; the inflated dollar grew weaker and weaker, periodically upsetting the international monetary system. To add further injury to American capitalism, workers struck the mightiest of all U.S. industries in late 1970 and showed signs that the pattern set at General Motors might be repeated elsewhere in the land.

This was the background to Richard Nixon's 1971 proclamation. In essence, his "New Economic Policy" signified that U.S. imperialism would take the high road of trade and financial warfare on an international scale and, at home, use every instrument of the government to keep workers and wages in line. It is now possible to make initial estimates of the impact of Nixon's "New Economic Policy." For one thing, it is increasingly clear that the inflation sweeping world capitalism today is intimately connected to the sharp escalation of U.S. economic warfare initiated on August 15, 1971.

Oil

The world energy crisis most clearly disclosed the aggressive policies of U.S. corporations in the intensified struggle for markets. Whether the decision to raise oil prices in the winter of 1973 was initially made in New York or in the Arab East is a moot point. What is clear, however, is that Washington made no move to resist the rise of world oil prices and that U.S. imperialism benefited from this development.

The major oil corporations worked in concert with Arab regimes as the crisis deepened.

Higher oil prices became one of the main generators of spiraling world prices generally. From synthetic fabrics to fertilizer, a host of essential commodities directly require petroleum byproducts.

Some efforts have been made to present the United States as a country that will suffer along with everybody else because of higher oil-import prices. These, it is true, have been helpful to the oil trusts in driving up domestic gasoline and heating fuel prices. But so far as the ebb and flow of U.S. profits is concerned,

U.S. capital has much to gain from the energy squeeze. The main factors were explained by Dewey Daane, a member of the board of governors of the Federal Reserve System, in Congressional testimony May 30, 1973, *five months before* the October War and its consequences.

"It should be noted, first," said Daane, "that not all of the increase in U.S. payments for oil imports will constitute a net drain on the U.S. current account balance. There will be substantial offsets in the form of increased U.S. exports to those oil-producing countries that do have sizable populations and development needs. There will be further offsets in the form of increasing earnings by U.S. petroleum companies engaged in foreign operations, and a reduced need for U.S. financing of the future expansion of the industry.

"Second, those oil-exporting countries that do add very substantially to their foreign assets over the decade will be seeking secure and profitable investment outlets for these funds. It seems likely that a substantial portion will be invested in the United States. . . .

"Third, other industrial countries in Europe and Japan will also be increasing their oil imports. They are, and will remain, much more dependent than this country on rising oil imports. . . ."

Nor will the nationalizations of the holdings of the oil trusts have a significant effect on profits. For these corporations still control the world markets where oil is consumed. "Few informed people dispute the oil industry's ability to survive and many even predict a fair amount of prosperity well into the future," wrote William D. Smith in the July 7 *New York Times*.

The impact of high oil prices in Europe and Japan has been far more serious than in the United States. Western Europe, it is estimated, faces a balance of payments deficit that will reach at least $20 billion in 1974, mostly because of the higher price of oil. This does not tell the whole story, however, because West Germany is expected to reap a balance of payments surplus of around $6 billion, so that the real impact on France, Italy and Britain, the hardest hit countries, is greater. In Japan, the cost of foreign oil, which accounts for 80 percent of Japan's energy needs, *quadrupled*.

Food

"Food is power," U.S. Secretary of Agriculture Earl Butz told *New York Times* correspondent William Robbins, as Butz stressed "the diplomatic leverage that world dependence on American grain provides." (*New York Times,* July 5.)

The statistics of the International Monetary Fund (June 1974) are equally eloquent.

· The United States exports 45 percent of world corn exports (the second largest exporter is Thailand with 5 percent). The wholesale price per bushel has risen from $1.37 in 1966 to $3.01 in March 1974, a rise of 220 percent.

· The United States exports 27 percent of world rice exports (with Thailand again second at 11 percent). Rice sold for $8.30 per 100 pounds in New Orleans in 1967. The April 1974 price was $30, 361 percent higher.

· The United States accounts for 94 percent of world soybean exports; prices have risen from $2.72 per bushel in 1967 to $6.34 in March 1974, up 233 percent.

· U.S. wheat exports comprise 32 percent of world wheat exports (followed by Canada with 21 percent and Australia with 12 percent). Wheat in Kansas City rose from $1.79 a bushel in 1966 to $5.82 a bushel in February 1974, up 325 percent.

These fantastic price leaps have paralleled a huge increase in the volume of U.S. exports, beginning in 1972, so that the recent profit increases are even greater. The *Commodity Trade Statistics* published by the United Nations on wheat, for example, show that U.S. exports increased from 21.3 million metric tons in 1972 to an annual rate of 32 million tons in January–March 1973, a 50 percent rise in volume. In prices, the increase was from $1.4 billion for 1972 to an annual rate of $2.4 billion in the first three months of 1973, a 78 percent increase.

Worth noting, moreover, is a recent development in the U.S. beef trade. This summer, prices began to fall back in agricultural livestock. Cattlemen sought U.S. *import controls* in order to keep beef prices up. Such controls have not so far been applied because 1974 beef imports have not yet been great, although the Agriculture Department has been pressuring foreign countries to limit their beef exports to the U.S. and has been asking Canada to import more U.S. beef.

This example illustrates the "upward ratcheting" effect in

world prices. So long as world demand for U.S. beef drove beef prices up in the United States, Washington sought free international trade conditions in order to keep the profits pouring in. When prices began to fall, however, protectionist moves were immediately initiated to prevent a return of prices to their old level.

Raw Materials

The hypocrisy bound up in the concept that raw-materials producer nations are somehow responsible for world inflation is limitless. All that one has to forget in this regard is the fact that the major imperialist powers control the marketing of raw materials—so that even when nationalizations are undertaken, profits are not seriously threatened. *But most of world raw materials continue to be owned by the major imperialist monopolies, above all by U.S. firms.* The inflation of the prices of other raw materials besides petroleum has provided a profit bonanza for the monopolists involved.

Devaluations

As prices rose the world over, U.S. capitalism reaped unprecedented benefits. Holdings in five of the seven major international petroleum corporations, a commanding position in vitally needed world food exports, global monopolization of raw materials—all contributed to record-breaking profits for American corporations in 1973–74. This was a central objective of the escalated offensive in world trade and finance signaled by President Nixon's "New Economic Policy" in 1971.

Furthermore, it is clear that one of the important causes of inflation lies precisely in the double devaluation of the dollar decided on by the Nixon administration. By May 1973 the Federal Reserve Board could calculate the following appreciations of foreign currencies against the dollar as compared to April 1971:

Australia	up 26.3%
Belgium-Luxembourg	up 27.7%
Britain	up 6.4%
Canada	up 0.8%
France	up 25.0%
Germany	up 31.6%
Italy	up 6.2%
Japan	up 36.2%

The devaluations in December 1971 and February 1973 succeeded in cheapening the prices of U.S. goods relative to those of Washington's major overseas rivals. U.S. exports once again were able to rise above imports. Concentration on the export trade greatly increased. *Business Week* magazine reported July 6, "U.S. exports of goods and services, as a percentage of GNP, have almost doubled—to nearly 8% in the last 10 years. For merchandise alone—excluding services, which are less mobile—exports now account for 12% of U.S. goods production."

The increasing export trade mounted on two devaluations of the dollar is a key cause of the rapid U.S. inflation that erupted in 1973.

Dollar devaluation both directly and indirectly contributed to higher prices in the United States. Its direct contribution comes from raising the prices of foreign goods in the U.S. market, after all, one of the main reasons for the devaluation to begin with.

The appreciation of foreign currencies against the dollar automatically raises the price of foreign goods in the U.S. market. A Japanese businessman complained to *Business Week* (July 6), "The rising cost of wages and materials . . . coupled with the revaluation of the yen, have already cost Toyota and Nissan their price advantage in the U.S. auto market, and by 1975 the electronics industry will be in the same fix."

But this is actually doubly inflationary. It not only means that cheaper cars are no longer available to U.S. consumers from abroad. *It allows American corporations to raise their prices on cars.*

A second important industry in which this effect is visible is steel. Foreign competition had in some cases formerly caused U.S. firms to actually cut steel prices; today they are jacking up prices to unprecedented levels. Between April and July 1974 the U.S. Steel Corporation raised its prices *23 percent.*

Shortages

A second important factor in the present inflation—the appearance of shortages in the U.S. economy—is also inseparable from the effects of devaluation. It has been asked, How can there be shortages in the United States, particularly when the central problem of world capitalism is generalized *overproduction,* with its consequent global struggle to find markets for goods and investment?

Yet this contradictory phenomenon is a consequence of the very character of monopoly rule. Monopolists deliberately curtail production to keep prices up. The United States witnessed the remarkable phenomenon of the oil firms virtually halting refinery building over a period of years, with all the consequent price rises and profit-gouging effects of the "energy crisis."

Here the question of tempo is also vitally important. The generalized saturation of markets that came as the postwar expansion of European and Japanese capitalism reached its peak does not preclude the continuation of business cycles within the overall context. The years 1970 and 1971 saw recessions in most advanced capitalist countries, but the selling off of inventories, dampening of wage increases, and government deficit spending paved the way for a new world upswing.

In fact 1972–73 saw a simultaneous rise of the economies of all the major powers, and this in itself sharpened inflationary tendencies. That is because prices always tend to rise more rapidly on the upswing of a business cycle. As production is expanding and more and more workers are hired, demand tends to run ahead of supply, pulling up prices. When this occurred on a global scale in the last two years, the result was a massive upsurge of demand, intensifying world trade. In the words of *Business Week* (July 6), "Buyers all over the world have been scrambling for supplies of everything from sugar to machine tools, irrespective of national boundaries."

But this happened when two dollar devaluations had greatly cheapened U.S. goods. The result, as U.S. exports soared, was sudden major shortages in the American economy and drastic price increases.

In the May issue of *Fortune* magazine, Lewis Beman vividly described the long "pre-NEP" (Nixon's "New Economic Policy") period of stagnating investment under the blows of world competition.

Under world conditions of saturated markets, investment is retarded because a big new investment *might not* find markets for its products. But the devaluation of the dollar, combined with a rising world demand that was fueled by deficits—especially in the United States itself—radically altered the situation. Beman writes: "The overvalued dollar had repressed the growth of many producers: directly, by creating new competition for them in the U.S. market, and indirectly, by eroding the overseas markets of their manufacturing customers. It took the double devaluation of the dollar—which raised the price of foreign goods by as much as 50 percent—to reverse these devastating trends. But when the reversal finally took place, basic manufacturers in the U.S. suddenly found that they had the lowest prices in the world. And they also had the longest list of customers."

"Keynesianism" Stymied

The foregoing effects of devaluation and sharpened trade warfare do not in and of themselves completely explain inflation. For inflation to take place there must be not only an increased demand and monopoly conditions whereby price increases can be imposed on markets, there must also be an increase of the money supply to fuel the new higher-priced purchases. But the world money supply is growing on an unprecedented scale—and it is this phenomenon that is sowing doubts about the ability of governments to bring the inflationary crisis under control.

Simultaneous economic expansion was accompanied by an even more rapid expansion of the money supply, resulting in a global expansion of the inflation rate. Keynesianism "works" on a national scale if the surplus purchasing power pumped into one country can, to some extent, be absorbed elsewhere in the world system. This was an important aspect of the U.S. economy within the context of the postwar world. Continuous U.S. deficits, above all to support the military machine, were not acutely inflationary as long as world capitalism was generally expanding.

Today, nations are following parallel inflationary policies, and inflation is rapidly "exported" from one country to another. Wherever the inflation rate is highest, high prices draw goods toward that country, pulling up prices elsewhere. Moreover, the resulting increase in world trade tends to draw the movement of world economies into closer synchronization.

This is especially reinforced by the large size of the U.S. economy relative to the world economy, so that the movement of the U.S. economy tends to pull that of the others toward it. If 1972–73 saw a parallel rise of the economies of the major powers, the threat in 1974 is already of a second international recession in the postwar period, barely two years after the first, with the danger of its being far graver.

The phenomenon of world inflation—whether it results from domestic budgetary policies aimed at artificially expanding purchasing power, or from manipulations in international exchange rates, again aimed at an artificial expansion of markets—expresses the inability of the capitalist system to thrive without continuous expansion of productive investment. Credit is expanded, and paper money is pumped into the world system to make up for the slack. This is a risky business.

Liquidity Crisis

"Credit inflation" is especially dangerous when, as is the case today, the world economy is beginning to turn toward recession.

A "liquidity crisis" inevitably occurs as a capitalist economy turns toward downswing. The threat is of this occurring internationally.

As corporations begin to find their sales declining, they are forced to borrow to finance swollen inventories of overproduced goods. Morever, especially in the United States at present, the beginning of an economic downturn has been accompanied by an *upsurge of capital spending*.

This historically unusual event undoubtedly corresponds to the new-found conviction of U.S. capital that it can, with sufficient cudgel in world affairs, continue to maintain its superiority in world markets. If two devaluations of the dollar brought the profit bonanza they did—why not more protectionism if and when necessary?

Nevertheless, the concurrence of heavy corporate demand for funds to finance inventories and for investment funds, riding on top of a 10 percent annual inflation rate, is driving interest rates to their highest levels in American history. Abroad, with even greater inflation rates, the interest rates are all the higher. In mid-1974, overseas inflation rates included 19 percent in France, 20 percent in Singapore, 26 percent in Japan, and 35 percent in Brazil.

"The Loans Are Eternal"

In this explosive situation, an international credit collapse becomes increasingly possible. All of the world's major banks are ever more deeply interlinked in the global expansion of credit. The bankruptcy of another enterprise quickly influences the rest, since they are all up to their chins in the same game—each has lent funds to others.

The collapses in June and July of the U.S. Franklin National Bank and of I.D. Herstatt in West Germany were symbolic. "Herstatt," *Business Week* reported July 6, "lost an estimated $200-million in foreign exchange dealings and was forced to close. . . . The Herstatt failure is proving costly for other banks that dealt with it, and it threw the financial markets of Europe into a panic. The rate on one-month Eurodollars jumped from 12.9% to 14.3% in a single day, and the foreign exchange markets on the Continent were nearly paralyzed."

Equally significant, however, were the paths followed to salvage these wrecks. In the United States, the Federal Reserve Board issued more than $1 billion in credits to Franklin. A consortium of world banks promised to back up the Herstatt failure. Thus the only answer to such problems is to expand the credit bubble even more.

On a state scale this takes on all the more importance. *Business Week* declared: "Eurobankers are already edgy about the billions they have lent to governments that may be pushed to bankruptcy by oil bills. . . .

"Italy is a real problem. The Italians, who face a $12-billion trade deficit this year, have already borrowed heavily in Eurocurrency markets. Now, says Vice-President David Devlin of First National City Bank: 'Italy can't borrow any more even with a government guarantee.' "

So far as the "Arab oil billions" are concerned, the real problem is rarely mentioned. After all, of what possible harm can it be to have up to $100 billion in investment funds available to pour into the world economy? *The problem is precisely the absence of long-term investment potentials. It is the clearest indication in international finance of the end of the long-term expansion.*

Business Week (July 6) expressed it in these terms: "The main channel for recycled wealth is the vast Eurodollar market, which has probably handled at least $15-billion in oil money since the price went up. But the money is going to only a relative handful of institutions, chiefly the London branches of giant

U.S. banks, and it is coming in only for very short periods. And short-term deposits are a pain because borrowers want the money for long period. Says one banker ruefully: 'The money is in overnight, the loans are eternal.' "

They are words that could easily presage a banking collapse on the order of the 1930s. On one side corporations—and governments!—want long loans; on the other side, banks want sufficiently high interest rates to cushion the risk. At some point the demands can diverge too widely.

Deflation

With parallel "Keynesian" policies of leading capitalist governments overinflating national economies, there are indications of a further parallel turn of these governments toward the "classical" solution of *deflation*. Government spending must be cut. Taxes must be raised. Workers must be laid off in sufficient numbers to dampen their wage demands, ultimately decreasing the level of wage increases, and opening to the respective powers needed room for maneuver in world competition.

Whatever their private and public second thoughts, the leaders of world capitalism are simultaneously moving toward international deflation, just as their economies simultaneously surged upward two years ago. This was the price world bankers demanded to come to Italy's rescue. In the United States the Federal Reserve is following stringent tight-money policies that can only end in a further sharp curtailment of production.

But this is the danger. When workers are being laid off on an international scale, when purchasing power is falling across the globe, the result could be a worldwide depression.

Go It Alone Over the Brink

And here is the crux of the matter:

No matter how far-flung their multinational investments, and no matter how much world capitalism increasingly comes to depend on expanded world trade, in the last analysis capitalisms are national. The basis of power of the competing ruling classes lies in their own states and in the control over "their own" workers that the repressive governmental apparatus makes possible.

The editors of the *New York Times* said July 2, "The real question is whether there is or can be a common Western purpose at all. Or whether in dealing with the explosive energy and petro-dollar crisis, go-it-alone policies will be followed that could destroy the benefits of the three decades of politico-economic cooperation, endanger the common defense structure and set off a worldwide depression."

But what else is international competition except "go-it-alone"? Every ingredient of the world crisis expresses *national needs*. Currencies are devalued in order to carve out bigger world markets. (The European Common Market can no longer even maintain a common EEC float.) Governments run deficits to shore up their own economies.

On a small scale, as in the example of backing the loans of I. D. Herstatt, or even bailing out Italy on a short-run basis, international capitalism can unite to protect specific interests. But it is utopian to believe that this can take place on a much wider scale.

Lenin stressed that the fundamental problem for imperialism is the contradiction between the expansive needs of capital on an international scale and national boundaries. This is the essence of the present inflationary-recessionary world crisis.

The imperialist governments will not plunge blindly into this catastrophe. They turned to the ideas of Keynes because they believed, with good reason, that capitalism could not survive another international depression. Nevertheless, the end of the long-term boom and the intensification of world competition have released forces that can no longer be contained within the safe limits envisioned by Lord Keynes. Rising unemployment and explosive inflation have become the inescapable "solutions."

14. THE SHORTAGE ECONOMY: CAPITALIST AMERICA IN DECLINE

by Sidney Lens

The full significance of the shortage economy extends far beyond its effect on prices. It is a fever chart of the basic economic and political ailments of the 1970s. It is a manifestation of a crisis —more properly, a blend of a half dozen crises—qualitatively different from anything we have ever experienced. The half dozen recessions since 1945 may have been, as the economists said, "adjustments" to rectify secondary imbalances. The current shortage-inflation-recession syndrome, on the other hand, reflects a breakdown—a breakdown of the Bretton Woods money system, the disarray of the dollar on the world market, the shattering of the *Pax Americana*. In sum, the shortage economy is a symptom of the *decline of American power.* The United States can no longer organize the world in its image, and can no longer impose the necessary *discipline* on its allies, on its satellites (such as Iran), or on its own national and multinational monopolies.

This crisis in power manifests itself in different forms at varying times—a supply slowdown, price-gouging and inflation, semipanic on Wall Street, a credit crunch, economic pressure on Washington's allies, and above all a drop in the living standards

Abridged from "Running Out of Everything," in *The Progressive* (October 1974). Sidney Lens, a Chicago-based labor leader, lecturer and world traveler active in peace and radical movements, has written extensively on both domestic and international political and economic issues. His most recent book is *The Promise and Pitfalls of Revolution* (Philadelphia, United Church Press, 1973).

of the American people. From the third quarter of 1972 through the second quarter of 1974 the real wages of 52 million workers in private industry fell by 8 per cent—the worst decline in living standards since the Great Depression. And it is going to fall further.

The First National Bank of Chicago, which is more candid about such things than are politicians, shows how the petroleum crisis alone must lead to a drop in living standards. The oil producing nations, it says, will be exacting $60 billion a year more from oil importing nations this year than last. Since the weak economies of such producers as Saudi Arabia, Iran, Libya, and Venezuela can, at most, absorb additional purchases from the United States, Western Europe, and Japan of $10 billion or $15 billion a year, that leaves a deficit for the West of $45 or $50 billion.

"This means," said the First National Bank in its August 1974 report, "that the importing country has to expand its export of goods and services to pay for the more expensive imports. To accomplish this, some resources that would have been used to produce goods for domestic consumption will have to be channeled into the production of goods for foreign consumption (exports). This means that *consumers' real incomes must decline because there is less real output available for the domestic population.*" (*Emphasis added.*)

How did this situation originate? Why has a country with such monumental resources—the envy of every nation on earth—become a "land of shortage"? How did three decades of unparalleled U.S. "prosperity" come to such an abrupt halt?

The answer lies in the peculiar circumstances of that prosperity: It was built on the quicksand of militarism, and the United States now cannot survive without militarism and cannot survive with it. During World War II, national income in the United States more than doubled and the capital equipment industry, in the words of the National Planning Association, was "nearly twice the size which would be needed domestically under the most fortuitous conditions. . . ." "Free enterprise" America required a vast new market to dispose of this surplus—or face depression. But the rest of the postwar world—friend and foe alike—was in economic chaos and not far from revolution.

Washington "solved" the problem in brilliant fashion. Any

nation willing to join the "American system" was given aid (some $150 billion in economic and military assistance), as well as the protection of America's military power, against internal revolution and Soviet pressure.

To prevent "disorder"—that is, revolution—the United States built the world's greatest navy, acquired 2,500 minor and major military bases abroad, stationed about a million troops overseas, and was prepared to intervene at a moment's notice against any government or force that threatened to secede from the "American system"—as it did in Korea, Vietnam, the Dominican Republic, Lebanon, the Congo, and other "trouble spots." In return for this military protection and economic aid, those who accepted the American arrangement had to pledge an "open door" for U.S. private trade and investment (as well as that of America's allies) and adherence to the Bretton Woods money system which made the dollar the international unit of exchange.

For a quarter of a century this *Pax Americana* worked tolerably well. The CIA and Pentagon intervened in dozens of countries to assure "stability," to overthrow governments it did not like, or to install right-wing forces it approved. But the cost was a shattering $1.4 trillion spent on militarism since 1945, causing budget deficits for all but three years since 1952, some of them as high as $25 billion, and an astronomical increase in the national debt. Every year but two (when there were small surpluses) America also suffered multi-billion-dollar balance-of-payments deficits. Two-thirds of the U.S. gold hoard fled the country, and as of 1972 about $82 billion were floating around the world, accepted by other nations because they were allegedly as "good as gold," though they were actually much depreciated in value. Finally, in August 1971, a staggering deficit of about $25 billion loomed on the horizon. Uncle Sam's credit was no longer sound, the dollar was shaky, and the nation needed to increase exports and decrease imports to keep its ship from foundering. In this circumstance President Nixon took the drastic step of devaluing the dollar—to make U.S. goods cheaper abroad, and foreign goods more expensive here—and he instituted wage controls in an effort to hold down costs for U.S. entrepreneurs so they could remain competitive on the world market.

It seemed like a simple and decent solution—except that other nations took countermeasures, and eventually the dollar, the economic pivot of American power, had to be devalued further, then abandoned to float at whatever price it could command. Today the international money system is in chaos, with currencies rising and falling 10 or 15 per cent against each other, and exporters and importers hedging sales and purchases by speculating on the currency market.

Domestically, the system of controls was a fiasco, like plugging a broken dam with a cork. The lifting of controls was just as bad. Controls led to shortages, which then accelerated inflation, and both problems survived. Neither controls nor the "free market" can cure our present sickness, for what is happening is that the tide of debt has reached our chins, and we are faced with an old mortgage to pay. We mortgaged our future to support militarism—so that we could exact discipline for the *Pax Americana;* now we must pay the mortgage by lowering our standard of living. Thus, by a long and circuitous road, we have arrived at the shortage economy, intractable inflation, and a looming depression.

As a result of the *Pax Americana,* industry burgeoned and capital became so concentrated, through merger and other devices, that today only 500 industrial firms account for three-quarters of industrial employment and two-thirds of sales. Under the New Capitalism our main industries—steel, rubber, autos, paper, certain foods, aluminum, electrical appliances, and others —are dominated by two to four companies each. Those companies, often interlocked with the same banking interests, conspire to *administer* prices. The Federal Trade Commission estimates that if the highly concentrated industries were broken up by antitrust action, prices in those industries (the heart of the economy) would fall by at least 25 per cent. Collusion sometimes goes further. Oil companies collude to win drilling rights at low cost, or collude to drive independents from the scene, or collude to cause a shortage in order to exact concessions—such as the Alaska pipeline and relaxation of environmental standards —from the Federal Government.

That seems to be the case with the paper companies as well. They not only administered prices but contrived a "shortage" to exert pressure for additional cutting rights in such national forests as Tongass and Chugach in Alaska. In 1973, however, the pressure for concessions from Government—perennial under the New Capitalism—was complicated by the existence of domestic price controls. International sales were not subject to controls, and the paper moguls took full advantage of this fact. In the first half of 1973, export of chips and pulp to Japan increased by 49.2 per cent, reducing to that extent the stockpile at home—hence, a paper "shortage." And what was so attractive about selling to Japan? A representative of the American Paper Institute put it candidly: "Other countries seem to be paying a higher price due to the Cost of Living Council's freeze on price increases."

The most insidious shortage of the whole shortage economy, of course, is the one in energy, and particularly in petroleum. Here all the dilemmas of American capitalism coalesce: We need a safe supply of oil not only for our economy but for our vast military machine. Under the profit maximization system, our Government is unwilling or unable to check the greed of the seven oil corporations, five of them American, which constitute a tight world cartel. But as the Seven Sisters contrive shortages and inflate prices, all the economies of the western world, dependent on the Seven Sisters for their fuel, totter. Each country seeks to repair its balance of payments difficulties at the expense of the others—through devaluations, floating of currency, trade restrictions, unilateral deals with the Russians, Chinese, and Arabs, and other makeshift devices. The fabric of the *Pax Americana,* already severely strained, shreds further. In 1973 not a single major refinery was built in this country, and in the previous five years only enough to refine 1.9 milion more barrels a day, though demand swelled by three million. Why is there a "refinery gap"? M. A. Wright, chief executive officer of Exxon, was disarmingly frank before a Congressional committee: "It is a problem of how much people want to pay for it [oil]. If they want to pay enough for it to make the market profitable in Europe, sure, we will sell it there. We are in business. . . ." From 1963 to 1972, the five largest companies increased crude oil production in the United State by 45 per cent, but outside the United States—where it was more profitable—by 97 per cent. The shift in refining was even more drastic, going up only 34 per cent in the Western Hemisphere and 176 per cent in the Eastern Hemisphere.

* * *

Such manipulation of the oil market, and through the oil market of national economies, is possible only because the U.S. Government helped the Seven Sisters become the largest cartel in history. For "national security" reasons—where have we heard that rationale before?—the State Department has since 1950 openly encouraged the five American firms and their British and Dutch partners to function as a tight cartel—aided, abetted, and protected by U.S. diplomacy and military power. Without that power American firms would never have gained their original oil concessions in Latin America and Canada; other foreign companies could enter this hemisphere only on sufferance of the State Department. Subsequently, State performed the same service for the U.S. firms in the Persian Gulf states, Africa, and Asia—in tune with U.S. economic and military aid. Nations that granted concessions received economic aid and military protection; those that did not were fortunate if the CIA refrained from overthrowing their governments.

The vise in which the Great Powers now find themselves, euphemistically called the "energy crisis," thus began with the formation of a Washington-sponsored world monopoly. It was tightened before and after the Yom Kippur war in the Middle East last year, when the oil producing nations suddenly realized their bargaining strength and doubled and redoubled the price of their product. Moreover, while the Seven Sisters were also exacting their pound of flesh, the oil nations took advantage of the Middle East war forcibly to buy up some of the foreign company holdings on their soil.

Thus a schism developed among the three actors in the drama —the United States and its allies (the consumer states), the Seven Sisters, and the producing nations. The producer states gained substantially. The Seven Sisters were hurt minimally— they lost some control over the extractive end of the industry, but remain a multinational monopoly in shipping, refining, and marketing; they will recover the extra royalties and taxes they must pay the producing nations—and more—from reductions in their U.S. taxes.

Only the consumer states lost heavily—though the United States lost least of all because more than two-thirds of its oil comes from domestic sources.

In effect, the "energy crisis" is a manifestation of a world-wide change in political fortunes: The socialist countries are growing stronger, and they can offer the Third World increasing diplomatic, economic, and military support; the Third World is beginning to feel a sense of growing control over its own destiny, and the Great Powers are in obvious decline.

A chart of the rise and fall of American power, which the shortage economy now punctuates, would look something like this:

1. From 1945 to 1965, steady growth; American foreign investments doubling, redoubling, and then redoubling again; living standards rising dramatically.

2. From 1965 to 1971, coincident with the Vietnam war and other crises, the gradual appearance of the credit crunch and all the problems associated with balance of payments deficits.

3. From August 1971 to the 1973 Yom Kippur war, the first clear evidence of a turnabout in international political power, and the consequent turnabout in economic fortune.

4. From the Yom Kippur war to the present, a "free world" in traumatic decline that can only end either in a "managed" reduction of living standards in the West or in a dreadful, unmanaged depression. Italy and Britain are already only a few steps from such a depression, and are thinking in terms of the kind of "austerity"—lower consumption levels—they were forced to adopt during World War II.

In this state of political decline, a capitalist America (and its allies) cannot avoid further economic pressure.

The danger is that the four countries that control the supply of copper (Chile, Peru, Zaire, and Zambia), now joined together, will be doing the same thing as the petroleum producing nations. The price of copper went up from 53 cents a pound in July 1973 to $1 in December. Five bauxite countries (Australia, Guinea, Guyana, Jamaica, Surinam), four nations that control natural rubber, and four that account for virtually all the tin exports may raise prices and create synthetic shortages in the near future. U.S. pressures may prevent concerted action here and there, but in the long run it will take place anyway, both because American power is limited and on the wane, and because, as the price of gold increases (it is now four times what it was in 1972), the inflationary pull becomes irresistible.

The economists of the Nixon and Ford Administrations are reacting to the shortage economy and inflation as if they were traditional problems, requiring only "adjustments" such as those that adjusted our six postwar "recessions"—monetary manipulation, fiscal changes, tax incentives, and the like. According to one of Nixon's former economic advisers, Paul W. McCracken, the cause of our troubles is that "we obviously have run out of plant capacity before we have run out of employable labor." Thus if we can "cool down" the economy, so that demand drops and steel companies can again operate at, say, 85 per cent of capacity instead of 95 per cent, all will be well again. Inflation will abate, and shortages will disappear as people buy less. If there is unemployment, the Government can provide a few hundred thousand public service jobs and increase jobless compensation. Such prescriptions have already proven themselves naive, for the economy *has* "cooled down"—we are in a recession—yet inflation shows little sign of slackening, nor are the shortages disappearing. And if the economy cools down much further, we may check inflation only to find a steep rise in unemployment.

President Ford, whose geniality temporarily obscures his Nixonite philosophy, is preparing to perform the feat of the century. He tells us he will reduce inflation without attacking its two major causes—military spending, which contributes nothing to the consumer economy and withdraws many billions of dollars, and monopoly, which incessantly fuels the inflationary fire. This is the kind of "Band-Aid" economics and diplomacy that brought us to our present despair.

The shortage economy tells us that Keynesian capitalism, which patched up the planless economy through deficit spending for forty years, has exhausted its potential and its usefulness. The *Pax Americana,* which organized the planet around the goals of the American military-industrial complex, is similarly passing into oblivion. We cannot live endlessly by going deeper into debt or by exploiting the peoples of other nations. We must learn to live by our own labor and ingenuity.

The shortage economy tells us that capitalism is in decline as a viable economic system, that it can only plunge us into depressions, international trade wars, monetary conflicts, and military confrontations. Not only radicals, but many populists and liberals as well, now recognize what Charles Beard and John Dewey told us in the 1930s—that our only salvation lies in a planned economy. Dean Acheson hinted at that back in November 1944, when he said that under another system—that is, socialism—the United States could adjust without being concerned with foreign markets, but that under our present capitalist system it could not have "full employment and prosperity" unless it found some way to dispose of its giant surpluses. The internal market of the nation can be controlled and shaped by the Government, which has political and police power to enforce its will; but the international market is something else again—here 150 or so sovereignties clash with one another, and there are no means to control them short of war, the threat of war, or the *Pax Americana* discipline the United States was able to exact for a quarter of a century.

Under a planned economy, by contrast with the so-called free economy, the Government could plan the allocation of resources to meet the needs of our people. It could begin by calculating a realistic balance of trade and money accounts around the world, and then determine how our $1.4 trillion gross national product should be apportioned after allowance is made for the outward flow.

An American planned economy in which the resources were put at the people's command would not be nearly so dependent on monetary and trade gyrations abroad. It could reorder its priorities to meet human needs rather than the greeds of private monopoly. Having determined that it requires so much for exports and can expect so much from imports and so much from its money accounts, the Government could proceed to set the level for minimum and maximum living standards. By controlling foreign trade through a state monopoly it could free itself from decisive dependence on such trade. Its surpluses could be channeled inward to improve living standards, and its factories could be redirected to meet the actual needs of people rather than the artificial demands induced to enhance private profits.

By slashing the $90 billion-a-year war budget and the 2,500 military bases it maintains abroad, the nation could attain a degree of prosperity and stability never known before. Instead of the tail (foreign trade, private monopoly) wagging the dog, the dog could finally wag its own tail. The shortage economy is a warning that we disregard at our peril, and it is an opportunity that must be seized.

15. A SOVIET VIEW OF THE CRISIS

by N. Inozemtsev

The ruling circles of the main capitalist countries intended, using possibilities connected with the scientific and technological revolution and expanding still more the state-monopoly regulation of the economy, to achieve a serious acceleration in the development of productive forces and, most important, a fundamental improvement in the economic position of and the social and political situation in their countries. On this basis, they wanted to consolidate the positions of capitalism and to change the general trends of present-day world development in their favor. However, life upset these calculations.

True, capitalism has succeeded . . . in bringing about a certain acceleration in economic development rates. Thus, whereas in the 1950s the annual increase in industrial production in the capitalist countries came to 4.8%, in the 1960s this figure was 5.9%, and in 1971–1973 it was 6.6%.

However, it has been confirmed once more that no state-monopoly measures can overcome *the cyclical nature of economic development* that is organically inherent to the capitalist mode of production or can rule out crises, slumps and sharp fluctuations in rates.

This is one aspect of the question, that of growth rates. An-

Excerpts from "Capitalism's Current Crisis Analyzed," in *The Current Digest of the Soviet Press*, Vol. XXVI, No. 33 (September 11, 1974). N. Inozemtsev is director of the USSR Academy of Sciences' Institute of World Economics and International Relations.

other no less important aspect is the fact that in today's conditions even relatively high rates—when they are achieved—do not save capitalism from very serious upheavals in various and highly important spheres of national economies and of the world capitalist economy as a whole.

One illustration of this is *the continuous development of inflation,* which has taken on literally catastrophic dimensions. G. Ford, the new U.S. President, has called inflation "public enemy No. 1."

Facts indicate that inflationary processes are becoming more and more uncontrollable and that governments are unable to cope with them. Inflation, which is engendered by a whole complex of causes and which reflects in the sphere of monetary circulation contradictions peculiar to capitalism, is in turn deepening these contradictions, impairing the economic mechanism and intensifying the instability of economic development.

Another vivid indication of the serious difficulties capitalism is experiencing is *the crisis in the system of monetary relations.* This crisis has manifested itself in repeated unilateral devaluations and revaluations of a number of national currencies, in the sharp fall (in the early 1970s) of the dollar's exchange rate and the virtual elimination of a firm relationship between the dollar and other currencies, in the rapid rise in gold prices, and in numerous panics on currency exchanges. This is a reflection of the profound contradiction between the so-called Bretton Woods system, which was created late in World War II and was based on the dominance of the dollar, and the actual balance of forces in the capitalist world today, which is characterized by a relative weakening of the U.S.A.'s position and by growth in the economic and financial might of the West European countries and Japan.

Power generation, an important sphere of the world capitalist economy, suffered a blow in late 1973. The *energy crisis* did not come about by accident. It was generated by a number of causes. These include the lag, first noticed a number of years ago, in the production of national primary energy resources behind the growing volume of energy consumption, the existing structure of the energy balance (in the U.S.A., oil and gas account for 7% and 3% respectively, of all proved reserves of various types of fuel, while their share in the country's power balance are

44% and 33%, respectively), and the transformation in most capitalist countries of imported oil into the predominant energy source. The causes include the speculative activity of the capitalist oil monopolies, as well as political factors, first of all Israel's aggression against the Arab states and the latters' retaliatory measures, which have been manifested, in particular, in steep price increases for oil. In other words, the roots of the energy crisis are to be found in the capitalist economic system itself, which impedes the rational and balanced utilization of power and other raw-material resources in the interests of society as a whole and obstructs the truly equitable and mutually advantageous international division of labor between the industrially developed countries and the developing countries. Thus, in mid-1973 the extraction of a ton of oil in the Near East countries cost the foreign monopolies only 75 cents, while its selling price was $21 or $22: It's no wonder that in 1973 alone the net profits of the five largest American oil monopolies reached $6,200,000,000.

What are the main reasons why the hopes that the leaders of the capitalist world pinned on the scientific and technological revolution and the further development of state-monopoly regulation have proved unfounded?

First, the fact that a profound contradiction exists between the objective need for planned development that is characteristic of present-day productive forces and the market anarchy and spontaneity that is organically inherent to capitalism. The requirements for a significant enlargement in the scale of production, long-range forecasting and planning and for improved management that are stimulated by this revolution are at variance with the unplanned and disproportional nature of the development of the capitalist economy, the competitive struggle among monopolies, as well as among various branches of industry, and the complex relationships that exist between large corporations and small and medium-scale production. Obstacles erected by private capital frequently appear on the path of the development of science and technology (for example, the oil monopolies in the U.S.A. and other capitalist countries have for a long time retarded the development of atomic power engineering and other fundamentally new energy sources). And, of course, the reactionary forces' desire to divert a large part of the discoveries of science and enormous material resources to military purposes is especially serious and dangerous. . . .

Third, in step with the growth of productive forces and the intensification of the processes of the international division of labor, which is logical in this connection, there is an increasing contradiction between requirements for the further internationalization of economic life and the national forms of production management, state-monopoly regulation on the scale of various countries, and the economic policies of the governments of individual countries. Capitalism is seeking a way out of this contradiction along lines of the economic integration of states and the growth of international monopolies. However, this involves more and more difficulties. Thus, the expansion of the framework of the Common Market in connection with the transformation of the Six into the Nine, the differences among its members over the creation of an economic and monetary union, the aggravation of the monetary and financial crisis and the energy crisis are all having a very painful effect on the European Economic Community.

The nature of the international monopolies today is illustrated quite convincingly by the following figures. By the beginning of the 1970s, the value of industrial goods and services sold by these monopolies had reached one-third of the gross national product of all the capitalist countries taken together.

Taking these figures into account, and considering the fact that the international monopolies easily bypass national customs barriers, are comparatively less dependent on fluctuations in currency exchange rates and can easily curtail production at enterprises in one country in order to organize it in another country where a cheaper work force, larger markets and higher profits are assured, it is not difficult to imagine the great opportunities that the international monopolies have to take advantage for their own purposes of the course of economic cycles in particular countries, their balances of payments, and the entire sphere of monetary and financial relations.

The expanding activity of the international monopolies, which inevitably clash with the economic policy of states and with their efforts in the field of economic programming, is a very graphic illustration of the limited possibilities of present-day state-monopoly regulation.

The aggravation of inter-imperialist contradictions, as well as of *contradictions between the capitalist powers and the developing countries,* is an important feature of capitalism in the mid-1970s.

In the postwar period, the action of the law of the uneven development of capitalist countries has been manifested with special force, and this has led to serious changes in the alignment of forces among them. This is convincingly indicated by the table below.

Major Countries' Percentage of Total Industrial Production of the Capitalist World

	1953	1960	1970	1973
U.S.A.	52.6	45.7	40.8	39.8
Japan	2.4	4.4	9.0	9.2
F.R.G.	6.6	8.8	8.6	8.1
Britain	8.9	8.3	6.1	5.5
France	4.5	5.1	5.0	5.0
Italy	2.4	3.2	3.5	3.1

In today's conditions the competitive struggle is becoming especially acute, in view of the fact that a process of the drawing together of the levels of the main industrially developed capitalist countries is taking place. For example, 20 years ago the per capita gross domestic product (in comparable prices) in the F.R.G. was 29% of the U.S. level, while in 1973 it had increased to 75%; the corresponding figures are 41% and 70% for France, 9% and 56% for Japan, and 16% and 51% for Italy. Naturally, this sharpens the competitive struggle of the states concerned, not only in the field of trade but also on capital markets, in the spheres of science, technology, etc.

As far as contradictions between the industrially developed capitalist countries and the developing states are concerned, the objective basis for this contradiction—the gap in levels for a number of indices—continues to increase (although on the whole higher rates are characteristic of the developing countries). Whereas 20 years ago the gross national product per capita in these states averaged $127 (in 1970 prices), which was 9.4%

of the corresponding index for the industrially developed countries, in 1973, although this product had increased to $260, it was only 7.5% of the developed countries' level. The developing countries, where 73% of the population of the nonsocialist world lives, account for only 18% of its gross domestic product.

The acute contradictions between the two groups of countries in the world capitalist economic system existed in the past too. But today new possibilities for resolving these contradictions have opened up before the newly liberated countries—possibilities connected with the growth of world socialism, with the different alignment of forces in the international arena, with the successes these countries have won in the struggle for political and economic independence.

It is now clear that the capitalist world is dependent to a great extent on deliveries of raw materials from the developing countries, and that no one is able to prevent these countries from taking control of their own natural resources. The struggle for raw materials has only started to develop; following the example of the oil producers, the countries that produce copper and bauxite, for instance, have begun to unite their efforts. All this indicates that the time of exploitation with impunity and the shameless plunder of backward countries is drawing to a close.

3.—Economic upheavals and the growing inter-imperialist contradictions are by no means the only object of concern in international capitalist circles. *Capitalism's contradictions in the social field* are making themselves felt just as sharply, perhaps more so. State-monopoly regulation has proved unable to ensure "social peace" and suppress the class struggle.

B.
Understanding
the Specifics
of the Crisis

SECTION A PROVIDED overviews of the crisis. It is now time to take up some of the specifics. Unfortunately, they do not always come neatly bound together like the homogeneous sections of a supermarket. Those that do are presented in the last two sections of the book. This section, however, contains heterogeneous readings, those which cannot be so easily pigeonholed. That a section of this type is needed—indeed essential—reflects the fact that the crisis is exceedingly complex, with innumerable facets, each interrelated, whose endless ramifications we can only begin to explore. Decades from now, different scholars with access to documents currently not available, with the luxury of time and emotional distance, and most important, with the knowledge of how the crisis was resolved (even if resolved only temporarily), will pull together many of the anomalies and disparate elements and present an integrated analysis of what is currently still unfolding. Living in the midst of the crisis, with the opportunity yet to change its course, we must operate in a different fashion. More positively, I would suggest that our current insight is not inconsiderable. To the contrary.

The first three readings in this section are among the most theoretical in the book and therefore (being *economic* theory) may require considerably more intellectual effort than one is normally accustomed to. I can only assure you it will be time well spent. Reading #16 by David Gold is an able summary of a most important book, *The Fiscal Crisis of the State,* by James

O'Connor. Most Americans probably believe that government spending is out of hand and got that way because of the shenanigans of a bunch of incompetent or woolly-headed politicians. O'Connor shows that this simplistic view is not true, that enormous government budgets reflect the expansionary and survival needs of the capitalist order. *The Fiscal Crisis of the State* is highly recommended for those willing to tackle a difficult but brilliant book.

Among most educated persons Karl Marx is recognized as one of the greatest thinkers in history. His contributions in economics, history, sociology and philosophy are widely acclaimed as long as they are not applied to the present era. To acknowledge that Marx may have something important to say *today* is to open the door to the possibility that Marx was right about other things, including the necessity for socialist revolution. Reading #17 by Roger Alcaly explains the Marxian view of the economic downturn and shows that it has considerable relevance. Perhaps his relevance extends to political matters as well! The final reading of this triad (#18), by Robert Zevin, is a breath-taking essay on inflation, long-run investment cycles, the Eurodollar system, and more.

The three readings which follow can perhaps be described as historical and descriptive. The first of these is by Richard J. Barnet and Ronald Müller (#19), taken from their widely acclaimed book *Global Reach*. It focuses on a key participant in the unfolding drama of depression, the multinational corporation. Two aspects of its operations are discussed in this selection; first, the adverse effect these behemoths have on monetary and fiscal policy, and second, their tendency to undermine the wages and employment of American workers. Multinational corporations do not confine their activities to the capitalist world alone. Instead they are eager participants in the expanding trade with Communist nations. Joyce Kolko (#20) explores some of the underlying factors making for present-day détente. Finally, returning more to the domestic scene, Victor Perlo gives us his interpretation of the destabilizing role military expenditures have played during the cyclical swings of the postwar era (reading #21).

The last group of readings in this section is mainly useful in providing us with information about selected aspects of the workings of the economy and projections concerning its future. Anyone who doubts the seriousness of the current decline need only consult reading #22, reprinted from one of America's foremost corporate periodicals, *Business Week*. There the reader will find that the long postwar boom has been built on a paper mountain of debt and that there seems to be no reason why it won't collapse. Rarely is one likely to read a more abject confession of failure. At the center of this bubble of debt is a credit and banking system increasingly in peril. Instead of maintaining liquid secondary reserves in the form of short-term government securities, banks in recent years have turned to making risky but profitable loans to corporations and consumers. Moreover, banks themselves have borrowed extensively in order to do this. How and why this process works—and perhaps more important, its implications—are carefully analyzed in an important article (reading #23) by Harry Magdoff and Paul M. Sweezy, the internationally known Marxist economists. Following this, reading #24, taken from the *Wall Street Journal,* presents the dismal status of productivity. The most important implication of this article is that unemployment is apt to shoot up sharply as the year continues. Inflation may ebb a bit, though to what rate no one of course knows. One enormous obstacle to a reduction of prices is the prevalence of monopoly. Reading #25, by Richard C. Edwards, points out that prior to the rise of monopoly at the turn of the century, prices used to go down as frequently as they went up. In recent years there have been suggestions that to avoid the hardships and inequities which accompany inflation, the economy should be indexed; that is, inflation should simply be accepted, and wages, contracts, bonds, etc., should be adjusted to accord with the change in prices. Reading #26, taken from the monthly periodical *New American Movement,* critically examines this proposal. Finally, this section concludes on the sober note it has maintained throughout by reprinting from the *Wall Street Journal* an article specifying a number of scenarios for a full-scale depression (reading #27).

Reading *Business Week* and the *Wall Street Journal,* I am reminded of a trip to the mountain speedway (or "racer dips," as they were called where I grew up), where one is pulled up the first big incline and then guided around the bend, slow and calm, before the rapid plummet. These publications are saying, "Hold on tight—here we go!"

16. JAMES O'CONNOR'S *THE FISCAL CRISIS OF THE STATE*: AN OVERVIEW

by David Gold

One of the most widely noted facts about capitalist economies today is the large and apparently expanding role of the state. Whether measured by the size of spending and taxation, the amount of regulation, or the involvement in price and wage decisions, state activity is huge. In addition, this same activity is the subject of a substantial amount of political conflict. Struggles over who will gain from expenditures and regulations, and struggles over who will pay, or avoid, the necessary taxes, have become commonplace.

Despite the many manifestations of the state's important role in the economy, social scientists have been slow in developing a coherent explanation of the phenomenon. James O'Connor's *The Fiscal Crisis of the State* (St. Martin's Press, 1973) is an ambitious and provocative attempt to fill that gap. In formulating a theory of the state budget, O'Connor has contributed to a rethinking both of the relation between the state and the economy and of the dynamics of accumulation and economic growth.

Especially written for this book. David Gold is affiliated with the Center for Economic Studies, Palo Alto, California, and is a member of the Union for Radical Political Economics (URPE).

The Structure of the Economy

Governments throughout the capitalist world and at all levels in the United States have been experiencing a crisis in their ability to finance the activities that they are being called on to perform. The fiscal crisis is the tendency for government expenditures to grow faster than revenues. This is a phenomenon which is directly observed and which can be explained as the logical outcome of economic growth under capitalism. To find out what this logic is, O'Connor argues, a theory of the government budget is needed. But the budget itself represents only part of the fiscal crisis of the state. The fiscal crisis "reflect[s] and [is] structurally determined by social and economic conflicts between classes and groups" (p. 2). The theory of the budget must explain these conflicts and must, therefore, articulate the links between the budget and the economy and society.

O'Connor begins with a model of capital accumulation and economic growth. He divides the economy into three producing sectors: the monopoly sector, the competitive sector and the state sector.

The monopoly sector is composed of firms whose scale of production is very large and who have substantial control over the markets on which they buy and sell. (Economists call such firms oligopolies.) Firms in the monopoly sector grow primarily through increases in the quantity and quality of their plant and equipment; that is, via growth in capital and improvements in technology.

The way in which the monopoly sector grows has two important implications for the economy. One is that there is a tendency for capital-based growth to utilize less and less labor. As capital-labor ratios rise in production, there is a tendency for labor to be "freed," in the sense of there being a slower growth in job opportunities over time. Thus, capital-based growth tends to create surplus labor.

The second important implication is that the growth process in the monopoly sector tends to create productive capacity, the potential for producing goods and services, faster than can be absorbed by private economy. If this gap between potential output and realizable demand is not filled, and existing capacity is not utilized, profits will fall. Firms will attempt to cut costs, reduce their use of labor and limit their future expansion. There will be a slower rate of capital accumulation and economic growth, and the economy will be more subject to periodic, long-lasting depressions. Thus, the inability to sell what can be currently produced leads to a decline in productive capacity over time. In a sense, the economy's potential expands too fast, which creates the exact opposite tendency, one toward stagnation.

The problem of surplus capacity is exacerbated by the fact that productivity growth is slowest outside of the monopoly sector. As the competitive and state sectors grow, there has been a tendency for their costs of production to rise rapidly. With production labor-intensive in these sectors, it is extremely difficult to gain cost advantages with the systematic use of capital and technology. Thus, the amount spent in these sectors grows both because the sectors are being called on to do more, particularly in the case of the state, and because what they do costs more.

In summary, surplus capacity is a problem because total demand does not grow as fast as monopoly-sector productive potential, and because the pattern of expenditures shifts away from the monopoly sector.

The monopoly sector, then, is the source of two problems, surplus labor and surplus capacity, which are derived from a single process, capital accumulation. The state has more and more frequently been called upon to deal with these problems, and this has been a major determinant of the growth of state expenditures.

But there is a second, parallel process at work. While monopoly-sector growth creates the problems that lead to the expansion of some key items of the budget, at the same time budgetary expansion is an increasingly important determinant of monopoly-sector growth. The state has taken over more and more of the costs of investment and of the costs of creating and maintaining a skilled labor force—it subsidizes basic research, builds highways and industrial parks, and pays for higher education, to give three examples of state expenditures that promote accumulation and growth. Thus, the relation between the monopoly sector and the state runs both ways. "In other words, the growth of the state is both a cause and effect of the expansion of monopoly capital" (p. 8).

The competitive sector is composed of firms which produce on a small scale and which have little control over the markets on which they buy and sell. Production tends to be unstable, since with little market power these firms are subject to fluctuations from competition, seasonality and changing tastes. Firms in the competitive sector grow primarily through the expansion of low-wage labor.

Because production is less predictable, employment in the competitive sector tends to be unstable, with a more rapid turnover of jobs and a higher average rate of unemployment than in the monopoly sector. Productivity growth tends to be low, and that which occurs is more likely to be passed on to consumers in the form of lower prices than in the monopoly sector. Wages and fringe benefits are lower and unions weaker. Many workers in the competitive sector are members of the working poor—they have jobs, sometimes more than one in a family, but they are still in need of some kind of income supplement.

Competitive-sector workers form the core of the marginal work force, and the problem of surplus labor surfaces as a competitive-sector problem. Some of these marginal workers have, for all intents and purposes, been driven out of the labor force and become a "permanent" welfare population. Others are in and out of the labor force, but when they are in, they work intermittently and receive the lowest wages. Competitive-sector workers increasingly turn to the state for economic support. Sometimes they must also struggle against the state, as they are among the first victims of the fiscal crisis.

With entry relatively easy, competitive-sector industries tend to be crowded and the return on capital tends to be lower than in the monopoly sector. There is a high failure rate, and competitive-sector capitalists feel continuously threatened. They, too, will often turn to the state, seeking protection from unions, from rising costs and from the incursion of monopoly-sector firms, as, for example, in agriculture. Fair-trade laws, right-to-work laws, small-business-loan subsidies and the like have been some of the results. However, many of these state activities benefit monopoly-sector firms far more, and the competitive sector has been far less successful than the monopoly sector in gaining support from the state.

The state sector contains two types of production activities:

production which is organized by the state itself, such as the post office, public education and welfare, and production which the state contracts out to private firms, such as military equipment, and research and development. Within this categorization, some production is considered as being completely within the state sector, while, in other instances, firms produce both for the state and for sale on markets. An example is the General Electric Corporation, a producer of military equipment as well as capital and consumer goods for private markets. GE is part of both the state and the monopoly sectors. This empirical overlap is a potential source of confusion in applying the concepts, but the reason for such a definition is a powerful one. Production for the state is undertaken under a different set of criteria than production for markets. There is less competition, the constraint on demand is from the state budget and is more explicitly a political one, and there is less pressure for cost efficiency in production. State production and state contract production have an important characteristic in common— neither is subject to the kind of discipline that is imposed by the market. Instead, if there is a logic to the production process, it is one derived more from the politics of the budget.

The State Budget

O'Connor next turns to an analysis of the budget. His "first premise is that the capitalistic state must try to fulfill two basic and often mutually contradictory functions—*accumulation* and *legitimization*" (p. 6). Not only does the state get deeply involved in aiding private investment but it also attempts to create or preserve social harmony. The state's support of accumulation is often in conflict with its desire for peace and harmony. The accumulation process under capitalism is inherently unequal, as some groups and classes reap more of the benefits than others. The state must try to find some justification for its intervention, or it will undermine the basis of its support. (Thus Nixon, in justifying his New Economic Policy in 1971, declared that: "All Americans will benefit from more profits.") Yet successful support of accumulation leads to surplus capacity and surplus labor power, which threatens social and economic stability.

O'Connor's second premise is that the budget, the sum of spending and revenue-raising actions, can best be understood by relating these actions to accumulation and legitimization. The two main categories of expenditures are social capital, which corresponds to the accumulation function, and social expenses, which correspond to the legitimization function. Social capital is those expenditures that contribute to private accumulation, either by improving the productivity of the labor force or by reducing the labor costs that the firm must meet. Examples of the first type of social capital expenditures are physical investments, such as highways, utilities, office buildings, and sports and convention centers, and investments in the skills of individuals, such as public education and research and development performed directly by the government or subsidized out of state funds. These expenditures increase productivity by adding to the amount of capital and improving the level of technology that members of the labor force work with. They clearly increase the ability of firms to accumulate capital and reap profits, but the costs are borne by the state. Examples of the second type of social capital expenditures are items in the budget which provide goods and services that the working class can consume collectively, such as hospital and medical facilities, and items that provide some insurance against economic insecurity, such as social security or unemployment compensation. These are items that would probably have to come out of wage payments, and therefore be subject to higher wage demands by workers, if the state had not absorbed the costs.

Social expenses are those expenditures which attempt to maintain social stability both in the United States and wherever U.S. interests are present throughout the world. They do not contribute to capital accumulation but become necessary because of the results of accumulation. Examples include the police and military on the one hand, and the welfare system on the other. O'Connor argues that the dual problems of surplus capacity and surplus labor have led to an attempted solution in the form of a warfare-welfare state. Military expenditures try to raise demand directly, via purchases of equipment, and are necessary to protect foreign activities of U.S. business. Welfare and other income supplement and social control expenditures represent the strategy employed to deal with a surplus population.

Many items of expenditure perform more than one function. The military budget, in addition to being an example of social expenses, also includes items of social capital. Much research and development is subsidized by the Pentagon, and there are a number of examples of skilled labor, such as airline pilots, where substantial training is obtained in the military. The inter-state-highway system was designed with both social capital (moving goods and people) and social expenses (moving troops) in mind. Similarly, the same public-education system will attempt to train and control, though it is often different social classes that are trained and controlled.

The state has three main methods of raising the revenue needed to finance expenditures: it can produce and sell goods and services and use the net proceeds for other endeavors; it can borrow from individuals, firms and banks, and from abroad; and, of course, it can tax.

Nationalized industries and state-run enterprises are much more common in Europe than in the United States. Neither in Europe nor in the United States, however, has the state been able to use this form of activity as a revenue raiser. In fact, since state enterprises draw on the government's borrowing capacity for their expansion, and since capitalists have successfully resisted the incursion of state enterprise into areas that are profitable for private ownership, state enterprises tend to worsen the fiscal crisis. They provide services for private capital, such as running unprofitable but important activities like railroads and the postal service, do not earn profits and draw on the state for financing.

Since World War II, government borrowing has grown as a source of state financing. But this, too, is limited. Bonds must have buyers, and governments have been forced to raise the interest rates they pay in order to find the necessary market. This raises interest costs, which must come out of budget revenues. Government bonds compete with private bonds for scarce funds, and this is frequently viewed as a limitation on the state's ability to expand its debt. Government borrowing also contributes to inflationary pressures, particularly when the federal debt is used as the basis for expanding the money supply at a rapid rate. Inflation not only worsens the fiscal crisis, by making government activity more expensive, but also imposes limits on the ability of the state to finance its expenditures via issuance of debt.

Taxation is the remaining revenue source. Taxes have always been a way for one group to exploit another. In the United States, this is clear when data on tax incidence is examined. Income from labor is taxed at a much higher rate than income from property, and people with very high incomes, most of which is from property, pay a smaller percentage of their income in taxes than middle-income individuals. The state is continually faced with the problem of trying to explain or hide this unevenness, a product of its attempts to aid accumulation, or else run the risk of losing much popular support; that is, losing its legitimacy. It is very difficult to expand the tax base or raise tax rates without clear justification. Thus, taxation is also limited as a means to obviate the fiscal crisis, partly because the main fruits of accumulation, profits, are largely exempt from taxation, and partly because the expansion of existing tax sources are resisted by those who would pay. Taxpayers' revolts threaten both legitimacy and accumulation.

The State's Options

The fiscal crisis of the state is a result both of the increased demands on the state which arise from the process of accumulation and growth that characterize contemporary capitalism, and of the inability of the state to expand the sources of revenue fast enough to meet these increased demands. In addition, the fiscal crisis and its effects come back to haunt the firms in the monopoly sector. Inflation and heavy taxation tend to encourage militancy among labor leaders and rank-and-file workers. As O'Connor argues:

> Sooner or later, the fiscal crisis begins to threaten the traditional conditions for "labor peace" in the monopoly industries. The fiscal crisis is at root a social crisis: Economic and political antagonisms divide not only labor and capital but also the working class. This social crisis and the fiscal crisis, which mirrors and enlarges it, finally work their way back into the arena where the decisive conflicts and compromises between labor and capital occur—the monopoly sector industries (p. 44).

The warfare-welfare "solution" is incomplete and the state searches for other options. One is to run a managed recession in order to reduce wage and price rises, and to bring interest rates down. This may ameliorate some of the backlash from the fiscal crisis but does nothing to fill in the structural gap between state expenditures and revenues. In addition, a recession that is too long or deep may seriously cut into capital expansion and plunge the economy toward depression, exactly the situation that state intervention is supposed to prevent. Thus, the managed recession strategy is a temporary one.

A second strategy, which has been attempted extensively in Europe and the United States, is to institute wage and price controls in those sectors where wage demands are the greatest. Thus, monopoly- and state-sector wages would be hit the hardest. The experience of the wage-control mechanism in the United States indicates that the problems of legitimacy which they raise are immense. They are extremely difficult to enforce, particularly when unions no longer accept the rationale for their use.

A third strategy is to search for ways of reducing the costs of state activities. O'Connor envisions the possibility of a social-industrial complex, a link between the state and the monopoly sector with the aim of increasing productivity in order to lower costs and relieve the fiscal crisis. A favorite of liberals, the strategy of the social-industrial complex would attempt to stimulate demand through spending on social rather than on military projects, and care for the surplus population through expanded welfare and income-supplement programs. Greater productivity would reduce the costs of budgetary items in the state sector. The problem here is that state-sector productivity gains are extremely difficult to realize. Also, substantial segments of capital benefit from the military program and fight hard to retain their privileges. For the time being, the social-industrial complex seems to have died with the McGovern campaign, but that does not rule out the possibility of a resurrection.

A fourth strategy was attempted during the 1960's nationally, in the early days of the first Nixon Administration, and at state and local levels, most prominently by Governors Reagan in California and Rockefeller in New York. This was an attempt to reduce the costs of welfare and other agencies that deal with the surplus population. This was both an attack on the living standards of those who have been forced out of the labor force and an attempt at increasing the available pool of cheap labor, particularly for competitive-sector firms. This strategy was essentially defeated by a coalition that included many monopoly-sector capitalists, who feared the resulting social unrest. Many states and localities, however, still operate from this perspective.

The lack of a clear alternative strategy implies a continuation of the past: inflation and fiscal crisis, warfare and welfare, recession and attack on the living standards of the working class. What O'Connor's analysis indicates is that the ability of the state to "solve" the current economic crisis is limited by the contradictory nature of the system as a whole. The issue is not just one of tinkering with budgetary devices but one of restructuring the productive apparatus itself. Until that happens, economic crisis and fiscal crisis will continue to be part of our way of life.

17. THE RELEVANCE OF MARXIAN CRISIS THEORY

by Roger Alcaly

In the most basic sense, crises can be said to dominate the dynamics of capitalist development because capitalism is a system of production for profit rather than production for use.[1]

Unpublished paper. Roger Alcaly teaches economics at John Jay College, CUNY, and is a member of the Union for Radical Political Economics (URPE).

[1] More specifically, capitalism is a system of commodity production, or production for market exchange, in which labor power is also a commodity. The emergence of labor power as a commodity presupposes the separation of the means of production from the masses of the population, and the concentration of these resources in the hands of the capitalist class, a "historical condition" which Marx notes "comprises a world's

This means, of course, that anything which endangers profits will eventually lead to cutbacks in production and rising unemployment—in short, to economic crises. Thus, the formal possibility of crises which exists in any economic system in which the acts of purchase and sale are not identical and hence are capable of rupture is vastly enhanced under capitalism where production will only take place if it expands the value of capital. Moreover, there are several systematic factors which operate in the course of capitalist economic development to depress profits and consequently aggregate economic activity. These elements turn the formal possibilities of crises into actual crises.

Capitalist economic development is propelled by the continual investment of capitalists' profits in never-ending search of still larger and larger profits. The capitalist, *qua* capitalist, has no choice in this regard. He is compelled to act in this manner by the competitive struggle for survival. As Marx wrote in Volume I of *Capital:*

> The capitalist shares with the miser the passion for wealth as wealth. But that which in the miser is a mere idiosyncrasy is, in the capitalist, the effect of the social mechanism of which he is but one of the wheels. Moreover, the development of capitalist production makes it constantly necessary to keep increasing the amount of the capital laid out in a given industrial undertaking, and competition makes immanent laws of capitalist production to be felt by each individual capitalist, as external coercive laws. It compels him to keep constantly extending his capital, in order to preserve it, but extend it he cannot, except by means of progressive accumulation.

The principal strands in Marxian crisis theory revolve around the effects of the reserve army of the unemployed on wages and profits, the ability of capitalists to realize full profits on

history. Capital therefore announces from its first appearance a new epoch in the process of social production." See *Capital*, Vol. I, International Publishers, p. 170.

Capital employs labor as long as it will produce a surplus or profit, while the laborer is "free" to offer his labor power for sale in the sense that "as a free man he can dispose of his labor power as his own commodity, and that on the other hand he has no other commodity for sale, is short of everything necessary for the realisation of his labor power." *Ibid.*, p. 169.

all they produce or are capable of producing, and the generation of profits themselves.[2] Each will be considered briefly in turn.

As accumulation of capital, or investment, proceeds, additional physical capital and labor power are required in order to expand production. The labor requirements depend on the pace of accumulation and on the relative importance of labor in the production process. The more rapid the rate of capital accumulation, and the more labor-intensive the production process, the greater will be the tendency for the demand for labor power to outrun the supply, eventually exhausting the reserves of cheap labor power provided by the reserve army of the unemployed and the noncapitalist sectors of production like subsistence farmers and the self-employed. The exhaustion of the reserve army of the unemployed, however, weakens a crucial element of capitalist discipline on wages. As a consequence, wages could be expected to rise, profits to fall, and the economic expansion to reverse itself.

The exhaustion of the reserve army, like the other major crisis tendencies of capitalism, can be offset to a certain extent by imperialist expansion. For example, export of capital to areas where labor is in more abundant supply, and cheaper, increases the overall rate of profit in two ways: the capital invested abroad earns a higher rate of profit than it could have earned at home, *and* the investment of capital overseas rather than at home tends to lessen the demand for domestic labor power and lower its price. In effect, the reserve army is simultaneously recruited at home and abroad.[3]

The crisis tendencies of capitalism should properly be viewed

---

[2] These crisis tendencies are generally referred to as crises arising from the exhaustion of the reserve army of the unemployed, which is discussed by Marx in *Capital,* Vol. I, ch. XXV, entitled "The General Law of Capitalist Accumulation"; realization crises or crises arising from underconsumption (see Paul Sweezy, *The Theory of Capitalist Development* [Monthly Review Press, 1968], ch. X); and crises arising from the tendency of the rate of profit to fall (see Marx, *Capital,* Vol. III, part III).

[3] Cf. Maurice Dobb, *Political Economy and Capitalism* (London, Routledge and Kegan Paul Ltd., 1940, pp. 231–32), who goes on to note that "this double gain is the reason why, fundamentally, the interest of capital and of labour in this matter are opposed, and why a capitalist economy has a motive for imperialist policy which a socialist economy would not have."

as the driving force behind imperialist expansion. This crucial aspect of the development of capitalism as a world-wide economic system cannot be pursued in the following discussion, which is confined essentially to a domestic perspective.

Capitalists might respond to the reduction of profits as a result of the exhaustion of the reserve army by introducing labor-saving technology which replenishes the reserve army by making part of the working population redundant. Wage discipline is thus restored. However, this line of attack opens up two other threats to the rate of profit and continued expansion. On the one hand, the relatively small incomes of the majority of the population limit their ability to consume the output that the economy is increasingly capable of producing. But consumption of all that is produced, or is capable of being produced, is necessary to keep the whole cycle going. In order to "realize" their profits, the major part of which will go into further accumulation, capitalists must sell their output at its value. If this can't be done, prices will fall, production will be cut back, workers will be laid off and accumulation will fall off. And once the recessionary sequence has started in any part of the economy, it is very difficult to contain because of the interdependencies among the various sectors. The same thing in effect will result if, in anticipation of their not being able to sell all that their firms are capable of producing, capitalists choose to keep some productive capacity idle and to hire fewer workers.

On the other hand, the increased use of physical capital per worker in the production process tends to restrict the basis from which profits are extracted. Profits arise essentially from the difference between the amount capitalists must pay workers and the amount they receive from the sale of the workers' output. The decreased reliance on labor in the production process thus tends to restrict the rate of profit unless there is a concomitant increase in the profit generated by each worker, a situation which will tend to occur to the extent that productivity rises. Thus, if the increased use of labor-saving technology is not offset by sufficiently rapid technological progress and by increases in productivity, it too can lead to a deterioration in the rate of profit and economic contraction. These interconnected pressures on the rate of profit preclude an uninterrupted expansion. Rather, they tend to produce the crisis-ridden pattern of development characteristic of capitalist economic history.

Moreover, the entire process of capitalist development takes place within the context of the "anarchy" of capitalist production; that is, within an industrial structure whose interrelated parts tend to be coordinated by the "invisible hand" of the market. Such a system is capable of magnifying disruption in any one sector and transmitting it throughout the entire economy, as was the case to a certain extent in the so-called energy crisis. The "anarchy" of capitalist production thus may be considered an independent source of crisis or, more appropriately, an important part of the framework within which the other crisis tendencies operate.

No matter how these tendencies interact to produce a fall in the rate of profit, the falling rate of profit eventually sets off a cumulative process of declining production and employment. Investment will eventually drop in response to a fall in the rate of profit, either because the fall in the rate of profit results in a decline in the funds available for investment or because capitalists have, or expect to have, more profitable alternative uses for their funds. In either case the economic contraction will be reversed only when the basis for profitable production is restored.

Economic crises therefore serve an essentially restorative function for capitalism in a very real sense if they are not accompanied by widespread unrest and the development of movements for social change which threaten capitalism's continued existence. By forcibly, and at great social cost, reestablishing the basis for profitable production, crises set the stage for subsequent expansions. For Marx, "Permanent crises do not exist." Rather, "these contradictions [of capitalism] lead to explosions, cataclysms, crises in which by momentaneous suspension of labor and annihilation of a great portion of capital the latter is violently reduced to the point where it can go on."

The classical way to deal with an economic recession has been to ride it out essentially on the backs of working people. This is the course advocated by more conservative members of the capitalist class and their economic advisers and is the tack being followed by the present Administration. Milton Friedman is reported to have called this the "bang-bang" approach to policy: restrict government spending and growth of the money supply, allowing unemployment to rise and the adjustment process to take place as rapidly as possible. Similarly, Nobel Laureate Friedrich von Hayek has recently argued that the "teachings of Lord Keynes are a seductive doctrine" which merely postpones, and thereby intensifies, the inevitable economic downturn.

The "Keynesian Revolution" was supposed to have eliminated the capitalist business cycle. Balanced growth at full employment, with stable prices, was presumably attainable with the aid of appropriate governmental macroeconomic policy. But the Keynesian doctrines, widely accepted by policy makers in this country since the tax cut of 1964, have not enjoyed a very long run. The root of the problem appears to be the relative lack of attention given to the profit squeeze which tends to accompany economic expansions. For example, Raford Boddy and James Crotty have shown that all the periods of expansion in the American economy between 1954 and 1970 have been characterized by a declining profits/wages ratio during the second half of their duration.[4] Yet this phenomenon and its implications have generally been ignored in the ideological structure generated by the work of Keynes despite the fact that Keynes himself and so-called "neo-Keynesians" or "left Keynesians" like Joan Robinson were well aware of its importance.

People making policy in the interest of capital can ill afford to ignore the behavior of profits over the course of the business cycle because capital is in essence self-expanding value, and a squeeze on profits interferes with this expansion. The paramount importance of profits to a capitalist economy is at least partially reflected in the attention this variable has been receiving from segments of the business press, newsletters of banks, like the Morgan Guaranty Trust Company and First National

[4] See Raford Boddy and James Crotty, "Class Conflict, Keynesian Policies and the Business Cycle," *Monthly Review* (October 1974). Their work draws on Michal Kalecki's "The Political Aspects of Full Employment," *Selected Essays on Economic Dynamics* (Cambridge University Press, 1971), pp. 138–45. Boddy and Crotty tend to attribute the fall in the profits/wages ratio solely to the exhaustion of the reserve army in the course of expansion. I prefer to see this development as the result of the interaction of the three crisis tendencies outlined above. More work obviously needs to be done in pinning down the precise nature of this interaction and in applying this set of explanations to a concrete situation such as the present one.

City, and the papers on economic activity published by the Brookings Institution, a prestigious "think tank" located in Washington, D.C. Capitalism's ideologues, on the other hand, cannot afford to recognize the profits squeeze which eventually accompanies expansion because its implications call into question their neat theories about the harmony of class interests.

In some respects the Hayekian position, with its recognition of the inevitability of the downturn and the consequences of the "Keynesian" attempt to eliminate this phase of the capitalist business cycle, is similar to the Marxian view outlined above. However, Marxian analysis is far more sophisticated. It recognizes that the capitalist state's stabilization policy must ultimately maintain some form of the business cycle in order to maintain profits. But it is also cognizant of the fact that the restorative effect of cycles on profits must also be balanced against the social unrest which is likely to accompany severe downturns, and full restoration of profits. This balancing act— one which James O'Connor describes more generally as involving the contradictory objectives of maintaining profitable conditions for capital accumulation as well as ensuring the continued legitimacy of a fundamentally exploitative system—constitutes the real problem of "fine tuning" which crops up so often in discussions of government macroeconomic policy.

With this in mind it is somewhat easier to sort out the various perspectives on the economy and economic policy. Conservatives tend to consider Keynesians silly for not understanding how the economy functions, while Keynesians view conservatives as naïve for not taking the political implications of economic policy sufficiently into account. Marxists, on the other hand, understand the tension arising from the relationship between the "economic" and "political" aspects of economic policy, because they view the system in class terms and see its "laws of motion" arising from the contradictions contained in the antagonistic capital-labor relationship.

18. THE POLITICAL ECONOMY OF THE AMERICAN EMPIRE, DECEMBER 1974

by Robert Zevin

The salient characteristic of the economy of the American empire which demands and defies explanation is a virulent price inflation rivaling or exceeding any inflation in history since the Industrial Revolution. It is useful to begin with a taxonomy of extant theories. First is the confluence of random accidents. These include bad weather and associated bad crops, the absence of anchovies off the coast of Peru, the devaluation of the dollar, the Yom Kippur War as a stimulus to the effective organization of OPEC, the ecology movement and perhaps the war in Southeast Asia. A variant of this approach has been constructed by Michael Harrington, who adds the predisposition of advanced capitalism to be vulnerable to such accidents, to invite such accidents, and to be unable to effectively respond to such accidents. A second explanation hinges almost exclusively on the Vietnam war. Because broad political support did not exist for the war, this argument holds that inflationary financing was the only political alternative and that the economy continues to suffer the dynamic consequences of that decision. The unique importance of the war is also incorporated in the Kondratieff Cycle theories, which hold that 1974 is an inflationary peak year in a fifty-four-year cycle and therefore generally analogous to 1920, 1866 and 1814 in American economic history. Fortuitously (and mysteriously), a war always precedes

Unpublished paper. Robert Zevin has taught economics at Simmons, Harvard, Berkeley and Columbia, and is at present an investment counselor in Cambridge, Massachusetts.

these years of peak inflation in the Kondratieff chronology. In addition, Kondratieff theories may or may not embody a long-term investment cycle, long-term demographic cycles or long-term cycles in the psychology of consumers, workers, businessmen and other decision makers.

Liberal-establishment economists have generally opted for one or a combination of the above explanations. In addition, they sometimes argue that the inflation is a result of a persistent deficiency of investment and capital formation which has been used to pay for unsustainably rapid increases in consumption, nonproductive state expenditures or both. The deficiency of investment is the one element which frequently appears in both liberal and right-wing explanations.

Otherwise, right-wing theorists (Milton Friedman, Hayek, *Barron's,* innumerable "gold bugs" and Wall Street letter writers, etc.) have generally embraced one or more of the following propositions. The political commitment of the federal government to full employment has made it increasingly unable and unwilling to permit normal cyclical contractions to keep inflation in check. This commitment has led the federal government to persistent deficit spending, with consequent inflationary effects. The Federal Reserve Board, by monetizing these deficits or monetizing administered monopoly price increases or union wage increases, has provided the real engine of inflation. Once begun, deficit spending and/or monetary expansion designed to produce full employment set off automatic accelerators. Inflation, coupled with the ready availability of reserves to the banking system and the demonstrable commitment of the government to fighting cyclical contractions, simultaneously encourages businesses and consumers to become greater debtors and ensures that their demands will be met. Thus, government deficits with inflationary financing spawn consumer and business deficits, and the inflationary creation of private credit to finance them. All this in turn can only lead to more inflation.

The more advanced the process, the more determined the federal government and the Federal Reserve Board become to prevent any cyclical reversal, because as the process advances, the financial vulnerability of businesses, consumers and banks is increased and even a mild cyclical dip threatens to touch off a chain reaction of financial disasters. In addition, everyone in the system acquires a vested interest in continuing inflation without which debts would become excessively burdensome to the debtors with unpleasant consequences for creditors as well.

Thus, the economy becomes addicted to ever larger injections of fresh money with ever lessening real results. Like most addicts it is destined to eventually OD. Finally, in many rightwing views this decay of the monetary system is accompanied by a decay of economic motivations, law, order and morality. Business and organized labor become dependent on the state for protection of the monopoly positions and monetization of their administered prices, as well as for a proliferating array of subsidies and special favor legislation. A growing mass comes to depend on welfare or other handouts from the state in preference to honest labor for honest pay. The whole society becomes hedonist, lawless, environmentally polluted and violent.

For the most part, left-wing observers concoct explanations consisting of an eclectic selection from those utilized by liberal or reactionary economists. Only James O'Connor's *The Fiscal Crisis of the State* comes close to offering a systematic analysis of inflation from a radical perspective. Even so, the primary purpose of the book is to explain the crisis described in its title. Hence any explanation of inflation is only implicit and incidental to this purpose. [See reading #1 in this section]

I reject the confluence of random accidents on methodological grounds as the last resort of defeated analysts. The war in Southeast Asia is simply too slender an economic event on which to base the mammoth inflation which now engulfs the capitalist world. At the height of the war, military expenditures were less than 9% of American gross national product, whereas during the Korean War they exceeded 12%. The symptoms of inflationary decay were also distinctly apparent before the major escalation of the war in the mid 1960's. The Eurodollar market alone—which began with the enactment of the Interest Equalization Tax in 1962—has clearly made a quantitatively far more significant contribution to inflation than all of the expenditures related to the war in Southeast Asia. The Kondratieff Cycle is more appealing, for a variety of reasons. First, the conformance of its regularity is compellingly consistent with events to date. Second, there is a good deal of evidence which suggests that the the immediate future will also conform to its predictions. The inflationary bubble of commodity prices seems to have been pierced already and is currently deflating at a frightening rate comparable to the 1920–21 experience. Third, we seem to be well into an empire-wide experience of depression, increasing unemployment, inventory liquidation, surplus capital and reduced capital-investment budgets, and a high probability of major financial failures and bankruptcies with attendant liquidation of financial credits. Fourth, the theory leaves its users free to supply a variety of alternative specific explanations of its mysterious periodicity. Explanations involving long-term demographic or social-psychological cycles are appealing and suggestive. I will pass them over here because they are peripheral to my main concerns.

The long-term investment cycle as an explanation of Kondratieff phenomena is easier to deal with and also conflicts directly with other explanations of inflation. Kondratieff himself and Schumpeter have tended to view long-term waves of economic activity as long-term investment cycles. In its simplest form this explanation holds that one or a combination of technological innovations require a prolonged period of massive investment. Because these investments are large and/or geographically extensive and/or form complex interdependent chains of facilities, a prolonged period of time elapses during which the aggregate of resources devoted to investment purposes is large and the resultant increase in the flow of consumer goods for final consumption is relatively small. Examples would include the interrelated development of harbors, canals, sailing ships, warehouses, inland steamers, cotton-growing and sheep-grazing agriculture, textile mills, iron foundries and machine shops between the Napoleonic wars and the U.S. Civil War. Similarly, the development of a world-wide railroad network, extensive wheat and livestock agriculture, steamship, agricultural processing, steel and chemical complex in the fifty years after the U.S. Civil War. For the most recent cycle, the leading sectors which have absorbed tremendous investment funds include facilities for manufacturing automobiles, trucks and aircraft, the products of those facilities which are themselves investment goods, a world-wide complex for discovering, producing, transporting and refining petroleum products and distributing them; a complex of petrochemical, plastics, synthetic-fibers investments; and the electronics industry in the broadest sense of that term; not to mention the highways, airports and suburbs which were made possible by or were required by these innovations. In this view the recent inflation reflects excessively high investment in these very industries at precisely the time when they have matured in the sense of having adequate or surplus productive capacity. This view is borne out (and the contrary view of *deficiency* of investment is contradicted) by recent statistics for gross private domestic capital formation as a percentage of national income. For the past nine years this percentage has been higher than for any other nine-year period since the end of World War I. It is similarly apparent that investment has been a very high percentage of total economic activity throughout the international sphere of American influence.

If we leave aside the institutional structure of control over resources, it is readily apparent that in some fundamental economic sense the empire at the moment has a surplus of crude petroleum reserves, automobiles, trucks, aircraft and the facilities for producing them, highways and numerous other products of the investment boom of the past quarter century. On the one hand, monopoly power and cartels maintain "artificially" high prices for such products as automobiles and crude petroleum; on the other hand, until this moment the appearance of scarcity has continued to stimulate extraordinarily costly marginal investments to increase the supply of the selfsame goods (offshore drilling and production, synthetic crude, new highways at costs in excess of $1 million per mile, etc.). These developments are quite analogous to the formation of steel and agricultural-products cartels in the late nineteenth and early twentieth centuries, as well as the expensive duplication of railroad trackage for intrarailroad competitive purposes.

A word should be added about the treatment of government expenditures for purposes of this investment-cycle analysis. O'Connor's observation that the growth of monopoly capital requires a disproportionate growth of government expenditures seems to be theoretically and empirically correct. The question is what portion of those expenditures are investments which are self-limiting in character because they make some actual contribution to the ability of the economy to produce more goods and services. Clearly, capital infrastructure such as highways, airports, public buildings, schools, hospitals and housing are of this character. If even these limited investment expenditures by government are added to private investment expenditures, the lopsided nature of the recent investment boom becomes even more apparent. In addition to these expenditures, government and private operating costs of education, health maintenance and scientific research all have at least in part the character of investment expenditures in that they result in improving the productivity of the work force. If these additional expenditures are also thrown into the comparison, we must conclude that the past nine years represent the dizzy heights of a historically tremendous investment boom.

A final point in favor of the Kondratieff Cycle explanation is that it calls for a sharp contraction in real economic activity characterized by rising unemployment, inventory liquidation, a reduction of real capital spending, severe financial system strains and sharp declines in price levels. There is at the moment every indication that each of those phenomena is already well under way.

I turn now to the right-wing explanations of inflation. At the outset it must be conceded that these theories have two very strong points in their favor. First, no other theoretical conception so adequately accounts for so much observed data. Second, no other theories or theorists can claim to have accurately predicted so much and so far in advance of what has actually happened and what appears likely to happen. I shall concentrate on those aspects of the empire's financial institutions and monetary system which are particularly illuminated by the right-wing point of view. It is indisputable that from the end of World War II until this year there has been a persistent secular tendency for the rate of growth of the domestic money supply to accelerate. It is also indisputable that there has been a persistent tendency for all levels of government, the business sector and the household sector to increase indebtedness compared to total assets or total incomes of those sectors. Both principal and interest debt servicing requirements have become ever larger portions of income for all three sectors. Even the banking system has more and more resorted to interest-bearing deposits and straight-debt instruments in order to meet the increasing demands for loans from other sectors. Superimposed on this tremendous growth of money supply and debt obligations has been an even more explosive growth of near-money credits and liquid assets. These include the spectacular growth in the circulation of credit cards, the creation of automatic overdraft checking accounts, and the growth of such near-money assets and liabilities as savings accounts, treasury bills, municipal notes, bankers acceptances and commercial paper—each of which has grown even more rapidly than the money supply itself.

The result of this process, compounded by inflation, is to increase the financial vulnerability of households, businesses, governments and banks. The further the process continues, the more these paper liabilities and assets become multiplied by serving as the foundation for the creation of still more liabilities and assets; the lower becomes the margin of equity available to businesses, banks and households to absorb any period of economic reversals; and the more the soundness and collectability of debts and other liabilities become dependent on the continued creation of new money and new paper assets, as well as the maintenance of stable or rising commodity prices. The obverse of all this is that the system becomes more and more vulnerable to a major chain reaction of financial disasters and collapses in response to less and less severe moderations in real economic activity or the rate of price increases. Hence government central banks and private banks become more and more determined to make good on their past excesses by extending, reextending and multiplying them in a variety of old and complexly new ways, all of which compound and accelerate the rate of inflation and the financial vulnerability of the entire system.

All of these effects are duplicated and multiplied in the international monetary systems of the empire. Since the 1940's the U.S. dollar has been the de facto international reserve currency of the empire. The United States has exploited its reserve-currency status to export a large and growing stream of dollars to the rest of the world ever since the end of World War II. Until the late 1950's a sufficient portion of these dollars returned to New York as deposits in banks or for the purchase of treasury bills to effectively disguise what was really happening. Ever since the late 1950's the United States has had a persistent and growing balance-of-payments deficit, and since the late 1960's it has had a deficit in current payments for goods and services alone as well. This was originally due primarily to the rapid economic development of Western Europe and Japan to the point where they became effective competitors. Since the formation of the OPEC cartel, the balance of payments of the entire capitalist world has been thrown into severe deficit. This persistent outflow of dollars has been used to pay for the far-flung military expenses of empire; to finance a massive diversion of investment from the domestic United States to other capitalist and to underdeveloped countries; and increasingly, as well, to pay for massive imbalances in the consumption of raw materials, manufactured goods and tourism services.

To the extent that these dollars returned to the United States, they became directly or indirectly deposits in New York banks. To the extent that the Federal Reserve System did not attempt to deliberately neutralize their effect, they contributed to a further growth of domestic credit. If they did not return to New York, these dollars found their way to the central banks of other major capitalist countries, where they were exchanged for Deutsche mark, francs, pounds, yen or whatever. In this way they contributed to an unwanted or at least unplanned expansion of the money supply of other major industrial countries in the empire and had the effect of exporting the American inflation to the rest of the empire. To the extent that these inflations reduced the international competitiveness or the domestic real incomes of Germany, France, England, Japan or any other country, they tended as well to export the military and investment costs of empire to these other nations.

The Eurodollar market is a special and quantitatively very important aspect of the international scope of the current inflation. In 1961 there was no such thing as a short-term Eurodollar market. Today, that market has created a supply of purchasing power roughly comparable to the entire domestic money supply of the United States. The proximate motive for the creation of the Eurodollar market on the part of major American banks and multinational corporations was the desire to evade the Interest Equalization Tax, "voluntary" guidelines for direct overseas investment and lending, and other regulations of the early Kennedy Administration designed to stem the balance-of-payments outflow. A closely related result was to create a money and banking system that escaped all regulation. Although Eurodollars (or more precisely, all expatriate dollars), considered as a distinct currency, are the second largest pool of purchasing power in the world, they are the only currency for which there is no central bank to act as either a rescue lender of last resort or a regulator of the growth of deposits and loans within conservative limits.

To the right-wing theorists this development is only part of a broader picture which shows the progressive deterioration of conservative self-imposed and regulatory constraints on the money and credit system. It is coincident with the development of certificates of deposit in the domestic banking market, instruments whose clear purpose is to evade the substance of many of the banking reforms of the 1930's. It precedes by a half decade or so the widespread resort of banks to debt capital, and it precedes by a little more than a decade the current state of extreme deterioration in the ratios of loans and capital to deposits, in the relative quality of loans and deposits, and in every other conceivable measure of the liquidity of the purely domestic operations of American banks, especially the very largest ones. In the right-wing view this process reflects both a waning commitment to prudent constraints, as the historic events which called them into existence fade further into the past, and a response on the part of both private and central banks to the accelerating pressures for more generous credit creation in order to keep the entire system from unraveling.

In any case, the Eurodollar system is a classic example of an undercapitalized, unregulated, overexpanded, private banking system. It is precisely comparable to the American system of state banks in the 1820's and the 1830's. The only true reserves of the system are in the form of deposits which various Eurodollar banks in London have with their home offices in New York or less frequently in London, Frankfurt, Paris or Tokyo. These total some $5 billion to $10 billion. However, these dollars are hardly "as good as gold," given the precarious positions of the home offices as well as the ambiguous commitment of their respective central banks to rescuing a monetary system which has grown to monstrous proportions outside of their control. As with the American state banking system, these slender reserves are multiplied through a complex round robin of interbank deposits, with each bank counting as reserves its gross credit against every other bank. As with the American bank state notes, one Eurodollar is not necessarily equal to another. Banks and private depositors make sharp distinctions between Eurodollar banks. For every participant in this market there exists some group of Eurodollar banks in which it is never acceptable to have a deposit or any other form of credit because of a presumed high degree of risk. This is exactly analogous to a New York bank in the 1830's refusing to accept a note issued by a bank in Memphis. Similarly, the bewildering array of conditions and interest rates under which each Eurodollar bank can obtain deposits from every other participant is precisely analogous to the complex schedules of discounts at which the notes of state banks are sold depending on the issuer as well as the place of sale.

. . .

Just as the monetary and investment analyses are parallel and in no significant way conflicting, so too is a Marxist point of view with each of them. Marxist analysis already incorporates a well-developed theory which accounts for investment or monetary cycles of any duration. What distinguishes a Marxist or other radical points of view from most of those already discussed, and characterizes them in common with some radical right points of view, is the belief that there is a secular progression from one cycle to the next reflecting the evolution, sharpening contradictions and ultimate disintegration of the capitalist system.

What changes can we identify over the past one, two or three fifty-four-year segments of the history of capitalism? The most persistent and obviously apparent trend is the growing relative importance of governments in the total economic system, no matter how measured. In every capitalist country, no matter when the Industrial Revolution began and no matter how large a role the state played at that point, the relative importance of government has increased irreversibly and without exception ever since. A perhaps related observation is the persistent trend toward increasing interdependence throughout the economies of the capitalist world and its less developed territories. It has become more and more difficult for any enterprise or region or country to effect an economic destiny for itself, independent of the course of the empire-wide economy. An orthodox Marxist analysis would suppose an increasing concentration of ownership and control over private productive capacity as well. However, the evidence on this point is far from clear. On the one hand, an increasing number of industries are characterized by the presence of very large firms with national or international scope of operation and some degree of monopoly power in product and factor markets. On the other hand, within many of these same industries the degree to which capacity is concentrated in the largest firms has declined over the past twenty-five or fifty or seventy-five years (for example, steel, aluminum, copper, petroleum production, refining and marketing, automobiles and computers). Especially since the end of World War II, leading American multinationals have been faced with an increasingly formidable array of new domestic and overseas competitors at the same time that they have continued to grow. Perhaps many of these new competitors will prove to be the ephemeral children of the late stages of a Kondratieff Cycle doomed to perish in the forthcoming contraction. Indeed, a rapid reconcentration of power in the hands of the very largest institutions is already under way in domestic and international banking as well as in certain other industries where access to credit is particularly vital.

I will return in a little while to the impact which these encroachments may have had on the perspective and behavior of the largest multinational corporations. I wish now to return again to the Eurodollar market specifically, and the explosion of money and credit more generally, to consider the quite different explanation of these phenomena in a Marxist framework. Let us accept as a premise for argument that monopoly capital or major multinational corporations have a persistent tendency to increase their productive capacity more rapidly than the natural rate of increase of effective demand for their products, given capitalist institutions which determine the distribution of purchasing power. Then, quite obviously, it is in the interest of monopoly capital to create new markets for its surplus productive capacity. This is the traditional Marxist explanation of the market-capturing function of the modern warfare state as well as the domestic market-creating functions of the modern welfare state. This point of view also provides a compelling explanation of the dynamic urgency with which the Eurodollar market has exploded.

Until quite recently, virtually all Eurodollar loans were made directly or indirectly to governments or enterprises outside the United States in order to finance some sort of investment. Major investment projects included the purchase of large computer systems, modern commercial jet aircraft, electronic-aerospace military systems, heavy industrial processing complexes (steel, petroleum refining, petrochemicals, fertilizers, automobile plants, foundries, etc.), raw-material exploitation and transportation investments (offshore drilling rigs, pipelines, supertankers), and the construction of roads, ports, dams and housing. With the sole exception of the construction of supertankers, all of these activities require the provision of capital goods and services in which American-based multinational corporations are preeminent. Thus, until quite recently, virtually every dollar lent in the Eurodollar market became a dollar of sales for a leading multinational American corporation. Also, virtually every such dollar came back in the form of a deposit in a Eurodollar banking institution. In this respect, the expansion of the Eurodollar market is quite analogous to the explosion of international lending from London, Paris and New York to Latin America, Africa, Asia and Eastern Europe at the end of the last Kondratieff Cycle.

However, there are important differences as well. First of all, the magnitude of this activity relative to the dimensions of domestic economic activity in the United States, Western Europe and Japan exceeds the relative comparison for the period preceding World War I by a factor of 5 or 10. Second, it has not been possible this time to pass on the burden of the loans which have been extended to some broader cross section of the investing public. The very corporations which have benefited have also assumed the risks of the loans made through their dominant position as depositors in the Eurodollar banking system. The loans themselves seem no more collectable than those made in the earlier period. However, the different distribution of the burdens of default may help to explain the seeming ability of the Eurodollar banking system to defy the laws of gravity. The multinational banks and the multinational manufacturers who are their depositors have a common interest in trying to maintain the integrity of the Eurodollar credit structure. Thus, just as in the late nineteenth and early twentieth centuries, when a loan matures it is reextended for a longer period of time in an amount sufficient to retire the existing loan plus interest. On the other side of the ledger, a maturing certificate of deposit is redeposited in an amount sufficient to cover the interest which has been earned. Thus, on paper, both the bank and the industrial depositor show that they possess real assets which are producing real profits. The fiction can be maintained as long as no one insists on turning these multiplying paper assets into something more nearly like real money. Everyone knows that any attempt to do so will have near-fatal effects on everyone. This syndrome is as old as economic history, which contains repeated examples of loans made from a metropolitan center to finance exports to peripheral areas. The peripheral areas, being unable to return a sufficient quantity of real economic goods to the metropolitan center in order to pay for the original exports, ultimately retroactively confiscate the original goods by defaulting on their loan obligations.

The Eurodollar market is only an especially clear case of how a Marxist analysis applies to the whole spectrum of the inflationary expansion of credit and the government's fiscal commitment to "full employment," all of which have the ultimate and futile purpose of trying to make effective market demand expand as rapidly as the productive capacity of monopoly capital.

. . .

In lieu of a summary of these analytical meanderings, I offer my future detractors some predictions which seem to me to follow from the foregoing considerations. First, the present inflation will end with a sharp deflationary, credit-liquidating, empire-wide economic contraction. Most likely it has already begun, but it could conceivably be staved off for another two to four years. A consequence of these events will be to further concentrate political and economic power in the hands of the already largest and most powerful private and government bureaucracies at the expense of their lesser competitors and everyone else. Second, there will be yet another Kondratieff Cycle, characterized by technological innovations in the service and state service areas analogous to the revolutionary applications which have already been made of computer and communications technology to the banking industry. Third, inflation will reappear throughout the empire sooner and stronger than one would expect from the past economic history of capitalism. Fourth, real per capita economic growth, throughout the empire will be lower for the next half-century than the 1½% to 2% annual range which has prevailed over the last two centuries or more. Fifth, the future life of the empire's political economy will be disturbed by increasingly frequent and severe battles among and between competing state and private centers of power. Sixth, this will reinforce the already evident tendency for the political economy of the empire to grow increasingly volatile and unpredictable in the short run.

Beyond all this, both the empire and the multinationals will survive for many more decades and perhaps longer than that. More likely than not, the empire as a governmental system will fall, while the multinationals will survive its decline.

19. THE NEGATIVE EFFECTS OF MULTINATIONAL CORPORATIONS

by Richard J. Barnet and Ronald Müller

Multinationals Undermine Fiscal and Monetary Policy
The dramatic spread of United States corporations overseas in the mid-nineteen-sixties has compounded the problems of the

Abridged from two articles in *The New Yorker* (December 2 and 9, 1974), which were based on *Global Reach: The Power of the Multinational Corporations* (New York, Simon & Schuster, 1975). Richard J. Barnet is co-director of the Institute for Policy Studies, and Ronald Müller teaches economics at American University (Washington, D.C.).

White House, the Treasury, and the Federal Reserve System. Keynesian fiscal and monetary policies, reasonably effective when the economy was less concentrated and only minimally dependent upon commercial and financial transactions taking place beyond its borders, are increasingly inadequate to manage the North American division of the global economy. It is sometimes argued that the dependence of the United States on the world economy is exaggerated. After all, exports and imports account for only a little more than ten per cent of the gross national product of the United States. But the true extent of the dependence of the United States economy on foreign operations cannot be gleaned by focussing on exports and imports. In 1970, about twenty per cent of all corporate profits were derived from abroad. For many of America's major corporations, foreign profits mean the difference between operating in the black or in the red. Moreover, the actual magnitude of foreign-derived earnings must include profits derived from exports and imports plus the substantial disguised or unreported profits obtained by transfer-price manipulations. If all these factors are considered, some thirty per cent of total United States corporate profits can now be directly or indirectly attributed to overseas operations. This increased dependence on foreign investment and the changed character of that investment have had profound effects on employment in the United States.

Between 1966 and 1970, there was an increase of fifty-three per cent in exports produced in the American factories of global corporations and a spectacular increase of ninety-two per cent in exports from their foreign subsidiaries—exports that, had they been produced in the United States, would have provided thousands of jobs for American workers, especially since much of this foreign production was in labor-intensive industries. According to a Department of Commerce study, the two hundred and ninety-eight American-based global corporations had an annual growth rate of over five per cent in overseas employment during these years and a growth rate in domestic employment of under three per cent. By the end of 1970, more than twenty-five per cent of all their workers were outside the territory of the United States. When more than a fourth of the payroll and the managerial energies of the leading industrial concerns go to workers outside the country, it is not surprising that the federal government finds it difficult to develop an effective employment policy.

There are other, equally dramatic indicators of structural changes in the United States economy. In 1961, the sales of all American manufacturing subsidiaries abroad represented only seven per cent of total United States sales. In 1965, the proportion of foreign to domestic sales crept up to eight and a half per cent, but in the late sixties, the picture changed abruptly. By 1970, according to Commerce Department statistics, foreign sales accounted for almost thirteen per cent of the total sales of all United States manufacturing corporations. In the quest for foreign profits, the American global giants were making more and more of their new investment overseas. In 1957, United States companies were investing about nine cents of every dollar of new investment in plant and equipment overseas. Again in the mid-sixties, there was an abrupt upward shift, so that by 1971 they were diverting a quarter out of every dollar of new investment to foreign expansion. When so many different indicators register changes in the same period, it strongly suggests that something important has happened. More specifically, what does it mean for the average American and the federal regulatory process when the economic environment created by America's largest companies is increasingly beyond the control of the government?

One aspect of the growing ineffectiveness of Keynesian monetary policy in controlling inflation is seen in the way credit restriction feeds concentration, not only for industrial corporations but for the banks themselves. When money is tight and there is intense competition for funds to lend, big banks, as one might expect, obtain such funds when small banks cannot. (The big banks, of course, have a ready set of prime borrowers—principally the large global corporations.) Thus, in 1973, according to the Federal Reserve, nine New York City banks, six of which belonged to the Rockefeller-Morgan group, accounted for more than twenty-six per cent of all commercial and industrial lending by banks in the United States. (There are two hundred and twenty banks, according to the Fed, which do virtually all the large corporate lending in the country.) About half of all the money lent by these New York superbanks goes to global corporations—with the result, as George Budzeika, of the New York Federal Reserve Bank, has noted, that about ninety per cent of the entire indebtedness in the United States petroleum and natural-gass industry, two-thirds in the machinery and metal-products industry, and three-fourths in the chemical and rubber industries is held by these same nine New York banks. "On the whole," Budzeika concludes, "New York City bank behavior in the past two decades has shown that it is very difficult to control large banks whenever demand for credit is heavy. The growth and profits of these banks—their very viability—depend upon their ability to satisfy the credit demands of their customers. These banks, therefore, are strongly motivated to find loopholes in control measures and to press credit expansion to a greater extent than may be deemed advisable by monetary authorities."

It is the big banks, the very ones whose lending policies must be controlled if the government is to manage the economy successfully, that, of course, have the resources to escape control. As for medium and small banks, Budzeika points out that "lack of information and limited skills prevent them from adjusting quickly to changing levels of monetary restriction." The ability of large banks to insulate themselves through international dealings and other techniques from the intended effects of tight credit policies means, he contends, that "the only way to restrain [them] efficiently is to reduce the over-all liquidity of the banking system." But that is a drastic remedy, with serious side effects. Because large banks can evade mild credit restrictions, serious efforts to cool the economy by means of monetary policy must be so Draconian as to create even higher unemployment and idle factories. But too high a rate of unemployment is politically unacceptable. Therefore, only moderate monetary policies are pursued, and since these affect only smaller firms, they further contribute to the very concentration at the heart of the problem—a classic "vicious circle" of the sort that has plagued the governments of poor countries for years. Thus, even in a period of rapidly rising interest rates, corporations' current borrowings are permanently accelerating much faster than their increase in current cash holdings. Interest-rate policy appears to have substantially less effect on the rate of credit expansion than in the past, because corporations continue heavy borrowing even when the Federal Reserve System is pursuing a deflationary credit policy. Similarly, when the managers of the economy wish to stimulate expansion of the gross national product, they must expand credit at an ever-faster rate, and this has inflationary effects.

The Keynesian vision of how to control international money transactions assumed a market in which national banks and national corporations transacted their business within the context of national boundaries. Money markets in each country, although affected by conditions in other countries, were more or less independent. At the same time, it was assumed that most financial transfers would be accomplished through banking institutions, not through intracorporate flows. Public institutions, it was believed, could control all this sufficiently to protect the soundness of the national currency, because the government would have, to use economists' jargon, "perfect information" about what the private institutions were doing with their money; that is, governments would be able to respond quickly enough to the behavior of banks and corporations to make effective changes in monetary policy. These assumptions no longer hold.

Multinationals and Unemployment

What does the concentration and globalization of the United States economy mean for the average American citizen? For the personal economic security of those Americans with a family income of twenty-five thousand dollars or less—about ninety-five per cent of the population? What has the new world economy meant for this group in terms of income and jobs?

A 1972 study made by Peter Henle, a labor specialist at the Library of Congress, and published by the Labor Department reveals "a slow but persistent trend toward greater inequality" for the period from 1958 to 1970.

The deterioration of income distribution appears to have gathered momentum in the same years during which the processes of concentration and globalization in the United States economy also became evident. Mere coincidence in time is not the same as a causal connection, but there is strong independent evidence for suspecting that the behavior of global corporations has materially contributed to the worsening pattern of income distribution.

The interaction of corporate concentration and productive-wealth concentration explains, in part, why income distribution is becoming more unequal in the United States. Because the industrial giants such as I.T.T. have absorbed thousands of smaller companies in the last generation, a share of stock in these corporations represented a much larger portion of America's productive wealth in 1970 than it did in 1950—and a significant part of the stock of the largest corporations is going to their own top managers. The managers are becoming owners, deriving an ever-larger proportion of their income not from their managerial skills but from the stock they own in their own corporations. A glance at the annual earnings of two hundred and twenty men in charge of some of America's largest corporations (there are no women) shows them to be at the very top of the income pyramid.

Concentration in the manufacturing, transportation, communications, banking, and other dominant industries has apparently led to further concentration of income-producing wealth, and hence to further concentration of income. As for the impact of globalization on employment, have the decisions of America's major corporations in the nineteen-sixties to make a quantum leap in foreign investment affected the job opportunities of the average American?

The whole subject of the employment impact of global corporations—whether they increase or reduce employment possibilities for American workers—is a matter of intense political debate. The global corporation cannot afford to be known as a job destroyer, which organized labor says it is. This issue is one that the corporation must either win or defuse if it is to gain the legitimacy it seeks. For this reason, the public charges and countercharges of unions and companies on over-all employment impact, though each side is armed with studies, must be understood as a form of political advertising. The battle of the studies aside, certain key industries are definitely undergoing unfavorable changes in their employment patterns, and these changes coincide with changes in the investment behavior of the companies dominating the industries. The first big wave of foreign investment, from 1958 to 1967, established American-owned corporate subsidiaries abroad to export products back to the United States; it affected such industries as shoes, textiles, electronics assembly, and leather. Factories in this country began to close down. (There remain twelve shoe manufacturers in Lynn, Massachusetts, which thirty years ago boasted thirty-six.) In the very industries that once were major employers of unskilled, semi-skilled, and part-time workers, basic goods formerly produced for both export and the American market are now produced abroad. Both Henle's and Schultz's [omitted] studies confirm the fact that unskilled, semi-skilled, and part-time workers suffered a greater decline in their share of the national income than skilled workers during the first wave of this foreign investment. But by the late nineteen-sixties underdeveloped countries—Singapore, Taiwan, Brazil—were demanding that local factories be more than simple assembly operations and that the skill level and number of jobs in their factories be increased.

Both the stiffening requirements of the underdeveloped countries and the savings to be achieved by the use of overseas skilled labor led to a second wave of export-platform foreign investment, in the late nineteen-sixties. More capital-intensive operations employing highly skilled workers were moved abroad during this period, contributing to the result, reflected in the Henle and Schultz data, that the share of national income going to *skilled* workers in the United States began to drop perceptibly. Not only did the transfer of investment from local factories to overseas factories affect those who were thrown out of work but it also exerted a downward pressure on wages generally. The threat to move, whether actually brought up in labor negotiations or not, had a sobering effect on labor militancy. Concentration and globalization have weakened labor's bargaining power, and the result, not surprisingly, is that middle-income and low-income workers are sharing less in the nation's wealth.

There is another reason, in addition to job displacement and the weakening of union bargaining power, that income distribution is becoming more unequal. Over the last few years, an ever-greater proportion of new investment dollars of the largest United States corporations has been invested abroad. By 1972, twenty-five cents out of every dollar was going into overseas plant and equipment.

[Robert Gilpin] sees a connection between foreign investment and loss of job and income opportunities for workers— particularly in the lower ranks of blue-collar workers. The creation of capital stock abroad does not create jobs for American workers as would a corresponding investment in the United States. (Whether the long-term impact is to create more jobs in the United States than would otherwise exist is, of course, a matter of controversy. But no one argues that putting up a factory in Taiwan will have anything but an immediate unfavorable impact on workers in Akron.) The return on foreign investment, which generates interest, dividends, and fees but not blue-collar wages for American workers, is thus a benefit to capital but not to labor. Gilpin pinpoints this in his report:

> The effect of foreign investment is to decrease the capital stock with which Americans work; this decreases the productivity of American labor and real wages below what they would have been if the foreign investment had not taken place. By one estimate, the annual rate reduction in labor's income is around $6 billion. This is obviously a rough estimate, but it serves to indicate that the export of capital benefits the owners of capital and management more than labor as a whole.

A critical aspect of income distribution is the job market. If employment possibilities increase, so will wages—not only because there are more jobs for more people to fill but also because employers in a time of labor scarcity must pay more. Thus, income distribution and employment are inextricably linked. The great statistical battle of the nineteen-seventies between the A.F.L.-C.I.O. and the principal lobby for global corporations, the Emergency Committee for American Trade (reinforced by the Department of Commerce and the Harvard Business School), is fought in a spirit of awesome scientific exactitude. The A.F.L.-C.I.O. has brought forth a mass of figures which show that American global corporations were responsible for a net loss of half a million jobs between 1966 and 1969. An Emergency Committee study of seventy-four representative global corporations shows "a major positive contribution" to the growth of employment in the United States—five hundred and twenty-eight thousand new jobs. Professor Robert Stobaugh, of the Harvard Business School, and others have used more recent information and come to an even more euphoric conclusion. "The aggregate effects of U.S. foreign direct investment on U.S.

employment" are so substantial and positive, he says, that they are responsible for saving or creating "a total of perhaps 600,-000 jobs." Stobaugh's study was immediately retailed to the public in large ads placed by corporations in major newspapers and magazines. Obviously, these extraordinary discrepancies reflect sharply differing perceptions of reality. It is primarily the differing assumptions under which numbers are fed to the computer that produce the widely disparate results.

The use of aggregate figures can have a mystifying effect. For example, the Emergency Committee's study states that the seventy-four sample corporations increased their domestic employment (exclusive of employment gains through acquisition) more rapidly than the average manufacturing company. Their rate of new-job creation was about sixty per cent greater than that of all other manufacturing companies. But these figures were derived from employment statistics covering a ten-year period. If one looks at the period from 1960 to 1965 and the period from 1965 to 1970 separately, a different picture emerges. (The justification for separating these two periods is that the pace of globalization greatly increased in the second half of the decade and the character of foreign investment changed in significant ways.) It appears, in fact, that the ability of corporations to create new jobs is drastically declining. In the first half of the decade, the sample companies were creating new jobs at a rate sixty-seven per cent higher than the national average, but by the second half their job-creation rate was just under five per cent higher. (It should not be forgotten that these are among the largest companies in the country; they expanded significantly inside the United States during the nineteen-sixties through mergers, and consequently should be assumed to be among the nation's largest employers.) In the latter half of the sixties, the rate of job creation in the entire domestic manufacturing sector registered a decline of more than eight per cent, but the decline for the sample companies was forty per cent. There is considerable doubt whether, as a long-term trend, the global corporation is going to continue having a positive impact on employment in the United States.

The Harvard Business School estimate that the global corporation has saved or created six hundred thousand jobs in the United States is arrived at this way: There are, according to the economist Raymond Vernon, of Harvard, two hundred and fifty thousand jobs in the headquarters of parent companies (mostly staff). If there were no direct foreign investment, the study concludes, the jobs of an additional two hundred and fifty thousand production workers and a hundred thousand supporting workers "would be lost." But the dominant question—"What would have happened if the foreign investment had not been made?"—and its predetermined answer constitute the basic assumption behind the analysis, and that assumption decisively affects the results. The labor studies assume, on the one hand, that a worker is infinitely employable in the United States if only the corporations will keep their capital in the country. On the other hand, the favorite studies of the companies assume that if a worker now employed by a global corporation were not working for the corporation he would be unemployed. Both assumptions are too simple; the battle remains inconclusive.

There is a certain fatalism in all these studies. The company computers operate on the assumption that foreign investment is "defensive"—that if the company did not locate a factory in a cheap labor market abroad, a Japanese or European company would take over the market and the displaced American worker would be unemployable. (Union computers, in contrast, act as if comparatively high labor costs in the United States make little difference in competition with foreign corporations.) But even assuming that all foreign investment is "defensive," there are ways to protect a market position other than building a factory in Taiwan. Companies could put more money into research and development in the United States to replace the diminishing stock of basic innovative ideas on which future production depends. Such an investment policy would have a greater domestic multiplier effect than foreign investment. One might also ask what would have happened to the American employment picture if corporations had not been so ready to sell their comparative advantage to their competitors by licensing technology to them for quick profits.

As for the over-all impact on employment over the last few years—whether negative or positive—the judgment, then, must be "not proved." Over the long run, the trends are unfavorable. As long as we talk about employment in the aggregate, there is little more to add. But if we look at the regional effects of foreign investment, the dislocation caused by closing factories in the United States and opening them somewhere else is obvious. On computer tapes, jobs may be interchangeable; in the real world, they are not. Two hundred and fifty thousand jobs gained in corporate headquarters do not, in any political or human sense, offset two hundred and fifty thousands jobs lost on the production line. When Lynn, Massachusetts, suffers a drastic decline in shoe-manufacturing jobs, its jobless citizens will find little satisfaction in reading about the new headquarters building on Park Avenue and all the secretaries it will employ. The changing composition of the work force and its changing geographic location brought about by the globalization of American industry are affecting the lives of millions of Americans in serious and largely unfortunate ways. The growing obsolescence of American labor in the scheme of the global corporation is potentially one of the most serious management problems of all.

20. THE SOVIET UNION, CHINA, AND THE CAPITALIST CRISIS

by Joyce Kolko

Faced with conflict in trade, a near saturation in effective demand both in the industrial states and the Third World, and a burgeoning productive capacity, many of the world's capitalists believed by the 1970s that they literally had no option but

Excerpts from "The Soviet Bloc, China, and the Capitalist Crisis," ch. 6 in *America and the Crisis of World Capitalism* (Boston, Beacon Press, 1974).

to look covetously at the vast potential market in the orderly economies of the Soviet bloc and China. In 1972 these appeared the only areas of the world where there remained a possibility of expansive and complementary economic relationships.

The Soviet "Life-buoy"

One of the most crucial explanations for the 1972 shift in American business confidence and the expansionary direction of the economy was the new turn in trade relations with the Soviet bloc and China. Pressures from the chief foreign trade-oriented industrial corporations and major American banks to evolve a new relationship had been mounting for some years. Yet as late as May 1970 the U.S. government vetoed Ford's participation in the huge Kama River truck plant. It took the acute economic crisis of 1971 to jar the Nixon Administration loose from its archaic ideological moorings and set it firmly on its new paths. For the Nixon Administration there also appeared the political benefit of using the lure of trade and better relations to isolate the Vietnamese from their chief suppliers and thereby forestall the inevitable American defeat in that war-ravaged country.

The American Interests

From the American viewpoint, one can easily calculate the enormous benefits for individual industries and the general economy accruing from the new relations with the Soviet Union and, to a lesser extent, with China. It is no wonder that one industry after another celebrated the new relations as Nixon's greatest achievement of his first four years and, most significantly, such acclaim comes from the most powerful U.S. industries and banking interests.

Starting in July 1972 with "history's biggest" single grain trade agreement, a $750 million transaction that may exceed $1 billion over three years, U.S. industries have moved with alacrity to secure their own contracts.

Oil and Gas

News of the most spectacular U.S.-Soviet trade deal began to emerge in November 1972 when it became known that multi-billion dollar barter contracts were being negotiated to develop the oil and gas fields of Siberia. One involved the development of the Yakutsk region in eastern Siberia to supply Japan and the West coast of the U.S. And in June 1973 the Soviets signed an agreement with a consortium of Occidental Petroleum and El Paso Natural Gas providing for a preliminary 25-year contract for $10 billion. The Japanese may join the project in the future. The deal requires an initial Western loan of $4 billion to construct a pipeline and a tanker fleet.

Even larger, however, is an agreement involving western Siberia which barters natural gas in return for $12.5 billion in goods and services over a 25-year period. Negotiating this contract was a Texan consortium of Texas Eastern Transmission, Tenneco, and Brown & Root. This massive accord was signed with the U.S.S.R. on June 29, 1973, with the direct encouragement of President Nixon. Involved in the financing of the transaction is a consortium of banks led by Citibank and Bank of America.

The U.S. has both the money to invest and the market for natural resources, especially oil and gas, at this particular moment in its history. The money invested and loaned would be used to buy goods in America, spreading the benefits across the entire economy, increasing employment, and improving the balance-of-payments. The Soviets were to repay the development loans with natural resources and at the same time expand their own internal consumer market. The recent Kremlin policy decision to sell the natural resources of Siberia opened prospects of trade and repayment on a massive scale which did not exist when Soviet exports were perceived as only crabmeat, caviar, vodka, and the like. At the June 1972 summit meeting in Moscow, Brezhnev described the Siberian riches—probably the world's largest petroleum deposits—to Nixon and showed him a map of "This wealth that we are prepared to share with you." An article in *Pravda* underlined Russia's interest in these prospects: "Mutually advantageous cooperation between Soviet organizations and American firms in developing . . . natural resources . . . could, in our opinion, be one of the most promising paths . . .[and] would create a lasting and long-term basis for expanding Soviet-American trade and economic . . . ties. . . ."

Financing the exploitation of these minerals, particularly gas and oil, will be a gigantic project, but it is one which the

Americans feel that only they can undertake. "Nothing so large has been tried before in world trade," said then Secretary of Commerce Peterson in the fall of 1972. Just a couple of deals such as the oil and gas projects, he added, would wipe out the Export-Import Bank's capacity of only $4 billion. In March 1973 the ExIm Bank extended the first credit of $100 million to the U.S.S.R. It was matched by private U.S. banks for 90 percent financing for purchases in the U.S. to total $225 million. Most of the huge sums, of course, will come from private investors. Washington officials and bankers expect bond issues "of a magnitude rarely before underwritten."

The Banks

In quest of the financing of the multiple and ever-expanding agreements between the Soviet Union and the U.S. corporations are the largest American banks. At a time when banks feel forced by competition to grant ever more risky loans around the world at marginal rates, the promise of Eastern Europe, with its ultimate stability and security, was a welcome blessing. "This provides a new business frontier for most U.S. banks," reflected the *Bankers Magazine* with satisfaction in mid-1972. David Rockefeller toured Eastern Europe in January 1973 and shortly thereafter Chase Manhattan won permission to set up a representative office. Thereafter, a rush of "eight to ten" western bankers a day, according to the president of Manufacturers Hanover Trust, began to visit the Soviet central bank in the hope of financing East-West trade. And inevitable rate-cutting started as Chase was rumored to have offered concessions in lending rates to get the largest possible portion of the business, and continued until interest margins barely allowed any profit.

Many other industries have secured contracts, some at difficult periods in their corporate lives. International Harvester was pulled out of the red by a Soviet order; General Electric has signed an agreement with the U.S.S.R. for a joint research and development project in nuclear reactors and gas turbines. General Motors is negotiating for another truck plant in Siberia, one supposed to be far larger than the Kama River $2 billion project. Control Data signed a ten-year agreement of up to $500 million for joint computer development. For every agreement already signed there are scores of corporations, including IBM, Boeing, General Dynamics, RCA, ITT, Reynolds Metal, Kaiser, Hewlett Packard, Litton Industries, Alliance Tool and Die, Caterpillar Tractor, and Gulf and Western Industries, bidding for the multiple projects authorized or contemplated in the U.S.S.R. As the Assistant Secretary of State commented, "It seems that nearly every time we open the *Wall Street Journal* or turn to the financial section of the *Times,* we find a new project with the U.S.S.R. discussed or announced."

One measure of the importance of this new trend was seen in July 1972 after Brezhnev's visit to the U.S., when David Kendall of PepsiCo called a meeting to establish a U.S.-U.S.S.R. Chamber of Commerce and only the presidents or board chairmen of 24 of the largest American industrial and financial corporations were invited to attend. Companies such as GE, GM, IBM, DuPont, Xerox, Bank of America, Armco Steel, Singer, Continental Grain, Textron, Pan Am, Occidental, and the like were represented.

The U.S. Government and Economic Ties

The U.S. government is working hard to achieve the environment of long-term economic relations and it has repeatedly tested the U.S.S.R. on a political level and found them cooperative.

In June 1973 the House Foreign Affairs Committee released a report with their assessment of the new relations with the U.S.S.R. They also found that the Russians' "moderation" was attested to by their response to mining the harbors and the massive bombing of the DRV, the elimination of the tax on Jewish emigrants, and the Soviet's response to the Watergate revelations. Further reinforcing this favorable view were the agreements on Lend Lease, the Polish decision to make a settlement on prewar government bonds, and Hungarian compensation for property nationalized in the 1940s.

The new détente was, according to the vice-president of Chase Manhattan bank, "born out of necessity." "Let's be quite honest," he amplified. "We do have a balance-of-payments problem and we have to look for new markets." And as Deputy Secretary of State Kenneth Rush noted in April 1973, "At a time when we have a trade deficit with most areas of the world, our balance of trade surplus with eastern Europe is particularly welcome."

The critical factor leading to a change in American political policy *vis-à-vis* the U.S.S.R. is which industries are interested and why. By their own account, the most powerful American industries believe that new relations with the Soviet bloc are important for markets, sources of raw materials, safe loans, and the production of goods. Such economic intercourse is also important to the Soviet rulers, and this fact is no less interesting to us here. That the Western capitalists will all fail in these goals, as they have in their other efforts, is another question entirely and reflects neither their intentions nor the overall patterns in their trade, but the contradictions in capitalism itself. But for Western capitalism in the 1970s there are no real options for an expanding market—save the artificial government stimulus of an expanded war economy, the contradictions of which I have discussed in the preceding chapters. But despite the best laid plans of the most powerful members of the ruling class and the full cooperation of the Nixon Administration, Congress was able to block or stall the promised MFN provision and the ExIm Bank credits. The long nurtured ideological biases are not so easily erased among those who lack direct economic interests. Those with power eventually will make their will felt, but it involves a struggle and the mere process of stalling may dampen Soviet enthusiasm and encourage them to look elsewhere for their economic desires.

The China Perspective

Although there had been considerable pressure from an important sector of the ruling class for some years to change American policy toward China, essentially for the same reasons that they advocated a shift with the U.S.S.R., it was, even more in China than the U.S.S.R., a fortuitous congruence of political and economic needs that dictated a revision in American policy between 1969 and 1971. As Assistant Secretary of State for East Asia Marshall Green pointed out, "it is hardly conceivable that this evolution in our relationship could have occurred at the time of the Great Leap Forward . . . or during the period of the subsequent Cultural Revolution in China. In other words, it would have been very difficult for these changes to have come about before 1969." Yet as early as 1968 Nixon prepared an undelivered speech outlining his ideas on a détente. Clearly, these views did not originate with him but had been articulated through prolonged consultation with the men of power and influence in the Republican party, men to whom a shift in policy toward both Communist powers was mandatory.

The promise of new economic relations with China for Western capitalism is considerably smaller than that offered by the U.S.S.R. After the U.S. eliminated the political restraints to expanded trade in 1971, China remained what Marshall Green called "one of the most conservative states in international financial dealings." By this he meant that China, uniquely in the world, was virtually debt free and insisted on balanced trade or paying in cash or bartered goods. Given the nature of Chinese exports, this posed a serious obstacle to anything more than limited sales to the coveted China market. By the end of 1972 only Boeing, RCA, and the wheat growers had benefited substantially from the new trade relations. For the few banks that have access to China, usually only one per nation, the prospects for profit are considerably greater than in the U.S.S.R., where the competition has virtually eliminated the profit margin.

In January 1973 the Chinese indicated that they would waive this ideological barrier to pay interest and indeed accept a disguised form of interest in order to purchase their major requirements. While this new position whetted the appetite of additional industries and banks and may lead to sales of oil refineries, mining machinery, and transport equipment, it soon became clear that the bulk of Chinese purchases would be with Japanese corporations for industrial supplies and with Australia and Canada for agricultural needs. The Europeans are actively trying to expand their trade relation, and the U.S. government in early 1973 set up an intermediary committee of leading businessmen to deal with the Chinese purchasing agencies to promote competitively American trade. Hostility between European, Japanese, and American rivals was aroused by early 1972 when RCA sold a communications network to China that the Europeans and Japanese had earlier wanted to sell but were prevented by the U.S. government's insisting it was strategic goods. From that time on the China market has become one of competitive struggle between the various Western and Japanese capitalists. Trade with the U.S. grew from zero in 1970 to over $600 million in 1973, but it is far less likely to expand in the manner of Soviet trade.

Since the Chinese do not aim at an expanded consumer goods industry, at least at this stage, the China market is structurally of a different composition and promise than the Russian for Western capitalists. Their focus is on power complexes, steel mills, refineries, and transportation equipment intended to facilitate distribution. And most of their contacts are with the Japanese.

While the effects of the Cultural Revolution are being moderated, although apparently not reversed, the Chinese, like the Russians, have divorced ideology from international state relations and have fully accepted the rules of *realpolitik*. In opening diplomatic ties with fascist regimes around the world, to the extent of economic aid, they have not restricted their contacts to simply correct formal relations but have lavished effusive praise on the Shah of Iran, the King of Ethiopia, and the governments of Ceylon and Pakistan, and others of similar character. Any understandings they may have had with the Americans regarding the liberation of Taiwan were not quickly forthcoming, other than their replacement in international bodies like the U.N., and the Americans doubtless are holding the future of Taiwan as a trump card in future political negotiations.

Conclusion

The Soviet bloc and China, while appearing potentially to hold in their hands the only "life-buoy" for a sinking capitalist system, have, in fact, been permitted to join the society too late. What will occur if the present uniform credit policies lead to the expected "slowdown" or recession of the economies throughout Europe, North America, and Japan? What will happen to the oil shortage, and the U.S. interest in the Siberian reserves? What can they do if stagnation and unemployment overwhelm the capitalist states, and the overexpansion of manufacturing in the Third World compound, with the fall in demand for raw materials, the crises in these areas? Can the Soviet bloc provide the escape when the political tensions, competitive devaluations, tariffs, and trade blocs ensue? Could the Soviet and Chinese markets save the situation if the biggest markets collapse simultaneously for all? Will the "secure" but low profit loans to

Russia save the banks forced into default? Merely to raise the questions shows how preposterous an affirmative answer would be.

The industrial capitalist states seek a supplementary market in the U.S.S.R. and China, but their primary market remains in Western Europe, North America, and Japan. And the lure of Soviet raw materials is generated by the current booming economy that makes their shortage the felt need of the system. The interest in new sources will diminish rapidly if there is a glut from falling demand. The position of banks throughout the world is already too perilous to gain any compensating security in loans to the Communist states.

21. ECONOMIC ASPECTS OF MILITARY SPENDING

by Victor Perlo

I

Military Spending and Inflation

That wars are engines of inflation is well known; in fact, every substantial war in U.S. history has been accompanied by inflation. And the wildest inflationary periods in other countries have been associated with wars. For 30 years the United States has had a permanently militarized economy. The same applies, in lesser degree, to other major capitalist powers and, to an even greater degree, to certain small capitalist states.

Militarization provides corporations with a cushion of high-

Excerpts from *The Unstable Economy: Booms and Recessions in the United States Since 1945* (New York, International Publishers, 1973), pp. 92–93 and 163–68.

profit business, enabling them to set and maintain higher profit margins in civilian markets. Fantastic markups of four or five times factory cost are applied to the sale of products originally developed for military use, for example, electronics. Efficiency in production for the military is a fraction of that in civilian production, and the corresponding multiplication of costs inevitably is transmitted, at least in part, to civilian sales of armament manufacturers.

Military spending on a large scale generally involves a distribution of purchasing power to servicemen, and munitions contractors and workers, not offset on the supply side by production of civilian goods, nor on the demand size by an equal collection of taxes.

This last point usually signifies deficit financing of military spending, which translates directly into monetary inflation. The effect, however, can be similar even when there is no deficit. The federal budget was, on balance, in surplus during the Korean War —markedly so in the first year of the war,—yet prices soared. Deficits were not exceptionally high during four of the first five years of massive U.S. intervention in Vietnam, and yet there was a marked acceleration of price increases.

In part, this is due to nonmonetary factors connected with a military buildup, the strengthening of monopoly power already referred to, and the sudden increase in demand that surges throughout the civilian economy in a war situation. However, this also takes a monetary form—a rapid rise in credit money—even when the government does not issue money through deficit spending.

The pertinence of militarization might be questioned, considering that countries with relatively little militarization show just as much inflation as those with a high degree of militarization. There is, however, a high degree of militarization in the capitalist world as a whole, especially in its most powerful country, the United States. With the growing cosmopolitanism of capital, the effects are spread throughout the areas of operation of giant multinational firms, most of which are based on the United States.

II

Militarism and the Business Cycle

War and militarism tend to *increase* cyclical economic fluctuations. Although World War II was followed by even greater booms in capitalist countries, so far no world crisis comparable to that of 1929 has resulted. Yet economic cycles since World War II have been more pronounced in the United States, the most highly militarized country, than in any other land.

In part, this results from the sharp fluctuations in military spending. "National defense" expenditures jumped from 3.9% of GNP in 1947 to 13.3% in 1952–53; dropped to 9.6% in 1956; increased to 10.3% in 1958; dropped to 7.3% in 1965, advanced to 9.1% in 1967, and declined again to 6.8% in 1971. These swings are considerably wider than those in that traditionally volatile component—plant and equipment investment.

Rapid increases in military spending have a doubly stimulating economic effect. At the start of a war or big peacetime arms buildup, the increased outlay usually far exceeds increased tax revenues. Civilian purchasing power is thereby suddenly increased, with no corresponding rise in civilian supplies. The resulting inflationary price increase initially stimulates productive activity. People buy consumers' goods, business enterprises buy capital goods and raw materials to beat higher prices and possible later wartime shortages. The arms buildup also directly stimulates a surge in capital investment.

At the end of the military buildup, and especially with the end of a war or any other decline in military spending, the opposite effects are equally marked. Capital spending and purchases of materials by armament manufacturers are radically reduced or completely ended. Workers are laid off as rapidly—in some cases, more rapidly than they were hired. The only asymmetry is in prices. The power of monopoly prevents any general reduction, and it is usually able to maintain the price uptrend, if at a slower pace.

On the other hand, all postwar administrations have manipulated the military budgets for economic purposes—to smooth out the business cycle, as well as to throw business to favored arms contractors. Contracyclical timing of the placing of military orders partly—but only partly—offsets the overall unstabilizing effect of military spending.

There follows a chronicle of cyclical development after the Korean War, with corresponding fluctuations in new military contracts:

Trough of recession: III, 1954 (Roman numerals represent quarters.)

Military contracts built up from an annual rate of $6.4 billion in the fourth quarter of 1953 to $16.4 billion in the third quarter of 1954, contributing significantly to checking the recession and starting a new upturn. The big strategic weapons buildup of the post-Korea period was the underlying driving force behind this increase, although economic motives hastened it.

Peak of the boom: III, 1957.

Military contracts dipped from $20.8 billion in 1956 to $18.8 billion in 1957, as part of a deliberate program to cut government spending for anti-inflationary purposes. This contributed to the outbreak of an economic crisis in the second half of 1957.

Trough of the recession: II, 1958.

Military contracts jumped from an annual rate of $16.9 billion in the third quarter of 1957 to an annual rate of $29.6 billion in the second quarter of 1958, exactly countering the cyclical movement. The military contract rise far exceeded the shift in any other area of the economy. The increase in residential construction—another plus factor—started later and was not so sharp.

Peak of recovery: II, 1960.

Arms contracts drifted downward from $24.4 billion in 1958 to $23.2 billion in 1960. This decline was not sufficient to set off a slump directly. But the failure of the 1958 increase to carry through contributed to it.

Trough of Recession: I, 1961.

Military contracts increased from $23.2 billion in 1960 to $26.0 billion in 1961 and $28.5 billion in 1962. There was a more rapid buildup in space agency contracts. Thus, military and space contracts, combined, contributed significantly to the recovery of the early 1960s.

With all the fluctuations, there was a steady uptrend in military contracts between the Korean and Vietnam wars, with the amount more than doubling between 1954 and 1964. Annual, quarterly, and sometimes even monthly contracts fluctuated around this trend and at crucial turning points were often deliberately designed to reverse undesirable cyclical trends, whether inflationary-boom or recessionary. Rarely was this purpose explicitly and officially proclaimed, but unofficial comment, the statements of anonymous White House spokesmen, and other evidence confirmed the purposive nature of the fluctuations.

Beginning with 1965, the rapid Vietnam buildup of military contracts gave several years of extra life to the tired boom and raised it to new heights. This added stimulation was primarily for military reasons; its economic consequences were side effects. Military contracts jumped from $27.1 billion in 1964 to $39.7 billion in 1966. The rise slowed down in 1967, when contracts totaled $42.3 billion; and ended in 1968, with contracts remaining at the 1967 level. Simultaneously, overall economic activity stopped increasing for a year, and then slowly moved forward until mid-1969.

Peak of boom: III, 1969.

Military contracts dropped sharply from $42.3 billion in 1968 to $35.5 billion in 1969. There was simultaneously a sharp decline in space contracts. These declines came about for economic reasons, as part of the Nixon administration's "anti-inflation" program. The decline in armament contracts preceded the reduction in U.S. military activity in Indochina that took place in 1970. The 1969 drop in armament contracts contributed significantly to the *timing* of the crisis of overproduction that began in the second half of 1969.

In fact, the main decline in activity, and the financial crisis, occurred during 1970, while munitions contracts remained at a level. No significant economic recovery occurred during 1971, despite an upturn in military orders in the second half of the year.

President Nixon and his aides distorted the significance of the decline in military orders and in the size of the armed forces, ascribing to it full responsibility for the increase and stubborn high level of unemployment.

Early in 1972, President Nixon signalled an intended fresh upturn in munitions contracts. His budget for fiscal 1973 called for new "national defense" obligational authority at an all-time high of $85.4 billion, up $10.2 billion from the authority actually granted during fiscal year 1971. Another $1.7 billion increase was called for in authority for spending for international affairs, much of which is to support military actions.

Accompanied by a big propaganda barrage about the alleged Soviet military buildup, this administration move foreshadowed a possible new round in the nuclear arms race, and the renewed savage bombing of North Vietnam which soon followed.

At the same time, the timing of the move was influenced by Nixon's desire to prime the pump through the favored method of big business—a sharp rise in military contracts—so as to improve economic activity prior to the 1972 presidential elections.

To summarize, armaments spending has been manipulated in every cycle for contracyclical economic purposes, generally as one in a collection of measures. In that sense, it has contributed to the early ending of several economic declines. On the other hand, on two occasions declines in military orders designed to "cool off" inflation, actually contributed to cyclical downturns, and in that sense added to economic instability.

Appraisal of results over the past two decades permits the conclusion that the stabilizing effect of contracyclical manipulation of military spending has been insufficient to offset the unstabilizing effects of fluctuations in military spending resulting from wars and arms buildups. Thus, on balance, the militarization of the economy has tended to increase cyclical instability.

22. THE DEBT ECONOMY

Business Week

I

The U.S. economy stands atop a mountain of debt $2.5-trillion high—a mountain built of all the cars and houses, all the factories and machines that have made this the biggest, richest

Reprinted from *Business Week*'s special issue (October 12, 1974).

economy in the history of the world. The next biggest capitalist economy is that of Japan, but it would take a sum more than one-third the gross national product of Japan just to pay this year's interest on the U.S. debt.

The U.S. is the Debt Economy without peer. It has the biggest lenders, the biggest borrowers, the most sophisticated financial system. The numbers are so vast that they simply numb the mind: $1-trillion in corporate debt, $600-billion in mortgage debt, $500-billion in U.S. government debt, $200-billion in state and local government debt, $200-billion in consumer debt. To fuel nearly three decades of postwar economic boom at home and export it abroad, this nation has borrowed an average net $200-million a day, each and every day, since the close of World War II.

It would be an awesome burden of debt even if the world's economic climate were perfect. It is an ominously heavy burden with the world as it is today—ravaged by inflation, threatened with economic depression, torn apart by the massive redistribution of wealth that has accompanied the soaring price of oil.

Two critically important questions must be asked about the U.S. economy today:

· Can all the debt now outstanding be paid off or refinanced as it comes due?

· Can the economy add enough new debt to keep growing at anything close to the rate of the postwar era?

If those two questions have been asked a thousand times in the past three decades, never have they been so hard to answer as they are today.

No one doubts that the U.S. economy will continue to need capital at a prodigious rate: money to build new homes, to provide additional government services, to combat pollution, to overcome the capacity shortages that are contributing to today's inflation. Yet the U.S. economy is leveraged as never before. There is nearly $8 of debt per $1 of money supply, more than double the figure of 20 years ago. Corporate debt amounts to more than 15 times after-tax profits, compared with under 8 times in 1955. Household debt amounts to 93% of disposable income, compared with 65% in 1955. U.S. banks have lent billions overseas through Eurocurrency markets that did not even exist in 1955.

And there are signs of tension everywhere: corporate debt-equity ratios and commercial bank loan-deposit ratios way out of line, consumer installment-debt repayment taking a record share of disposable income, the huge real estate market in desperate trouble despite all that the federal government has done to save it. Never has the Debt Economy seemed more vulnerable, with a distressing number of borrowers and lenders in precarious shape. The consensus among economists today is that the economy still is not overborrowed. "But we may indeed be approaching such a point, especially in the banking system," warns economist William Gibson of the Brookings Institution in Washington. Adds Fletcher L. Byrom, chairman of Koppers Co.: "Outside of one or two industries where there is an excessive amount of debt, I am not sure large industrial companies are that heavily leveraged. But a whole lot of small and medium-size companies are really stretched out."

"The real question comes down to 'Where is the economy going?' " says Charles E. Fiero, executive vice-president and treasurer of Chase Manhattan Bank. The answer is not reassuring because the economic outlook is dark both here and abroad. Not one Western industrial power, the U.S. included, has been able to bring inflation under control, while efforts to control it have brought the world closer to a major economic slump than at any time since the 1930s. Meanwhile, just the first year's payment of those swollen oil bills has brought such nations as Italy and Britain perilously close to economic ruin—a horrendous danger in a world where multinational business and multinational financial institutions have bound nations more tightly together than ever before. Serious trouble in one nation could infect all nations in the twinkling of an eye. It has been three months since the failure of Germany's Bankhaus I. D. Herstatt—a tiny bank compared with the titans of international finance—and the foreign exchange markets still have not fully recovered from the blow.

No Right Answer

Americans took on their enormous burden of debt with the expectation that personal income and corporate profits would continue to grow year after year and that government economic policy would remain essentially expansionary. But inflation, while adding greatly to the need to borrow, has slashed the share of income—corporate and personal—available to pay off debts, and an expansionary government economic policy would only add to the inflationary pressures.

In fact, governments everywhere are caught in an awful bind —forced by inflation to follow restrictive policies but keenly aware that too much restraint will crush borrowers and lenders alike. Nowhere is that conflict more apparent than in Washington, where months of restraint by the Federal Reserve produced a severe liquidity squeeze in the U.S. economy but did little or nothing to slow the rate of inflation. Now the Fed seems to be easing a bit because the liquidity squeeze, especially among the banks, and the threat of recession seem the most pressing concerns. Further, it is finally getting some overdue help from government fiscal policy. Yet continued inflation limits how much easing the Fed can do, even with help from the White House, and raises the threat of still another turn toward restraint further down the road.

"There are so many arguments for coming off where we are gradually and not going from one extreme to another," warns Professor Milton Friedman of the University of Chicago. Otto Eckstein, professor of economics at Harvard and president of Data Resources, Inc., a Lexington (Mass.) consulting company, agrees. "The surest way to mess things up down the road," he says, "is by putting the financial system through the squeeze it has been put through every few years. You can't keep shotgunning the economy."

Yet both the Fed and the White House, petrified by both inflation and recession, seem unable to avoid swinging first this way and then that way, and the impact on the Debt Economy is devastating. Between monetary and fiscal restraint, the economic outlook at best is for sluggish growth, and, that being the case, it is safe to assume that the economy will not be able to borrow as much as it needs in the months and years ahead. And it is prudent to assume that not all borrowers will be able to pay off their debts as they come due.

A Choice of Disasters

It is not even possible to pick between recession and inflation as the greater threat. Recession would strike an immediate blow at the Debt Economy. But Robert W. Stone, executive vice-president of Irving Trust Co. in New York, warns: "If inflation is not brought under control, then the conditions are that sooner or later we will have a recession of substantial depth and length. The question is what kind of economic setback to expect. Most of us would rather have a setback now. It will be more pronounced than two or three years ago but less pronounced than two or three years from now."

Most observers expect at least some trouble with the U.S. economy in the months ahead, with only the extent of the trouble, and the damage it will do, in doubt. Nearly all agree that the economy is particularly susceptible to damage if there is a serious recession.

Fiero of Chase sees only a mild slowdown ahead. But, he says, "If we are going into a protracted and deep recession, that will undoubtedly make the ability to service debt more of a problem." Barry Bosworth of the University of California warns: "If we have a major recession, firms may not have the cash flow to meet their debt payments and may not be able to roll over their short-term debt. Because of the current financial structure, the system cannot withstand a recession as well as it could in the past." Herbert E. Neil, Jr., vice-president at Harris Trust & Savings Bank in Chicago, puts it more bluntly: "A major downturn in business activity would cause a much sharper increase in liquidations and bankruptcies than at any time in the past 30 years."

And then there is the most pessimistic view of all: the specter of a chain reaction of defaults by borrowers and failures by lenders, thrusting the world into deep depression. It is not the 1930s, and governments and central banks are now more knowledgeable, better able and more willing to aid institutions in trouble, as the Federal Reserve aided Franklin National Bank and the German central bank aided the victims of the Herstatt disaster. Yet the dangers are greater than in the 1930s. The amounts at risk are greater, and so is the leverage, here and abroad. Perhaps the greatest risk is in the billions lent to borrowers whose ability to repay has been compromised by the high price of oil.

It is not just a company here or there whose ability to repay is in question but that of the developing lands that borrowed heavily and of such powers as Italy, which borrowed $10-billion from the private financial markets of the world. This is money owed to banks whose own liquidity is all too often stretched dangerously thin. Should a colossal borrower such as Italy default—and the threat is very real—it could possibly send big banks toppling faster than central banks could respond. At the least, a default by Italy on its loans would cause a serious world-wide contraction of credit.

In the end, the world may very well escape disaster, but there is no way it can escape change. The very assumptions on which the U.S. built its Debt Economy, for instance, must be rethought. Not in the foreseeable future will any nation pile up debt as rapidly as this nation. It has become obvious, too, that the more leveraged an economy, the less scope there is for such traditional economic weapons as monetary policy. The concept of what constitutes appropriate government economic policy will have to be rethought in the years ahead.

A Generation of Consumers

The fact that so many borrowers have borrowed too much must also be considered. It is absolutely certain that the whole capital-raising process will come under tighter government control than ever before. Even though government attempts to manipulate private markets have so far done more harm than good, it seems reasonable to expect more attempts by government to allocate what credit there is to those who, for social or political reasons, seem most worthy of it. The net result of the crisis in the Debt Economy will be to thin out the ranks of those who can borrow and those who can lend. All the antitrust laws in the world will not prevent a still greater concentration of wealth in fewer hands because to the extent that there is a crisis in the Debt Economy, only the biggest and fittest will survive.

The stunning thing about the Debt Economy is how rapidly it grew. In 1946, the total debt of the U.S., public and private, was only $400-billion, and nearly 60% of that represented U.S. Treasury debt. But in 1946 the U.S. had an economy starved of the good things in life by depression and war. Consumers raced through the liquid assets they had piled up during the war and, having spent them, borrowed so they could keep on buying. To meet their demands, corporations began piling up debt at an accelerating clip. Meanwhile, federal spending—and borrowing

—stayed high, and borrowing by local government became a new fact of life for the financial markets.

Yet what happened during the 1940s and 1950s was only a prelude to what happened after 1960. It took 15 years, from 1946 to 1960, for total U.S. debt to double, but only 10 years, from 1960 to 1970, for it to double again. The key economic indicators—gross national product, personal income, corporate profits, and the like—have all grown by 500% or so since World War II. The key debt indicators have all grown by three and four times that amount, and the sharpest gains have come since 1960.

Corporations have tripled their debt in the past 15 years. Treasury debt, which hardly grew at all in the late 1940s and 1950s, has jumped by $180-billion since 1960. Installment debt, mortgage debt, and state and local government debt have all climbed by 200% or more since 1960, and the debts of federal agencies have climbed by more than 1,000%. New demands for money bred new sources: the commercial paper market, which was a nickel-and-dime affair until the 1960s, and the Euro-currency markets, which were not even born until the 1960s. Leasing became a billion-dollar business during the 1960s. The neighborhood bank became a multinational bank holding company that frequently became as voracious a borrower of funds as the companies to which it lent.

The equity markets could not supply more than a tiny fraction of the new money that business needed, so corporations turned more to the debt markets. The stock market did sell substantial quantities of equities in the 1960s, but the money mostly went to finance emerging industries—lessors and franchisers and conglomerates—and seldom to finance basic industry. The long-term markets became congested, so companies borrowed more short term. This country's futile attempt at capital-export controls turned companies that had been modest suppliers to the international money markets into major international borrowers.

Every theory that business ever had about how much debt it could take on got thrown out the window, and much the same was true for consumers. Certainly the lenders scrapped every theory they had about what constituted a safe burden of lending, and nowhere was that more true than at the commercial banks. Loans jumped twice as fast as deposits, risk assets (loans and investments) grew twice as fast as bank capital. "The only place where I do think we have an overleveraged position—where capital is really extraordinarily low—is in the banking industry," says Friedman. But since banking is the nation's biggest industry, an overleveraged banking system is very scary.

The Federal Reserve has moved against the borrowing binge three times in the past decade—in 1966, 1969–70, and again this year—to almost no avail. And restraint has invariably been followed by ease—frequently excessive ease. The net effect of a decade of monetary policy has been to raise the cost of money to record levels, all but destroy the stock market, intensify the squeeze on liquidity in virtually all sectors of the economy, and force companies to leverage their equity at ever higher levels to support the inflated working capital requirements. Certainly monetary policy, and fiscal policy as well, have had little lasting impact on the rate of inflation. And it is inflation, more than any other factor, that is behind all the borrowing that is going on today.

Cutting the Growth Rate

"Inflation has forced corporations to do far more external financing than they ordinarily would," says Tilford C. Gaines, senior vice-president and economist at Manufacturers Hanover Trust Co. in New York. Gaines estimates the increase in the nominal values of inventories and accounts receivable alone has increased corporate financial needs by $30-billion this year. To the extent that funds generated through depreciation fall short of replacement costs—an ever-widening gap during periods of inflation—corporations are obliged to finance more and more of their capital spending externally.

Consumers have cut their purchases of big-ticket items. Yet the price of these items has gone up so rapidly that the decline in new installment debt is smaller than the decline in actual purchases. The slowing in the rate of residential mortgage lending does not reflect exactly the decline in housing starts because the average home mortgage loan is $30,400 today—21% higher than the average loan of 1970. Inflation has spending by state and local governments going up faster than any other sector of the economy.

So now the nation's burden of debt is like a string drawn very taut: $2.5-trillion in debt outstanding and more money needed to keep the economy growing, while the ability of borrowers to repay what they owe and to find more money is very much in question. The string has not broken, and it may not. The energies of every economist, of every government official, of every lender and borrower will be directed in the weeks and months ahead to keeping that string from breaking. Yet no one knows the precise breaking point and, while there are schemes and theories galore, no one really knows how to ease the tension, either.

II

The U.S., like the world around it, is in sad shape today. Having borrowed too much in the expectation of perpetual plenty, Americans are desperate for answers to questions for which there are no pat answers.

If there is a remedy for today's inflation except recession, it has not been found, all of President Ford's brave hopes this week notwithstanding. It is not certain that the $1-trillion transfer of wealth from oil-consuming to oil-producing nations can be carried out peacefully, and if the oil bill is hurting the U.S. less than most nations, it hardly matters because all nations are so closely tied together today. Even if this country's oil bill is comparatively modest, the U.S. already carries a burden of debt so heavy that it is doubtful that all of it can be repaid and almost certain that not enough more can be borrowed to keep the economy growing as it has since World War II.

Finally, and most distressing of all, it is not at all certain how graciously Americans, or any other people for that matter, will accept what is plainly today's (and history's) economic reality: that there is no such thing as perpetual plenty and no party that does not eventually end.

No more to borrow. The U.S. has tried to do too much with too little, and that cannot go on forever. Even if the U.S. is not overborrowed now—a most debatable point—it cannot continue to pile up debt as it has in the postwar era because the sort of government policies that would permit that to happen would simply feed inflation. "We have passed the point of no return," mourns Albert M. Wojnilower, an economist at First Boston Corp. in New York.

It is inevitable that the U.S. economy will grow more slowly than it has. Government economic policy will be more restrictive —and, at the same time, more imposing because it is also inevitable that government will attempt to take on still more of the job of channeling what capital there is to where it seems needed the most.

Some people will obviously have to do with less, or with substitutes, so that the economy as a whole can get the most mileage out of available capital. There will be fewer homes and more apartment houses built because apartment houses represent a more efficient use of capital. It will be harder to launch risky new ventures because the needs of existing businesses will be so great.

Indeed, cities and states, the home mortgage market, small business, and the consumer, will all get less than they want because the basic health of the U.S. is based on the basic health of its corporations and banks: the biggest borrowers and the biggest lenders. Compromises, in terms of who gets and who does without, that would have been unthinkable only a few years ago will be made in coming years because the economic future not only of the U.S. but also of the whole world is on the line today. **First things first.** Put simplistically, as long as corporations stay healthy, they can pay taxes and provide people with jobs. As long as people have jobs, they, too, can pay taxes, and they can buy goods. But when corporations fall sick, people lose jobs and stop buying. Nobody pays taxes, governments and local authorities are not financed, and everyone—corporations, consumers, federal and local administrations alike—goes broke or gets embedded more deeply in the debt spiral.

If corporations are healthy, these things do not have to happen. Corporations are the key to whatever can be done to unwind the Debt Economy with the least possible pain, partly because it is in the corporate area that debt has increased most spectacularly and partly because it is in the corporate area that the increase is doing the most damage. Chairman Reginald H. Jones of General Electric Co. put it very bluntly in testimony before the Senate Subcommittee on Economic Growth, headed by Lloyd M. Bentsen (D-Tex.). "We have," said Jones, "a picture of business going deeper into debt, faced with declining return on investment, unable to attract sufficient equity funding, unable to keep up with inflation in its depreciation charges, and subsisting on a thinner and thinner diet of retained earnings."

Yet it will be a hard pill for many Americans to swallow—the idea of doing with less so that big business can have more. It will be particularly hard to swallow because it is quite obvious that if big business and big banks are the most visible victims of what ails the Debt Economy, they are also in large measure the cause of it. President Ford's anti-inflation package may make perfect economic sense, but he will find it very difficult to sell Congress on his proposal to levy the same 5% tax surcharge on the worker making $7,500 a year and the corporation making a thousand times that much—especially when the package also contains some tax breaks for corporations.

Facing it squarely. Nothing that this nation, or any other nation, has done in modern economic history compares in difficulty with the selling job that must now be done to make people accept the new reality. And there are grave doubts whether the job can be done at all. Historian Arnold Toynbee, filled with years and compassion, laments that democracy will be unable to cope with approaching economic problems—and that totalitarianism will take its place.

Governments find it handy to blame the oil-producing nations for all that has gone wrong, but it is in the nature of elected officials to find others to blame for their own mistakes. The world's great economies were running out of control long before the first shot in the Yom Kippur War was fired, and all that the oil situation has done is to hasten an inevitable day of reckoning. Moreover, it is a day of reckoning made inevitable by forces set in motion three decades ago, in those heady days after the end of World War II.

The first promise that every postwar government made to people sickened by both depression and war was that a new era had dawned in which there would be neither—only limitless growth and prosperity for all. The industrial nations would regain their glory, the developing nations would achieve it. And for a quarter-century, governments actually did seem to be making good on that promise. Between 1945 and 1970 the world enjoyed the longest boom on record—fueled in large part by borrowed money. Business borrowed at a prodigious rate to make the stuff, consumers borrowed at a prodigious rate to buy it, governments borrowed at a prodigious rate to support armies and build roads and schools. The $2.5-trillion debt load of the U.S. is just a part of a total world debt load that could top $10-trillion. **Too many dollars.** And then, suddenly, it all began coming unstuck for reasons that are not totally clear even today—except that no boom goes on forever.

Among other causes, the U.S. flooded the world with an unprecedented quantity of unwanted, inflationary dollars. The death throes of the international monetary system sent billions of dollars crossing frontiers faster than anyone could count them—far faster than any government could counter them. Most basic, though, was that the world's hunger for goods—for cars instead of bicycles, for beef instead of chicken—simply outstripped its financial resources. That bred inflation, which bred more debt, which bred more inflation, and so on in an ever-worsening spiral. And then came the oil situation to make an awful situation unbearable.

But promises, once made, are not easily forgotten. The world's financial resources may be strained to the breaking point, but the demand for money has hardly slackened at all. It requires money beyond the ability of the average person to imagine just to keep the world's great economies where they are—some $200-billion in net new external capital to support the U.S. economy alone in 1974.

Finding the capital. Looking beyond this year, the U.S. demand for capital through 1985 will total—according to a study just completed by the New York Stock Exchange—no less than $4.69-trillion, counting internal as well as outside funds. The total expenditure of other countries will be even more if the Debt Economy does not drag them down. According to GE's Jones, in 1973 Japan put 37% of its gross national product into gross private domestic investment. The figures for France and Germany were 28% and 27%—and for the U.S. only 15.7%.

But whether the U.S. or any other country will in fact be able to make this kind of investment depends very largely on its ability to finance by some means other than going deeper into debt. For stock markets all over the world have been making it horribly clear that corporations are sick—and they are sick largely as a result of their overdependence on debt.

The recent destruction of stock prices reflects, more than any other single factor, the extraordinary recent build-up of debt. In the U.S., this build-up has been gaining momentum, and its acceleration has coincided with the debacle in equity values. As economist Henry Kaufman of Salomon Bros. points out, the increase in U.S. debt averaged a relatively reasonable 6.2% annually in the 1950s and 6.9% in the 1960s, but it zoomed past 9% in the first three years of this decade: The stock market, as measured by the average price of equities, has been sinking like a veritable stone since 1970.

If corporate debt continues to increase so rapidly, corporate interest payments will regularly exceed the combined total of dividends and retained earnings. And when this happens, corporations are not only intensely vulnerable to cyclical downturns but are also being run for the benefit of creditors rather than stockholders.

At least one solution must be to make capital more easily obtainable in the form of equity—and in the U.S., at least, it is not too late for this to be done. What is essential, in the opinion of John C. Whitehead, a senior partner of Goldman, Sachs & Co., is to increase both the incentive to save and the incentive to place savings in "opportunity" investments.

Looking at the U.S. picture alone, nonfinancial corporations invested nearly $540-billion between 1969 and 1973. About $290-billion came from depreciation, $60-billion from retained earnings, and a net $40-billion from stock sales. On the debt side, a net $75-billion was raised by bond issues, and $75-billion more was raised through bank loans and through commercial paper.

The NYSE estimate for plant, equipment, and inventory additions through 1985 is $2.65-trillion. If this were to be raised in the proportions of the last five years, corporate equity would rise by $500-billion, but debt would soar $750-billion. Since the resulting interest burden would certainly bring about—well before 1985—the bankruptcy of most U.S. corporations, it is something less than desirable. One alternative would be to reduce the level of expenditure. But if this were taken far enough to bring debt down to safe levels, it would result in such painful unemployment—and hence such dislocation of world trade—as to be equally undesirable.

Another alternative would be to correct the imbalance between equity and debt, and although this would certainly not provide a panacea for the world's problems, it would do a great deal to get the economy back on a sounder footing—and permit the U.S. to help keep other economies afloat. Among the steps that might be taken:

AVOID CREDIT ALLOCATION. Through the Federal National Mortgage Assn. and other agencies, there has been allocation of credit—and it has been something less than successful. It has failed to provide enough funds for the mortgage market, but it has made funds unavailable to other markets. If debt in the economy is to be reduced to reasonable levels, the first step is to put these agencies back into the budget and finance them through taxes rather than through borrowings—thus at least avoiding additions to the debt burden.

ENCOURAGE INVESTMENT FROM ABROAD. The NYSE strongly endorses increasing the supply of funds by eliminating the withholding taxes on dividends and interest from U.S. securities held by foreigners. The exchange's committee on International Capital Markets has estimated that an additional $4-billion to $6-billion of capital could flow into U.S. securities if these taxes were eliminated—and the committee was working with information accumulated before the rise in oil prices vastly increased the dollars in foreign hands.

CHANGE DEPRECIATION BASIS. Chrysler Corp. Chairman Lynn Townsend believes business should be allowed to base depreciation on replacement cost rather than on historical cost. "The net book value of plant, property, and equipment in the steel industry is about $14-billion," he says, "but the replacement cost at today's prices would approach $78-billion." If depreciation were put on a more realistic basis, retained earnings would of course be reduced. But since business' tax burden would be reduced considerably more, cash flow would be improved—and the need for external financing substantially cut.

MAKE DIVIDENDS TAX DEDUCTIBLE. Robert Eisner of Northwestern University favors the idea that dividends, like interest payments, should be tax deductible for the corporation paying them. To avoid revenue loss to the Treasury, it might be more practical to gradually reduce the amount of debt interest that is deductible—at the same time progressively increasing the deductible percentage of dividend payments.

A corollary of this plan, intended to encourage savings, would be to increase the deductibility of dividends to individuals while reducing that of individuals' interest payments. Since deducting interest is of less benefit to low-income than to high-income borrowers, its gradual elimination would insure that the benefits of the discouragement of debt and the encouragement of savings were not confined to any single group.

REDUCE CAPITAL GAINS. An alleviation of the capital gains tax is essential, in Senator Bentsen's view, if the individual investor is to return to the equity market, and President Ford's new proposals favor the principle. Bentsen has introduced legislation that would increase the amount of an individual's income that could be offset with capital losses and would progressively reduce the taxability of capital gains according to how long an asset is held.

The effects. It is obviously impossible to quantify precisely the improvements in the Debt Economy that might be brought about by these suggestions. There are too many imponderables involved. To take just one: It is far more likely that large quantities of oil dollars would be reinvested long term in the U.S. economy if the economy were seen by potential investors to be sounder. And if large quantities were reinvested long term, the whole capital supply picture would change for the infinitely better.

In any case, it seems fair to speculate that the amount to be raised in the public markets through the sale of equity might be increased so that the additional amount of debt required would be no more than the additional amount of equity.

There would thus be a relatively minor deterioration in debt-equity ratios. And the removal of governmental demand from the debt market, coupled with the infusion into the capital pool of an indeterminable but substantial sum from overseas as a result of eliminating withholding, would make interest rates substantially lower—so that interest coverage would be greatly improved.

It is hardly necessary to add that initiatives such as these could not instantly repair the damage done by 30 years of ever-increasing reliance on debt. But they would go a long way toward undoing the harm—and toward insuring that capital formation provides a much more solid base for the future than it has for the past.

23. BANKS: SKATING ON THIN ICE

by Harry Magdoff and Paul M. Sweezy

> By means of the banking system the distribution of capital as a special business, a social function, is taken out of the hands of the private capitalists and usurers. But at the same time, banking and credit thus become the most effective means of driving capitalist production beyond its own limits and one of the most effective vehicles of crises and swindle.
> —Marx, *Capital*, vol. 3

The specter haunting today's capitalist world is the possible collapse of its financial institutions and an associated world economic crisis. The miasma of fear is hardly surprising in the light of the coincidence in many capitalist countries of seemingly uncontrollable inflation, declining production, and instability in financial markets. The banking and credit community is showing increasing signs of weakness. Thus, in the span of one year the United States witnessed the two largest bank failures in its history (U.S. National Bank in San Diego and Franklin National Bank in New York). In addition, according to a report in the *Wall Street Journal* of December 18, 1974, more than a dozen European banks reported big losses or failed in 1974.

The state of mind of the ruling classes of the leading capitalist countries was well illustrated in an article in *Le Monde* (October 22, 1974), Europe's most prestigious newspaper, entitled "The Bankers of New York Begin to Feel the Wind of Panic."

Reprinted from *Monthly Review* (February 1975). The authors are the well-known editors of *Monthly Review*.

According to the paper's special correspondent in New York, he was told by a well-known American banker:

> "It is not impossible that the monetary authorities will be led in the near future to make dramatic decisions, such for example as freezing certain long-term deposits in the banks (deposits established against the issuance of CDs, i.e., certificates of deposit for which there is a very active market in the United States). It is not even possible to exclude the possibility of a panic which would drive depositors to withdraw their funds."
>
> These somber prognostications, made during a luncheon attended by some ten people, raised no objections from the other guests, whose analyses in other respects however were quite different from those of our interlocutor, a man with world-wide experience, not confined only to the United States.

Superficial apologists are inclined to gloss over these warning signals by dwelling solely on the special and, by implication, unique errors of the banks that collapsed, thereby ignoring the fact that these so-called errors are merely distorted reflections of more basic difficulties besetting the money markets. The more responsible financial leaders of the capitalist class tend to speak more frankly. For example, Robert V. Roosa, a partner in Brown Brothers Harriman and former Undersecretary of the Treasury, observed last August, according to a *Washington Post* dispatch:

> "There has been a loss of confidence in the [financial] machinery most of us took for granted. There is a fear, a kind of foreboding." It is "not too much," Roosa added, to say that these concerns are similar to the kind that prevailed in the 1930s. (Published in the *Boston Globe,* August 5, 1974.)

And the chairman of the Federal Reserve Board, Arthur F. Burns, in a major address to the latest convention of the American Bankers Association (October 21, 1974) also went back to the Great Depression as a point of comparison for today's critical conditions. While he did not specifically identify the decade of the 1930s, he could not have meant anything else by his opening sentence: "This year, for the first time in decades, questions have been raised about the strength of the nation's, and indeed the world's, banking system." Rather than sweep this notion under the rug, as one might expect from a conservative government official charged with the responsibility to sustain the public confidence and faith on which banks rely to stay in business, Burns went on to spell out in considerable detail why such fears are justified, tracing the problems to the fact that the "goals of profitability and growth have been receiving more and more attention [by bank managements]." He did, of course, utter the necessary endorsement of faith in the banks, but made it clear that it does not rest on the liquidity and stability of the banks themselves. Instead, he pointed out that "for the first time since the Great Depression, the availability of liquidity from the central bank has become . . . an essential ingredient in maintaining confidence in the commercial banking system. . . . Faith in our banks . . . now rests unduly on the fact that troubled banks can turn to a governmental lender of last resort." (Full text of Burns's speech in *The American Banker,* October 23, 1974.)

Why is it that matters have been permitted to reach such a state—where banks can't stand on their own feet and must hopefully rely on the government to prevent collapse? Why, indeed, when there are long-established laws and regulatory bodies—notably, the Federal Reserve Board itself—designed to prevent precisely the dangerous developments analyzed coldly and competently by Burns in the aforementioned speech? Surely, the reason can't be ignorance. The relevant data about the operations of the large commercial banks are available to the Federal Reserve Board, and are publicly distributed by the Board itself, from week to week. Moreover, the important changes, showing increasing sources of instability, are not new, but, as we shall show below, have been developing since the early 1960s and accelerating since the mid-1960s.

The answers to these questions are not to be found in ignorance, absence of wisdom, or lack of will power. What has to be understood is that the ruling class and government officials could hardly have prevented the present situation from developing no matter how much they may have wanted to. The overextension of debt and the overreach of the banks was exactly what was needed to protect the capitalist system and its profits; to overcome, at least temporarily, its contradictions; and to support the imperialist expansion and wars of the United States. Those who now complain and tremble over excesses are the very same people who helped bring them about, or at the least did nothing to forestall them, for fear of bringing down the whole financial network. This should become clearer as we examine some of the key facts.

Before we get into the workings of the banking system in these years of inflation and credit expansion, we should understand that there are two sides to the debt explosion: (1) capitalists borrow as much as possible not only from necessity but, more importantly, as a way to increase their individual profit rates, and (2) banks and other institutions aggressively increase their lending as a means of maximizing their own profits. The first point can easily be seen with a simple arithmetical illustration.

Investment—First Stage
Let us assume that a capitalist has invested in a manufacturing process .... $ 1,000
Profit
Assume that he makes a gross profit of 20% on this investment .... $ 200
Assume further that he pays 50% of profits in taxes . $ −100
_____
He then makes a net profit of 10% on his investment $ 100

Investment—Second Stage
The capitalist decides to double his capacity, but, instead of plowing back his profits, he borrows another $1,000 by issuing bonds. The capital in his business then consists of
Stock investment .... $ 1,000
Bonds .... $ 1,000
_____
Total capital .... $ 2,000
Profit
Gross profit (20%) on total capital .... $ 400
Assume bondholders are paid 6% interest on their $1,000 of bonds .... $ −60
_____
The capitalist then has, after interest payments .... $ 340
Deduct the 50% he pays in taxes .... $ −170
_____

The capitalist now gets a profit rate of 17% on his
    original $1,000 invested .... $ 170

This arithmetic of profits (in our simplified example, a potential increase in the profit rate from 10 to 17 percent) is
what lies behind a good deal of the vast expansion of long-
term debt shown in Table 1.

TABLE I

Investment in All U.S. Corporations

Year	Long-term debt bonds and mortgages	Direct investment by owners of the corporation: stocks	Long-term debt as a percent of stock investment
	Billions of dollars		
1940	$ 49	$ 89	55.1%
1950	66	94	70.2
1955	98	113	86.7
1960	154	140	110.0
1965	210	161	130.4
1970	363	201	180.6

SOURCE: U.S. Bureau of the Census, *Statistical Abstract of the United
States: 1973*. Washington, D.C., p. 479.

As can clearly be seen from Table 1, the rapid accumulation
of corporate capital since the end of the Great Depression involved both equity investment and debt, but the growth in the
use of bonds and mortgages far outpaced that of stocks. Stock
investment (equity capital) increased $112 billion (from $89
in 1940 to $201 billion in 1970), while debt capital (bonds
and mortgages) grew by $314 billion (from $49 in 1940 to
$363 billion in 1970). This shift to much greater use of debt
capital has two origins: (1) the drive to increase profit rates,
as explained in the foregoing arithmetical example; and (2)
the constant pressure to increase the mass of profits, even
though, as in Marx's words cited at the outset, this means
"driving capitalist production beyond its own limits," and means
relying on debt because of the insufficiency of funds capitalists

are able to generate internally or through flotation of new stock issues to finance expansion. Note that we are now discussing all corporations (financial and nonfinancial); the impulse to rely on borrowed money for investment capital extends over the entire spectrum of capitalist enterprise.

As much as this long-term debt of corporations has grown, it has nevertheless proven to be insufficient to appease the capitalist appetite for accumulation. And hence corporations, with the collaboration of the banks and other financial institutions, began to depend more and more on short-term borrowing as a means of obtaining capital both for new investment in plant and equipment and for their everyday operations. Salient facts on these changes for all nonfinancial corporations are shown in Table 2.

TABLE 2

Short-term Debt of Nonfinancial Corporations

End of year	Bank loans	Other borrowing (a)	Gross National Product originating in nonfinancial corporations	Bank loans as percent of GNP	Other borrowing as percent of GNP
		Billions of Dollars			
1950	$18.3	$ 1.4	$151.7	12.1%	.9%
1955	25.6	3.0	216.3	11.8	1.4
1960	37.7	6.8	273.1	13.8	2.5
1965	60.7	8.8	377.6	16.1	2.3
1970	102.5	24.3	516.1	19.9	4.7
1974 (first half)	183.6	37.6	727.9	25.2	5.2

a. Includes commercial paper sold by corporations on the open market and loans by finance companies.

SOURCE: Data for borrowing are from *Flow of Funds Accounts 1945–1972* (Board of Governors of the Federal Reserve System, August 1973) for 1960 and previous years; *Federal Reserve Bulletin,* October 1974, for the period after 1960. Data for gross national product originating in nonfinancial corporations are from *The Economic Report of the President* (Washington, D.C., U.S. Govt. Printing Office, 1974) for the data prior to 1974; and the *Survey of Current Business,* October 1974, for first half of 1974.

Especially noteworthy in the data presented in Table 2 is the marked difference between the years before and after 1960. Bank loans increased in the decade of the 1950s, but pretty much in line with the general expansion of nonfinancial corporate business: bank loans as a percent of nonfinancial corporate GNP were 12.1 in 1950 and 13.8 in 1960—a rise, but not an especially significant one. Other short-term borrowing also grew in this period, but in 1960 it was still small potatoes. Now look at the decisive change that begins with 1960. Between 1960 and 1974 bank loans grew at a much faster rate than nonfinancial business activity, the ratio of the former to the latter almost doubling: from 13.8 percent in 1960 to 25.2 percent in the first half of 1974, while at the same time other forms of short-term borrowing spurted forward.

Still more interesting is the acceleration in the dependence on bank credit. Thus, if we examine the rate of increase of this dependency (as expressed in the column of Table 2 headed "Bank loans as percent of GNP"), we find that reliance on bank credit increases by 17 percent between 1960 and 1965, by 24 percent in the next five-year period, and by 27 percent in only three-and-a-half years from the end of 1970 to the end of June 1974.

While this kind of debt acceleration helps keep the economy going by "driving capitalist production beyond its limits," the dependence on debt produces limits of its own. If we assume for the sake of argument that the sale of bonds and mortgages and the granting of bank loans can keep on increasing endlessly, business borrowers can still absorb this expanding debt only as long as they can make enough profit to meet the rising interest payments. Eventually, if the debt load keeps accelerating, the interest on the debt begins to choke off profits and hence also the incentive, as well as the financial ability, to keep the underlying accumulation process going.

The capitalist answer to this dilemma up to now has been to feed the fires of inflation. As interest burdens increase— the result of larger debt as well as higher interest rates stimulated by the huge demand for money capital—capitalists raise prices to meet these obligations. And as price hikes spread throughout the economy, the need for even more borrowing follows. Thus debt obligations, interest charges, and prices chase each other in the upward spiral of inflation.

Thus far we have examined only one side of the problem: the demand for money by business, assuming in effect that there is no end to the supply of money. To a certain extent, this is a tenable assumption, but only if one also assumes that the government's money-printing presses go mad and end up producing a hyperinflation that destroys the country's currency. Short of such a runaway inflation, we are beginning to see obstacles emerging in the ability of the banks to keep on supplying credit at the accelerated rate of the past. It is true that the banks, in pursuit of ever more profits for themselves, have tried to keep up with the demand for loans. But in doing so they have stretched themselves so thin that their own liquidity is in question, and legitimate fears have been raised about the possible collapse of the financial system.

To understand this aspect of the problem we need to review a few simple fundamentals of how commercial banks operate. The traditional function of such banks has been to act as a depository (safekeeper) of money. Individuals and business firms place their money in these banks in the form of deposits in checking or savings accounts, which the banks should always be able to return on request. The banks in turn accept these deposits because they can make a profit by using the major part of them either to buy bonds or to make loans. Bankers base their operations on the assumption of a certain pattern of withdrawal of deposits by customers, i.e., that only a certain portion will be withdrawn each day. To meet these withdrawals, banks keep a reserve of cash. Since one cannot be too sure that there may not be unexpected surges of deposit withdrawals, an additional part of the deposits is invested in short-term U.S. Treasury bills and notes. The prices of these investments do not fluctuate very much and, more important, they can be sold almost instantaneously in the money market to raise cash, should deposit withdrawals suddenly increase. On top of this, banks invest another part of the deposits in longer-term bonds of the U.S. Treasury, other government bodies, and corporations. On such investments banks make more money than on short-term debt instruments, their disadvantage being that the prices of these bonds fluctuate, which means that the banks can lose money if they are forced to sell when prices are down. Still more profitable for the banks than bonds are loans to businesses and consumers, but these cannot normally be turned into cash until they mature, so they provide little or no protection against a sudden dash by depositors to withdraw funds. Hence, for the sake of safety, banks have traditionally maintained a pattern of investment which consists of retaining a margin of ready cash and then distributing their money-making assets among a variety of notes, bonds, and loans.

Against this background look at Table 3, which shows how banking practices have been changing in recent years and why doubts have been arising about the general viability of the banking system.

The rise in the percent of loans to deposits between 1950 and 1960 is not especially noteworthy. Cash reserves in banks (and in business firms) were still very large, reflecting the cash accumulated during the Second World War. Further, the fact that 56 percent of the deposits of the large commercial banks were loaned out still left the banks in a fairly secure position, with comfortable reserves in cash and short-term securities to meet emergencies. It is the inexorable growth of the percentage of loans to deposits since 1960 that cries out for attention. The heating up of the economy under the stimulus of the Vietnam War and the consequent kindling of the flames of inflation induced an expansion of the bank-lending activity beyond any traditional understanding of the so-called fiduciary responsibility of the banks, a process that endangers the safety of the money left for safekeeping and begins to bump against the ultimate ceiling of how much money banks can lend.

Clearly, the banks cannot lend out all of their deposits; some part must be held in reserve to pay depositors who wish to withdraw their money and to cover losses arising from defaulted loans. While there is no trustworthy guide to the "proper" ratio of loans to deposits, the persistent rise in the ratio, especially since 1970, reveals that even apart from their responsibility as safekeepers of other people's money, the banks are fast approaching the absolute limit (100 percent) of the deposits that could be loaned out. Thus, as shown in Table 3, by the end of 1974 the large commercial banks had committed 82 percent of their deposits to loans; the same pattern is seen in the large

New York City banks—at the heart of the country's main money market. To see this in perspective, it should be noted that the highest ratio of loans to deposits in U.S. banks between 1900 and 1970 was 79 percent (and that in only one year, 1921); in 1929 the ratio was 73.1 percent. (Calculated from data in U.S. Bureau of the Census, *Historical Statistics of the United States, Colonial Times to 1957,* Washington, D.C., 1960).

How the banks were able to reach the extraordinary ratios of the 1970s will be explained below. But for the present it should be noted that a sizable part of the deposits recorded in Table 3 are far from what would be considered "normal" deposits of banks. No less than 40 percent of the deposits of the large New York City banks consists of large certificates of deposit, money borrowed by banks to facilitate the rapid growth of loans beyond otherwise practical limits; and half the increase in these deposits between 1965 and 1974 was generated by the sale of these specially issued short-term certificates of deposit. But more on this later.

This is not yet the whole story. In their search for profits and since they are bumping against limits to their outright lending power, the banks have introduced and are expanding a new technique of lending, called "standby letters of credit." (See *Business Week,* February 16, 1974, p. 120.) For a fee, they guarantee the IOUs issued and sold on the commercial paper market by big corporations. In other words, the banks commit themselves to paying the borrowed money if the corporations default. Since it is the financially weaker corporations that need such bank guarantees in order to sell their IOUs, this type of "indirect loan" is itself of the shakier variety. These letters of credit are not reported on the balance sheets of the banks and are therefore not included in the loan figures shown in Table 3. If they were included, the 1974 percentages of loans to deposits would be even larger than those shown.

Why this mad rush by the banks to expand loans? There are two basic reasons: the lust for profit and the pressure of competition. Banks operate according to the laws of capitalism expounded by Marx. Their dominant motive is the continuous search for ways to expand profits: by accumulating capital and by increasing their rate of profit. They search in every nook

TABLE 3

Loans and Deposits: Commercial Banks

LARGE COMMERCIAL BANKS (a)

End of year	Loans	Deposits	Loans as percent of deposits
	Billions of dollars		
1950	$ 31.6	$ 87.7	36.0%
1955	48.4	105.3	46.0
1960	71.6	127.2	56.3
1965	120.3	181.8	66.2
1970	188.8	266.8	70.8
1974	319.3	389.4	82.0

LARGE NEW YORK CITY BANKS

End of year	Loans	Deposits	Loans as percent of deposits
1950	$ 9.9	$25.1	39.4%
1955	14.2	27.9	50.9
1960	18.6	31.0	60.0
1965	31.8	45.7	69.6
1970	45.5	63.2	72.0
1974	78.9	93.5	84.4

a. Banks that had total deposits of $100 million or more on Dec. 31, 1965. SOURCE: Data prior to 1974 are from various issues of the *Federal Reserve Bulletin*. Data for 1974 are from *Federal Reserve Statistical Release H.4.3* for the last week in 1974.

and cranny of the economy, using salesmen, newspaper and television advertising, testing new devices—all geared to opening up new opportunities both for lending large amounts to business firms, real estate operators, stock market speculators, finance companies, and also for extending small loans (at even higher rates of interest) to the garden-variety of citizen. This incessant drive for business and profits goes on even as the banks' lending potential (as shown in Table 3) narrows; in this fashion, they are being true to their nature as capitalist entrepreneurs.

The second stimulus for the ballooning of loans is the competition among the banks themselves. Turning down the request for a loan to an established customer always carries with it the threat that the borrower will shift his entire banking business to a competitor. If the customer is a big corporation, there is every reason to expect that another bank will stretch itself

TABLE 4

Liquidity of Large Commercial Banks

End of year	*Cash Reserves(a)*	*U.S. Treasury Bonds(b)*	*Short-term U.S. Treasury Notes(c)*	*Cash + All Treasuries as a percent of total deposits(d)*	*Cash + Short-term Treasuries as a percent of total deposits(d)*
		Billions of Dollars			
1950	$13.7	$33.7	n.a.	54.0%	n.a.
1955	14.9	30.1	n.a.	42.7	n.a.
1960	14.0	30.2	$ 8.2	34.7	17.5%
1965	16.3	24.3	8.6	22.3	13.7
1970	20.2	28.1	10.3	18.3	11.4
1974	29.5	23.4	7.9	13.6	9.6

n.a.: Not available.

a. Cash in vault plus reserves with Federal Reserve banks, as required by the Federal Reserve Board.

b. Bonds here include bills, certificates, notes, as well as bonds.

c. All treasury securities that mature in less than one year.

d. The data on deposits used as the denominator are those given in Table 3.

SOURCE: Same as Table 3.

to latch on to a new source of business, even if the loan in question does not measure up to "sound" banking practice.

Both of these pressures—the drive for profits and the need to protect one's already existing market—lead to a larger and larger share of relatively unsafe loans in the banks' portfolios. It should be noted that the very ease with which the larger corporations can get loans facilitates their carrying on their own business affairs beyond safe limits, as clearly seen in the steady decline in the ratio of liquid reserves relative to what the corporations owe. (See "The Long-run Decline in Corporate Liquidity," in MONTHLY REVIEW, September 1970.) And the harder it becomes for the corporations to repay their bank loans (because of declining liquidity), the more the banks are obliged to grant further loans to prevent borrowers from going bust and thus defaulting on the backlog of loans. As willing or unwilling collaborators in the process by which the large corporations operate closer and closer to the edge of the precipice, the banks are themselves drawn nearer to the same edge, for they can manage to lend at such a furious rate only by impairing their own liquidity. What has been happening on this score is shown in Table 4.

The last two columns of Table 4 are measures of the liquid position of the banks. In other words, they show what percentage of deposits can be got hold of quickly by bank managements to pay back depositors' money in case of an upsurge of withdrawals. The decline in liquidity shown in the penultimate column of this table (the persistent decline from 54 percent in 1950 to under 14 percent in 1974) should come as no surprise after one has examined Table 3, for this decline has been a necessary complement to the increasing percentage of loans to deposits. (This inverse relation is not precisely complementary because of the growth of bank borrowing, as will be explained presently.) Yet even this meager liquidity ratio exaggerates the reserve position of the large commercial banks. First, in order for a bank to qualify as a depository for U.S. Treasury funds, it must keep a specified reserve of U.S. treasuries to back up the government's deposits. Hence, not all of the treasuries included in this liquidity ratio would be available to meet sudden large drains on deposits. Second, the data shown in the third column represent what the banks originally paid for the bonds. (This is standard accounting practice for bank assets.) The market prices of bonds, however, go up and down: as interest rates rise the prices of bonds go down, and vice versa. For example, if a bank wanted to sell a 20-year, 3-percent Treasury bond which had been bought for $1,000 (and so recorded on the bank's books), all that could be realized on that bond in the market at the end of 1974 would have been about $550. Furthermore, if several big banks began to unload their bond holdings quickly, the market price would drop even further.

It follows that the data in the penultimate column of Table 4 overstate the degree of liquidity, sharp as the drop shown has been. A more realistic picture is given in the last column of the table, where only the short-term treasuries (those with a maturity of less than one year) are counted. And here we see the same pattern: a persistent decline in liquidity, dropping by almost half from 17.5 percent in 1960 to 9.6 percent in 1974.

There is an interesting feature here that is worth noting. If you look at the first column, you can see that cash reserves have been rising since 1960, not as much as the growth in deposits but a significant increase nevertheless. The reason that the banks did this was because they were forced to in order to live up to the requirements of the Federal Reserve Board. But for the next most liquid asset—short-term treasuries—there is no such pressure from the Board. What the banks do with respect to short-term treasuries is their own business. So here the investment by the large commercial banks was actually *reduced* somewhat between 1960 and 1974 while their liabilities in the form of deposits were more than tripling during the same period.[1]

Liquidity ratios are not the only way of looking at the safety problem. Traditional theory of good banking practice points out that while loans are a source of risk, banks protect themselves by maintaining special reserves in reasonable anticipation of a certain percentage of defaults, and in the final analysis rely on the bank's equity capital (bank stockholders' original investment plus accumulated profits) to make good on unexpected loan losses (thus preventing loss of deposits). But here too the ratio of equity capital to outstanding loans has been steadily dropping, most noticeably since 1960, as pointed out by Arthur Burns in the speech quoted above:

> . . . this enormous upsurge in banking assets [in other words, increase in loans] has far outstripped the growth of bank cap-

---

[1] One of the common illusions concerning this subject is the belief that even if bank liquidity is inadequate the Federal Deposit Insurance Corporation (FDIC) is at hand to protect the savings of depositors. The truth is that the FDIC is only an insurance company and can therefore rescue depositors only to the extent that it has enough assets to cover bank losses. Thus, as an insurance agency the FDIC was designed to deal with occasional breakdowns of one or more banks, and not with a major financial catastrophe. The dimensions of the problem can be seen from the following facts. According to the last annual report of the FDIC, the deposits covered by FDIC insurance amounted to $465.6 billion at the end of 1973. Against this the FDIC had $8.6 billion: $5.6 billion of assets, plus the right to borrow, according to existing law, $3 billion from the U.S. Treasury.

ital. At the end of 1960, equity capital plus loan and valuation reserves amounted to almost 9 percent of total bank assets. By the end of 1973, this equity capital ratio had fallen to about 6½ percent. Furthermore, the equity capital banks had been leveraged in some cases at the holding company level, as parent holding companies have increased their equity investments in subsidiary banks by using funds raised in the debt markets. Thus, the capital cushion that plays a large role in maintaining confidence in banks has become thinner, particularly in some of our largest banking organizations.

For a better understanding of Burns's argument we should know something about bank holding companies. A "loophole" in the amendments to the 1956 Bank Holding Company Act has been used by most of the big banks to expand their activities into a diverse range of non-traditional financial operations. What happens is that a holding company is set up which owns a bank and at the same time may own, for example, mortgage, finance, and factoring businesses. A number of these bank holding companies have gone to the money market to borrow funds in order to carry on this variety of operations, and in the process have used some of the borrowed money to increase their equity investment in their own banks. This is what Burns is referring to: even that small ratio of equity capital to assets is overstated, since some of the equity is really only debt owed by the parent company.

And now we come to where the dog is buried. How do banks manage in practice to keep on extending loans to reach such percentages as shown in Table 3? Normally, banks get resources to meet the demand for loans by increasing their capital, attracting additional deposits, or selling off investments in bonds. As we have just seen, the increase in equity capital was insufficient to support the explosion in loans. Nor have deposits increased sufficiently. Finally, the banks did not want to take the losses that would result from selling off all or a major part of their bond holdings, assuming that they could do so without destroying the market for bonds. So beginning in the 1960s the banks themselves have become major borrowers in order to enable them to indulge in their furious rush to lend. In the process they have created a complex network of borrowing and lending throughout the business world which not only further stimulated the inflationary process, but also resulted in a kind of delicately balanced debt structure that is constantly in danger of breaking down. Now let us look at the facts as shown in Tables 5 and 6.

Before discussing the significance of the facts presented in these tables, let us first explain what some of the headings mean. The first item, money borrowed "From Federal Reserve Banks and others," is a catchall, which includes among other things a usually relatively small amount of money that the Federal Reserve Banks lend for a short period to help banks maintain their required reserves, and money borrowed by banks on their promissory notes and other collateral.[2]

The series on "Federal funds purchased" represents, in large measure, borrowings for one business day of excess reserves from other banks willing to lend their funds. There are other borrowing devices included in this category, which as in the case of the federal funds were originally designed to cope with temporary adjustment problems of the banks. But these devices became transformed during the 1960s to meet an entirely different purpose: a tool by the biggest banks to mobilize the maximum of money resources, through going extensively into debt, in order to accelerate the pace of lending.

Still another method of borrowing developed by the big banks in the 1960s was the issuance on a large scale of negotiable certificates of deposit (CDs) in minimum amounts of $100,000. These too are short-term debts of the banks. Funds raised in this fashion are used to create new loans by the banks which, in addition to being usually of longer duration than the life of

---

[2] A description of these various devices, including loan participation certificates, bank-related commercial paper, as well as other items covered in Tables 5 and 6, can be found in Robert E. Knight, "An Alternative Approach to Liquidity, Parts I-IV" in the *Monthly Review* of the Federal Reserve Bank of Kansas City, December 1969 and February, April, May 1970. A shorter version of these questions can be found in Donald M. De Pamphilis, "The Short-term Commercial Bank Adjustment Process and Federal Reserve Regulation," in the *New England Economic Review* of the Federal Reserve Bank of Boston, May/June 1974. This is a summary of a more detailed treatment in one section of Federal Reserve Bank of Boston Research Report No. 55 by the same author, *A Microeconomic Econometric Analysis of the Short-term Commercial Bank Adjustment Process.*

TABLE 5

Short-Term Borrowing by Large Commercial Banks

————— *Borrowed money (billions of dollars)* —————

End of year	From Federal Reserve Banks and others	Federal funds purchased (a)	Large negotiable certificates of deposit (b)	Eurodollars(c)	Total	Short-term borrowing as a percent of total loans outstanding(d)
1950	$0.7	—	—	—	$ 0.7	2.2%
1960	1.8	$ 1.4	—	—	3.2	4.5
1965	6.2	2.6	$16.1	—	24.9	20.7
1970	1.5	18.8	26.1	$7.7	54.1	28.7
1974	4.8	54.0	92.2	4.0	155.0	48.5

a. The data for 1960 and 1965 are from a special series designed by the Federal Reserve Board, based on the 46 most active commercial banks in the federal funds market. The data for these years are not comparable with those for later years, but are given here to indicate the trend. The data for 1970 and 1974 include, in addition to federal funds purchased, securities sold under agreements to repurchase identical or similar securities, and sales of participations in pools of securities.

b. These are short-term certificates of deposit issued in minimum amounts of $100,000.

c. These data are the reported "Gross Liabilities of Banks to Their Foreign Branches." According to the Federal Reserve Bank of New York, *Glossary: Weekly Federal Reserve Statements,* this item is often used as a proxy for Eurodollar borrowings, though these data include some other types of transactions between domestic banks and their foreign branches.

d. The data on loans used as the denominator are those given in Table 3.

SOURCE: Same as Table 3.

the CDs, do not necessarily mature at the same time. This puts the banks under constant pressure to refinance the CDs when they become due, hopefully by issuing still more CDs.

Finally, there is the resort to Eurodollar borrowing. This in effect means the borrowing by U.S. banks from their branches abroad, and is based on the dollar deposits in these foreign branches. This method began to be used in 1966, but became especially important during the credit crunch of 1969. As can be seen from the data for this item shown in the accompanying tables, this method is used intermittently.

There are various technical aspects to these data which need not be gone into here. The important thing is to understand the

TABLE 6

Short-Term Borrowing by Large New York City Commercial Banks

——————— *Borrowed money (billions of dollars)* ———————

End of year	From Federal Reserve Banks and others	Federal funds purchased(a)	Large negotiable certificates of deposit(b)	Eurodollars(c)	Total	Short-term borrowing as a percent of total loans outstanding(d)
1950	$0.4	—	—	—	$ 0.4	4.0%
1960	1.0	$ 0.8	—	—	1.8	9.7
1965	2.5	1.4	$ 6.9	—	10.8	34.0
1970	0.2	5.5	7.9	$5.2	18.8	41.3
1974	1.7	13.6	31.7	2.8	49.8	63.1

a. Same as in Table 5, except that the earlier data are based on a series for eight New York City banks.
b. Same as in Table 5.
c. Same as Table 5, except that the figure for 1974 is estimated, based on past ratios of Eurodollar borrowing by New York City banks to all commercial banks.
d. Same as in Table 5.

SOURCE: Same as Table 3.

speculative nature of the enormous debt expansion by the banks —both as borrowers and lenders. On the one hand, the banks are gambling that businesses will be able to repay their loans despite (a) declining corporate liquidity, and (b) the fact that many firms are borrowing to pay for investment in plant and equipment that will take longer to produce the income needed than is required by the loan repayment schedules. On the other hand, the banks are speculating on being able to support this large and growing lending by having recourse to the mercurial money markets. How rapidly this short-term borrowing has grown and how dependent banks have become on this type of debt to expand their loan load is shown in Tables 5 and 6. From Table 5 we learn that the reliance on short-term borrowing by the large commercial banks reached a point by the end of 1974 such that it represented almost 50 percent of outstanding loans. Even more striking is the case of the large New York City commercial banks, where, as can be seen in Table 6, 63 percent of their outstanding loans is accounted for by short-term borrowing.

It is also important to understand the degree of uncertainty involved in these various forms of borrowing by the banks. They are almost all interest-sensitive, which means that the quantity of such borrowing can fluctuate very widely over relatively short periods, depending on the interest differentials for various types of borrowing. Arthur Burns in the previously quoted speech refers to the "volatile character" of these borrowings. And it is on these foundations that the equally volatile structure of loans, which keep the economy going, is based.

In short, the commercial banking structure, and the entire business world that relies on this structure, is skating on thin ice that is getting progressively thinner.

Why haven't the powers-that-be done something about this? As noted above, there is good reason to believe that all this has been well known for some time by the government agencies set up to prevent such menacing developments. From time to time, these agencies, and in particular the Federal Reserve Board, have taken steps to moderate one or more abuses, only to find that the financial community either found a loophole in the regulations or discovered another avenue to stretch out the debt load. Basically, the regulatory agencies were helpless, despite all their bold stances, because they too were committed to the same ends as the ruling financial and other business circles: to increase profits and to expand business opportunities, with all that these ends entail, including imperialist expansion and the Vietnam War. Rowing in the same boat as the business community, the regulators had to close their eyes to the dangers, trusting in lucky stars. Once the excesses began to reach a critical point it was too late to retreat, for too much disturbance of the intricate and complexly interrelated debt structure could all too easily break the thin ice.

The transformations described here also illuminate how fanciful are the myths of economists, Keynesians and non-Keynesians alike, who insist that they can produce a smoothly running capitalist economy by manipulation of such matters as fiscal policy, interest rates, and the money supply. The point is that all such devices do not get to the heart of what makes the capitalist economy go.[3] At best, they cover up for a while the contradictions of the capitalist system—contradictions that cause eruptions at one time or another—with the credit and banking arrangements being, as Marx long ago explained, at the center of capitalism's vulnerability to crisis.

The advanced thinkers of the ruling class are well aware of the inadequacy of the traditional nostrums as well as of the potential threat of a United States and world-wide depression. They are therefore searching for new and more reliable ways to keep the ship from sinking. It is possible to discern from the business press two important approaches emerging. One is to get the government's finances more actively engaged in salvaging business and banking firms that begin to flounder. This, however, has certain limits, for it entails widening the money and credit stream, and thus reinforcing the inflationary trend. (Over $1 billion, and by some estimates close to $2 billion, was lent by the Federal Reserve to Franklin National, merely the 20th largest commercial bank at one time, to keep the institution's head above water until some sort of reorganization could be effected, and to sustain public faith in the banking system, thus avoiding a possible flood of withdrawals from other banks. Imagine what would be required if one of the real giants began to gasp!)

The second, and more basic, line of thought is to create a firmer financial foundation for business, so that corporations can rely more on equity capital and less on debt. For this, a greater rate of profit would be needed by business. But that alone would not be enough. The government would have to step in more actively: first, to mobilize federal finances to fatten the equity position of industrial and financial firms; and second, to rationalize monopoly capital by weeding out the weaker firms.

---

[3] In addition, hands of the policy-makers are usually tied. It is impossible to devise consistent policies that can at one and the same time handle the conflicting pressures on a capitalist economy: for example, the need to finance the military budget; to keep the money markets in shape to absorb the debts of federal, state, and local government; to support the dollar abroad; to improve the balance of payments by attracting foreign funds and stimulating exports; to try to keep inflation from getting completely out of hand; to see that the banks have enough money to rescue tottering corporations; to keep the economy expanding at a rate sufficient to provide jobs for the labor force, etc., etc.

Within the limits of capitalism, measures of this sort can have only one meaning: to cut into the living standards (wages and welfare) of the working class, the old-age retirees, the petty bourgeoisie, and smaller businessmen. This is the only way that profit rates can be beefed up and finances procured to strengthen the equity capital position of the bigger corporations.

Here lies the challenge to the working class and whatever allies may be available to it. Above all, it is necessary to destroy prevailing illusions about the possibility of regulating capitalism in such a way as to produce prosperity for all classes. The ruling class will soon be sharply drawing the class issues with the hope of stabilizing their own affairs. Only by facing up militantly to the fundamental class nature of the impending struggle, which means challenging capitalism as such, does the working class have a chance to protect its true interests.

24. WAGES, PRODUCTIVITY AND PROFITS

by Alfred L. Malabre, Jr.

The cost of labor is soaring.

Wage boosts in the first year of major-labor contracts averaged about 10% in the first three quarters of 1974, nearly twice the comparable 1973 rise. But the actual cost of labor—up at an annual rate of 14% so far this year—has climbed even more swiftly in a spiral that many economists believe may worsen.

One reason many analysts view the trend as "ominous" is that

Excerpts from "Real Cost of Labor Outpaces Pay Gains as Productivity Lags," in the *Wall Street Journal* (October 31, 1974). Alfred L. Malabre, Jr., is a staff reporter of the *Journal*.

it could soon begin to erode company profits sharply and trigger increasing layoffs. So far, corporations generally have managed to boost their prices even more rapidly than labor costs have risen; a ratio of wholesale prices to labor costs climbed about 10% in a recent 12-month period, with most of the rise coming recently.

Lagging productivity is a major factor in the extraordinary labor-cost spiral, analysts say. Over the full post–World War II era, output per man-hour in private industry has risen roughly 3% a year. But this year this productivity measure has been falling steadily. In the third quarter, it fell at an annual rate of 3%, reaching the lowest level in more than two years.

Productivity gains, of course, tend to offset rising pay levels. If a widget-factory worker wins a 10%-an-hour pay boost but also turns out 10% more widgets each hour, the cost of his labor remains unchanged. But if there isn't any increase in his productivity, the cost of labor per widget rises 10%. And if his productivity declines, the labor cost climbs more than 10%. This is what has been happening on the U.S. labor front in recent months.

Looking ahead, analysts see several factors suggesting that pay —and labor costs—will continue to increase substantially while productivity lags.

"There's little hope for any strong pickup in productivity," Mellon's Mr. Robertson says. He also anticipates an intensifying demand by union leaders for "large catch-up wage increases" because prices generally have risen faster than pay. He notes that the buying power of the average worker's weekly paycheck, after federal tax payments and inflation are taken out, has declined about 8% over the past two years.

The productivity lag, economists say, is tied to the overall economic situation. Traditionally, as business activity slows down— and many forecasters believe the economy now is in the early stages of a full-fledged recession—productivity tends to drop. This isn't because workers suddenly grow lazier. Rather, employers normally hesitate to lay off workers in such situations, uncertain that business will turn really sour. The upshot is that productivity declines as actual production falls faster than employment is cut back.

Experience shows, by no coincidence, that labor-cost increases tend to accelerate as a recession deepens. In the process, the cost increases begin to outstrip price boosts, which in any event grow more difficult for companies whose sales may be flagging. As a result, the aforementioned ratio of prices to labor costs usually turns sharply down. Layoffs grow more frequent as employers struggle to limit the labor-cost spiral. Despite such tactics, however, profit margins generally begin to shrink.

At present, analysts say, business is at the deceptively painless stage where the labor-cost climb hasn't quite yet begun to bite sharply into profits or prompt massive layoffs.

An analyst at Irving Trust Co. in New York views the situation this way: "As labor costs continue to jump later this year and during 1975, they are bound to begin taking a toll—and two of the major casualties will be corporate profit margins and the employment picture."

Some economists say that another factor limiting productivity gains—and thus tending to push up labor costs—is industry's increasing need to ensure that new facilities are nonpolluting and safe for employes. Nearly 10% of plant-and-equipment spending is mainly for such purposes, according to a recent survey by McGraw-Hill Inc. That compares with an estimated 3% in 1967.

"Slower productivity gains are part of the price of trying to clean up the environment and make plants safer and healthier places to work," says a Commerce Department economist who keeps a close tab on capital-spending trends.

Analysts see additional long-term developments that may increase the cost of labor. After remaining flat through most of the 1960s, union membership is on the rise. Many economists expect the trend to continue because professional people and employes of state and local governments increasingly are joining associations that are tantamount to unions. Membership in such groups rose nearly 30% to about 2,300,000 during a recent five-year period. Overall union membership rose about 5% in the same span. Roughly one-quarter of the U.S. labor force currently belongs to a union or similar employee association.

While there are notable exceptions, unionized workers generally command higher pay levels than their nonunion counterparts, Labor Department studies show.

Union contracts containing cost-of-living "escalator" clauses are another factor that some analysts believe could tend to intensify labor costs. Workers covered by such agreements still amount only to a small fraction of the country's labor force, but it's a rapidly growing fraction. At the beginning of the year, about four million union members were covered by escalator clauses, but since then about another 1,000,000 have gained such clauses in their contracts. Analysts anticipate a rapid spread of such agreements.

In any event, the country's labor-cost climb remains generally less severe than in most major countries. In a recent three-year period, according to a Labor Department study, unit labor costs rose more slowly in the U.S. than in any of nine other major countries. In many countries costs rose several times faster than in the U.S. The main reason for the relatively good U.S. record, the study shows, is that U.S. pay gains were much smaller than in most lands. As a result, there was less of a gap between productivity and pay increases in the U.S.

25. THE IMPACT OF INDUSTRIAL CONCENTRATION ON THE ECONOMIC CRISIS

by Richard C. Edwards

Why, in the current crisis, is there *both* high inflation and high unemployment? The simultaneous existence of these two ills makes this crisis different from any others in the American past. It directly raises a more fundamental question: Has the structure of the economy itself changed?

Most people realize that the U.S. economy has increasingly

Unpublished paper. Richard C. Edwards teaches economics at the University of Massachusetts, Amherst, and is a member of URPE.

fallen under the control of huge monopolistic and internationally based firms—companies like GM, IBM, Exxon, GE and ITT. Yet the increasing dominance of these firms is one of the missing —or seriously misrepresented—elements in recent discussions of the deeping economic crisis. Inflation has been blamed on the Arabs, on excessive government spending, on crop failures, on consumers who spend too much, on workers who try to protect their wages—in short, on just about everyone but the corporations which control the economy. Similarly, unemployment is blamed on lack of "investor confidence," on the failure of consumers to spend their incomes on automobiles, or on high interest rates. Do the big firms make no independent contribution to the crisis?

The argument of this paper is that increased corporate dominance of the economy has fundamentally changed the way prices and employment levels get determined. Although increasing concentration cannot fully explain the peculiar nature of the current crisis, neither can the current crisis be explained without a better understanding of the role of large, monopolistic corporations in our economy.

Increasing Corporate Control

The facts of corporate dominance appear to be relatively simple. This is often obscured by the government's confidentiality rules and its failure to collect the relevant statistics—for example, comparable data on assets, share of the market, employees, and profits for the largest firms in each industry.

But in a careful recent study, economist William Shepherd presented convincing evidence of the wide extent of market power.[1] The private sector, if one includes private-sector production for government use, accounts for approximately 85% of all the goods and services produced in the United States; in 1973 the private-sector output totaled $1,125 billion. Shepherd's contribution was a methodical identification of all those industries in which the leading firms exercised "substantial market power," i.e., monopolistic or oligopolistic control. He concluded that a "reasonable minimum estimate" would be that 35% to 45% of

[1] William Shepherd, *Market Power and Economic Welfare* (New York, Random House, 1970).

private sector output was produced where "substantial market power" existed.

The conservative nature of Shepherd's estimates should be emphasized—the actual extent of monopoly power may be considerably greater. Moreover, in the industrial core of the economy—manufacturing, finance, utilities, transportation, communications—the concentration is particularly high. Table I gives some examples of these highly concentrated industries.

TABLE I

*Examples of Industries in Which Leading Firms
Have "Substantial Market Power"*

INDUSTRY	NUMBER OF "LEADING FIRMS"	APPROXIMATE SHARE OF THESE FIRMS IN RELEVANT MARKETS
telephone equipment	1	80–90%
computers	1	70–80%
heavy electrical equipment	2	70–80%
iron and steel	4	50–60%
drugs	4	70–80%
soaps	3	60–70%
aircraft	3	80–90%
aluminum	3	80–90%
dairy products	3	60–70%
cereals	2	60–70%
soup	1	90%
motor vehicles	3	90–100%
petroleum refining	4	40–50%
industrial chemicals	4	60–70%
aircraft engines	2	90–100%
copper	3	60–70%
photographic supplies	1	60–70%
metal containers	2	80–90%

SOURCE: Shepherd, *Market Power and Economic Welfare,* pp. 152–53.

Another view of the role of big corporations in the economy is gained by measuring their operations as a proportion of the total economy (see Table II). The seventy-eight largest companies, all giants with assets in 1968 in excess of $1 billion, owned 43%

of all assets and captured an even larger share (49%) of the total profits in manufacturing.[2]

TABLE II

Concentration of Assets and Profits in American Manufacturing Corporations, First Quarter, 1968

CORPORATIONS HAVING ASSETS OF:	NUMBER OF COMPANIES IN CATEGORY	ASSETS OF FIRMS IN CATEGORY AS PERCENT OF TOTAL MANUFACTURING ASSETS	PROFITS OF FIRMS IN CATEGORY AS PERCENT OF TOTAL MANUFACTURING PROFITS
$1 billion and over	78	43	49
$250 million to $1 billion	194	21	20
$10 million to $250 million	2,165	22	19
under $10 million	185,000*	14	12
Total	187,437	100	100

* Estimate

SOURCE: *Studies by the Staff of the Cabinet Committee on Price Stability,* p. 92.

As these data demonstrate, large parts of the U.S. economy are now in the hands of enormous companies which operate domestically as monopolists or oligopolists and which have huge resources to use in exercising their power and expanding their influence. They own most of the factories, land, and other assets; they produce most of the goods, especially in key sectors of the economy; and they capture an even larger share of the profits.

These fundamental facts of the U.S. industrial structure need to be incorporated into our understanding of the causes of the crisis.

Monopoly and Inflation

Inflation is not, of course, caused solely by industrial concentration. But the increasing domination of the economy by large

[2] *Studies by the Staff of the Cabinet Committee on Price Stability* (Washington, D.C., 1969), p. 92.

monopolistic firms does bear a direct relation to tendencies toward inflation in capitalist economies.

The key to the relation between monopoly power and inflation lies in the pricing of big corporations. A consequence of their market power is these firms' ability to maintain prices, to pass along cost increases in the form of higher product prices, and even to profit from further cost increases in their world of "cost-plus" pricing. These firms often raise prices and sometimes hold prices constant, but they almost never reduce prices.

The general effect of a pricing system in which some prices rise, some remain constant, but none or only a few fall, is inflation.

For those firms experiencing increases in demand for their products—firms such as the sugar companies and other food processors or the oil companies—the price increases spell spectacular profits. Amstar, the biggest sugar company, riding the tide of the 300% increase in sugar prices over the preceding year, reported that third-quarter profits were up 250% over the second quarter of 1974. Great Western United, the largest beet-sugar refiner, reported a profit increase of 1,120% in the third quarter.[3] These companies' profits were so spectacular that they are now under federal investigation for price fixing. More significant, the oil companies reported profit increases ranging from 38% (Exxon) to 104% (Standard of Indiana) in the first nine months of 1974 as compared to the same period the previous year. These latest increases came on top of those large increases so widely reported earlier in the year (a survey of the twenty-five largest oil companies indicated that 1973 profits jumped nearly 53% over 1972).[4]

On the other hand, those monopolistic firms experiencing constant or even declining demand do not correspondingly reduce *their* prices. The domestic automobile industry, stuck with the overweight, gas-guzzling models popular before the energy crunch, reported new-car sales that were sharply lower. GM's third quarter, 1974, sales were down 22% compared to a year

[3] *New York Times* (October 23, 1974), pp. 63, 73; *Oil and Gas Journal* (February 18, 1974), p. 32.
[4] *New York Times* (November 1, 1974), pp. 55, 57; (November 2, 1974), p. 37.

earlier. Yet in contrast to the standard lessons of supply and demand analysis which indicate that falling demand should be accompanied by falling prices, the auto companies *raised* prices —by a whopping $900–$1,000 per car, on average, over the initial price of the 1974 models.[5]

Sales in the fourth quarter plummeted further, yet not until January did the auto companies respond—and then with their "rebate" plan, which was both temporary and offered price cuts lower than previous price increases.

The evidence on increasing industrial concentration indicates that a significant part of the economy is now controlled by firms that have sufficient market power either to profit from the inflation or to resist downward pressures on prices. In either event, concentration tends to exaggerate the pressure toward inflation.

Monopoly and Unemployment

There is another side to the relation between concentration and the economic crisis. While concentration tends to generate chronic pressures toward inflation when demand is high, the corporations' ability to control prices means that slack times produce not lower prices but instead higher unemployment. Firms use their market power to maintain prices as demand falls. But lower demand means that the corporations can sell less of their product. Inventories build up, and the corporations must cut back production. Massive layoffs begin.

The auto industry in the last few months of 1974 began filling up acres of their back parking lots with new cars which could not be sold at the high monopoly prices. By the beginning of December, Chrysler had a three months' supply on hand, and the other companies were not far behind. Rather than reduce prices to stimulate sales, workers were laid off. As 1975 began, hundreds of thousands of auto workers were out of jobs. Workers who had earlier paid the higher monopoly prices for consumer goods during the inflation were now being forced to pay for the downturn by becoming unemployed.

Thus concentration exacerbates problems in both directions. In boom periods (or industries) it produces higher prices; in bad times (or depressed industries) it throws more people out of work. In any phase of capitalism, workers face job uncertainty

[5] *Ibid.* (October 26, 1974), pp. 41, 43.

and production is anarchic; the market, with flexible prices, is supposed to make the necessary and painful adjustments quickly. But the presence of monopoly means that even this relief is increasingly impaired.

Increasing Concentration, Crisis and Antitrust

Whenever the ill effects of industrial concentration are noted, the standard prescription given is a "vigorous antitrust policy." Why not simply break up these monopolies and oligopolies, and "restore" competition?

The problem, of course, is that monopolistic corporations with their overwhelming power are not some unfortunate aberration in American capitalism. By and large, they *are* American capitalism. The evidence cited above indicates that antitrust policy, to be effective, must be directed not just against a few misbehaving firms, but rather against those several hundred firms which control between a third and a half of the total private-sector output.

The present U.S. industrial structure is the product of 150 years of development. The central fact about the growth of American capitalism is the increasing concentration and centralization of capital in ever larger and more powerful corporations.

The long-term trend toward concentration is strikingly evident in the percent of assets held by the largest corporations (see Table III). The series begins in 1925 only because that is the earliest estimate available; but were the information available for preceding years, it would undoubtedly show the same trend. Moreover, the projection into the future is equally obvious.

The problems created by concentration have grown alongside the growth of monopoly. In the nineteenth century, when the U.S. economy was still fairly competitive, prices went down as often as they went up. During times of scarcity, as during the Civil War, prices shot up; but afterward they returned gradually to their previous levels. Overall, prices were no higher at the end of the century than at the beginning.

Monopoly power started to be important in the economy around the turn of the century. And so did long-run inflation. Prices doubled from 1914 to 1920 and never returned to 1914 levels, even in the depths of the Great Depression of the 1930's.

Since 1940, consumer prices have fallen in only two years: in 1949, by 1%, and in 1955, by less than 0.5%. 1975 will set a

TABLE III

*The Percentage of Total Assets of All Manufacturing Firms
Held by the Largest 100 Manufacturing Firms*

YEAR	% HELD BY LARGEST FIRMS
1925	35.1
1931	42.3
1939	42.4
1948	40.1
1955	43.8
1960	46.0
1965	47.6
1971	48.9

SOURCE: *Studies by the Staff of the Cabinet Committee on Price Stability* (*op. cit.*), pp. 45, 92; U.S. Bureau of the Census, *Statistical Abstract of the United States; 1973* (Washington, D.C., 1973), p. 483.

new record in American history: twenty years of consecutive price increases.

Moreover, unemployment problems may have become more serious at the same time. The 1930's saw the highest and most prolonged levels of unemployment in history—fully deserving the title "Great Depression." The 1970's, though unlikely to have unemployment as high as the 1930's, likewise promises to be a prolonged period of high unemployment.

The "vigorous antitrust policy" so often prescribed cannot be expected to stand against these long-run and fundamental changes in the structure of capitalism. The economic dislocations engendered by such a policy, not to mention the absurdity of the government's attempting to undertake a massive deconcentration program against the wealthiest and politically most powerful "interest group" in capitalist society, rule out the possibility of a meaningful antitrust policy. The current docket of five antitrust cases—including the three instituted by the Federal Trade Commission while its chairman is barnstorming the country in defense of "vigorous antitrust"—indicates the purely cosmetic character of the capitalist antitrust program.

Concentration and Crisis Policies

The heavy concentration of economic activity in the large industrial corporations places certain constraints on governmental policies designed to combat inflation. In general, the increasing control exercised by big firms makes the standard remedies less effective.

As Royal Little, living member of *Fortune*'s Business Hall of Fame and founder of Textron, recently declared: ". . . the surest cure for inflation is a severe recession." [6] Recessions and depressions—by throwing workers off the job and reducing consumer incomes—reduce aggregate demand and undermine the upward pressure on prices.

But with the expansion of the monopolistic core of the economy and the resulting wider impact of inflexible pricing policies, the recession or depression required to stop any given level of inflation must be correspondingly more severe. Recessions must be ever deeper, more prolonged and more severe to overcome the effects of monopolistic power.

In the case cited earlier, that of the automobile industry, a decline in demand of 20% to 30% was still insufficient to halt the price increases. Only after thousands of unsold cars had accumulated and hundreds of thousands of workers were unemployed were the (temporary) rebates put into effect. Clearly, the decline in demand required in the auto industry in order to stop inflation, much less actually to register price declines to offset price increases in other industries, implies a deep recession indeed.

If it were true in all industries, as it apparently is in autos, that a 20% to 30% decline in demand would bring little impact on inflation, then of course the depression as antidote to inflation would be almost worthless. But despite increasing concentration, much of the economy—especially in activities such as personal services, retailing and other service industries—remains competitive. And in the competitive sector, prices continue to work pretty much as expected. For example, when small electronic calculators first became available, only a few companies produced them and the high prices meant large profits. But soon

[6] Royal Little, "Listen to the Painful Lessons of 1920," *Fortune* (February 1975).

other firms entered the industry and prices (and profits) were bid down. (Unable to keep competitors entirely out of the market, the large firms are now moving to establish market control based on massive advertising and brand identification; the smaller firms, which had successfully competed in price, will probably not have the resources to follow suit and will lose their markets.) In competitive industries like the beef industry, temporary shortages cause price rises but eventually result in expanded supply and lower prices again.

But almost no one can raise the huge amounts of money needed to open a new oil or sugar refinery. And even a business that could raise the money might think twice before taking on such powerful opponents. So the oil and sugar companies do not have to worry much about their skyrocketing profits attracting more competitors.

Moreover, declining demand drives prices in the competitive sector down, as is indicated by the complaints of the cattle farmers, gasoline retailers and other small businessmen whose profits are squeezed. These groups, along with the unemployed workers, tend to pay the costs of "the surest cure for inflation."

Industrial concentration also means that the other anti-inflation policy—wage and price controls—is less effective as well. Expansion of the large firms implies that economic transactions increasingly occur *within* these firms rather than between firms. But internal transactions are based on internally set prices, which prices are shielded from governmental scrutiny. More important, the international scope of the big corporations permits them to escape domestic controls by switching production abroad, as the oil companies' transferral of refining capacity from the continental United States to the Caribbean islands demonstrates.

The ultimate effect of such efforts is the translation of wage and price controls into simply wage controls. As happened in the recent past, such controls eventually become discredited and cannot be maintained except with unacceptably harsh repression.

Concentration and Future Crises

The changing industrial structure will also affect future crises. Just as the data cited above indicate that aggregate concentration has increased since 1925, so can we expect that there will be increasing concentration beyond 1975. And as the economy continues to fall more completely under the control of the big companies, the pressures toward inflation, high unemployment in the cyclically depressed industries, and the concentration-related weaknesses of the aggregate policies will all get worse.

One way of summarizing this point is to say that the crisis of the 1980's will likely be much worse than the one we are now in. The price of enjoying the "benefits" of capitalism, like all prices, is going up!

26. INDEXING THE ECONOMY:
A BRIEF PRIMER

by Timothy Nesbitt

At the first of President Ford's mini-summits on the economy in September, 28 experts met for what the business press billed a knock-down battle of ideas.

Most of the contestants dueled with dull old swords—slashing budgets, cutting taxes, even brandishing again the double-edged threat of wage and price controls. The only hint of any new inflation-fighting strategy came from Milton Friedman of the University of Chicago. Instead of trying to lick inflation, he invites us to join it. Just inflate all things equally, he says.

Indexing the economy means hitching all wages, prices, and monetary values to some standard measure of inflation, like the Consumer Price Index (CPI), and then letting go the reins.

Friedman calls his proposal a pain-killer, not a cure. But in

Abridged from "Riding the Inflation Escalator," in the *New American Movement* (October 1974). Timothy Nesbitt is a member of the *New American Movement* newspaper collective.

Brazil, where the plan has been in effect since the military take-over in 1964, indexing is touted as the only way to combine a holy war against inflation with the endless crusade for economic growth. The "Brazilian solution" has created a permanent state of siege for the working class, with real wages shrinking like rations.

Here, the aim of the indexers is to "express all transactions that have a time value in terms that eliminate the effects of infla-tion." In every area of the economy, there is an amazing readi-ness to scrap the old free market in favor of the indexers' lesser evil—"impartial and automatic adjustments to general price movements." But the effect of an indexed economy may be less than impartial.

Labor Plays Catch-Up

This is labor's problem. With inflation now threatening to double the cost of living every six years, it takes a lot of bargain-ing, threatening, and striking just to keep up. Real wages in July were down 5.3% from the year before.

Thus cost-of-living escalators can look good from both sides of the bargaining table. But it wasn't always so. Back in 1939, after a decade of deflation, John L. Lewis of the CIO said of the cost-of-living proposal: "It is economically unsound, socially un-just, and politically unwise."

After World War II, however, labor was forced to change its tactics.

In 1948, with all controls off the economy and inflation steam-ing at today's double-digit levels, General Motors surprised the United Auto Workers with an historic offer—the first unlimited cost-of-living escalator in a major union contract. UAW chief Walter Reuther accepted, and the 1948 compromise offered regular cost-of-living and productivity increases for the union and the security to do some long-term planning for GM.

Since then, the popularity of cost-of-living escalators has varied directly with the rate of inflation. In the early 60's, the Steelworkers accepted a 3-cent ceiling on their CPI adjustments, then dropped the clause entirely. The UAW, too, accepted an escalator ceiling in 1967—just before the onset of the Vietnam-fueled inflation. Three years later they had to strike to get it lifted.

Now both unions have unlimited cost-of-living escalators, adjusted quarterly, and calculated to increase hourly wages one cent for every equivalent rise in the CPI. Their members are among more than four million workers in the private economy covered by such automatic adjustment.

However, among non-union and small-union workers, the total covered by full CPI escalators is only 600,000. Overall, including government employees, fully protected workers number just 10% of the work force. Some of the rest are covered by partial or limited cost-of-living clauses. But it is this other 90% that pays in full for that 5.3% decline in real wages. These men and women bear the brunt of this inflation, while those well insulated with full CPI protection have more or less made a trade, explicit in that first UAW contract, of long-term safety for long-term status quo.

Big Money Schemes

Now the process has been complicated by the indexing schemes of several big commercial banks. New York's Citibank came up with "floating rate" notes keyed to the daily fluctuation of U.S. Treasury bills. These notes started paying well above the legal interest rates of any savings and loan, and they're rising still. Other banks followed suit. Now money is flowing from the savings banks in torrents.

So the savings institutions are fighting back with indexing schemes of their own. One plan, recently recommended by the president of the Federal Home Loan Banks, calls for variable-rate mortgages. These would enable the savings banks, with a nod from their federal and state regulators, to offer higher, more competitive interest rates.

But the built-in cost for a home buyer who accepts a variable-rate mortgage could be enormous. If such a system had been in effect in 1966, for example, a monthly mortgage payment of $123 would have swelled to $148 two years later. Any new home owner who accepts a variable-rate mortgage will have to be protected with a full cost-of-living escalator on the job.

But if indexing works for an autoworker and can keep him up to date with his payments on the house, there must be something in it for the Milton Friedmans of the country. The answer is obvious—lower taxes.

As the income system works now, anyone keeping up with or getting ahead of inflation will find him/herself spiraling with the upwardly mobile into successively higher tax brackets, thus paying higher and higher percentages to the government. This is particularly annoying to conservatives like Friedman. According to their thinking, the government causing this inflation with its unrestrained spending is also reaping the benefit with inflated tax revenues.

The argument is a personal one. Business should have no such complaint. Argus Research recently estimated that, while corporate profits have risen at a compound rate of 10.6% since 1969, the effective corporate tax rate—thanks to loopholes like the oil depletion allowance—has actually dropped from 43% to 34% in the same period.

Yet a bill introduced by Senator James Buckley of New York, and supported by Senators Proxmire and McGovern, calls for indexing the income tax structure to benefit both businesses and individuals. Inventory and capital gains would be deflated accordingly, while personal deductions and income brackets would be adjusted upward according to yearly changes. Security payments are tabbed to rise with every 3% change in the CPI. The Buckley bill would index government securities too.

What are the consequences of an indexed economy? Brazil is one case history. According to the *Wall Street Journal,* the rate of inflation there under indexing dropped from 90% in 1964 to just 15% last year. But wages declined even more. The "Brazilian solution" was no more equitable than the bureaucrats who controlled it. Then, when barrels of higher-priced oil started rolling ashore in the first quarter of this year, inflation quickly escalated to 35%.

Obviously, an indexed economy absorbs all price increases indiscriminately and bloats accordingly. This happens without indexing. But with it, the price hikes of an oil company or the manipulations of a grain dealer are not only passed on, but legislated as well. Where corporations are strong and their pricing power unchecked, they will have all the more leverage to press for successively larger shares of the consumer market. Marginal, small, more competitive industries will be forced out of existence or into conglomerates. And prices, which are hardly the products of free market forces even now, will become powerful instruments of rule.

27. HOW A WORLD DEPRESSION JUST MIGHT HAPPEN

by Lindley M. Clark

Are the U.S. and the rest of the industrialized nations headed for a depression?

The Gallup Poll reports that 51% of the American people think that the U.S. is moving in that direction. And some knowledgeable analysts fear that the entire industrialized world may be poised on the brink of some such disaster.

Most economists, it should be noted, believe that such fears are overblown. "Everyone thinks that things will work out," says Norman Robertson, senior vice president and chief economist of Pittsburgh's Mellon Bank. However, he adds, "no one is sure precisely how."

To understand how all this might happen, it's necessary to consider a little background.

In late 1972 concern and confusion began spreading swiftly in the U.S. and the University of Michigan's Survey Research Center reported a drop in consumer confidence. Price inflation, suppressed for more than a year by controls, was accelerating once again, though business activity still was strong and the stock market was rushing toward a new high.

Excerpts from "World Depression? Analysts Doubt Crash—but Some Tell How It Just Might Happen," in the *Wall Street Journal* (November 7, 1974). Lindley M. Clark, Jr., is a staff reporter of the *Journal*.

Early in 1973 the economy's rate of growth began slowing, and the market started a long and sickening slide. Economists agreed that the business pace of 1972 and early 1973 had been too fast to be sustained.

Then things really began getting worse.

First, poor harvests in the U.S. and abroad helped shove up food prices. Later, in October 1973, the Arab oil-producing nations embargoed shipments to the U.S. In combination with their fellow members of the Organization of Petroleum Exporting Countries, they started sharply increasing the price of their oil.

With inflation zooming into double-digit territory in the U.S. and elsewhere, Michigan's consumer-sentiment index hit a new low. Businessmen were puzzled but not quite as worried as consumers. Although the gross national product, in terms of 1958 dollars, began dropping in the year's first quarter, many firms found that sales and profits, in terms of 1974 dollars, were better than ever. When the Arabs lifted the oil embargo, some businessmen thought their troubles were over—but that proved temporary.

In mid-1974 the Fed began sharply slowing the growth of the nation's money supply; this is defined as currency plus bank checking accounts. In the process, the Fed seems to be slowing the inflated economy. Meanwhile, the U.S. and other oil-consuming countries are paying additional tens of billions of dollars to members of OPEC, which is made up of both Arab and non-Arab nations. "The annual rate of revenue of OPEC countries has increased from $15 billion in 1972 to an estimated $90 billion to $95 billion as of January 1974 and to $110 billion to $115 billion by mid-September 1974," according to Walter J. Levy, the veteran New York oil consultant.

One result: Huge deficits in the international accounts of most major industrial nations. In theory, these countries could devalue their currencies to try to balance their books. But deep devaluation would mean even more inflation, partially by raising the price of imports, and the oil-producing countries have promised that the price of petroleum will keep pace with the prices of everything else.

So far, the Arabs, whose generally undeveloped economies can't absorb these huge amounts of funds, are investing much of their newly gained wealth through private banks in Europe and the U.S. These banks, in turn, have lent money to some of the oil-consuming countries. This is what is meant by recycling—a term that has begun to show up more and more in the newspapers.

The term recycling suggests to many observers a measure of safety. The U.S. and other countries pay the OPEC nations for their oil, OPEC lends the money to banks in the U.S. and elsewhere, and the banks then lend the money to countries that need it. Thus, in this view, everything works out fine.

But others are less sanguine, and they see the OPEC funds pushing the world into a recession in this way:

Even if all needy nations were the soundest of credit risks, prolonged recycling would produce a pyramiding of debt—and interest costs—that some nations eventually would find insupportable. And, of course, some nations aren't the soundest of risks. "What recycling really means is piling debt upon debt, and more, realistically, bad debt on top of good debt," Federal Reserve Chairman Arthur Burns said recently. "All the talk about recycling, in my opinion, is an escape from reality. The reality is that the financial problems caused by high oil prices are simply unmanageable."

The private banking systems of the industrial countries are already stretched tight; they have been financing inflated domestic economies in a period when domestic governments have been tightening monetary policy to check inflation. Already, some major international banks in the U.S. have grown reluctant to accept so-called petrodollars—that is, the dollars that OPEC nations get for their oil.

Then suppose the OPEC nations keep the oil price at its already-high level or even raise it. Assume that they remain eager to invest the money, but private banks are no longer willing and able to handle it. Because of the lack of funds, some oil-importing countries find that they can no longer get money to finance new oil purchases—or even to pay the interest on old loans. One or more major nations, in effect, might go bankrupt, perhaps declaring a moratorium on international loans.

Such a development could trigger a series of events, none of them happy. Defaults or "postponement" of debt repayments would put tremendous pressure on lending banks.

Countries that could no longer afford the oil they needed would obviously face deep cutbacks in domestic business and drastic energy-conservation measures—as well as inability to pay for other imports besides oil. If the U.S. and other stronger nations failed to bail out the weak, the upshot could be spreading economic collapse.

No. 1 on everybody's list of major "weak" countries is Italy.

To a lesser extent, the U.S. and other industrial nations share the problem of Italy. Their economies were in trouble even before the oil problem appeared. Now the huge oil payments pose the risk of financial collapse and depression.

There is a second way that the oil-producing nations could wreck the world economy. As the more pessimistic analysts see it, these nations could keep the oil price high and simply refuse to invest all of the money they receive; they could, in other words, elect to bury the money in the sand.

Some economists say tough talk by U.S. officials has increased the Arab countries' fears that any assets they hold in Western countries are in danger of being seized. "The fear of confiscation is very real," Mr. Wolman of Argus Research says.

A massive pullout of funds would raise enormous problems. Recycling may or may not be a good idea, but without Arab investments, there simply wouldn't be any funds to be recycled. Countries might try huge inflation and deep devaluation— or drastic curtailment of their economies. In either case, the eventual result could be disaster. So far, however, the Arabs haven't shown any inclination to follow this bury-the-money course.

The industrial nations, however, don't need the Arabs to push them into depression; these countries are capable of doing it all by themselves. The U.S. and most other nations are trying to check domestic demand to get inflation under control. By overdoing this battle against inflation, the pessimistic analysts say, the nations could end up in a depression.

This overemphasis on the anti-inflation battle is the chief way the industrial nations could push themselves into a depression. But there are others. "They could get into competitive devaluations in attempts to boost their exports and help pay for oil," one economist suggests. "But sooner or later, they would be selling goods for less than they cost, and there's no future in that."

Inflationary policies wouldn't lead to immediate depression, but economists are sure that they would bring eventual financial collapse and at least deep world recession. "One of the chief dangers I see," one analyst says, "is that industrial nations won't realize that they share common interests in this situation and will instead try to help themselves at the expense of their neighbors."

So far, the oil-producing countries have largely avoided long-term investments—in real estate, common stock and bonds. But some analysts fear that the oil nations will start using much of their money to buy Western companies at the currently depressed prices.

Early in the oil crisis, one wag suggested that the solution for the whole problem was simply to sell to the Arabs General Motors and U.S. Steel and then to have Washington nationalize the companies. Analysts now think that the Arabs are fearful enough of some such development to forgo any early foray into the U.S. stock market.

C.
The Crisis in
Europe and Japan

THE GREAT DEPRESSION spawned Hitler and World War II.
Some think the current crisis may result in equivalent horrors,
even the holocaust. All we can be certain of is that fundamental
changes lie ahead. In this section we survey some of the other
advanced capitalist countries, including France, Great Britain,
West Germany, Italy and Japan. (Following the survey, reading
#34, taken from the Marxist newsletter *Economic Notes*, points
out that "world-wide inflation" is a misnomer. It is not descriptive of conditions in the socialist world, except Yugoslavia, the
most market-oriented of the socialist countries—many would
even call it more capitalist than socialist—and the one most
integrated into the capitalist world economy. Unfortunately, this
article does not include China and Cuba, because of a lack of
comparable data. Neither, though, has inflation. The point is
that inflation, at least at this juncture in history, is a disease
specific to capitalism. For a brief discussion of what socialism
means, see the final paragraphs of the introduction to Part III.)

Of the above-listed countries, least stable is Italy. While its
economy has boomed, the current slowdown, along with monumental oil-induced deficits, has brought it to the brink of bankruptcy. There is much talk of fascist coups d'état, and right-wing
plots are uncovered with alarming regularity. What may be
shaping up is a bloody confrontation, even civil war, between
those who prefer a fascist solution and those—mainly the industrial working class—for whom Communism is the answer. Political violence has already become a regular feature of Italian life.
Reading #32, by Ray Vicker, reprinted from the *Wall Street*

Journal, provides an accurate rendering of the chaotic mood that now prevails. But it is wrong to imply, as the article does, that Communist participation in a future Italian government—the "historic compromise" sought by the CP—is antithetical to capitalism. Not only will the Communist party likely provide honest government, as it has in Bologna, but a governmental role at this point ultimately means accepting responsibility for keeping labor in line. Its "responsible" and conciliatory attitude toward wage restraint helps explain the increasing wildcat strikes in defiance of party leadership. In addition, the CP is now on record that it will not challenge Italy's membership in NATO. For these reasons, the *Wall Street Journal* to the contrary, U.S. capitalism has little to fear from Communist *participation* in a new Italian government (except in the unlikely event it is used as a wedge to gain full-scale control). Nonetheless, it is not obvious that it will occur, or if it does, that it will not provoke widespread violence, a coup d'état or civil war.

Meanwhile the economic crisis poses fundamental and unprecedented questions: What happens if Italy can't pay its bills? *Business Week,* in an article published elsewhere in this volume (reading #22) posited that "it could possibly send big banks toppling faster than central banks could respond." Will private banks continue to pour in good money after bad in an attempt to keep Italy afloat and preserve their previous investments? No one knows the answers to these questions, only that time is running out, with no solutions in sight.

Almost as bad off is Britain. Plagued by a past record of mediocre growth, a present that is increasingly violent (as terror from Northern Ireland spills over into England), there is an understandable need to live in the future. Development of the North Sea oil off Scotland, starting in the late 1970's, many hope will make Britain independent in energy. But the *present* reality is one of massive deficits. Britain, like Italy, can solve its problems only by forcing its working class to take bitter medicine, as the conservative (and pessimistic) London *Economist* points out (reading #30).

But if decisive action is what is needed, the existing context is one of indecision and stalemate. Two elections were held in 1974, each resulting in miniscule Labour victories. The British also seem equally divided on whether to remain in the Common

Market. Raymond Williams (in reading #31) assesses the situation from a position to the left of the Labour party and believes that the social contract offered by the latter—basically a deal to cut money wages in return for social benefits including food and housing subsidies—is politically the last hope of capitalist democracy.

France, too, is plagued by a massive payments deficit, as well as by rising unemployment (especially in autos), 17% inflation and a rash of strikes. These are described in reading #28 by *New York Times* correspondent Clyde H. Farnsworth. Germany, on the other hand, though faltering, remains strong, as indicated in reading #29 from the *Economist*. Its trade surpluses continue, its inflation rate is merely single-digit, and much of its unemployment is experienced by the large contingent of foreign workers from Turkey, Yugoslavia, Italy and Spain. The latter may receive two thirds of their net pay in unemployment benefits, but it is a bit unseemly to casually remark, as the *Economist* does, that therefore "there is no immediate economic hardship."

The other pillar of postwar strength is Japan. Hard hit by the oil crisis, and currently coping with a 25% inflation, Japan has nevertheless succeeded in expanding its exports and maintaining its employment. Nonetheless, many firms such as Matsushita, a top appliance and TV maker, are in trouble (reading #33, from *Business Week*). Under fire is the traditional job security every Japanese worker expects as an article of faith. Unlike America, where workers flit from job to job or are fired periodically, once hired in Japan, a worker stays on for life. The commitment is two-sided. This system is now in jeopardy.

As the general crisis of capitalism unfolds, there are two main situations to be watched, one economic, the other political. A crucial difference about this decline as compared to that of 1957 is that the world economies are now synchronized. In 1957 the boom abroad helped lift America out of its slump. Today, in contrast, all economies are moving downward together. The parallel is 1929.

Finally, almost everywhere one turns, one reads of the growing likelihood of fascism, coups d'état and the erosion of democratic institutions. Italy is an obvious case in point, but there are private right-wing armies being organized in Britain, and right-wing Japanese manifestoes are dramatically signed in blood. Historians tell us that democracy cannot withstand inflation rates of 20%; nor will it likely survive a deep depression. One is prompted by the situation to put forth the following thesis: capitalism in its youthful days required an expansion of democracy to free it from the shackles of feudal restrictions. In the era of its decline, it must slough off its democratic forms and enforce harsh authoritarian controls to preserve its existence and ward off the threat of socialist revolution. In its heyday, capitalism was progressive, extending both freedom and prosperity. In its decline, its achievements are all but being eroded away. The burden of proof has shifted to those who seek to justify its continued existence.

28. FRANCE'S ECONOMY IS IN GROWING DIFFICULTY

by Clyde H. Farnsworth

The difference between the American and French economies, as the chief of the French Employers Association, François Ceyrac, sometimes says, is the difference between a vehicle of four and of two wheels. When the four-wheeled vehicle stops, it remains upright. The two-wheeler stops, and it falls over.

Lately the two wheels Mr. Ceyrac sees in France have shown signs of jamming up. Inflation is at 17 per cent, or twice the rate last winter. The oil price boosts that followed the October war in the Middle East last year represent an added tax on national

Reprinted from the *New York Times* (December 1, 1974). Clyde H. Farnsworth is a member of the reporting staff of the *Times*.

revenues this year alone of $7.5-billion, or $400 for each French family.

A former Finance Minister and élite-born technocrat who recently completed his first six months as the third President of the Fifth Republic, Valéry Giscard d'Estaing has tried to deal with the financial problems by getting people to consume less.

Through tight money and selectively increased taxes for corporations and higher-income individuals, he has sought to control inflation and divert resources to exports in order to redress the balance of payments deficit.

So far nothing seems to have worked. The President's popularity is at a new low. Personal criticism of his style of leadership is mounting. Job fears, combined with growing militance in the labor force, have created a potentially explosive social climate.

What's happened essentially is that credit has been so tight that it has forced many small and medium-sized businesses into an unsavory choice of decisions: Bankruptcy, reduction of the labor force, cancellation of investment plans, appeals to the state for special aid.

The Auto Industry's Plight

Bigger corporations are better insulated, but are still running into serious troubles especially in the auto industry. Companies are having difficulty getting normal bank credit, and so are consumers. A prospective auto buyer, for instance, has to pay 40 per cent down and the rest in 21 months at interest rates approaching 20 per cent.

Predictably, car sales have plummeted. But the construction, textile, shoe, chemical and printing industries are also affected. One French banker who keeps watch over bankruptcy trends said: "The weakness now permeates all sectors of the economy." The bankruptcy rate is 35 per cent more than a year ago.

On the other hand price increases have not slowed. Companies are selling less at higher prices. The main effect of the credit restrictions has been to reduce the number of jobs.

The French unemployment figures are not really comparable with those of the United States. But even by the French standards of measurement—the number of persons registered as looking for work (in the United States you don't have to be registered to be counted)—the total of 600,000 is up 40 per cent over a year ago. Union organizations say the true figure is closer to 800,000 and will probably top 1 million during the winter.

One young Frenchman looking for work last week was told the only place he might be able to find a job, in competition with a handful of other applicants, was in the unemployment office itself.

With jobs growing scarcer and prices still unacceptably high, the Government has been unusually reluctant to put any curbs on wages. These are rising by 20 per cent over a year ago to provide a real increase in purchasing power of from 3 to 5 per cent.

The hope was to choke off social unrest, but French mail deliveries have been halted for six weeks by a strike of sorters demanding an additional $40 a month raise. Miners in Lorraine, Paris garbagemen, workers in state radio and television are among other groups that have stopped work. Mountains of garbage are still being removed from Paris streets, even though the garbagemen have gone back to work. Essentially it is the lower paid who want more. Two-thirds of all French workers still make under $350 a month.

The Government is also counting on its latest unemployment insurance program to keep the social atmosphere calm. Those laid off because of economic conditions are guaranteed up to a year's full pay. Socialist Leader François Mitterrand says, because of technicalities in the plan, no more than one out of two of the unemployed, will get the benefits. Youths, women and unskilled temporary workers are likely to be excluded, he says. Mr. Mitterrand and other critics see Mr. Giscard d'Estaing deliberately promoting unemployment to curb inflation.

In the present structure of the economy the reduction of 1 percentage point of inflation is at a cost of 80,000 jobless. So to get the inflation rate down from 17 to the target figure of 6 to 7 per cent could be at the expense of some 800,000 fewer jobs, a chilling prospect for a country prone to periodic revolutions.

Externally the economic policies have not really worked either. In trade and services, including the oil accounts, France will run a deficit this year of $6-billion to $7-billion. The Government had banked on a big export drive to narrow the deficit.

But with the United States facing its deepest postwar recession and with most other European economies in similar straits, there aren't many buyers.

The deficit is being financed by borrowing. But the French, like the Italians and the British, may find it difficult to borrow.

Faced with these economic problems, France has been trying to promote deeper union in the Common Market, in hopes of mustering some kind of collective bootstrap operation. But the old divisions between France and her partners over whether or not to work with the United States, especially in the energy and monetary fields, have tended to check progress.

Then again, if conditions get much worse, all countries including the United States (where many Europeans see the danger most pronounced) could decide to turn inward, concentrating on their own internal problems and reviving protectionist, nationalistic policies.

Mr. Mitterrand thinks that capitalism itself is under siege. "The current period can lead to an immense upheaval," he said, "because the mechanisms of the marketplace, both at the national and international level, are incapable of resolving the economic contradictions."

29. THE DETERIORATING SITUATION IN WEST GERMANY

The *Economist*

The policy of severe economic restraint that the German chancellor, Herr Helmut Schmidt, has pursued since the oil crisis

Extracts from "Will the German Belt Be Loosened?," in the *Economist* (November 16, 1974).

has been notably successful in keeping inflation to a current level of 7%, but it has failed on three separate scores. It has been unpopular with the electorate, as the setback his party suffered in two recent state elections has reminded him. It has been unpopular with trading partners, who have resented the tight-fisted way in which Germany has tried to export its way out of a slowdown at home. Worst of all, domestic industry is now faced with many of the problems of low order books and redundancies that have hit other European countries.

But now a substantial shift in policy seems near. Last month Germany's respected, government-financed, economic research institutes forecast that there would be around a million unemployed later this winter.

Germany's historic obsession with inflation has again prevailed. The threat of recession in the wake of the oil crisis prompted the government last autumn to cancel most of the anti-inflationary package it had introduced the previous May, but looming double-figure inflation kept it from easing up more than was absolutely necessary.

Herr Schmidt gave a hint that he, and his finance minister, Herr Hans Apel, may be cooking up something bigger when he said last weekend that 6% inflation was still easier to bear than 4½% unemployment.

In some ways Germany's economic picture looks gloomier now than it did a few months ago. What growth there has been this year has gone entirely into exports, leaving Germany with even bigger surpluses than last year. But domestic industry is sluggish and there is now a feeling that export orders too may start to level off, particularly with the American economy in a worse state than forecast. To no one's surprise, the car industry is doing badly, although car buying at home has not actually dropped off as much as feared earlier. German petrol prices, after getting perilously near to the pychological DM1 per litre (76½p per gallon) after the oil crisis, have been forced down again by easier supply and more competition. Textiles, too, after a rough patch for the past year or two, have been cheered up by a German shopping spree, perhaps prompted by the early winter and a change in fashion.

But the building industry, one of the main sufferers, still shows no signs of picking up. Large numbers of private flats, started when the inflation scare was at its height and property seemed the only reasonable hedge, remain unsold and without much prospect of finding buyers until well into next year. Prestige offices and shops are taking months and years to let. The troubles of several German banks are well known. But more unexpected names, like Rollei, the camera makers, suddenly crop up announcing major retrenchment programmes and large-scale sackings. A lot of small businesses are giving up altogether and bankruptcies so far this year have been up by nearly 50% on a year ago.

With 3% unemployment, Germany's immigrant so-called guest workers too are beginning to feel uneasy. When the oil crisis broke, an immediate ban on further recruitment promptly turned off the tap for these workers, mainly from Turkey, Jugoslavia, Italy and Spain. Now unemployment among foreign workers is rising faster than the average, mainly because they are concentrated in troubled industries like cars and construction. Like their German colleagues, foreign workers get two-thirds of their normal net pay as unemployment benefit, so there is no immediate economic hardship. But unless the economy picks up again quickly they may have to go home.

So far the Germans feel that this year's economic discomfort has been worth it. Although inflation was unofficially forecast to reach 10% or more, it peaked out in the spring at 8% and is now running at an annual rate of only just over 7%. Chancellor Schmidt confidently forecasts that it will go on dropping to around 6% by early next year.

The Germans have been lucky in the timing of their anti-inflationary efforts: just when they badly needed to be seen to be successful this summer some world commodity prices were coming down with a bump, easing the pressure on the country's raw material imports. At the same time the drop in the D-mark exchange rate allowed exporters to raise their prices in foreign markets while keeping them down at home.

Anti-inflationary luck may also hold on another front: this winter's wage round may be kept down to below 10%, a rate most other countries would regard as splendid. Last winter things went less well. Public service employees, one of the largest groups of workers, put in a 15% wage claim which, after a few token strikes by transport workers, postmen and dustmen, got them a 12%–13% rise. This was the signal for double-figure increases all round which economic experts said could only mean double-figure inflation rates in the later part of this year.

But in the event industry absorbed much of the extra where it could not pass it on in higher export prices, something it could afford thanks to a comfortable profit cushion. This year industry can afford no such thing (investment in real terms is already well down on last year), so the German unions are back to exercising the impressive restraint which makes countries like Britain so envious.

The steelworkers have already settled for 9% (although bonus payments and fringe benefits may push this up to 12%). Public employees last week put in a complicated claim which even the government's presumably pessimistic calculation put at just below 10%. The government immediately made all the expected noises about this being far higher than warranted by the economic situation, and may even manage to beat the union down a bit. It is fully aware that anything under 10% would be a great help in facing the 4m metalworkers who are next in line for a pay rise.

30. CAN THE BRITISH MUDDLE THROUGH?

The *Economist*

The first Wilson government was so worried by the current account deficit of 1964—which turned out to be £382m—

Extracts from "Healey's Heel," in the *Economist* (November 2, 1974).

that it slapped on an emergency 15 per cent import surcharge, cut public spending and went to the International Monetary Fund for help. In the first nine months of 1974 the current deficit has been running at an annual rate of £3,860m, over ten times as large as then, but nobody much bothers. Instead, as Mr. Denis Healey prepares his inflationary budget, the question is how far he dare go to save jobs at the risk of feeding inflation.

Today's jumbo-sized deficit is ignored for two understandable but misguided reasons: (1) At least two-thirds of the deficit comes from higher oil prices; as oil-consuming countries are bound to run a deficit of the order of £80 billion over the coming 12 months, it has become fashionable in Britain—but alas not in other countries—to think that good neighbourliness requires each deficit country to borrow recycled petrodollars rather than balance its own national books. (2) The residual non-oil deficit has been shrinking.

Events will very soon shatter both these illusions. The improvement in its non-oil deficit in recent months bodes not well but ill for Britain's future. As the chart shows [omitted], the volume of British exports has been nearly static; export earnings have been breaking new records only because export prices have risen by a third in the past year. The volume of imports has fallen, thanks to stagnation, although import prices have kept the bill rising. The main gain has come from an unhealthy improvement in the terms of trade through higher export prices. This brings short-term benefits at the expense of lost orders in the future.

The precise loss of export competitiveness in recent months is hard to measure. Up to the middle of this year Britain's export prices were more than holding their own with major competitors'. This was because of the greater depreciation in sterling, down 19 per cent on a trade-weighted basis since the pound floated in June, 1972, and thanks as well to the success of the first two stages of Mr. Heath's wage controls. However, wage costs have been rising faster in Britain than abroad and America's export prices figures are not as high as they look since they include food and commodities whose prices shot up but with which Britain does not compete. As for Germany's prices, they perennially count less in selling German exports than quality and delivery.

When the crunch comes, there will not be much help available to Britain from outside. Mr. Healey has found little sympathy from exactly the friends he would like to have. The strong credit-worthy countries like America and Germany are not, in practice, very interested in recycling either spare petrodollars or good neighbourliness. To many Americans, recycling means that creditworthy countries must borrow more than they would otherwise need from the Arabs to lend to bad credit risk countries who need more than they could otherwise borrow; and thus prolong an intolerable situation where a few dictators in sparsely populated deserts, with their hands on the oil taps, hold the world to ransom in a way which must ultimately destroy the international monetary system. Better short-term misery, they say, to break the oil cartel, particularly if it helps cure world inflation in the process.

There are only three ways of moving resources into the payments balance:

(1) By a slowdown or a fall in activity sharper in Britain than elsewhere. The volume of Britain's imports would then presumably fall by more than foreigners' imports of British exports.

(2) By direct action to limit imports while keeping up domestic demand.

(3) By a fall in British export prices relative to competitors'. Devaluation would do this at a stroke; a successful wage freeze would produce the same result much more slowly.

The first of these policies—a deliberate attempt to solve the problems by higher unemployment—would mean subjecting Britain to a worse slump than in the 1930s. Imports take perhaps a quarter of total expenditure at the margin (about one-fifth overall). To cut imports by the equivalent of 5 per cent of gdp would mean lopping 20 per cent off expenditure. No government could consider this and survive.

The last solution—a successful wage freeze—is now too little too late. It might have worked a year ago if the wage explosion could have been prevented, but the winter fiasco of strikes, three-day week and the February election stopped that. A wage

freeze still must be part of any answer, but is not sufficient on
its own.

The best sort of import controls would be quota restrictions
with the licences auctioned, the proceeds going to reduce other
taxes on prices. Britain's ability to run a deficit and borrow without default is limited; imports will have to be cut relative to exports one way or another. In a rational world it should matter
little to other countries how they are cut but in the real world
of painfully won liberal trade it does.

The arguments against trade controls are that: (1) they encourage an import-substitution-led rescue from recession which
is worse than an export-led rescue because it means industry
would concentrate on its least competitive activities instead of
where it can sell most competitively on world markets; and (2)
the strongest countries are the most likely to retaliate and Britain cannot afford to antagonise America and Germany, let
alone the rest of EEC and Britain's former Efta trading partners
as well.

A deliberate devaluation might not invite the same retaliation.
It would not anyway seek to remedy the oil deficit—the indus-
trialised world has rightly forsworn the path to competitive devaluation. It would be aimed at finding a truer value for balancing Britain's uncompetitive exports against its non-oil imports.
At present, although sterling is nominally floating, the Bank of
England is keeping it above a true market value by borrowing,
with help from Britain's public authorities and nationalised
industries, from anywhere it can. But should Britain try to restore its export competitiveness at one shot in a big bang devaluation or allow the rate to float slowly down?

In favour of the big bang devaluation is that the exchange
rate might seem as likely to go up after it as to go down. It
would not then be in the interests of petrodollar holders in London to withdraw their funds, as the damage would already have
been done. With a sliding devaluation there would be every incentive to do so.

Against the big bang is that it would have to be very big to
make a worthwhile dent in the deficit, perhaps 15–20 per cent.
And it would make the deficit worse before it made it better—
the so-called J-curve effect where the higher price of imports hits

immediately but the increased volume of exports takes time to come through. Against it, too, is that it would give another puff to the prices of imports, so making the job of controlling wages even more acute. Outside holders of sterling might well conclude at that point that Britain really was headed for a hyper-inflationary spiral and a mass flight from sterling would make this a self-justifying prophecy. Who could blame them?

Politicians naturally reject all these unpleasant solutions. The government also rejects rising unemployment and a wage freeze. But if it does not grip one or other of these nettles Britain will fall into the patch and be stung by every single one at once. The choice, however unpleasant, must be made. It should be made soon.

31. BRITAIN AFTER THE ELECTION: THE SIZE OF THE CRISIS

by Raymond Williams

In its seven months in office as a minority government, Labour had in fact put through a series of important measures to protect the living standards of working people: notably a freezing of rents, an extensive program of food subsidies, improvements in pensions, and repeal of the anti-union legislation on which the Conservative offensive against the working class had been centered. Labour had acted, in fact, as a good social-democratic government, and it had built support where it mattered: among

Abridged from *The Nation* (November 2, 1974). Raymond Williams is a Fellow of Jesus College, Cambridge, England. His latest book is *The Country and the City* (New York, Oxford University Press, 1973).

the unskilled working class, where its vote seems to have materially increased, and among its own activists and the independent Left, who were more solid in its support than at any time in the last ten years. February had been a desperate defensive battle; October was not only a partial consolidation but in deeper terms also a defensive battle against the kind of cut in living standards which the state of the economy makes almost inevitable. In real terms it is estimated that during the last year there has been an average 5 per cent cut in living standards, because of rising oil and commodity prices and the large deficit in the balance of trade. Most estimates suggest a further cut of 10 per cent in the next year or eighteen months, and there were real choices, not so much about whether it would happen (the parties, naturally, didn't stress that) but about how it should be distributed. At a time like this, over a two- or three-year period, a social-democratic program makes considerable sense. Both Conservatives and Liberals would have directly attacked the working-class standard of living; Labour at least will attempt to maintain it. It was in this situation that I, for example, went back to speaking for Labour candidates for the first time in ten years.

There are now three critical questions: What is the character of the crisis which Labour must attempt to survive? What is the political character of the party's program? What are its chances to survive as a government?

Take the last question first. Labour's lead over all other parties in the House of Commons is only three seats, and these could disappear in two lost by-elections. But the real situation is more complicated. Among the smaller nationalist or regionally based parties there is probably enough support to make the solid lead at least thirteen; and for the next year or two, given Labour's commitment to establish separate assemblies in Scotland and Wales, perhaps as high, on many issues, as twenty-five or thirty. With one important question ignored, this would insure parliamentary survival for at least three years. But the question of membership in the Common Market may wreck these calculations. Labour will now get a real renegotiation of the terms of entry, and the chances are that the government will then approve and recommend them. But there is a commitment to both a special party conference on the issue and a national referendum. The referendum, given government backing and the support of the leadership of the two parties, could probably be won. But most signs are that the organized party is still against entry, and there is a powerful group in Parliament and in the leadership which is also against it. The possible permutations make any forecast impossible, but the chances of a split, sometime next spring, must be reckoned as high. That is the only real question about the immediate survival of the government.

What happens about the Common Market will also affect the political character of the Labour program. As it now stands, it is the most radical social-democratic program, including some actual Socialist measures, on which Labour has taken power since the war. Its enemies said during the election that carrying out this program would turn Britain, irreversibly, into a Socialist state. That is nonsense, but the full program would complete the transition to a modern social democracy. Will it be carried out? The problem is that it is a bundle of measures, and that everything will therefore depend on the timing. If the Left is defeated or isolated on the Common Market, the program is unlikely to get further than the modernization of capitalism and the corresponding improvement of the welfare state. On the other hand, if the Left wins on the Common Market, and Britain withdraws, nothing less than Socialist policies, including the crucial and thus far avoided question of real controls over capital, could possibly save a Labour Britain. If the Left wins on the Common Market but fails to carry full Socialist alternative policies, the conditions will have been created for a decisive swing to the right. Politically, therefore, the situation is exceptionally complicated and volatile, beyond what will be at first the placid formalities of a new and confident Labour government.

A key issue in the election was the plausibility of what Labour calls its social contract with the unions. This needs precise analysis. In real terms it is a deal to cut real personal wages in return for an increased social wage (food and housing subsidies and welfare benefits). The cut in the money wage is meant to improve the competitiveness of British industry, and there will also be an attempt to improve industrial investment, by direct state involvement and control. It is an interesting program, and it might in the short term succeed. The crucial factor that is missing, from a Socialist point of view, is any convincing element of control over capital. Without this, and under international pressure, it could turn into simple wage restraint and would then, eventually, be defeated by the unions. Moreover, there has as yet been little frank explanation of the substitution of a social wage for part of the personal wage. As inflation is now running at about 17 per cent, direct personal wage increases need, after allowing for taxation, to be above 25 per cent if disposable income in real terms is not to be cut. Since the general situation will impose a cut of 10 per cent somewhere, the pressures and dangers are obvious. The social contract is thus very easy to attack. The Right attacks it as unworkable; the Left as anti-working class. In fact it is the only set of proposals which could keep the existing political system together. As a basic program it looks like the last formula of capitalist democracy. Therefore it will need to be watched in practice with the closest attention. If it proceeds as proposed, it will undoubtedly lead to many painful political clarifications.

Of course the election took place during a mood of profound general pessimism. In a period of major crisis in the international capitalist economy, Britain, despite some recent marginal improvements, is weak and exposed. Most people are banking on the supply of North Sea oil by the late 1970s to initiate a period of recovery. This estimate is certain to underlie Labour strategy; the government will try, politically, to get through the three or four years to that period and then move ahead on the upswing. In local terms that is not implausible. Like the social contract politically, North Sea oil is economically the last chance for capitalist democracy in Britain. That is the size of the crisis during the next five years.

I said that I spoke in this election for Labour candidates. But now that they are in it is time for Socialists to return to their own perspectives. There are solid defensive reasons for getting and keeping a Labour government in power. The alternatives on the Right are extremely dangerous—not so much the private armies, which in that form are ludicrous—but the capitalist state, with its available and hardening political parties, and still with a majority of public opinion. It is a paradox that the Labour government is the last real chance for capitalist democracy in Britain. As the pressures mount, and the real contradictions come into the open, it will be vital not only to maintain an independent Socialist program—in part as a form of struggle within the Labour Party itself—but to work directly for public support of Socialist measures: the very opposite, in fact, of the mood now forming, of leaving it to the Labour government.

32. CHAOS, ITALIAN STYLE

by Ray Vicker

The parliament building here, like so many other structures in this ancient capital city, has seen better days. But then, to hear Italians talk, that's only fitting—considering the state of the country these days.

A representative comment comes from the proprietor of a souvenir stand on the Piazza Navona who says: "I wouldn't claim that everybody in parliament is a crook, for there are some good people there. But there are so many crooks that it makes it difficult to tell the good from the bad. Most of them are dons like in the Mafia, only looking after themselves, their relatives and their friends."

This assessment, comparatively speaking, is generous. Alberto Bondi, a 41-year-old concierge at a downtown office building, flatly states that "politicians only want to line their own pockets." The Italians have never been overly fond of bureaucracy anyway and have traditionally regarded the government as an adversary to be outwitted through tax evasion and by winking at laws.

Extracts from the *Wall Street Journal* (November 25, 1974). Ray Vicker is a staff reporter of the *Journal*.

The roots of the chaos are clear enough. Italy is beset by rampant inflation—currently around 25% annually—but the country's political leaders and bureaucrats, instead of taking decisive action, seem more intent on living up (or down) to their highly unflattering public image. Periodic scandals erupt in the press. Public payrolls are so top-heavy with political appointees that 36,000 agencies, many of them of questionable utility, are listed on government rosters.

And the troubles mount. In recent days, two would-be right-wing coups were thwarted. American offices in the country are targets of bombs. Communist-led street demonstrations are so common that they command only cursory attention. (The strong Communist Party, which has recently commanded 27% of the Italian vote, has, of course, much to gain from the current unsettled conditions.)

Meanwhile, at the top, the same game of political musical chairs that has brought Italy 36 governments in the last 30 years goes on. Aldo Moro, veteran politician of the dominant Christian Democratic Party, recently announced his agreement to form a minority cabinet with support from all center-left parties.

But it doesn't end the country's troubles. Italy's foreign-trade deficit this year is expected to be about $8.75 billion, more than double last year's deficit. Pointing up the country's financial woes, the Common Market recently in effect gave Italy three more years to repay a loan that initially fell due five months ago.

Unemployment in Italy stands at around 1 million, or 5.8% of the labor force, and is rising fast. Yet strikes proliferate, some of them protesting layoffs. The mail service is nearing collapse. Judicial confusion has reached the point that it takes 12 years for an average lawsuit to work through the courts—and anyone arrested may well be crammed in a crowded jail for a year or more before being charged.

Bureaucracy, in the worst sense of the word, reigns supreme. When a worker retires, the paperwork is so slow that the first pension check doesn't arrive for a period of anywhere from six months to three years. Hospitals are running out of money because they can't collect public-health monies from officials. Even a complaint to the police about a robbery can't be filed except on an official form, procurable at a tobacco shop for about 75 cents. So labyrinthine is the network of bureaucrats that a special breed of expediter, the *spicciafaccondi* has developed. Such persons know whom to contact for a necessary signed paper, which official can be bribed, which ways applications can best be speeded through government channels. The fee for all these favors is whatever the traffic will bear.

As a measure of Italy's current confusion, there is already talk of a "historic compromise" that would bring the Communist Party into the central government to share power with the long dominant Christian Democrats. The prospect frightens Washington, particularly because Italy has such a pivotal position in Europe. From the U.S. viewpoint, the whole southern fringe of the continent, with the possible exception of France, is a trouble area where Communists are either gaining strength or are waiting in the wings for possible benefits from future internecine struggles. (And even in France, a strong Communist party worries American diplomats.)

Nevertheless, at least for the moment, the party isn't pushing too hard to gain a foothold among the bureaucracy, which is so widely regarded as inept. "Who would want to be in government with all the problems facing Italy today?" asks Luciano Barca, the Italian Communist Party's chief economist and a member of its ruling politburo. It is a rhetorical question, to which he adds: "We certainly aren't knocking on the door to enter the government. But we do believe that a party such as ours, with four million grass-roots votes, should be in position to contribute something to solutions."

Luicano Barca believes that history is working inexorably—and peacefully—to bring the Communists into Italy's government. He adds: "We aren't talking about tomorrow morning or the short term, nor are we talking long term. It will be in the medium term."

Consensus among political observers is that the crunch may come next spring [1975]. All parties seem interested in delaying a new election and major political decisions until next year, although any serious right-wing coup attempts could upset that time schedule. "In any emergency," Mr. Barca says, "we would be willing to go into the government to fill a vacuum, though we don't expect such a possibility." Then, bluntly, he adds: "There will be no coup from the left, either."

"Things are going to get worse before they get better," says

Mr. Bondi, the concierge. "The politicians will help make it worse." From Mr. Bondi's point of view, things are bad enough as it is. He earns about $270 a month for working 14 hours a day, six days a week, performing janitorial and watchman chores in a building that has 14 offices. A two-bedroom apartment goes with the job. But despite this perquisite, he, his wife, and two daughters (aged 10 and seven) have trouble living on his income, two-thirds of which goes for food. "Most of the time, we eat pasta," he says—and the price of pasta has nearly doubled in the last year. Recently, Mr. Bondi's wife was hospitalized, and about $600 of her medical expenses wasn't covered by insurance. "That wiped out our savings," he says.

Mr. Bondi distrusts the Communists, as does Mr. Marsili, the restaurant manager. However, Mr. Marsili is more concerned with present woes than future politics. "People don't eat out as much as they did," he says mournfully, explaining that business is off 10%. "And why not? I have had to put up my prices by 30 to 40%." To illustrate his point, he picks up a menu from a table and points to "Pizza Primavera." "This was 600 lire [90 cents] last year, and now it is 800 [$1.20]."

As inflation rages, the tensions in Italy are exacerbated by a feeling among the nation's poorer citizens that they are being hit the hardest of all. Italy's professional class is widely believed to be dodging the inflationary bite by widespread tax evasion. "Everybody who is making big money cheats on income taxes," says one woman matter-of-factly.

Whether this is indeed the case is beside the point; it is *believed* to be the case. And observers believe this frustration and feeling of injustice have far more to do with the rising Communist vote here than has any political philosophy. The 27% Communist total could rise to 29% or 30% in the next election. But as one diplomat in Rome puts it: "This is mainly a protest vote."

33. A JAPANESE GIANT IN TROUBLE

Business Week

In Japan, it is an article of faith that an employee, once hired, can stay with the same company—very often in the same job—for the rest of his working life. So it came as a shock when a corporate giant so successful and well-known as Matsushita Electric Industrial Co., the Osaka consumer electronics and appliance maker, recently switched 2,000 workers from offices and production lines to door-to-door selling, and let it be known that layoffs are contemplated.

In few other ways could President Masaharu Matsushita and Chairman Arataro Takahashi—"the two wheels that drive Matsushita"—so strongly illustrate their awareness that the Japan of the late 1970s will be a very different place from the supremely confident nation that roared out of the 1960s on the back of a super-growth economy. That growth has disappeared under a series of hammer blows: President Nixon's devaluation of the U.S. dollar that made Japanese exports to this country more expensive; the Arab oil embargo and subsequent quadrupling of oil prices; and the rising cost of raw materials. Today, like all major Japanese companies, Matsushita is awakening to a whole new world dominated by the twin headaches of inflation and recession.

It will be a particularly testing time for the company's 62-year-old president, Masaharu Matsushita. Though president since 1961, the youthful-looking Matsushita, who married the daughter of founder Konosuke Matsushita and took the family name, has always been overshadowed both by his father-in-law

Reprinted from *Business Week* (November 16, 1974).

and by Chairman Takahashi. But Konosuke Matsushita (the name is pronounced Mah-tsu-shta) retired last year and is reportedly in ill-health. Takahashi, though tough and still going strong, is 71 years old.

Says the venerable Takahashi: "Today we face a kind of situation that is unprecedented in Japan." A sudden end has come to 18 glorious years of 10%-plus annual growth that thrust Japan from the rank of a third-rate nation into the front rank among the world's industrial powers. And for even powerful companies such as Matsushita, whose Panasonic and National brand TV sets, phonographs, radios, and other consumer appliances generate annual sales of nearly $5-billion—one-third of the industry—the years ahead promise to be tradition-shaking.

Inflation and recession are bound to cut into sales of Matsushita's lucrative domestic market for such postponable purchases as $430-color television sets. Color TV already has penetrated 87% of Japanese households. Even more serious, Matsushita's labor union wants a wage hike next spring as large as last spring's 34% boost.

Beyond this, Matsushita's big export market, booming under forced draft to take up some of the slack of a depressed domestic market, is running into import quotas in Europe, which seriously threatens its export volume.

Matsushita's woes reflect the fundamental economic problems of the nation. Japan, more than any other country, is caught fast between worldwide recession and the soaring costs of energy, raw materials, capital, and labor. Indeed, its gross national product is expected to decline by as much as 2% in real terms this year. Recovery is expected in 1975, but few economists or business leaders see an annual growth rate of more than 6% for years to come.

Although other nations, including the U.S., would rejoice at a 4% to 6% growth rate, it is small enough in Japanese terms to demand a massive psychological and physical restructuring. For one thing, it probably will require a return to the discipline and sacrifice of the early days of the postwar economic miracle, when Japan swept world markets by the sheer force of imagination and manpower—and its cheap energy. But the Japanese people, who had in their grasp the good life of steaks, second homes, and foreign vacations before the Arab oil embargo changed the economic ground rules for the world, are not likely to return to the old life of unbroken and unquestioning toil without a protest.

'Upheaval, disruption'

The seeds of that protest are evident. The long-term Credit Bank of Japan surveyed economic experts recently and found them agreed that the outlook for the nation in the second half of the decade is "upheaval," "crisis," and "disruption." The experts predict growing "mass movements" by consumers, labor, and other citizen groups unless the government speeds up social welfare and unless corporations recognize their social responsibilities and allow unions to participate in management, adopt the five-day week, and improve working conditions.

The signs of change are already evident. The growth-at-all-costs philosophy that has cursed Japan with one of the world's more polluted countrysides is being severely challenged. Labor, once hardworking, docile, and cheap, is now definitely not cheap. Nor is it so hardworking and docile. Even the consumer is getting testy about the safety and pricing of products. Matsushita found this out in 1970–71, when housewives boycotted its color TV sets for eight months and forced a 17% slash in the price of those sets in response to the revelation that the company was building its market in the U.S. by selling TVs for considerably less than in Japan. These pressures are all beginning to have a compound effect on the profitability of Japanese companies.

Right now, of course, the twin devils of recession and inflation are having the major impact on Japanese balance sheets. Even the largest and most efficient are feeling the lash. Toyobo Co., the nation's biggest yarn spinner, is about to cut 2,200 workers from its payroll. Auto makers are full of hollow cheer that September's 12% drop in sales was the smallest decline since January. And the big appliance makers—Sony, Sanyo, Hitachi, Toshiba, and Matsushita—all are experiencing double-digit profit declines.

While Matsushita's sales are up substantially from last year's $4.2-billion, profits for the first nine months plummeted 16% below the 1973 figure. One Tokyo analyst estimates that profits for the full year could drop a sickening 22% below last year's $242-million. Such a decline would mean the Matsushita's profit margin has been cut in half since 1970—from 8% to 4%.

The Japanese government and business establishment are watching this trend with some concern. While consumer appliance manufacturing contributes only 2% to the Japanese gross national product, its importance goes beyond such measurements. Like Toyota and Datsun cars, Panasonic and Sony TV sets and radios have been conspicuous for establishing the international reputation for the quality of Japanese products.

More tangibly, in energy-conscious Japan, consumer electric appliances produce more money with less energy input than such products as steel that contribute more heavily to GNP. Last year the appliance industry earned $2.9-billion in foreign exchange for Japan, compared with $5.3-billion by the steel industry. But every $330,000 (100-million yen) spent on energy produced $5.5-million worth of appliances vs. $1.3-million worth of steel.

Can Matsushita Cope?

So it matters greatly to Japan when Matsushita, which dominates one of the country's great growth industries, falls on bad times. And it matters even more whether a generation of managers, which has known two decades of good times, is geared to make the dramatic moves required to rebuild profit margins and deal with the social uproar that such measures may evoke.

Drama and the confusion, anxiety, and exhilaration it brings with it, do not appear to be President Matsushita's cup of saké. A mild-mannered man, he was almost unknown outside the company until his father-in-law's retirement. And even to insiders he remains an unknown quantity. "We know less about M. Matsushita than about K. Matsushita," admits one employee.

What is known about the younger Matsushita hardly suggests he is a charismatic man capable of providing inspirational leadership. His critics, for example, suggest that he proved rather more successful at picking up the founder's philosophy than the management skill that, in 50 years, turned a $50 investment in a facility that made electric light plugs into a consumer appliance giant with a global reach.

Certainly a rare interview granted to *Business Week* was redolent with such saws as, "It is a condition that no enterprise will come out with pollution if it knows this is against the wishes of the populace." It was as though the years of public uproar over the chemical waste that caused the crippling Minamata disease never occurred.

And when asked to comment on a statement attributed to him in a "message from the president" in the company's 1973 annual report, a look of puzzlement crossed his features. "I did not say that," he said. "It does not correctly represent what I have in mind. Maybe somebody drafted it and put it there with my picture." While most president's messages are ghost-written, it is a rare chief executive who does not know what words have been put in his mouth, particularly, as in this case, when they refer to a corporate reshuffling.

Matsushita claims to feel no strain from having to work under the omnipresent shadow of the founder. "I feel more heavily," he says, "the burden of running one of the biggest enterprises in Japan." It was an awareness of that burden that presumably prompted the elder Matsushita several years ago to plead with Arataro Takahashi, then an executive vice-president, to forego retirement and stay with the company. Takahashi moved up to the chairman's spot when Konosuke Matsushita retired.

While politic corporate executives are fond of the "two wheels driving Matsushita" image, there is no doubt which wheel provides the more thrust. A Tokyo banker obliquely presents his view of the two by stressing that Takahashi is a "superstar in financing" and "a kind of Godfather" at Matsushita. Takahashi obviously makes many of the basic decisions at the company.

But even though Takahashi is still vigorous, it seems likely that the younger Matsushita will have to make more and more of the difficult decisions in the years to come. Certainly, there will be plenty of tough decisions to be made. The appliance maker, along with key rivals Sanyo and Sony, badly miscalculated the effect that higher oil prices would have on the economy. It expected only a 10% fall-off from last year's record domestic sales of 6.3-million sets. But over-all appliance sales are off 25%, leaving about 2.3-million sets in warehouses and incurring heavy financial carrying charges.

A Devastating Blow

For Matsushita this is exceedingly rough because TV set sales account for more than one-third of its total revenues. While color TV sales are off only 15%, and price hikes have cushioned even that unit decline, Matsushita is hard hit because 80% of its color receivers are sold in the domestic market, and color is the high-profit item. Not much else is filling the gap, either. The market for other Matsushita products, including several big sellers such as motors, radios, and semiconductors, is fairly soft. Nor do industry executives expect a dramatic recovery. Says Takashi Takesita, a Sanyo executive: "We are now going to a plateau for household appliances in Japan."

No one can expect the corporate research laboratories to come rapidly to the rescue anymore. "In the past, demand decline often led to dramatic new products," says Haruyuki Mizuno, an analyst at the big Tokyo brokerage house of Yamaichi Securities. "But color TV is a very big item and so far no new big item has been found to substitute for it."

Compounding the slow growth is the sudden rise in the cost of labor and raw materials. These two factors are largely responsible for the sharply reduced profits outlook facing all the major appliance makers. A Nomura Securities research officer points out that while Matsushita's predicted 22% drop is the largest anticipated, Hitachi can expect an 18% decline, Sanyo, 17%, Sony, 11.5%, and Toshiba, 9%. (Hitachi and Toshiba are major factors in the industry although consumer appliances account for less than half their sales.)

Wages vs. Productivity

The only consolation that the appliance makers have on the energy and raw materials fronts is the prospect that the biggest surge in prices may well be over. Prices may still rise, but the effects cannot possibly be as devastating as they have been thus far.

Labor costs are something else again, as the unions strive to catch up with inflation. Last spring, Matsushita granted its 53,-000 labor union members—out of a total Japanese workforce of 85,000—an average wage increase of 34%, which more than met the Japanese unions' national target. Now the company faces the near certainty of a similar increase next year. "If we allow such high wage hikes," warns Takeshi Asozu, Matsushita's director of labor relations, "our international competitiveness will be lost." Asozu argues that Matsushita workers will have to settle for 10% to 15%.

"No way," is the blunt response of Keiichi Takahata, Matsushita's burly labor leader. Takahata, pointing to the 25% inflation rate, says that if Matsushita does not grant a 30% hike, it
can expect a "rough spring offensive."

That sort of increase will be tough to swallow—even if a
recovering economy does boost color TV sales. During the past
five years, automation and improved assembly techniques have
enabled Matsushita to achieve annual reductions of about 10%
in production time per unit, which more than offset earlier wage
increases. "But," says Executive Vice-President Yasuharu Na-
kagawa, "this year's 34% wage increase really offsets the productivity increase. It is virtually impossible to achieve such an
increase in productivity."

Matsushita has managed to make up some of the difference
by recent price boosts, such as the 20% hike in refrigerators
and 40% to 45% increases in heating appliances. But there is a
limit to what domestic consumers can pay. And the Japanese
consumer appliance industry's exports also are being endangered
by its rapidly rising operating costs. A recent survey by the Industrial Bank of Japan warned that the country's electronics
industry will lose its overseas competitiveness as early as next
year because of spiraling material and labor costs. That is grim
news for Matsushita, which generates 20% of its sales from
exports.

What is grim for Matsushita, of course, is music to European
manufacturers that have fought a losing battle against Japanese
imports for years. In Italy, where the flood of Japanese tape re-
corders has swelled from 20,000 a year to 461,000 since 1970,
industry spokesmen have become "downright spastic," as one
observer puts it, at the mere mention of Japanese competitors.
That is why Britain, France, Italy, and the Netherlands have
slapped quotas on Japanese imports.

But now the Europeans see the tide turning. "Their situation
is going to be really tough in France," says the president of a
French electronics company. "Without their cheap price, what
have they got?"

A Multinational Solution

The Japanese, having arrived at the same conclusion, are just
beginning to move from being simply exporters to becoming

multinational operations. Assembly plants are cropping up in the world's less-developed countries, especially in Asia and Africa, where labor is still plentiful, easily trained, and cheap. The products from those plants are still highly competitive in major markets in the industrial countries.

Within the past two years, for example, Matsushita has set up joint ventures or subsidiaries in South Korea (for color TVs and radio), Iran (for rice cookers, blenders, and meat grinders), and Spain (for black and white TVs and air conditioners). The company's 27 manufacturing subsidiaries abroad generate annual sales of $330-million.

Nor is the overseas expansion aimed solely at cashing in on foreign low-cost labor. Matsushita and its brethren want to manufacture inside major markets and so avoid trade barriers. Matsushita and Sony are building TV factories in Wales. Sanyo is setting up a joint-venture TV facility in Australia. Sony and Sharp Corp. are establishing color TV plants in Brazil, and the boldest foreign adventure is Matsushita's acquisition of the television division of Motorola in the U.S.

Many of the new foreign operations are formed as joint ventures, and given the sweep of nationalism around the world, that is not too surprising. Asian countries especially are demanding bigger shares for nationals. In Thailand, where Matsushita established its first post-World War II overseas plant, the parent company originally had a majority interest. Now it is down to 49%. The Japanese are resigned. "It is the tendency all over," shrugs Matsushita's Eisaku Onishi, deputy director of overseas operations. "We don't object to that. What we are interested in is getting a good partner. And that is difficult, very difficult."

Also not too surprising is that manufacturers in the industrial countries are beginning to fret about the Japanese setting up house on their turf. Listen to Arrigo Castelli, president of Magnetofoni Castelli, Italy's largest portable tape recorder company: "Before, they were only dumping their goods when export markets elsewhere quieted down on them," he complains. "Now, they look as if they want to come in here on a permanent basis."

Castelli's anxieties are echoed by an official of the British Radio Equipment Manufacturing Assn. "It seems to us it is difficult enough with eight companies already making color TV sets in Britain, without having to split up the market 10 ways," he says, in reference to the new Welsh plants of Sony and Matsushita. "It will be dog eat dog and hard for anyone to be profitable."

Hayata Tokizane, managing director of Matsushita's TV department, rejects suggestions that Japanese are unwanted guests. "We did not go into Wales. We were asked in. And we decided to use as many local components as possible, so we can contribute to the development of the local economy." Tokizane is indignant at the charge that the Welsh plant might gain Matsushita access to the European Community and benefit from low wages in that depressed region of Britain.

The Pressures of Society

Matsushita's difficulties are throwing an increasing burden on the company's marketing men, who in turn are putting pressure on the research laboratories in Osaka for a more vigorous flow of new products and components to supplement the 10,000 already being turned out in Matsushita's 63 Japanese plants and in its growing empire abroad. Products now on the drawing board include a TV set that produces a three-dimensional picture, a flat profile TV, and an improved solar battery.

But even developing new products is not as easy a job as it used to be, admits Shunkichi Kisaka, managing director of Matsushita's product development. "In the past," he says, "you could get the respect of the public by developing technically new products. But now there are other things to be considered—to save natural resources, to consider safety more, to conserve energy, and to avoid pollution."

Kisaka cites just how this is affecting his work. In recent years, TV makers went to wider angle picture tubes, of 110 to 120 degrees, to achieve a big picture in a stylishly shallow cabinet. But now, because the wider angle tube consumes more energy, designers are swinging back to the older 90 degree tube. Kisaka's researchers also are under pressure to come up with a fireproof TV cabinet. And Matsushita's brass is also pushing for a solar battery that will not use scarce silicon or pollution-related cadmium sulphide.

But the pressure that top Matsushita management is exerting upon employees such as Kisaka for new products is nowhere near so intense as the pressures for change being imposed upon Masaharu Matsushita and Takahashi by economic and social forces. Takahashi is the first to admit that "we are in a transition period." Just how men like Takahashi and Matsushita handle the transition will decide the future profitability of their company.

For example, there is the politically and socially flammable decision of whether the Matsushitas of Japan can afford the luxury of a "lifelong employment" policy. So far, most companies have held the line, although Yashica Co., a major camera maker, is so deeply in trouble that it is thinking of laying off 40% of its work force. And both Toshiba and Hitachi have tentatively confronted the issue giving some employees three- to four-day "holidays" at slightly reduced pay.

Seeds of Dissatisfaction

But even at Matsushita, where the singing of the company song brings workers to assembly-line pitch every morning, the possibility of layoffs is being considered. "We do have a kind of labor surplus in some departments," says Chairman Takahashi. "Our company will try to rationalize operations. If sales go down, then the next step would be to reduce production. And then it would be a question of how to deal with excess labor and facilities."

Part of the rationalization is going on in the TV department run by Hayata Tokizane. Tokizane readily admits that new, integrated processes are being included in one reorganized assembly line, where set production is off 15%, that will effect a 30% manpower cut. With Matsushita pushing more of its production overseas and exports running into barriers, the company could soon be faced with closing domestic plants and laying off workers.

The possibility of layoffs is certain to stir up workers who already are beginning to become more independent—and less hardworking. A recent tour of a Matsushita factory unearthed one assembly-line worker who, during a temporary stalling of the line, settled back to read the paper. That is behavior that Japanese managers expect from American workers but hardly from their own breed of *stakhanovites*.

The dissatisfaction with the old ways is also showing up

among younger, aspiring managers. Young Matsushita executives, for example, are growing a touch tired of having to warble such words as "let us bind together a world of blooming flowers and a verdant land in love, light, and a dream" every morning before squaring off to fight the business wars of the day.

The emergence of a more searching generation of Japanese obviously is disturbing to those reared in unquestioning acceptance of the old virtues of loyalty and gratitude. Yet another tradition that may be in danger is the time-honored distribution system. Competitors such as Sharp, followed by Hitachi and Toshiba, are trying to cut prices by going straight to the retailer and thus eliminating the middlemen who clog up the system and keep prices high.

Matsushita is loath to follow suit. For one thing, it has a wholesale company that takes a cut of the profits before sending products to retail outlets. But competitive pressures may force Matsushita's hand.

That Matsushita management will make the necessary adjustments to surmount Japan's current economic difficulties is not in question. What may be in question is whether it possesses the necessary flexibility to adjust to the social and economic changes pressed upon it in the coming years.

Chairman Takahashi insists that "we have no serious problems that we cannot solve." But it appears likely that in the future, President Masaharu Matsushita may well find it fruitful to transfer his formula for relaxation to his executive suite. Matsushita's formula is based upon four tenets: "To try to be as optimistic as possible. To try to joke and laugh. To read books. And once or twice a week to play golf. It circulates the blood to give new ideas."

34. INFLATION NOT WORLDWIDE: PRICE STABILITY IN THE SOCIALIST WORLD

Economic Notes

First National City Bank of New York reports in its "Monthly Economic Letter" (9/74) that "a worldwide inflationary chain reaction has caused prices to soar." The article analyzes erosion of buying power in "industrialized and less-developed countries." Whereas the less-developed nations suffered from an inflation rate of 18.7% (median—or middle of the range) or 19.1% (mean or average), the industrialized nations were burdened only with a median inflation rate of 11.1% (mean, of 12.6%). The period under consideration was approximately the twelve-month period ending in mid-1974.

Three comments are in order:

1. The only socialist country included in the entire list of 50 countries is Yugoslavia—and Yugoslavia is hardly representative of the socialist countries, as will be seen below. The other 12 socialist countries were excluded.

2. The "less-developed countries" listed by First National are all dependent on the "industrialized countries." They are the victims of imperialism. It is no accident that workers and peasants in the former colonies—and present neo-colonies—are suffering from inflated prices.

3. The inflation rates for the socialist nations are far below those of the "industrialized" nations. Intellectual honesty demands that socialism's advantage be noted.

Excerpts from "Inflation Not Worldwide," in *Economic Notes* (October 1974), a monthly published by the Labor Research Association (see Suggested Readings).

SOCIALIST COUNTRIES LISTED BY ILO: CONSUMER PRCE INDEX

COUNTRY	1966	1970	1971	1972	1973	1974	(month)
East Germany	100.1	100	99.8	99.3			
USSR	99.6	100	99.9	99.7			
Bulgaria	96.5	100	99.9	99.9			
Czechoslovakia	91.5	100	99.7	99.5	99.8	99.7	(Jan-Mar)
Romania	98.0	100	100.8	100.8			
Poland	94.5	100	99.9	99.8	100.3	103.9	(Jan-Mar)
Hungary	97.7	100	102.0	104.9	108.7	110.3	(June)
Yugoslavia	74.5	100	115.6	134.8	163.7	199.2	(June)

SOURCES: *1973 Yearbook of Labour Statistics,* International Labour Office, Geneva, 1973. *Bulletin of Labour Statistics,* First Quarter, 1974, ILO, Geneva, 1974.

Contrary to popular opinion, prices of consumer goods in the socialist countries have not been caught in the surge of skyrocketing prices hitting workers in the capitalist countries.

Latest figures from the International Labour Office (ILO), which collects and publishes labor information for the United Nations, indicate that consumer goods prices in 1972 were lower than in 1970 in the USSR, the German Democratic Republic, Bulgaria, Poland, and Czechoslovakia. Romania and Hungary had price increases of less than 5%. Only Yugoslavia experienced sharp price rises: 35% in two years.

Unfortunately, comparable data on prices are not available for the People's Republic of China, the Democratic People's Republic of Korea, the Democratic Republic of Vietnam, Albania, Cuba, and Mongolia.

1974 statistics are available only for four socialist countries. They show that in the twelve-month period ending in March, 1974, prices fell slightly in Czechoslovakia, while they rose only 4% in Poland. In the twelve-month period ending in June, 1974, prices rose only 1.2% in Hungary, although they rose 18% in Yugoslavia.

The median price increases for the four socialist countries was therefore 4%, while the average price increase was 5.8%. The median for the industrialized capitalist countries was almost three times that of the socialist countries—and the average price rise was more than double!

The USSR, the GDR, Bulgaria, and Romania, whose data

are not yet available for 1973–74, probably experienced slight, if any, rising consumer prices. Why? Because between 1963 and 1972, a period of ten years, prices fell slightly in both the USSR and the GDR—and rose only 3% and 4% respectively in Bulgaria and Romania. In contrast, during the same period prices rose 60% in Japan, 59% in Britain, 47% in France, 37% in the USA, and 34% in West Germany.

The statistics prove that prices do not have to rise. Workers' control of the economy under the slogan: "production for use, not for profits," can ensure stable prices for the working class.

D.
The "Energy Crisis"

So MUCH PERNICIOUS nonsense has been fed to the American people about the so-called energy crisis that it is difficult to present an overview that does not simply repeat the clarifications provided in readings #36, by Pugh and Zimmerman; #37, by Richard Kronish; and #38, by Michael Tanzer. Each of the latter, in presenting an account of the crisis, exposes a different facet of petro-corporate manipulations, showing them, though, to be the urgent responses to authentic problems. From the point of view of the dominant Seven Sisters,* the key to the situation was a sharp decline over the postwar period in the rate of profits. Nothing could be more serious. Prospects for a reversal of this trend were anything but rosy. Not only were independent producers and distributors carving out larger niches in the domestic market, but OPEC (the Organization of Petroleum Exporting Countries—often incorrectly referred to as Arab but also including Venezuela, Nigeria and Iran among others) menaced the very foundations of the private cartel. In addition, a growing environmental movement, already making life difficult for the Alaskan pipeline, threatened to jeopardize long-run plans to develop new sources of energy.

* Exxon, Mobil, Texaco, Gulf, Standard Oil of California, Royal Dutch/ Shell and British Petroleum. The first five are U.S.-owned and have dominated the American economy for decades. In 1929, for example, all were among the top twenty corporations. In 1972 they received about 10% of *all* profits made by U.S. industrial corporations, an eye-opening achievement when one considers the enormous profits made by other super-giants such as GE, GM, IBM, DuPont and U.S. Steel, not to speak of those of the scores of regular-sized giants such as Deere, Singer, General Foods and Borden.

This is the context in which shortages began to develop even before the October war and the embargo. There is considerable evidence (as the readings show) that these shortages were artificial, a contrived plot to jack up the price of oil. Not without success! As a consequence, profits soared, as mentioned in reading #35, originally an ad by the Oil, Chemical and Atomic Workers that appeared in the *New York Times*. If these profits are so desperately needed for the exploration and development of new sources of energy, why, this ad asks, are they being invested in real estate, entertainment and the purchase of a department-store chain?

To believe oil and government officials—at least on those days when they are not pointing the finger of blame at the Arabs —*we*, the greedy American people, are the real culprits. What chutzpa! After decades of throttling us with gas-eating monsters and victimizing us with a wasteful, inefficient *system* of transportation, one designed to maximize gasoline and automobile profits, they now have the gall to blame the *victims* for the crisis *they* have created.

The situation is filled with complexities and contradictions. First, the American transportation system reflected an implicit alliance between oil, autos and construction (the latter on both roads and suburban housing). That confluence of interest has now been shattered. Second, the short-term benefits to the oil companies have been enormous. As mentioned previously, profits are soaring but competition on the home front has also been undermined while the ecology movement has been dealt a severe if not fatal blow. On the other hand, what appeared to have begun as a series of moves designed to increase *company* profits has been transformed by the Middle East war, Arab nationalism and growing Soviet power into a threat to long-run profits, even greater than what had existed previously. I am referring, of course, to the new and powerful bloc of Arab and Iranian capital. Most of the readings in this section discuss one or another aspect of this situation.

Even more important, perhaps, is the damage barrelhead increases have inflicted on the world capitalist monetary system and the danger that weak links, like Italy, might cause the entire structure to topple, or at least be plunged into a devastating depression. Reading #40, by the Belgian Marxist Ernest Mandel, addresses itself to these issues and to a discussion of what options exist for petrodollar investment. At the same time, however, the overdependency of Europe and Japan on imported oil has served to improve the competitive position of the United States.

In this welter of rival interests and uncertainty, the U.S. government is attempting to set a policy that simultaneously increases the profitability of the oil companies, props up the failing domestic economy and shores up the shaky world monetary system. It is not clear what will emerge. My impression is that debates are proceeding vigorously—some might call this floundering—in the highest councils of government, but that no final decision has yet been taken. However, an informative article by Leonard Silk in the *New York Times* (reading #39) sets forth what I believe is the central thrust—that is, to maintain a permanent structure of high oil prices. These are to be publicly justified by the need to create monetary incentives so that the oil companies can develop alternative sources of energy, including oil. Oil companies, as the readings show, and as one might expect, have invested heavily in coal, natural gas, uranium reserves—in other words, the entire gamut of energy sources.

Along with high fixed prices—subsidies if you prefer—there will be a concerted effort to undermine the OPEC cartel. Cartels are rarely stable formations. Moreover, it is difficult to evaluate the durability of a political cartel as unique as this, one which few believed even possible a decade ago. For this reason I include, without comment, for the reader to consider, a lengthy quote from a student of business organization on the optimum conditions for cartel maintenance. This passage was written years ago by an economic theorist who had in mind a cartel of business corporations and not one of governments. But the economics of cartel management is similar enough to believe it a useful overview both in the situation at hand and the developing possibilities in other raw materials, especially bauxite, but to a lesser extent copper, tin, chromium and manganese.

> The industry should consist of relatively few firms in order that our job of inspection and co-ordination may be easily handled. . . .
> The demand for the industry's output should be highly in-

elastic at its precartel price, so that any reduction of output will cause a perceptible increase in the industry's total revenue. Such inelasticity simplifies our task of selling our members on the advantages of co-operation and the unwisdom of chiseling once some part of monopoly profit has been realized. That is, we prefer that the advantages of mutual restraint should be capable of easy demonstration.

Likewise, the success of the cartel will be assisted if we can secure control of the better supplies of some essential raw material and so render the entry of new producers more difficult. Our task will be further simplified to the extent that the industry consists of firms which must incur high overhead costs in order to operate efficiently. A large optimum size for the firm will increase the difficulty faced by potential competitors in raising capital and make easier our task of driving out newcomers who give battle with firms of less than optimum size.

Finally, we should wish to organize our cartel in an industry which in the short run is unprofitable without co-operation, modestly profitable with it. This condition will serve to discourage chiseling among the members since there is a good prospect for profits for everyone if restraint is practiced, and the probability of profits for no one if our admonitions are ignored. If the industry is so lacking in hope that some firms face bankruptcy even if they play the game, desperation may drive them to cut prices or exceed their quotas on the chance that they may survive through a policy of beggaring their more honest or less enterprising neighbors. If the industry is already earning appreciably more than the prevailing rate of return on capital, its members are probably thinking in terms of expansion rather than contraction, and if our cartel cannot long delay the entry of new firms, they are right to do so. In any event, the higher the rate of return, the sooner (presumably) we should expect the assault on our position by outsider capital.

(Donald Dewey, *Monopoly in Economics and Law* [Chicago, Rand McNally, 1959], p. 22)

But if pressure and arm-twisting from afar fail to reduce OPEC power, more direct approaches are possible. War talk is growing. Previous readings have alluded to this growing possibility, but reading #41 is devoted exclusively to some aspects of the arms build-up in the Middle East. There are some who believe that the Vietnam fiasco precludes new American adventures elsewhere. Such sentiments, overstating the power of public opinion, are more in the nature of wishful thinking. Accompanied by repression and propaganda—our lives will be said to depend on oil—there is no reason why a determined ruling bureaucracy will forgo in the present the traditional military prerogatives it has used in the past.

Moreover, a recent article in *Commentary* magazine by a Johns Hopkins professor, Robert W. Tucker, argues the military case of invading the area from "Kuwait down along the coastal region of Saudi Arabia to Qator." As this area contains almost half of OPEC production, such an attack promises success at a modest cost. "Since it has no substantial centers of population and is without trees, its effective control does not bear even remote comparison with the experience of Vietnam." Those advocating war assume, perhaps correctly though perhaps not, that the Soviet Union will limit its response to sharp but ineffective condemnations at the U.N. Still, there are grave risks. A milder measure, perhaps a CIA-sponsored coup in Libya, ridding the mainly conservative Arab world of its most militant anti-imperialist leader, Muammar el-Qaddafi, might be sufficient to induce the oil producers to resume their "rightful" subordinate role.

The drama has just begun, and like the spinning roulette wheel, where it ends no one knows. It is all but certain, however, that all the government's missiles and all the government's marines cannot put the old system back together again.

It is worth asking, in conclusion, whether a nationalized energy industry is a viable and meaningful alternative. Apart from the political infeasibility of stripping power from the mightiest members of the capitalist class, there is a technical problem involved: much oil production takes place outside the United States; it is not ours to nationalize. Nor, by and large, are tankers. Even more important, nationalization within a capitalist context invariably has led to minor changes at most. If nationalization is not part of a general restructuring of the entire economy away from production for profit to production that genuinely meets people's needs, the basic problems remain. In the meantime, the prospects remain grim: more likely than not, ahead of us looms war or depression, or quite possibly both.

They can't rob us blind

We, the refinery workers of America, are about to take an unprecedented step in the relationship between worker and employer.
We're going to open up one of the most secretive industries in America to public scrutiny.

We're the Oil, Chemical and Atomic Workers, the people who make the petroleum products that keep America running.

We hope to influence the industry we've served long and well to make some basic changes in the way it treats its workers and the public.

We all know the effects of inflation. We feel them every time we buy food or clothing. Every time we buy gasoline or pay our utility bills. We don't need any lessons in economic theory; we can see what's happening every time we struggle over our family budget, then read about huge profit increases for corporations.

What Causes Inflation?

Increased oil prices were responsible, directly or indirectly, for almost half of last year's increase in the cost of living, according to a congressional study. So what causes high oil prices?

They're partly due to increased prices for foreign crude. But not entirely.

Oil industry profits are up 146% since 1972, 360% since 1961. We may be paying more for foreign crude, but we're also paying a lot more for industry profits. The oil companies would like to believe they need all the money they're making—$17 *billion* in 1974 alone—to find more oil.

But we know different.

Being inside the industry, we have a pretty good idea of how it works. And how, as workers and consumers, we're being robbed blind. We took a good hard look at where the money we pay for oil goes. And we found some interesting things.

We knew the extra money wasn't going to pay our salaries.

Since 1961, the refinery labor cost of refined products has risen one one-hundredth of a cent per gallon— to slightly more than seven-tenths of one cent per gallon—while the price of a barrel of refined products has increased from $3.85 to $10.10. Proportionately, the refinery labor cost per barrel has been cut in half, from 7.1% of the total cost in 1961 to 3.3% today.

Obviously, the money's going somewhere else. We found that oil executives got average salary raises of more than 21% last year.

They got an average *increase* of more than *$22 per hour.*

Their *raise* was almost four times *our total wages.*

The Monopoly Game.

We found that oil companies are using tremendous amounts of money to buy up other companies. Some of them are energy companies, giving them a horizontal monopoly in energy to go along with their vertical monopoly in oil. Oil companies control most of America's natural gas, 50% of its nuclear fuels, seven of the fifteen largest coal companies,

and Inflation
if we open our eyes.

We're going to tell you why oil prices are so high.

How the oil industry causes the inflation that robs our paychecks.

And... what we can do about it.

most of the oil shale leases and most of the geothermal energy leases.

They're also investing heavily in chemicals and other petroleum derivatives. Between 1961 and 1967, the industry spent as much on chemical plants as on oil refineries. They're using their current profits to invest in plastics, fertilizers, building products and other downstream applications of oil. They're even investing in companies that have nothing to do with oil. One company spent a sum just about equal to its entire 1973 profits to buy a *department store chain*.

Other companies are putting their money into real estate, entertainment, commodities and other areas that will never give the public one drop of oil. And finally, the oil industry spent huge sums on illegal campaign contributions in 1972, to influence government supervision of their activities.

If the oil companies have all that money to spend on executive raises, outside investments and political contributions, they must be making too much money.

The money we pay for oil shouldn't go for *anything* except finding, refining and delivering oil.

The industry *can* and *should* lower its prices.

A Fair Price For Labor.

At the same time, it can afford to pay its workers a decent wage. While the industry has prospered, we've suffered. In 1966, our average wage was $3.45 an hour. Today, we get $3.27 an hour in 1966 dollars. For some of the most dangerous, unhealthy work in America.

What To Do?

We can't let the oil industry get away with blaming workers and consumers for our nation's ills. When we recognize what's really behind our inflation and energy problems, we can begin to do something about them. But if we allow corporations to continue playing off one segment of the public against another, we'll never get to the real root of the problem.

They may keep trying to rob us. But if we open our eyes, they can't rob us blind.

The Oil, Chemical and Atomic Workers.
We want a fair shake. For us, for you, for America.

This originally appeared as a full page advertisement in the *New York Times*, December 16, 1974.

36. THE "ENERGY CRISIS" AND THE REAL CRISIS BEHIND IT

by Dave Pugh and Mitch Zimmerman

Seven giant companies have long dominated world oil—almost everything from the well-head to the gas pump. Five of the seven are U.S.-owned, and more than half their oil and their profits come from overseas.

Through joint ventures and agreements, the seven have spun a web of power that covers most of the globe—and they have used this power for decades to limit oil production. Why? History has taught Big Oil that surpluses of oil and free-swinging competition mean lower prices and lower profits. But by agreeing among themselves to limit the amount of production, prices can be kept artificially high.

The big companies have an additional reason for limiting U.S. oil output. It is far more profitable to import foreign oil and gasoline. Production costs in the Middle East average 12 cents a barrel (42 gallons), twenty times cheaper than in the U.S. Refineries, too, are cheaper to build and operate overseas, because wages and taxes are lower and they can operate without expensive pollution controls.

So for more than twenty years, the companies have deliberately cut back on U.S. energy development.

Excerpts from booklet entitled "The 'Energy Crisis' and the Real Crisis Behind It" (San Francisco, United Front Press, June 1974). Dave Pugh is a staff member of United Front Press, an anti-imperialist pamphlet publishing and distribution group. Mitchell Zimmerman is a free-lance writer currently working on a book on imperialism and underdevelopment, and is co-author of *Dr. Spock in Vietnam*.

· Between 1956 and 1972, the number of new oil wells in the U.S. steadily tumbled—with total drilling declining from 208 million feet to 86 million feet per year.

· In the 1950s and 1960s, the major oil companies capped over 20,000 flowing wells in California alone, with an estimated capacity of 5 billion barrels of oil.

· Between 1968 and 1972, U.S. oil companies built only one major new refinery in the U.S.

· Since the early 1950s they have opposed government research and development of alternate energy sources, such as shale oil and coal gasification.

In short, the oil industry itself imposed severe limitations on the development of U.S. energy to maximize their profits.

But Then: A Profit Crisis!

By the end of the 1960s, however, the big international companies faced a number of serious problems. First and foremost, nationalist and popular governments around the world were fighting to regain control of their natural resources from foreign companies. The oil companies were hit hardest in the Middle East—where Arab governments demanded higher prices, control over production levels, and a growing share of ownership.

In the U.S., independent refiners and dealers were cutting into the markets of the major oil companies. Independent gas stations eliminated the green stamps, credit cards and tigers-in-the-tank, and kept prices down through "gas wars" with the majors. Their share of U.S. gasoline sales rose from 10% in 1960 to 25% in 1972.

Finally, the environmental movement was interfering with a number of profitable Big Oil plans for plundering our natural resources. This movement delayed the Alaska pipeline, stopped offshore drilling and strip mining, fought against air pollution, and delayed the construction of unsafe, nuclear power plants.

Here was the real crisis—a profit crisis for the big oil companies. Although they were still making enormous profits, the *rate* of profit was slipping—and this was something they could not tolerate.

Enter the Energy Crisis

Exxon treasurer Allan Hamilton bluntly stated the companies' position: "*Unless profit levels become such that the oil industry is confident its investment will bear fruit, the supply of oil will not be forthcoming."* Big Oil decided to use its world-wide power over supplies to create shortages that would send prices through the ceiling.

Although oil executives probably met secretly to nail down the timing and details of the energy crisis, they had already laid the basis by limiting the supply of oil here and abroad. All that was required was more of what they had been doing all along.

In the period from 1968 to 1972, the industry began to beat the drums for the energy crisis—and to take steps to make this threat a reality. "The era of cheap fuel is over," declared the business publication *Fortune* in November 1970. "Everywhere there is talk of an 'energy crisis.'"

But at the same time, in secret reports not meant for the public, they admitted the real situation: "Oil supply, particularly crude oil, remains in potential surplus relative to the market." So said the top planners for Standard Oil of California in a December 1968 study that recommended the big oil companies limit their Middle East production to keep prices high. (*San Francisco Chronicle*, March 27, 1974.)

The energy crisis was underway. From 1968 to 1970, the government of Iran pressed the Iranian Oil Consortium to boost production. But the Consortium, an international group including Exxon, Gulf, Texaco, Mobil and other U.S. companies, refused. In the same period, the U.S.-owned Arabian-American Oil Company (Aramco) kept Saudi Arabian oil production level, despite government requests to produce more oil.

Meanwhile the companies continued to cut back U.S. oil output. From 1972 to 1973, U.S. crude oil production actually dropped 2%. In addition, the use of refineries was reduced from 90% in 1970, to 85% two years later.

First Shortages

The oil companies gave the energy crisis a test run in the winter of 1972–73. The companies refused to order as much foreign oil as they themselves predicted would be needed. The result was a shortage of fuel oil in several northeastern U.S. cities that winter, and a sharp increase in the price.

In the spring and summer of 1973 the oil companies really began to clamp down. In many areas of the country, gasoline was in short supply, and prices began to rise. By May, 1200 independent gas dealers had been driven out of business.

These events represented minor successes for Big Oil and their energy crisis. But it would take something much bigger to push gasoline prices completely out of the 30 to 40 cents-per-gallon range. The Arab oil embargo and price hikes provided them with a golden opportunity to put the energy crisis in high gear.

The Oil Embargo

When the Arab-Israeli war broke out in October 1973 eight Arab oil-exporting governments declared an embargo against the United States, South Africa, Portugal and the Netherlands— all countries that were supporting Israel. They followed this with a series of dramatic increases in the price of their oil.

In a larger sense, these moves represented heavy blows against the power of the Western oil giants (mainly U.S.) that had dominated Middle Eastern oil production for decades. But in the short run, the actions of the Arab governments presented the companies with an opportunity to boost their profits.

By creating shortages of panic proportions, the oil giants could ram through enormous price increases on the retail level. And both the shortage and the price increases could be blamed entirely on the Arab countries.

The Companies Had Plenty of Oil

To put the embargo in perspective, the U.S. only gets a small (though rising) portion of its oil from the Middle East. Over 60% of the oil we consumed in 1973 was produced in the U.S. and another 17% of our oil came from Venezuela and Canada. Before the boycott started, the U.S. was getting only 13% of its oil from the Middle East.

Even during the Arab embargo, however, there were enormous leaks to the U.S. Millions of barrels of "embargoed" oil went to Europe and the Caribbean—then the oil companies quietly routed it to the U.S. In addition, the companies increased imports from Iran, Indonesia, and elsewhere.

Where were the shortages? According to *Oil & Gas Journal,* imports for October, November and December 1973 were actually 32% higher than for the same three months of 1972.

While we were sitting in long gas lines at Christmas time, oil was pouring into the U.S. in record quantities!

Yes, there was a shortage of gasoline at the gas pumps—but there was no shortage of oil waiting in storage tanks and pipelines.

· In January 1974 the oil companies were pressured into revealing that their oil stockpiles were 5% higher than the year before.

· This was confirmed by *Platt's Oilgram,* a daily business service that oil companies subscribe to for about $400 a year. The Oilgram reported in January 1974: "Storage tanks are, in fact, full to the brim in northwest Europe, the east coast of the United States and in Italy."

Oil imports did begin to fall off in February, but it was for a different reason—to help Big Oil wipe out the smaller independents. The *New York Times* reported (February 22, 1974): "Some of the nation's major oil companies are deliberately reducing their imports of crude oil," to keep it out of the hands of independent refiners. The article also noted they could make higher profits refining it in Europe.

Gas Lines Vanish Overnight

When the Arab governments officially lifted their embargo in March, the oil companies and the government promptly released their enormous reserve to promote the illusion that the boycott had mainly been responsible for the shortages. But at every stage of the game, the shortages had to do with decisions of the oil companies to boost their rate of profit by raising prices.

What About Price Increases?

First of all, since over 60% of the oil we consume is from U.S. wells, nothing the Arab oil producers do has any effect on the cost of producing this oil. Yet the price of U.S. crude oil rose from $3.50 to $7.00 per barrel—pure profit for the oil companies.

Secondly, we're paying much more at the gas pump than is needed to cover increased taxes to Arab governments. From March 1973 to March 1974, Arab oil producers raised their taxes from $1.75 to $7.00 per barrel, or about 17 cents a gallon. (One barrel = 42 gallons.) But in the same period, gasoline prices rose almost 30 cents a gallon—not just for gasoline made from Middle East oil, but for *all* gas we buy here.

Finally, a special arrangement with the U.S. government allows the oil companies to deduct all payments to foreign governments from the U.S. taxes due on their huge overseas profits. Thanks to this "foreign tax credit," Exxon, Gulf, Texaco and the others paid no taxes whatsoever on their $6.1 billion in foreign profits last year. In effect, Big Oil is overcharging us twice—once with higher prices at the gas pump, and once in extra taxes we pay because they evaded theirs.

Higher prices in the Middle East have been used by the oil companies as an excuse to boost prices—not just in the U.S., but in Europe, in Japan, and in the poorest countries of the world, that can least afford costlier oil.

Big Oil's Big Gains

In the short run, the energy crisis has been a great success for Big Oil. The 1973 profits of the ten biggest U.S. oil companies were $7.8 billion—up 51% from 1972. Independent refiners and dealers are being weakened or driven under. And a host of environmental and health safeguards are in danger: Offshore drilling is starting up again, air pollution controls are being relaxed, construction of the Alaska pipeline has begun, lower safety standards are being pushed for nuclear reactors, and the companies are pressing to cancel safety restrictions on the nation's coal mines.

As the icing on the cake, the oil companies will profit from a $10 billion program of government subsidies called "Operation Independence"—which President Nixon claims will make the U.S. self-sufficient in energy by 1980. Oil company executives are unanimous in saying this goal is impossible to meet. But they are glad to go along with this hoax, because most of the subsidies will go to oil companies.

For the last decade and a half, the oil giants have been gaining control over "competing" energy sources to make sure they don't compete too much. The oil companies have become giant energy combines. They now own 54% of the country's coal reserves; 73% of natural gas supplies; and 45% of the uranium reserves. They are rapidly acquiring concessions for oil shale and geothermal energy (underground hot springs) as well. The only thing they haven't been able to corner is solar energy. So far the sun hasn't been up for sale.

And now, $5 billion of the "Operation Independence" money is slated for research and development of nuclear energy. As the third largest contractor for nuclear reactors in the world, a Shell-Gulf partnership will get a big cut of this. And Exxon and Arco both have a big stake in turning uranium into nuclear fuel.

Now that the price is right, and now that Big Oil itself stands to receive the profits, it's full steam ahead on alternate energy sources—especially if our taxes will pay for it.

37. RESPONDING TO OPEC: AN ASSESSMENT OF OIL CARTEL OPTIONS

by Richard Kronish

The transfer of power at the point of international production thus nears completion. The OPEC countries threaten, certainly within the next decade, to force the oil companies entirely out of crude pricing and crude production. What remains for the companies is the limited and, in the context of the modern structure, far less profitable role as transporters, refiners, and merchandisers of crude petroleum. Phillips Petroleum, for example, recently identified its return on investments in combined refining, distribution, and marketing properties as only 0.17 per cent in 1971 and 1.92 per cent in 1972. The major oil firms have, how-

Excerpts from *Socialist Revolution* (September-October 1973), pp. 28–46. Richard Kronish teaches sociology at the University of Massachusetts, Boston.

ever, successfully grappled with other serious challenges to their hegemony. There is no reason to expect that they will not make a further attempt to defend their profitability and dominance. In the present setting, four alternative courses of action for the companies stand out. The major firms can attempt to:

1. increase the supply of petroleum available from alternative sources;
2. turn to alternative fuels;
3. prompt military intervention;
4. restructure the industry, making "downstream operations" more profitable.

In examining these options, it is important to keep in mind that they are not mutually exclusive.

A veteran oilman described the first alternative to *Forbes:*

> We don't have the oil in the U.S. to meet our future requirements. Either we are going to have our future committed to those crazy Arabs or we are going to develop Southeast Asia, the West Coast of Africa and the West Coast of Latin America as alternative sources—and hopefully, build the Alaskan pipeline.

Oilmen have certainly tried to develop alternative sources of petroleum. After a three-year struggle with conservation groups, the extensive lobbying efforts of the companies to construct an Alaskan pipeline have prevailed. Nevertheless, the Alaskan reserves are inadequate to forestall reliance upon the OPEC members. According to one estimate, the Alaskan reserves, while the "greatest discovery in the history of the U.S. . . . will merely offset declining production in the Lower 48."

The oil companies have also actively sought to discover new foreign sources outside the Middle East. In recent years, fully ninety-five per cent of new exploration efforts have been outside the Persian Gulf. Efforts have particularly centered on the offshore areas of Southeast Asia, where military regimes have not (yet) adopted OPEC's aggressive posture. In Indonesia, for example, the terms between the government and the oil companies are, according to *Fortune,* "exceptionally favorable to the oil companies." In contrast with the division of revenue with the OPEC members (approximately 79:21 against the companies before the 1972–73 price increase), in Indonesia the companies receive sixty per cent of the total output.

The offshore areas of South Vietnam have also attracted considerable American interest. In May of 1973, according to the *New York Times*, oil companies—including Jersey Standard, Mobil, Gulf, and Standard of Indiana—submitted bids for rights to drill for oil off the coast of South Vietnam. Oil officials have, however, interlaced high hopes with concern over the political situation. Indeed, the importance of the political regime in South Vietnam has led *Forbes* to suggest that oil may be "the hidden factor in the Vietnam equation."

While the international oil companies and the Nixon administration appear committed to a politically "satisfactory" government in Saigon, even the achievement of this goal—however unlikely in reality—does not significantly mitigate in the near future the reliance of the advanced capitalist countries upon the OPEC members for crude petroleum. In the first place, it is highly unlikely that Southeast Asia can supplant the Middle East as the primary source of crude imports. In Indonesia, anticipated production for 1975 is no more than the (1972–73) two-million-barrel level of Libya. While it is true that much of the vast archipelago remains unexplored, known reserves account for only about five per cent of the world's total. By contrast, the countries of the Middle East sit on seventy-five per cent of the world's 670 billion barrels of proven reserves, while Saudi Arabia alone accounts for twenty per cent of the total. Secondly, "the long gestation period between planning and actual production in the petroleum industry" means that it may well take until the end of the 1970s before production begins in earnest. Finally, it is quite possible that Indonesia, if not South Vietnam, will follow OPEC's path and perhaps even affiliate itself with OPEC. Alternative petroleum sources thus appear to be inadequate and potentially subject to the same actions that the OPEC members have taken.

The major companies have also responded to the OPEC challenge by turning to alternative sources of energy and transforming themselves into "energy companies." Natural gas, which accounts for approximately twenty-five to thirty per cent of all

energy consumed in the United States, has, for example, historically been associated with the search for oil. All the majors now
engage in the production of natural gas and account for perhaps
sixty per cent of production and reserve ownership. Atomic
energy has also come within the control of the petroleum giants:
oil companies, headed by Kerr-McGee, Jersey Standard, and
Gulf, now control forty-five per cent of the known domestic reserves of uranium. The petroleum companies have also made
considerable investments in potential sources of energy such as
oil shale, Canadian tar sands, and even underground steam.
Finally, beginning in 1963 with Gulf Oil's purchase of Pittsburgh & Midway Coal, the petroleum majors have acquired a
number of leading coal companies. At the present time, oil companies own two of the three largest coal producers, five of the
largest ten, and seven of the largest fifteen. Peter Barnes has
quite correctly predicted the consequences of the majors' concentration of energy resources:

> there will be less inter-fuel competition and higher prices,
> all to the companies' benefit and at the public expense. . . .
> Some of this has already started to happen. In the last two years
> (1969–71), for example, coal prices have jumped 79% on the
> average and more than 100% in some localities though demand
> and production both rose at about the same 5% rate. . . . The
> situation has been much the same in natural gas, the one fuel
> whose interstate price is federally regulated. Oil/gas companies
> . . . have been pressing the Federal Power Commission for
> enormous gas rate increases.

While major oil companies' efforts to dominate the entire field
of energy have increased both the prices of "competitive" fuel
and their own profits, it is unlikely that in the near future the
development of alternative sources of energy will significantly
reduce the dependence of the advanced capitalist countries upon
the OPEC members for crude petroleum. Coal, for example,
the most abundant of the fossil fuels, requires either deep or
strip mining, both of which "are objectionable because of human
hazards or environmental depredation." "Clean" coal with a
low sulfur content lies largely in a few western states. Trans-
ported to mid-continent markets, it costs twice as much as local
coal.

Oil-shale deposits might supply enough oil for a hundred and fifty years. However, there is scant possibility of producing shale oil in large volume before the Eighties, because of the huge investment and long lead times required to build the necessary plant and pipelines. At the present time, the extraction of oil from the tar sands is also not profitable.

The use of nuclear energy is also limited in the short run. The twenty-nine "conventional" nuclear fission reactors now operating in the United States employ only uranium-235 as a raw material. U-235 is relatively rare (comprising less than one per cent of all available uranium) and is "in danger of depletion in a few decades." Accordingly, attention has been devoted to the fastbreeder nuclear reactor, which produces more fuel than it consumes. The fastbreeder reactor is, however, extraordinarily dangerous, producing radioactive wastes with lifespans of over two hundred thousand years. In any case, operation of the fastbreeder cannot be expected before 1990. Use of controlled thermonuclear power (fusion), while a "clean, cheap and virtually inexhaustible source of energy," similarly cannot be expected to replace petroleum in the near future. Indeed,

> success is decades and billions of dollars away. Estimates of the time when fusion power will be feasible range from 20 to 100 years.

While the major companies have profited, then, from their expansion throughout the energy field, it is unlikely that the development of either alternative sources of petroleum or alternative sources of energy will permit the international oil companies to overthrow their dependence upon the OPEC members for crude petroleum.

Direct United States military intervention, perhaps against the Libyan or Iraqi governments, offers another possible means for breaking OPEC's power. According to the *New York Times,* "the Arab world"—undoubtedly with recollections of Marines landing in Lebanon in 1958 following the overthrow of the pro-Western regime in neighboring Iraq—views the possibility of direct military intervention "as real." Nevertheless, direct United States military intervention at this time appears unlikely in the light of likely Arab resistance, possible Soviet intervention, and an uncertain response at home. Somewhat more likely is clandestine action by the CIA along the lines employed in Iran in 1952. At the present time, however, the United States government seems primarily intent on exploiting the ideological and territorial divisions within OPEC in an effort to splinter its unity. American support coupled with the fear of internal radicalism has drawn the conservative governments of Kuwait, Abu Dhabi, Saudi Arabia, Pakistan, and Iran into a "virtual alliance."

The uncertainty of these efforts to reduce OPEC's bargaining leverage, if not to crack OPEC itself, have not, however, left the major oil firms without an alternative. As profits from production decline, the majors seem to be determined to make downstream operations more profitable. Putting downstream operations on a "moneymaking basis" is, however, no mean task. The majors must restructure downstream operations and production. In the first place, the majors must effect increases in the prices of refined petroleum products, particularly gasoline (which represents sixty-five to seventy per cent of the revenue of refined products) both absolutely and relative to crude prices. Then, in order to maintain prices and profits in marketing at a high level, the majors must significantly reduce the number of gasoline service stations that now operate. In addition to reducing the number of stations, the majors must also reduce the share of the market garnered by independent marketers (or nonbranded stations). Throughout the late sixties, independents continuously increased their share of the total gasoline market, capturing 25.6 per cent of the market in 1972. As long as the majors were primarily interested in realizing the enormous profits locked in the crude barrel, the market losses sustained by their stations were no great concern. The majors' new interest in securing high prices and profits in marketing puts the independents, which have tended to be a source of price competition, in an entirely different light. To secure control over marketing and to put marketing on a "moneymaking basis," the majors must reduce the share of the market held by the independents. Indeed, in order to boost their own profits, rather than the profits of the branded stations, the majors must restructure their relationship with those who operate the majority of service stations. Since the 1930s, the major oil companies have preferred to lease their stations to dealers who would work long hours on their own (at low pay) rather than have to pay employees who might not have as much incentive to sell extra gasoline.

With marketing far more profitable, the majors may well decide to re-assume direct ownership control of the stations. The total number of stations, for example, peaked in 1968 somewhere between 200,000 and 230,000 (exact figures are not available), remained static in 1969 and 1970, and slowly diminished in 1971 and 1972. This slow decline reflects the majors' gradual reduction in their own stations. In the first five months of 1973, however, the Federal Trade Commission estimates that more than 1200 independent stations closed, while thousands of stations—particularly independent stations—faced gasoline rationing imposed by their suppliers, the major oil companies.

Finally, as gasoline prices have risen and as a consequence made it more attractive for the majors to operate service stations outright, the major companies have raised the rent and cancelled previous rent waivers for leased branded stations, "some of them on unreasonably short notice."

The impetus for these changes has been the so-called "gasoline shortage" of the summer of 1973, which itself followed on the heels of the fuel oil scare of the previous winter (1972–73). Before looking more closely at the shortages, it is worth considering the explanations of the major companies. The majors have rooted the shortages in the controls imposed by Nixon's Phase II over petroleum pricing. The majors have also charged environmental groups with exacerbating the shortages, particularly by blocking construction of new refineries.

The available evidence, however, discounts these charges. While the petroleum price freeze may have increased the attractiveness of gasoline relative to fuel production, a government investigation determined that "in spite of the firms' protestations to the contrary, Humble (Jersey Standard), Texaco, Mobil, Shell, Atlantic Richfield, Cities Service, Phillips and Marathon probably could produce more fuel at present control levels." Similarly, according to General Lincoln, former director of the Office of Emergency Preparedness, the "Cost of Living Council/

Price Commission staff have concluded . . . that the oil industry can make a profit on current prices of No. 2 [fuel] oil, and they know it."

The majors' second charge is somewhat more complex. They claim that the shortage of domestic refining capacity developed in the late 1960s as the gap between new construction and increasing demand rose to over one million barrels per day by 1972, and that environmental groups have played a role in this by blocking construction of new refineries, particularly on the Maine coast. Neil Rolde, former executive assistant to the governor of Maine, challenges, however, the assertion that environmental groups were responsible for blocking refinery construction in Maine. Rolde observes that

> from our standpoint in Maine . . . [Lichtblau's charge] is a misleading statement. In the recent past, we have had two serious proposals before us for oil refineries. Of these, the more serious was the proposal by Occidental Oil to build a refinery for Libyan crude in the foreign-trade zone at Machiasport, Me.
>
> It is true that there was opposition to this project by environmental groups in Maine. But the lion's share of the opposition came from the major oil companies, which were determined not to let Dr. Armand Hammer's company get a foothold in the United States for importing oil and thus break through the oil import quota barrier.
>
> Had it not been for the unrelenting opposition of the major oil companies, a refinery would have been built at Machiasport because, at the time, both environmental laws were weak in Maine.

The major companies also limited new refining construction in a second way. By restricting refinery profits (through the posting of crude prices at a premium), the majors effectively discouraged independent companies from entering refining. In any case, what engendered the fuel and gasoline shortages was not the price freeze or the impending shortage in refinery capacity. It was, quite simply, a decline in refinery capacity utilization.

The decline in heating oil inventory which left the industry short during the winter of 1972–73, like the decline in gasoline inventory which left the industry short during the summer of 1973, had a simple explanation: the utilization of refinery capacity during the first four months of 1972 averaged 84.2 per cent, 3.0 per cent lower than in 1971 and fully 6.5 per cent lower than in 1970, despite an increase in demand. Federal officials entreated the industry to increase refinery output sufficiently.

Notwithstanding government urgings, refineries east of the Rocky Mountains operated at only 89% of capacity in the final quarter of 1972. . . . This was the beginning of the first peacetime petroleum product shortage in the U.S.

The failure of refineries to increase utilization sufficiently continued during the first five months of 1973, despite a 7.4 per cent increase in demand for gasoline, and produced "the gasoline shortage which occurred during the peak summer season."

Responsibility for the decline in refinery output rests heavily on the very largest of the major firms. According to the Senate report, the ten largest refineries—Jersey Standard, Indiana Standard, Texaco, Shell, Gulf, Mobil, ARCO, Sun, Sohio, and Standard of California—"were the major contributors to the drop in refining capacity utilization during the first four months of 1972 below that of 1971 in spite of demand exceeding production." Finally, the available evidence militates against the notion that crude shortages drove the top ten refiners to cut back refinery operations. Standard of New Jersey, Shell, and Gulf refused in fact to avail themselves of any of the additional crude allocated to them.

While a crude shortage did not drive the top ten refiners (with the possible exception of Sohio, a large net crude buyer) to curtail their refining operations during 1972, an inability to obtain sufficient crude-oil feedstocks did force small (and especially independent) refiners to limit their operations. What is more, there is evidence to suggest that the major companies were primarily responsible for the crude shortage experienced by the smaller refiners. In the first place, two Federal Power Commission economists . . . have charged that the major companies are withholding production on nearly one million acres of the nation's richest offshore oil lands. The second piece of evidence requires some explanation. Many smaller American refineries, especially those inland, have traditionally not been "in a position to economically utilize imports." To some extent, this may reflect the shape, direction, and operating rates of the nation's pipeline networks. In any case, most foreign crude has a very high sulfur content that many inland, independent American refineries are not equipped to process. The FTC charges, however, that the major firms have been

> preventing many independent refineries, particularly those in the Midwest, from obtaining sufficient supplies of "sweet" crude. Therefore these refineries are running far below capacity.

The major companies have made good use of the fuel shortage of the winter of 1972–73 and the gasoline shortage of the summer of 1973, shortages that they themselves largely created. With independent refiners curtailing their operations and with the majors reducing their sales of gasoline to independent marketers, more than 1200 independent service stations closed their doors during the first five months of 1973. As the FTC observed, "the major integrated oil companies are . . . taking advantage of the present shortage[s] to drive the only viable long-term source of price competition, the independent marketer, out of market after market." At the same time, the shortages were enormously profitable.

The production boycott imposed by the Arab members of OPEC following the October War has provided the major companies with still further opportunity to restructure downstream operations. *Business Week* reports that during 1973, as a whole,

> some 10,000 gas stations have gone out of business, nearly 5% of the 218,000 stations that existed when the year began.

And now, the target is no longer just the independent marketer. As a Texaco dealer puts it,

> last summer, it was the independent gasoline dealers who were badly hit by gasoline shortages. Now it's the people who lease gasoline stations who are being driven out of business.

The boycott has also permitted the major companies to create an atmosphere where they can override the demands of environmental protection groups. Clean-air standards, for example, have been put to the side throughout the country. The atmosphere of crisis has also permitted further price jumps as the majors have passed on the OPEC increases plus a little something extra.

Despite the majors' success thus far, it is still too early to determine the overall success of the majors' attempt to restructure the industry. Indeed, the drama is merely unfolding. The new strategy, much like the structure imposed upon the industry by the old Standard Trust, contains a highly vulnerable side. Should the OPEC members decide to integrate forward and develop their own refining and marketing operations and/or choose to sell their crude to independent refiners and marketers,

> improving those "downstream" profits won't be simple. New competition from Arab-owned companies and independents could depress prices.

Under these circumstances, it is likely that the major companies will again turn to the federal government for assistance. It is important, however, to recognize and not mystify the genesis of the structure that maintained the predominance of the major companies for some thirty-five years. That structure emerged from fierce political struggle between the majors and their opponents. The majors are now engaged in another struggle to structure the industry in accord with their new needs. Public anger against the majors coupled with pressure from petroleum independents struggling to survive could limit the success of the majors' efforts.

38. THE INTERNATIONAL OIL CRISIS: A TIGHTROPE BETWEEN DEPRESSION AND WAR

by Michael Tanzer

Recent events have drastically changed the equilibrium of the international oil industry, with major repercussions for all countries of the world. The industry is still in a state of flux, and the new equilibrium is far from clear at this point. To understand the present situation, it is necessary to review at least the recent historical background.

Changing Times

Up until the beginning of the 1970s the Big Seven (five American and two British-Dutch international oil companies) dominated the industry through their ownership of the great majority of the world's low-cost oil as well as their vertical integration into the refining, marketing, and transporting of oil. The economic power of the Big Seven was backed in turn by the power of their home governments, of which the Anglo-American overthrow of the Mossadegh government in Iran in the early 1950s was one single visible effect.

In the 1960s, however, the combination of the enormous potential oversupply of cheap oil from the Middle East (with costs at about 10 cents per barrel) and the competition from profit-maximizing newcomers to the international oil industry

Reprinted from *Social Policy* (November-December 1974), an abridged version of the next-to-last chapter of Tanzer's *The Energy Crisis: World Struggle for Power and Wealth* (New York, Monthly Review Press, 1975). Michael Tanzer is an economic consultant in New York City.

led to a steady decline in the market price of crude oil. During this period, the Organization of Petroleum Exporting Countries (OPEC), which was born in 1960 in response to the companies' cuts in the posted prices of crude oil, was a relatively weak organization. (The significance of the posted prices was, and is, that producing-country taxes on crude oil are calculated as a fixed percentage [then about 50 percent] of the posted price, regardless of the market price; thus, in 1960 if posted prices had been cut by 20 cents per barrel, the governments would have gotten 10 cents a barrel less from the companies whose profits would have been increased by that same 10 cents per barrel.) However, OPEC generated sufficient pressure to stop the oil companies from cutting the posted prices any further, so that government revenues per barrel remained constant and the declines in market prices were reflected in declining per barrel profits for the companies.

Nevertheless, the per barrel drops in company profits were more than offset by increases in the volume of production, so that company profits on total crude oil sales rose over the 1960s, even if at a much slower rate than OPEC government revenues.

A plausible "static" economic projection at the end of the 1960s would have been more of the same for the 1970s. The reasons for this belief were that the governments were too diverse and disunited by their short-run economic self-interest to agree on a common front against the consumers.

Now, as the reader is quite aware, the 1970s projections based on these assumptions rank with Herbert Hoover's "Prosperity is around the corner" as among the worst in history. Rather than continuing to decline, crude oil prices have jumped as much as tenfold since 1969. Exactly why this dramatic reversal took place in the 1970s is not fully clear even now, but with the benefit of hindsight we can trace some of the forces which led to the change.

Why the Desert Winds Blew

An important underlying force was the growing weakness of American imperialism in the mid-1960s and after, culminating in its defeat in Vietnam, which was already apparent and irreversible by the end of the 1960s. The whole Vietnam experience (which had gravely weakened the American economy through inflation and balance of payments problems) had also generated a strong antiwar, anti-interventionist mood in the American people. This made it increasingly unlikely in the late 1960s that the U.S. government, the strongest ally of the Big Seven, could intervene physically in the Middle East as it had before.

A second underlying factor was the smashing Israeli victory in the June 1967 war. In hindsight it can be seen that this abject defeat of the Arabs, combined with continued U.S. support for Israel, made it very difficult for any Arab government, no matter how reactionary, to fail to use the ultimate trump card of the "oil weapon" when war broke out again, as it did in October 1973.

On a more immediate level, one of the most significant changes seems to have been the overthrow of King Idris in Libya and the taking of power by Colonel Muammar el-Qaddafi in September 1969. Today, it is hard to realize that in the period before Qaddafi took power the OPEC governments used to bargain with the international oil companies for months and years in order to gain additional crumbs of the potentially enormous oil pie. In the hands of Qaddafi, who is a fiercely anti-imperialist (and anticommunist), religiously ascetic Arab nationalist, Libya's bargaining position was used to whipsaw the international oil companies. In turn, the achievements of Libya virtually forced the rest of OPEC to use them as a standard for the Teheran Agreement of February 1971 which raised posted prices sharply; Libyan prices were further raised in the Tripoli Agreement of March 1971.

Another factor in Qaddafi's success was that he adopted a policy of ordering the companies to cut production if they would not agree to his demands. This was particularly effective in Libya where newcomer oil companies like Occidental Petroleum were heavily dependent upon Libyan production for their total company profits, and hence were in a much weaker bargaining position than the Big Seven which had vast worldwide oil supplies.

While due credit should be given to Libya (as well as Algeria, with which it worked closely) for these aggressive tactics, there are strong indications that the "fight" at Teheran was fixed from the start.

According to the testimony of an oil company insider, the critical turning point in the early Libyan negotiations was the refusal of the major international oil companies, particularly Exxon, to help Occidental Petroleum resist Libya's demands. Thus, Occidental had requested the major internationals to agree to provide it with crude oil from their other sources in the event it found its Libyan supplies reduced, but the majors refused. This predictably forced Occidental to cave in to Libya's demands for increased prices and taxes, which demands predictably the majors would then have to meet.

Surely, if the majors really wanted to keep oil prices down they could easily have provided Occidental with some of their low-cost crude from other countries. Their failure to do so suggests one or both of the following. First, that they wanted prices to rise, which would happen if Occidental agreed to Libya's demands in order to save itself from nationalization. Second, that they wanted to eliminate Occidental as a strong competitor, which would happen if Occidental refused the Libyan demands and was nationalized or had its production cut back. In either case, the companies could only gain by refusing support to Occidental.

Government for Business

There is additional evidence that the international majors had the interrelated goals of increasing foreign crude oil prices and eliminating competition. For one thing, raising the prices on foreign crude oil would not only increase the profitability of the majors' U.S. oil, but also the profitability of their other energy sources such as natural gas, coal, and uranium. In particular, since it was already foreseen around this time that the United States in the 1970s would be far more dependent on crude oil imports than in the 1960s, there was increasing pressure to end the United States oil import quota law. This law, which restricted imports of foreign oil, had kept the price of domestic crude oil more than $1 a barrel above that of foreign crude oil.

In fact, in February 1970, President Nixon's own task force studying the law had recommended its abolition and replacement by a steadily declining tariff. This new system would sharply reduce the majors' profits on both foreign and domestic crude oil. While Nixon, who always was favorably disposed to big oil (and vice versa, as evidenced by oil industry contributions of over $5 million for his 1972 campaign), rejected his commission's recommendation, it must nevertheless have been clear to the majors that there was considerable danger in that direction. If the price of foreign crude were increased to the level of U.S. crude, then the oil import quota law could be safely abolished without threatening the majors' profits. Thanks to the rises in foreign crude oil prices triggered by the early 1970–71 negotiations, this was accomplished six months before the 1973 October War.

The necessary piece to complete the picture of a revitalized cartel is the U.S. Justice Department's removal in January 1971 of antitrust restrictions on the American companies negotiating at Teheran. According to U.S. government officials, this was done to give the American oil companies the ability to present a common front at the negotiations. This was purportedly needed because of the administration's concern with "national security" and its fear that, if harmonious agreement was not reached, the United States might lose access to Middle Eastern oil.

Whatever the U.S. government's motivation, the removal of antitrust restrictions on the U.S. oil companies opened the door for them to make comprehensive plans for worldwide cartelization. That the companies took the opportunity to drive a truck through this opening appears to be confirmed by a top Justice Department official. In announcing in mid-1974 the end of the antitrust clearance, an assistant attorney general gave as reasons that the coordinating body of the companies (the London Policy Group) which "was to be an ad hoc organization had become a quasi-permanent institution for oil company cooperation." He noted: "Studies within it tend to approach sensitive competitive areas of supply, cost, demand, control of downstream distribution, and possible exclusion of independents by means of exclusive buying-back arrangements."

At the same time, some of the fruits of such efforts were being uncovered by an investigative body representing the nation's 5,000 prosecuting attorneys, which found that the major oil companies were pursuing "anti-competitive practices and tactics":

> The group, a committee of the National District Attorneys Association, said that a five-month probe had uncovered enough preliminary indications to warrant formal antitrust investigations and prosecutions by local district attorneys across the country. . . .
>
> Not only are the oil companies showing monopolistic tendencies in petroleum production and sales, the prosecutors charged, but they are also attempting to gain control over the entire energy industry.

The U.S. government's role in the 1971 negotiations is also quite revealing, in that it reportedly undercut the nominal common front of the oil companies vis-à-vis the producing countries. President Nixon sent Undersecretary of State John Irwin to Teheran in mid-January of 1971, ostensibly to show the U.S. government's support for a common effort by the oil companies to resist higher taxes and prices. In fact, Irwin undercut this effort by advising that the talks be divided into separate discussions with the Gulf countries and Libya and Algeria, thereby leaving the companies open to leapfrog tactics by the OPEC countries.

While many people, such as Professor M. A. Adelman of MIT and Senator Frank Church, have attributed this action of the State Department, which contributed to the future rapid upward spiral of oil prices, to "bungling," another interpretation is quite possible. For one thing, the U.S. government and the State Department in particular have been close to and strongly supportive of the major U.S. international oil companies. Since the major oil companies wanted higher crude oil prices, the State Department's action could be just one more in a long history of service to the companies. Moreover, rising crude oil prices along with increasing oil company profits could well be seen by the American government as helpful to the U.S. economy as a whole. This would be true because the increased cost of importing oil would reduce Western Europe's and Japan's balance of payment surpluses, while the U.S. balance would benefit from the increased oil company profits.

Give a Little, Take a Little

The Teheran and Tripoli agreements of 1971 and the "participation agreements" of 1972 seem to mark a new era of monopolistic control of oil supplies, this time shared by the companies and the OPEC governments. From these agreements the OPEC governments got a sharp increase in posted prices and in their per barrel revenues, as well as a minority share of the oil companies' production, with the promise of a majority share by the early 1980s. At the same time, however, with the previous oversupply of crude oil now under control, the market prices of crude oil rose even more rapidly than the posted prices and taxes, and the per barrel profits of the companies soared.

From a market low of perhaps $1.25 per barrel in 1969—of which about 10 cents was cost, 95 cents government taxes, and 20 cents company profits—by the middle of 1973 the market price had risen to about $2.50 per barrel, with $1.50 for the government and 80 cents for the companies. Both parties had gained significantly here, but while the government's per barrel revenues had increased by about three-fifths, the companies' had quadrupled.

In addition, the countries had received the right to buy participation in the oil production end. While this was a relatively good deal for the countries, it was not all bad for the companies since it also reduced the pressure for total nationalization. At the same time, "buy back" provisions of the oil agreements allowed the companies to go on selling most of the oil produced in the countries. This was extremely valuable in a world of increasing, artificially created scarcity. The fact that the governments were still largely tax collectors—since they sold back most of the "participation oil" and therefore did not get into the refining and marketing areas—made them much less of a threat to the operations of the major companies.

All this of course was but prelude to the vast changes in the wake of the 1973 October War. The cutback in Arab oil production, as well as the embargo on sales to the United States, created near panic buying which sent market prices of crude oil skyrocketing. In this context the OPEC countries attempted unilaterally to fix the division of crude oil revenues between the governments and the companies at an 84:16 ratio in their own favor. Thus, in two stages, the posted price of Arabian Light was raised from $3 per barrel before the war to over $11 per barrel by December 1973. The governments' per barrel revenues from this Arabian Light thereby leaped from less than $2 per barrel to over $7 per barrel.

This attempt by the OPEC governments to set the level of crude oil profits was undoubtedly a blow to the big oil companies. More direct blows were also sustained from the Iraqi nationalization of all American and Dutch oil interests. In addition, the new climate destroyed the timetable for gradual transfer of majority ownership of the oil fields. Instead of 51 percent for the governments by 1982, it appears that something like 60 percent in 1974, possibly escalating in the future (the deal negotiated by Kuwait in 1974), will be the minimum goal of the OPEC governments.

On the other hand, the developments stemming from the October War have also had their bright side for the international oil companies, and particularly the Big Seven. Thus, even the original OPEC target, now abandoned, of an 84:16 split on profits still would have left a profit for the companies on Arabian Light of $1.20 per barrel, or 50 percent more than the per barrel profit level before the October War. Moreover, the OPEC split was based on setting posted prices at 40 percent above what it considered market prices. But, since most crude oil is sold in integrated channels within the international companies, there was no guarantee that the companies were not selling their crude oil at prices far above OPEC's estimates of what market prices would be in arms-length deals. Certainly with crude oil being auctioned after the October War at prices in the $15–$20 per barrel range, it is highly unlikely that the international oil companies were selling crude at OPEC's estimated $8 per barrel level. Hence, in reality the companies were able to use their control of market prices to increase their crude oil profits well above OPEC's target limit.

In addition, the real impact of the speeded up movement for majority participation and ultimate nationalization is far from clear. As long as the OPEC governments combine these steps with agreements to sell back most of the crude oil to the companies, for them to market, then the effect may be more one of form than substance. What the companies are primarily interested in is the quantities of oil which they can draw and the per barrel profits on each, and if satisfactory arrangements can be made for them on these questions, they are quite willing to accede on formal questions of legal title. Witness the much ballyhooed "nationalization" of the oil industry by the Iranian Shah in 1954, which was the figleaf which imperialism installed in place of the real nationalization by Mossadegh.

The real danger to the international oil companies is nationalization in which the government of the oil-producing country takes command of the crude oil supplies and either uses them internally, by building indigenous refineries, or markets them directly to foreign buyers. This would mean that the oil-exporting countries could deal directly with foreign governments or refiners or marketers in consuming countries, thereby cutting off the oil companies' crude oil and gas profits, and ultimately their refining profits. Little wonder then that the September 1973 Libyan nationalization discussed above brought the State Department into quick action on behalf of the majors, just as fear of real nationalization in the leading oil-exporting countries has pushed the major oil companies to seek concessions for oil and gas exploration all over the world.

The Poor Pay More

Who are the losers from these changes in the international oil industry? Insofar as the price of crude oil has shot up tremendously, all oil-importing countries have been hurt, but obviously some have been hurt more than others. In human terms probably the most badly hurt will be the great majority of underdeveloped countries which rely on imported crude oil for their main energy source. This is because their economies are always in such weak condition that any adverse event can easily topple them; as one third-world representative discussing the impact of the energy crisis on these countries put it, "In an anthill the morning dew is a storm."

Thus, the World Bank has lamented that oil price increases, which have jumped third-world oil imports from $2 billion in 1969 to $15–20 billion in 1974, have completely wiped out all the effects of foreign aid given in recent years. If the World Bank is not simply shedding crocodile tears over this event, then it should hide its head in shame, since its own policy of not only refusing to lend money to governments of underdeveloped countries for use in developing their oil sectors, but actively opposing such activities, has contributed heavily to the drastic plight these countries are now in.

In any event, for a country like India, the increased foreign exchange bill for crude oil imports, to well over $1 billion in 1974, equals more than one-third of its total exports, and undoubtedly means that imports of other vital commodities, including foodstuffs and fertilizers, will have to be cut. The result, in the poor underdeveloped countries, then, is not adequately measured by percentage changes in GNP, but is truly registered in bellies bloated from malnutrition and increased death.[1]

No Capitalist Monolith When It Comes to Profit

The second group of losers are the developed countries of the world, but the relative extent of their losses depends in part on the proportion of their energy supplies made up of imported oil. In this regard Japan is worst off, with Western Europe in the next worst position, while the United States is much better off, particularly because most of the profits of the international oil companies return to the United States. In fact, it has frequently been suggested that the United States has not been averse to certain aspects of the energy crisis, since it has weakened Western Europe and Japan to its own benefit—witness the rapid strengthening of the dollar vis-à-vis other currencies following the October War. This is a point to which I shall return later.

Even within the United States, however, there are winners and losers from the energy crisis. The major winners, of course, have been the oil companies, and to a secondary extent the defense industries which have been strengthened by the increas-

---

[1] Given this, it is most heartening that the OPEC countries have expressed their willingness to provide financial assistance to the oil-importing third-world countries to help alleviate this situation. Moreover, an OPEC country, Algeria, took the lead in proposing the historic April 1974 United Nations special session on raw materials in developing nations. At this General Assembly meeting an oil loan fund was established for the poorest countries, and support provided for all third-world countries to raise prices on their own raw materials so as to help change the historically unfair terms of trade between underdeveloped and developed countries.

ing world tension. Major losers have been the giant auto industry and its supplying satellites, the electric and gas utilities, as
well as the widespread leisure industries dependent on the automobile and travel, such as motels, resorts, boating, summer
homes, etc. One of the things which is likely to come out of this
energy crisis is a sharpening of tensions between capital invested in different industries of the economy, particularly insofar as there is suspicion that the crisis has been artificially
created by the oil companies and/or that they are not doing
and will not do enough to overcome it in the future.

Thus, the recent demands of many members of Congress for
a more active government role in the oil industry, ranging from
gathering data on energy resources and prices all the way to
establishing a government energy corporation, reflect not only
pressure from ordinary constituents. They also must be responding to demands from leading sectors of big business that the
state move to help restore equilibrium among various industries of the economy.

While the amount of capital invested in the auto and related
industries and the utilities is obviously enormous, the oil-military complex has up until now had the dominant say in American government circles. Undoubtedly the strugggle between the
large sectors of industry which have been hurt by the energy
crisis and the oil-military complex will not end quickly. Thus
we have the recent lawsuits which have been brought by various
utility companies charging the oil companies with illegal restraint of trade which increased the cost of fuel supplies. In
the long run, however, what is most likely is that within the
United States there will be compromises worked out such that
at least American industry as a whole gets adequate energy
supplies.

Tightrope Balance
Given this general background, we can now turn to the critical question, Whither the international oil industry? Because
of the enormous size and influence of this industry, the question is largely synonymous with, Whither the international
economy?

The problem reduces to two related questions: How can the
importing world continue to pay for the oil it needs; and what

might be done with the enormous monetary reserves that the OPEC countries could pile up? (At the 1974 level of revenues, OPEC countries could take in well over $500 billion by 1980, a sum greater than total world foreign exchange reserves.)

Without drastic modifications, the future situation seems untenable for Japan and Western Europe. The latter's oil imports, which amounted to $10 billion in 1969 and $20 billion in 1973, are expected to jump to $50–60 billion in 1974. This means Western Europe's oil imports already amounted to 10 percent of its total export revenues in 1973 and could reach 20–25 percent in 1974. For Japan the situation could be even worse. Oil imports rose from $2 billion in 1969 to $7 billion in 1973, at which point they already amounted to over 20 percent of total exports, and in 1974 the proportion could reach one-third. Clearly, for Western Europe and Japan as a whole such levels of oil imports are not sustainable for very long. Moreover, the gravity of the situation is compounded by the fact that within Western Europe some countries, notably Italy, were in serious financial straits even prior to the recent oil changes.

The United States would also tend to be hard hit in the balance of payments area because not only have prices jumped, but U.S. imports are rising much more rapidly than those of Western Europe or Japan as U.S. production levels off. Thus, U.S. oil imports have risen from $3 billion in 1969 to $8 billion in 1973, and an estimated $25 billion in 1974, which would amount to about one-fourth of total exports.

However, the key to the better position of the United States is the enormously growing foreign profits of its international oil companies. While current data are not readily available, even if the oil companies were making only $1.00–$1.25 a barrel on OPEC crude oil, this would amount to about $10 billion. Moreover, many more billions of dollars are clearly being made from refining and marketing abroad, since foreign product prices have also shot up greatly. With these profit inflows helping to offset the cost of America's oil imports, the share of total exports needed to pay for vital oil supplies for the United States would tend to be relatively low compared to those of Western Europe and Japan. And when one takes into account the fact that much of Western European trade is within the bloc, so that its net exports to the outside world are far lower, then it is even more likely that the changed oil situation would be a relatively greater burden on Western Europe. Furthermore, the United States has more room to maneuver in that it can increase production substantially within its borders by producing from formerly unprofitable shut-in wells, in addition to expanding quick-return development and exploration drilling, an option which is not open to Western Europe or Japan.

Thus, one key effect of the changes in the international oil industry is a drastic shift in economic power from Western Europe and Japan to the United States.

In response to this situation, each developed country has been frantically and unilaterally seeking its own way out. One method has been for each country to seek to increase its exports, but since most of the developed countries' trade is among themselves, this clearly cannot be a solution for all of them. Another route has been to negotiate direct government-to-government barter deals with individual OPEC countries, swapping a range of developed-country goods for crude oil. For example, by early 1974 France had tentative agreements with Saudi Arabia, Abu Dhabi, and Iran to trade Mirage jets and petroleum refining and industrial equipment for crude oil; similar deals were also announced for Britain, West Germany, and Japan. However, there are many barriers to a large number of such deals being finally consummated. Nevertheless, they do pose serious problems for the United States, since presumably in such direct government-to-government deals the oil companies would not get their usual profits. This would then cut into the protective cushion the American companies form for the U.S. balance of payments.

Therefore we are left with the following conclusion. At present prices of oil, in the next few years Western Europe and Japan would be badly hurt while the United States would be greatly strengthened vis-à-vis these countries. However, since the United States has a big stake in investment and trade with Western Europe and Japan, a collapse there is not to U.S. advantage and hence to be avoided. It is quite conceivable, however, that the U.S. strategy is to try to walk the tightrope of benefiting from Western Europe's and Japan's weakened position in the short run while not allowing the latter's situation to deteriorate to complete collapse.

Now, after the October War, the United States is in an even better position to sit back and watch the treasuries of Japan and Western Europe being relatively quickly emptied, figuring to share these riches with the OPEC countries. If and when a point is reached where oil prices threaten to harm the United States, either directly or through a collapse of the other developed countries, then it could use its power to try to pressure the OPEC governments to reduce prices, with the ultimate threat being military intervention.

However, since military intervention would raise the danger of confrontation with the Soviet Union as well as of prolonged guerrilla warfare in the Middle East, it will not be chosen lightly. But it is a very real possibility. Trial balloons were sent up after the October War by everyone from Senators Fulbright and Jackson to Secretary of State Kissinger to Secretary of Defense Schlesinger. But with the American people sick of war and suspicious of the oil companies and the president (according to the polls at that time the majority of people blamed the oil crisis on the oil companies and the government and not the Arabs) intervention may not have been tenable. Instead such warnings may have been directed at preserving the privileged position of U.S. oil companies in the Middle East. That is to say, the saber-rattling may have been a not so subtle way of warning the OPEC governments not to truly nationalize American oil companies in the Middle East nor to set prices so as to reduce the companies' profitability sharply.

In any event, this is a most tricky and dangerous game for the United States, threatening to plunge the world into a war—or a major depression. Ironically, a major economic crash in the Western world would also help "solve" the oil problem by drastically reducing the demand for oil and hence putting strong downward pressure on the price. Indeed, the developed countries have long been teetering on the edge of a financial breakdown which would precipitate a major world depression; the international oil crisis might yet be just the factor necessary to tip the world economy over the precipice. After all, nothing on the world scene indicates the degree of coordination necessary among capitalist powers to prevent the recurrence of a severe depression.[2]

[2] The OPEC countries do not have the power to stop this process of decline, because its roots run much deeper and lie in the basic rivalries in the developed capitalist world. Given the likelihood that an economic deluge is in the cards regardless of what OPEC does, the only rational course for its members is to pile up as much money and resources as possible aboard their own Noah's Ark.

Moreover, in a fundamental sense what is involved as a result of increased OPEC crude oil prices is the long overdue need for a sizable shift of real resources from the developed countries to the oil-producing countries. The huge economies of the developed countries are certainly capable of making these resources available, not only to the oil-producing countries but also to all the world's underdeveloped countries.

39. U.S. OIL PLAN: HIGH PRICE IS KEY

by Leonard Silk

United States strategy for dealing with the international oil crisis continues to unfold, layer by layer. Last week's major development was the disclosure by Secretary of State Kissinger of American plans to negotiate a new $25-billion special oil fund for relending petrodollars to Western nations in deep balance-of-payments deficit.

Now comes the unveiling of the American plan for narrowing the gap between Western energy needs and dependency on im-

Abridged from the *New York Times* (November 27, 1974). Leonard Silk, a financial columnist and member of the editorial board of the *New York Times,* is the author of *Nixonomics: How the Dismal Science of Free Enterprise Became the Black Art of Control* (New York, Praeger, 1972).

ported oil from producers of the Organization of Petroleum Exporting Countries.

It is basically a high-price, high domestic production strategy.

The new plan was disclosed this week in a forum at Yale University, by Thomas O. Enders, Assistant Secretary of State for Economic and Business Affairs. Mr. Enders is regarded by insiders as the chief architect of Secretary of State Kissinger's energy policy including the International Energy Agency, the oil-sharing program for industrial nations, and the $25-billion petro-dollar recycling fund.

The rationale for the new United States strategy for closing the energy gap stems from the massive Project Independence report, released two weeks ago by the Federal Energy Administration.

That report set forth two basic patterns that would result from either (a) acceptance of an $11 price per barrel of crude oil in the world market or (b) early reduction of the world oil price to $7 a barrel.

As the F.E.A. data indicate, the rate of growth of domestic production would be much faster at $11 than $7, and there would be a far greater drag on the growth of oil consumption. By 1985, at the $11 price, according to the F.E.A.'s study, the expanded supply of oil—plus expanded output of coal and nuclear energy—could eliminate the need for imported oil.

But at the $7 price per barrel of oil, the gap could widen to about 13 million barrels a day, or more than half of all the United States' petroleum needs. The American dependency—and probably foreign dependency as well—on OPEC oil would increase rather than narrow, according to the F.E.A. projections.

The startling news broken by Mr. Enders at Yale—startling against the background of repeated declarations of high American officials that OPEC nations must reduce their exorbitantly high prices—is that the United States is now founding its strategy on the $11 price. This assumes, incidentally, a "real" price of that magnitude, one that would rise step by step with other goods, if world inflation continues.

Without following the Project Independence blueprint slavishly, nor limiting his analysis to the United States alone, Mr. Enders stated that the present high world prices—starting at about $10 a barrel F.O.B. for Persian Gulf crude—had started a worldwide oil boom.

"Substantial finds of oil have been reported from Mexico, Peru, China, Indonesia," he said, "and the wave of exploration is just beginning."

He estimated that the finds already made represent the possibility of new production a few years from now of 10 million barrels a day—"and more will follow."

OPEC members will try to sustain the high price by cutting production. They are now working at less than three-quarters of capacity, according to Mr. Enders. How long they can sustain the existing price will depend on how fast the world market develops for oil. Thus cuts in consumption—resulting primarily from the high price of oil—in the United States and by other major industrial users is crucial to breaking the cartel, if it is to be broken.

Mr. Enders implied that the United States thinks the cartel could fall apart. If demand is restrained, and new supply from non-OPEC producers comes to market, negotiation of the required cutbacks in production by OPEC would become more and more difficult: "First clandestine, then open violation of production quotas would occur. Ultimately all efforts to sustain the artificial price would collapse," he said.

Paradoxically, however, the United States is worried that such a downward break in world oil prices could come too soon, and be devastating for heavy American and other Western investment in the development of alternative energy sources, based on the assumption of a continued "real" oil price of $11 a barrel.

What is important, Mr. Enders argues, is that all the major oil companies adopt policies having the effect of creating stable investment expectations at a level of return roughly equivalent to current oil prices, protected for price increases; he wants "an international agreement to embody this fundamental decision."

This is what, in informal discussion, he called the Catch-22 of the United States position: It is designed to reduce Western dependency on foreign oil and ultimately break the OPEC oil price, but when the oil price comes down, the United States and its partners will hold up their own oil prices to protect high-cost domestic production.

In other words—for the sake of illustration—if the world oil

price dropped to $5 a barrel before the Western oil coalition—
which might be called anti-OPEC—was ready, the United States
and its partners would continue to pay $11 to their domestic
producers.

Foreign oil would then enter this country only at about the
$11 price, with the United States Government collecting the $6
difference, whether via a tariff, through a Governmental oil-
importing agency, or some other device. The foreign oil would be
sold to domestic distributors at a price that would not shake
current domestic production or jeopardize domestic investment
in future energy development.

Thus as the price for foreign oil came down before 1985—and
Mr. Enders made clear that he expected it to come down substantially—the United States and its partners would move toward
a two-tier cost structure for energy: "One that assures the consuming countries their desired degree of independence; the other
balances a constant demand and growing supply for imported oil
at prices that diminished, or even reversed, the accumulation of
assets by producers," he said.

If this country and others do not follow such a strategy, he
said, new investment stimulated by current high prices would
proceed anyway, if less rapidly. But when the world price fell—
later and less markedly—much of the investment now undertaken would no longer be viable. It would either have to be
protected after the fact, or the United States and others would
have to "succumb again to the comforts and vulnerabilities of
reliance on cheap imported oil."

Does this plan make sense? Is it in accord with the facts and
reasonable expectations about the way nations—not only the
European nations and Japan but even the United States itself,
with Congress and the voters generally exerting their influence
on Government—can be expected to react to what is clearly an
extremely costly, long-term program for stimulating and protecting domestic oil and other energy producers?

J. K. Jamieson, chairman and chief executive officer of the
Exxon Corporation, who was on the program with Mr. Enders at
Yale, found the United States plan "over-optimistic." Mr. Jamieson said the F.E.A. had overestimated future oil production in
this country on several accounts.

For instance, he maintained that the F.E.A. was expecting far too much from secondary and tertiary oil recovery. "All fields are already under secondary recovery," he said, "and there is no current technology for tertiary recovery that would not require energy inputs in excess of the energy output."

Mr. Jamieson also believes that the United States Government has been overoptimistic on nuclear power and other energy sources. However, the Project Independence report was relatively cautious about the rate of growth of other energy supplies, even including coal.

Prof. James Tobin of Yale, a former member of the President's Council of Economic Advisers, raised questions about the cost of the program and whether it was the most economic way either to protect the United States oil supplies or to deal with the problem of the transfer of wealth to the OPEC countries.

Mr. Tobin argued that there might be cheaper ways "to buy insurance"—as through increased storage or stand-by production capacity.

The political feasibility of the Kissinger-Enders plan is also questionable. Other nations, such as France, might refuse to go along—and, if the United States and its partners did succeed in driving down the world oil price, the outsiders would have a clear cost advantage in production and competition in world trade— in effect, a free ride resulting from the sacrifices of "anti-OPEC."

Questions can also be raised about the very heavy emphasis on expanding production at high cost and the relatively light stress on conservation. President Ford has thus far backed an essentially "voluntary" program of restraining consumption, resisting proposals even for moderate increases in gasoline taxes.

But the new program could send gasoline taxes far higher— unless, as is possible, the United States still had, in addition to two tiers for world and domestic prices, two or more additional tiers for "old" and "new" oil produced in the United States, as now.

Mr. Jamieson of Exxon estimated that, at an average price of $11 a barrel for crude oil, the price of a gallon of gasoline in the United States would be 88 cents—far higher than the price at the pump that would result from even a 20 cent rise in the gasoline tax.

In response to criticism that the Administration had under-stressed conservation and in fact had no real conservation plan,

Mr. Enders disclosed that a new daily and weekly monitoring program would begin by which the F.E.A. would measure the shortfall, if any, between oil consumption and a target for restrained fuel consumption.

If the United States did fall behind the President's goal of a reduction of 1 million barrels a day in consumption—that is, below what it otherwise would have been, not an actual reduction—he might propose a stiffer plan for cutting consumption.

Mr. Enders said the President "will make final his Project Independence proposals for submission to Congress in January" —and at the same time, the new International Energy Agency would consider joint decisions on conservation and energy investment policy.

He suggested that going it alone was not a viable energy policy for any oil-consuming nation today, and that over the coming decade, only the United States and Britain can go to self-sufficiency—all the others would "remain vulnerable to a new embargo."

Meanwhile, all the nations would be vulnerable, he said, "to financial crisis, and if the United States and Britain can solve the price and financial transfer problem by going self-sufficient, the only way Europe and Japan can is by cooperating with each other and with us."

Behind the United States position on energy, as developed by Mr. Enders, is the belief that the only way the United States can get a handle on the crisis is via its international dangers—and that is also the only way Americans can be brought to see the urgency of the crisis.

The steady and vastly mounting flow of arms to the Middle East, from France, the United States and others, to pay for oil imports, is one dimension of the problem to which Mr. Enders did not address himself. But that may be the most critical dimension of all.

And the most paradoxical aspect is that the United States, in fighting to bring down the OPEC price, means to keep its own price high.

40. THE EMERGENCE OF ARAB AND IRANIAN FINANCE CAPITAL

by Ernest Mandel

The increase in oil prices since the October War of 1973 has considerably increased the currency incomes of the oil-producing countries, especially the Arab oil producers and Iran. This enormous income—estimated to reach $75,000 million during 1974—can be utilized in the following ways:

1. It can be hoarded, that is, held by central banks in the form of backing for national currencies or in the form of gold or currency hoarded by private proprietors.

2. It can be placed on a short-term basis in foreign banks or international institutions or utilized to purchase public short-term bonds in the imperialist countries (treasury bonds).

3. It can be spent unproductively on importing materials that do not enter into the process of reproduction of commodities: arms, luxury items, and so on.

4. It can be used to import productive goods serving to accelerate the accumulation of capital and the production of commodities within the oil-producing countries. (Imports of food and consumer commodities serving to reproduce the labor force also fall into this category.)

5. It can be put into long-term investments abroad. Here several categories must be distinguished:

Abridged from "An Arab and Iranian Finance Capital Emerges," in *Intercontinental Press* (November 4, 1974). Ernest Mandel, editor in chief of the Belgian weekly *La Gauche,* is the author of the two-volume treatise entitled *Marxist Economic Theory* (New York, Monthly Review Press, 1969).

· investments in liquid values (stocks and bonds)
· nonliquid investments
· buying of shares in industrial, financial, commercial, or transport companies and the creation of new firms of this type with participation in the management.

Of these five forms of utilization of "petrodollars," only the first has a deflationary effect on the economy of the imperialist countries and may therefore be considered a supplementary, although extremely marginal, factor in the economic recession now under way. To speak, as do certain politicians in imperialist countries, of "sixty thousand million dollars withdrawn from the Western economy" because of the balance-of-payments deficits of some imperialist countries is to forget that the majority of this $60,000 million remains in the West or is returned there in the form of payment for supplementary commodity purchases or in the form of various investments.

In fact, the opposite thesis has much greater foundation. By being placed on a short-term basis in American or European banks, petrodollars feed the inflation of credit and thereby the inflation of paper money rather than contributing to deflation.

At present, it is difficult to estimate the proportion in which the income of the oil producers is divided among the five means of utilization mentioned above. In general, however, it can be estimated that $30,000 million will be used in 1974 to increase imports of commodities and to make various investments within the oil-producing countries (categories 3 and 4), while $35,000 million will be invested abroad (categories 2 and 5), the rest most probably being hoarded.

The investment programs already planned by the oil-producing countries for coming years are extremely extensive. Saudi Arabia has developed a five-year plan whose budget is about $60,000 million (at the current value); Algeria has a four-year plan for 1974–77 calling for $22,000 million of investments. Kuwait plans to invest more than $4,000 million in the 1974–75 fiscal year alone. It can thus be predicted that the cumulative balance-of-payments deficits of the imperialist countries arising from the high oil prices, all other things being equal, will diminish considerably in coming years because of the increase in the supplies of equipment, patents, and technical assistance they will send to the oil-producing countries. This is not true of the balance-of-payments deficits of the semicolonial countries that do not export oil; their deficits threaten to worsen.

A New Finance Capital Emerges

At the Tenth World Congress of the Fourth International, many delegates were surprised, and probably even a little shocked, at our assertion that the enormous and rapid accumulation of capital in the hands of the owning classes of the oil-producing countries due to the big rise in oil prices was giving rise to the emergence of a new, autonomous Arab and Iranian finance capital.

Since that time, what had appeared as a potential tendency has fully flowered. The purchase by the shah of Iran of 25 percent of the stock of the West German Krupp trust was the generally perceived signal of the appearance of a new, independent sector of international finance capital.

Finance capital is banking capital (money capital) that is invested in the productive sector (industry, transportation, etc.) and participates in the control of these sectors, even monopolizing that control. In this sense, it is distinct from *rentier* capital, which is content to hold stock portfolios and clip coupons.

The case of the Iranian bourgeoisie, which henceforth will be represented in the administrative council of the Krupp trust, is in no way an isolated example. In the field of real estate, the Kuwait Investment Company, founded in 1961, has bought the island of Kiawah in the United States, where it intends to create a big tourist center. It has taken a predominant share of a redevelopment project in the center of the city of Atlanta, Georgia, also in the United States. It has launched a gigantic public offer (a total of $260 million) for the St. Martin's Property Corporation in London. It has also acquired control of two maritime companies, one linking Cyprus and Britain, the other linking England to Ireland.

In the Arab countries themselves, Arab finance capital, associated with big imperialist monopolies (with the Arabs often holding financial and political control), is engaged in a whole series of major industrial projects. The Saudi Arabian company Petromin, together with the Marcona international consortium (including American, Japanese, and West German groups), is building a $500 million metallurgical factory in the Jubail region of Arabia. The Arab Maritime Petroleum Transport Company owns four oil tankers with a total value of $240 million. The emirate of Abu Dhabi is launching a $300 million project to build a liquefied-gas factory on Das island in association with an American and a Japanese group.

Veritable banks and investment companies (in which Arab or Iranian finance capital is generally dominant) have been created in association with the greatest names in imperialist finance capital in order to finance industrial and other projects. Some examples are: the Union des Banques Arabes et Françaises (Crédit Lyonnais); the Banque Arabe et Internationale d'Investissements (with a consortium of thirteen European banks); the Compagnie Arabe et Internationale d'Investissements.

The balance sheet is clear: We are dealing here with the activity of enterprising finance capital and not with a parasitic rentier capital.

Just Stooges for the Oil Trusts?

Two objections have generally been advanced to our thesis that a new autonomous Arab and Iranian finance capital has emerged.

According to the first group of critics, the Arab and Iranian governments and businessmen are nothing but stooges for the oil companies, particularly of the Rockefeller group (Exxon, formerly Esso). A number of factors have been variously cited in support of this objection: the enormous superprofits raked in by these trusts since the October War; the fact that a not negligible part of the petrodollars are deposited in the Rockefeller-controlled Chase Manhattan Bank; the sensational reentry of the Rockefeller group into the Egyptian market; the policy of Kissinger (a former adviser, very well paid, of Rockefeller) obligating Israel to gradually withdraw from some of the occupied Arab territories.

It is incontestable that these trusts have made fat profits from the oil price increases decided on by the governments of the cartel of oil exporters. It should be stressed that this includes not only American trusts, but European ones as well, Royal Dutch Shell and British Petroleum, for example. There is no reason to deny that there is a certain confluence of interest between the Arab and Iranian finance capital (and governments) on the one hand and the imperialist oil trusts on the other.

But it is one thing to affirm that there is a certain confluence of interest between two separate and autonomous groups of capitalist proprietors and quite another thing to affirm that there is an identity of interests between them or that one group is clearly subordinate to the other. It is sufficient to examine the development of the "oil crisis" during past months to see that the thesis of an identity of interest between the Arab and Iranian owning classes and the imperialist oil trusts is untenable.

During the last meeting of the OPEC (Organization of Petroleum Exporting Countries), it was decided not to change the sales price of oil, but only to increase the charges and taxes payable by the trusts. The exporting countries warned the Western consumers that any new increase in the consumer price would be the result not of an arbitrary decision of the Arab and Iranian governments but of the refusal of the trusts to pay for the taxes by reducing their superprofits.

More important than that decision, which nevertheless had a symbolic value, is the fact that the governments of the Arab countries are now transferring ownership of the oil wells—to their own benefit and at the expense of the imperialist trusts. Exactly how the nationalization of Aramco corresponds to the "interests" of the Rockefeller group is a mystery that our critics have yet to shed light on.

It is obvious that what unites all these owning classes is not a common political interest or project, but the possibility at a given moment in the history of international capitalism in decline of *profiting from a major redistribution of the surplus value extracted on a world scale from the proletariat and semiproletariat.* This redistribution is to take place at the expense of the imperialist bourgeoisie and to the profit of the bourgeoisie of *certain* semicolonial countries.

To get an idea of the enormous haul that is involved here, one must take account of the fact that the average cost of extracting one barrel of oil in the Middle East does not exceed 10 to 12 U.S. cents. Two years ago, the oil companies were asking $2 to $3 for that barrel! Today, they are selling it for $11.65 (to which, obviously, must be added the profits they make in transportation, refining, wholesale reselling, etc.). But of that $11.65, the amount of surplus value going to the owning classes of the exporting countries was $9.23 before October 1, 1974, and has been $9.74 since that date. Before October 10, 1974, $2.42 remained in the hands of the oil companies ($1.99 since that date). *That still represents more than ten times the cost of extraction!*

Once upon a time, the surplus value was divided 90% for the oil trusts and 10% for the local owning classes. Later, the proportion moved to 75%–25%, then to 67%–33%, then to 50%–50%. It has now been turned around to 20%–80%, if one considers only the price of the oil exported by the producing countries. Taking account of all the profits made by the trusts in transport, refining, distribution, and so forth, the division is still not very far from 40%–60%.

Revenge of the Third World?

The second objection to our thesis of the emergence of an autonomous Arab and Iranian finance capital comes from a diametrically opposite direction from the first. It affirms that it is not a question of a re-division of profits among possessing classes, but rather of a general revenge by the "Third World," a counterattack of the "poor countries" against the "rich countries." There are countries, this thesis runs, who have based the whole of their "prosperity" on "cheap energy." This era has now been turned around. The *peoples* of the "Third World" are now going to improve their living standards at the expense of the rich *peoples*. Furthermore, is it not true that most of the petrodollars are held by state or public institutions? How can one talk of "finance capital" when one is dealing with public property? Won't the income in dollars benefit all the inhabitants of the exporting countries?

Let us state right off the bat that the claim that the Arab and Iranian banks and investment companies are all or nearly all public institutions is vastly exaggerated. The Kuwait Foreign Trading Contracting and Investment Company has 25% of its stock in private hands. In the Kuwait Investment Company, the private shares account for as much as 50%. In most of the joint banking ventures referred to above, the private stockholders are not all foreigners; some are Arabs. Their share of the stock approaches or surpasses 50%.

Next, let us recall that in the semicolonial countries the separation between "public" and "private" is often largely fictitious, just as it was during the era of primitive accumulation of capital in Europe during the sixteenth, seventeenth, and eighteenth centuries. The sheikhs, emirs, and kings treat the public budget as their own private domain. Corruption, theft, and extortion are the classic sources of *private* accumulation of capital by the high dignitaries and functionaries of all these countries.

The assertion that the "Arab masses" as a whole will benefit from the oil price increase is true only in the exceptional and marginal cases of very sparsely populated countries like Kuwait.

The notion of "Arab solidarity" is scarcely appropriate as far as distribution of investment of surplus value is concerned. In this regard, let us cite the British daily *The Guardian* of October 9, 1974: "The fact is that immense question marks hang over the security and profitability of large-scale investment in the Third World. And in this respect, the Gulf oil rulers or the shah of Iran operates on as faultless a capitalist basis as any corporation or bank in London or New York."

If that's where "Arab solidarity" stands, even more of the same goes for "solidarity of the peoples of the Third World." Of an expected net oil income for 1974 of $75,000 million, the oil-exporting countries will accord only about $3,000 million to the semicolonial non-oil-exporting countries in the form of aid. That is but a fraction of the additional expenses that will be imposed on these countries by the rise in oil prices.

To be sure, the investment of a part of the growing income of petrodollars in some Arab countries and Iran will accelerate the economic development of these countries. They will thus end up having an infrastructure, including an infrastructure for heavy industry, which will favor their industrialization. That, after all, is what capital, finance capital included, accomplished in other countries, in other epochs, and under other circumstances. But here it is a matter of a *capitalist* development, which in no way will guarantee a rapid, not to mention automatic, rise in the living standards of the masses (except, we repeat, in half-empty countries like Kuwait and Libya).

41. PETRODOLLARS FOR PHANTOMS: THE ARMS BUILD-UPS IN IRAN AND SAUDI ARABIA

by Michael T. Klare

Without doubt future historians will speak of 1973 as a "watershed" year in United States relations with the oil kingdoms of the Persian Gulf. In October the principal Arab oil suppliers, led by Saudi Arabia, imposed an embargo on petroleum exports to the United States as a penalty for U.S. support of Israel, and later U.S. Secretary of State Henry Kissinger embarked upon an unprecedented diplomatic campaign designed to mobilize Arab support for the U.S. peace plan in the Middle East. While the embargo and diplomatic blitz filled the headlines and captured world attention, another set of events—involving substantial U.S. weapons sales to friendly Persian Gulf powers—contributed significantly to the upheaval in American relations with the area:

· First, on February 21, 1973, Defense Department officials acknowledged that Iran had contracted to buy over $2 billion worth of U.S. weapons in what government officials termed the biggest single arms deal ever negotiated by the Pentagon. Included in the deal were 175 modern jet fighters, 500 helicopters, air-to-surface missiles and other advanced weapons.

· Next, on May 26, the Pentagon confirmed that the White House agreed to sell advanced military aircraft—including F-4 Phantom fighter-bombers and F-5E supersonic fighters—to Saudi

Excerpts from "The Political Economy of Arms Sales," in *Transaction* (September-October 1974). Michael T. Klare is the author of *War Without End: American Planning for the Next Vietnams* (New York, Knopf, 1972).

Arabia and Kuwait. Although both countries later joined the oil embargo and provided substantial economic support to the nations battling Israel, these offers were not withdrawn.

· Finally, In the last week of August, Shah Muhammad Reza Pahlevi of Iran became the first foreign leader to be invited to place orders for America's newest jet aircraft, the Grumman F-14 Tomcat, in the first instance of a Third World country being permitted to purchase a major new U.S. weapon ahead of our principal allies in NATO.

These decisions constituted a radical shift in U.S. policy on weapons exports to the troubled Gulf area. Whereas during most of the post-World War II era U.S. policymakers favored a policy of restraint in arms sales to the region, under the Nixon administration the United States has become the principal arms supplier to the Persian Gulf Kingdoms and has authorized deliveries of highly sophisticated and potent weapons. According to one American official, the United States is selling Iran "most everything short of atomic weapons." Although this policy shift is usually attributed to the growing Soviet presence in the area (as reflected by Soviet military aid to Iran and South Yemen), the dramatic increase in military sales is in fact motivated by several interrelated political-military objectives:

1. To encourage and assist Iran and Saudi Arabia to assume the role of regional "police" powers, and thereby to insure America's continued access to the area's petroleum wealth.
2. To help defend the region's conservative monarchies against internal threats to their continued rule, and thus to facilitate the first objective.
3. To discourage the Soviet Union or any other external power from challenging America's role as the principal supporter of the Gulf autocracies.

These concerns are complemented by powerful economic considerations—particularly the pressing need to offset the mounting flow of U.S. dollars to major oil producers. (The recent price increase alone will provide the oil states with another $40 billion.) By selling modern weapons to the Gulf powers, it is argued, the United States can repossess some of the "petrodollars" that otherwise would pile up in Middle East bank accounts and presumably pose an independent threat to U.S. economic stability. National security and economic health are thus closely linked in the Pentagon's rationale for increased arms exports to these countries; any restriction on such sales, Deputy Secretary of Defense William P. Clements told Congress in 1973, "decreases the potential contribution of sales . . . to strengthening both free world security and the U.S. economy and balance-of-payments position."

Although U.S. arms sales to the Gulf states do not yet match its spending on the area's oil products, they are already considerable and rising rapidly. Between 1971 and 1973, for instance, Iran and Saudi Arabia jointly spent $3.6 billion on American weapons, or three times what they spent during the preceding 20 years. Iran, which has now replaced West Germany as the principal importer of U.S. military aircraft, is expected to spend upwards of $9 billion on U.S. arms by the end of the decade; Saudi and Kuwait purchases, while not as staggering, are nevertheless expected to enrich U.S. weapons manufacturers by several billions of dollars.

The choice of Iran as a regional police power is entirely logical from the State Department's point of view: Iran has long constituted a key link in the cold war chain of alliances designed to "contain" Soviet influence in Eurasia, and the shah has consistently opposed an increased Soviet role in Gulf affairs. When Washington sought to extend Iran's military role to include policing of the entire Gulf area, it found a ready reception in Tehran, where the King of Kings, Shah Pahlevi, has entertained grandiose schemes of resurrecting the great Persian empire. In pursuit of his dream in 1972, the shah seized several small islands in the Strait of Hormuz which had been claimed by the United Arab Emirates, and Iranian commandos have been deployed in Oman to help overcome the Dhofari rebels. Iran now has the strongest naval force in the Gulf, and the shah has announced plans to extend Iran's "defense perimeter" to the western Indian Ocean; he has already negotiated a basing arrangement with the government of Mauritius. When the advanced weapons now on order from the United States are delivered, Iran will possess the strongest military force between the Mediterranean and the Indian Ocean and will rank among the world's top ten military powers.

Saudi Arabia has emerged as a major regional power only

within the past few years, but already the United States has striven to provide King Faisal with a modern military apparatus. At present some 350 U.S. military and civilian technicians are stationed in the country to help train Saudi soldiers to operate the new U.S. weapons being supplied under the Pentagon's Foreign Military Sales program. Saudi Arabia is expected to spend at least $1 billion on U.S. arms in the next few years, and the total sum could go much higher. Although the emphasis presently is on developing the country's defensive posture, the delivery of naval vessels and F-4 fighter-bombers will invest Saudi Arabia with the capacity to help police the entire Gulf region—a task that is energetically being advanced by Washington. "We think that Saudi Arabia has been a voice of moderation in the area," Assistant Secretary Sisco told a congressional subcommittee in 1973. "We believe that it is in the mutual interests of the United States and Saudi Arabia for the forces of moderation to retain the upper hand in this area."

For this strategy to succeed, however, it is obvious that both Iran and Saudi Arabia must continue to be governed by authoritarian, pro-Western regimes. To this end, the United States is assisting the internal security forces of both countries. In Saudi Arabia, a team of 40 U.S. advisors is providing technical assistance to the Saudi Arabian National Guard, which, according to Representative Les Aspin, "is simply a private army of Bedouins under the control of one of the sheikhs." Similarly, the United States has long provided arms and training to the Imperial Iranian Gendarmerie, a paramilitary security force.

The dual requirements of a pro-Western police presence in the Gulf and the perpetuation of conservative regimes constitute the basic rationale for the massive flow of American arms to the area.

At present, the most likely participants in a destabilizing arms race in the Persian Gulf are Iran and Iraq, which share a 600-mile-long border. Both nations have ample oil revenues with which to purchase modern arms, and both are allied with great power patrons who feel obliged to match or better the equipment supplied by their rivals. Moreover, there are divisive issues in abundance which could trigger an armed conflict. Tehran is worried about Iraqi aid to Baluchi and Khuzistani separatists in Iran, while Baghdad fears Iranian support to the Kurdish forces now battling government troops in the northeast; Iraq has complained about Iran's military presence along the Shatt-al-Arab River (Iraq's main outlet to the Persian Gulf and a common boundary); and there is an unresolved border dispute which periodically ignites violent clashes. Fueling these traditional problems, of course, are the ideological and political differences separating the anti-Communist monarchy in Tehran and the radical Ba'ath party in Baghdad. Although the USSR has provided Iraq with modern arms (including MIG-2 interceptors) worth approximately $1 billion, it has not kept pace with the U.S.-sponsored arms buildup in Iran, and it is likely that Baghdad will feel compelled to approach Moscow for further weapons deliveries—thus encouraging the shah to acquire still more arms, and so on.

Clearly, the Iranian-Iraqi rivalry will remain in an inflammatory condition for some time to come. In the long run, however, it is likely that the most dangerous Gulf rivalry will develop between America's two closest allies in the region: Saudi Arabia and Iran. Shah Pahlevi's announced intention of extending Iranian hegemony over the entire Gulf region cannot fail but provoke Saudi fears and animosities in view of their historical religious and political conflicts with Persia. (Saudi Arabia and Persia are aligned with rival Moslem sects, and there are strong ethnic animosities between the Arabs of the southern Gulf and the Aryans of Iran.) Thus, although U.S. arms policy is based on the premise stated by Assistant Secretary Sisco that "Iranian and Saudi Arabian cooperation, inter alia, is of key importance as a major element of stability in this area," it is possible that the shah's military build-up and aggressive Gulf policy will trigger a conflict with the increasingly well-armed Saudis.

Even if war is averted, the growing sales of costly military hardware will strengthen the rule of authoritarian governments while at the same time diverting scarce resources from the social and economic development programs that alone can redress the inequities prevalent in these societies. While increased oil revenues will assuredly mean wealth and affluence for some, it is obvious that most of the Gulf's residents will continue to live in abysmal poverty. In Iran, where defense expenditures consumed a whopping $2 billion in 1973, per capital income remained at only $500. And as long as the Gulf's petroleum wealth is controlled by the giant oil concerns and a handful of local families, there will be glaring gaps in income—both between classes and nations—and thus a constant danger of war and revolution. Accelerated arms deliveries can only escalate the destructiveness of any clashes that do occur, and can never alleviate the problems which arise from the very structure of the area's political and social fabric. Only a meaningful redistribution of political and economic power—recognizing the unique contributions and traditional aspirations of the area's diverse minorities—offers any promise for a "stable structure of peace" in the Persian Gulf region.

E.
Food Inflation

WITH THE POSSIBLE EXCEPTION of gasoline, nothing in the current inflationary crisis has been more frightening or more upsetting than the skyrocketing food prices. For some Americans it has meant hunger and malnutrition. One hears of woeful tales of elderly shoplifters and the increased use of dog food for human consumption. All but the wealthy have had to modify their diets to accord with economic necessity. Cartoons abound of shoppers racing their carts to the check-out counter, one step ahead of managers, who are trying to put a higher price stamp on their wares. But the situation, of course, is no joke. Vast numbers are no longer able to make ends meet, while a growing sense of despair exists that the spiral will go on forever.

Most people are as puzzled as they are worried by what has been happening. Given what passes for answers, confusion is not unnatural. We are told that the high food prices reflect the complex interaction of rising demand and reduced supply. Had it not been for a bad harvest here, a Russian wheat deal there, and an assortment here, there and everywhere of other unexpected once-in-a-lifetime events, such as the failure of the anchovy "harvest" off Peru, prices would have remained as they were. These explanations have often been accompanied by predictions that prices will soon come down. Of course, in the aggregate, they never do. Underlying these explanations is an assumption that the food economy—meaning by this term everything relating to the production and distribution of food, from the farm to the supermarket—is basically competitive. This is endlessly trumpeted by economic theorists who probably could not distinguish a heifer from a sow. The heart of orthodox micro-economics is an elaborate model of pure or perfect competition. But in an era of monopoly capital, its practitioners are hard put to locate real-world situations where they can apply the complex theories they have so painstakingly mastered. Agriculture, then, more for its past than for its present, has been seized upon as the one sector of the economy which wards off total irrelevance. Elementary textbooks lovingly apply all the theoretical paraphernalia—shifting curves of supply and demand, their price elasticities, etc.

There is only one problem. Basically it's not true! By that I mean that farming is merely one step in a process whose entirety is largely monopolized. We would laugh out of court any claims that the petroleum industry is competitive because local gas stations compete. Agriculture must be seen in this light. Moreover, farming itself is frequently monopolized as agribusiness increasingly moves into lettuce, grapes, and other fruits and vegetables. More important, government intervention in the form of crop purchases and soil-bank schemes have had the effect of raising prices and cartelizing large sections of agricultural production. Even if we accept the presence of competition at the extreme ends of the process—in farming and retailing—in between is a vast, complicated network of monopolistic practices. One wonders how many economists, droning on about supply and demand, have ever heard of Iowa Beef, a giant meat packer, or Cargill, one of a handful of oligopolistic grain dealers. Perhaps theorists might become a bit more aware of reality were they to read institutional data like the following testimony from a Senate hearing concerning the source of Thanksgiving food: "The Smithfield ham comes from ITT, the turkey is a product of Greyhound Corporation, the lettuce comes from Dow Chemical Company, the potatoes are provided by the Boeing Company and Tenneco brought the fresh fruits and vegetables. The applesauce is made available by American Brands while both Coca-Cola and Royal Crown Cola have provided the fruit juices." (Quoted in William Robbins, *The American Food Scandal,* pp. 10–11.)

Moreover, there is every indication that less visible links in the food chain are permeated with sordid and illegal practices. That this is really the situation and not exaggerated, intemperate and uninformed prejudices is confirmed by readings #42 and #43, reprinted from the respected *Wall Street Journal,* an impeccable pro-business source. The first selection, one of a number that could have been chosen, illustrates how manipulation works in the market for meat, while the second offers an explanation for the spectacular run-up in the price of sugar. Monopoly in foods is hardly confined to meat and sugar. It is almost everywhere: Campbell sells 90% of all soups; four firms have cornered almost all of the breakfast-cereal market; Del Monte rules over canned fruits and vegetables much as Gerber does baby food. One indication that monopolization of foods is growing and leading to higher and higher prices is that middlemen (to some degree a polite euphenism for monopolistic canners, packers, processors, etc.) now receive 60 cents of every dollar spent on food, instead of the 50% received two decades ago. (The preceding data are taken from reading #45, which provides a general overview of the increasingly monopolized food economy.) The presence of monopoly also explains why economists who project future declines in the price of food on the basis of increases in the supply of grain are likely to be wrong. They ignore the situation of the industry as a whole. This is not to say that from time to time declines in food prices will not take place. To the contrary—but such moments will be the exceptions that prove the rule.

Not long ago I argued in a classroom that the propping up of reactionary regimes by the various military wings of American imperialism had the effect of costing Americans their jobs when corporations relocated to where labor was forcibly docile (fascist regimes don't play games!). However, I suggested somewhat facetiously that it did mean that bananas were cheaper, having in mind the CIA coup of 1954 in Guatemala. The latter toppled the liberal Arbenz regime, which was promising to distribute unoccupied land to the peasants. Such a reform threatened to jeopardize the availability of cheap labor to the giant United Fruit Company. I see now that I was essentially wrong. United Fruit (now United Brands) had other, loftier plans for its bananas. No doubt the inflationary story of Chiquita (reading #44) has its amusing aspects, but its implications are anything but funny. It is part of the unending process of the monopolization of the American economy, bringing with it higher prices and a transfer of income from poor to rich.

Monopolization in food is more than a question of price. What we eat has less and less taste, as any aficionado(-a) of tomatoes knows well; our foods are adulterated to such an extent—and this is common knowledge—that they contain large numbers of harmful, even life-threatening, substances. Finally, we are pressured into buying enormous quantities of profitable but nutritionally valueless, even harmful, junk foods. Regarding the latter, an orthodox economist might snobbishly remark, "It's a free country. You don't have to buy what you don't want." Try telling that to a busy parent whose child begs for a Hostess Twinkie, which she saw lusciously advertised on television. The truth is that people, especially the poor, pay more for Chiquita bananas (and scores of other products) because they are led to believe through manipulative advertising that Chiquitas are better when they are not. Unfortunately, as long as food is produced by corporations for profit, we can expect a continuation of these and other pernicious developments.

Finally, it is necessary to come to grips with the international aspects of the problem. (Omitted, and beyond the scope of this book, is the dreadful tragedy of mass starvation over much of the face of the globe, as well as the shameful American response to it.) Reading #46 is an analysis of the Soviet wheat deal and of the key and expanding role which food exports play in alleviating the deficits in America's balance of payments. In this way, food links up with energy and the rest of the international aspects of the contemporary crisis. Putting it all together is the final reading (#47), which summarizes the findings of a food project undertaken by a special group (PEA) of the Union for Radical Political Economics. (On these organizations, consult Suggested Readings.)

Our discussion of the crisis in food began with soaring prices and finished with the balance of payments. The truth is the whole, as Hegel once said, and the whole is an international capitalist system. Those who would seriously seek to roll back the food prices ought to be aware of the fact that they must challenge an entire social system.

42. THE MEAT MARKET: FREE OR RIGGED?

by Jonathan Kwitny

Every market day, in a ramshackle old house on Chicago's
Near North Side, Lester I. Norton produces a price report known
nationally in the meat trade as the Yellow Sheet. He has worked
on the report since it started in 1923, and has been its publisher
since 1948.

The [industry] sources estimate that half the wholesale meat
sales are directly governed by that price: They are contracted in
advance for delivery on a particular date and priced "at the
sheet"—that is, the meat will be sold at the price Mr. Norton's
report says is prevailing in the market on the day the transaction
is consummated with perhaps an adjustment for transportation,
processing or other costs.

Mr. Norton doesn't dispute these estimates. But he does dispute the suggestion—increasingly being made—that prices in the
Yellow Sheet are manipulated, mostly by major packing companies, for whom a price swing of a penny or two a pound on
carcass meat can mean millions of dollars in profits.

Meat brokers, wholesalers, processors and even some packers
poured out accusations of price-rigging in recent interviews with
this reporter.

No one interviewed by The Wall Street Journal questioned
Mr. Norton's integrity, or his desire to quote prices fairly. But
they contended that the Yellow Sheet's staff of nine elderly reporters (Mr. Norton calls them "mature"), working by tele-

Excerpts from "'Yellow Sheet' Guides Prices of Most Meat, but How
Reliable Is It?," in the *Wall Street Journal* (December 6, 1974). Jonathan
Kwitny is a staff reporter on the paper.

phone, are hopelessly unable to cut through the clever devices of men trying to jimmy the market.

"They got a hell of a lot of people lying to them," says John Sullivan, vice president of United Brokers Inc., Chicago, one of the few sources who didn't object to his name's being used. "A bunch of people saying they sold higher, and a bunch of other people saying they bought lower, and very few honest people in between."

The tales of price manipulation—combined with stories of racketeering, bribery and extortion in the meat industry, detailed in this newspaper in September—create an almost Alice-in-Wonderland picture of how steaks, chops and hamburger wind up priced the way they are in American supermarkets.

The Yellow Sheet reporters, mostly former packing-company employes, interview hundreds of sellers, buyers and brokers by telephone daily to determine the prices charged for various kinds and grades of meat.

Mr. Norton acknowledges that his reporters probably discover only 25% of what he calls the "open market" sales on a given day. No one is under any obligation to phone information to the Yellow Sheet or to respond to its requests for information. Moreover, most sales aren't considered open-market because they are based on the prearranged contracts often governed by the Yellow Sheet itself. So the Yellow Sheet may reflect only a small part of the day's sales. Some industry sources say the sheet's sample may be much less than 10% and therefore would be easy to manipulate.

Yet the sheet fills a need. "Nobody likes the damn Yellow Sheet," says Roy Lee Jr., a Houston consultant and former president of Iowa Beef Processors Inc., the world's largest beef firm. "Still, [it's] the best reflection of market price that's in existence and . . . everybody uses it."

But protests have been muted. Most of the buyers, sellers and brokers interviewed for this article insisted that their names be withheld. One prominent Chicago broker said, "If these packers figure you're hurting them, they're not going to give you any meat to sell."

Various sources displayed invoices and other records, however, indicating that the real price of meat among insiders in the stockyards district of Chicago, for example, often is quite different from the prices reported in the Yellow Sheet.

The sources complained that manipulation is largely responsible for the unprecedented swings in prices that have beset the wholesale meat industry in the past few years, clipping ranchers on the low end of the swing and the meat-eating public on the high end.

Several sources said that supermarket chains keep prices geared to the upper end of the spectrum, even when the Yellow Sheet price drops temporarily. One former packinghouse executive asked, "Why should the chains lower prices if they're just going to go right back up again?"

"There's something wrong in the meat business to account for these wide gyrations in price," says an official of the U.S. Department of Agriculture. "It didn't used to happen. I have a lot of suspicions about things that go on in this business not being ethical, but you can't put your finger on it."

Many sources in the industry did try to put their fingers on it. They described three basic manipulative devices:

First Alleged Scheme: the packer-to-packer highball. Hypothetical example: A major packing company has several 100-carload contracts to deliver beef "at the sheet" as of the close of market on a Thursday. That afternoon, with the market lingering around Wednesday's close of, say, 61 cents a pound for the particular grade of beef involved, the packer approaches another packer and asks to buy two carloads of the beef to fill an alleged shortage. The first packer bids 63 cents a pound. The deal is transacted and reported to the Yellow Sheet, which—accurately—reports a closing transaction of 63 cents, and doesn't mention names. Thus a two-carload sale (a carload contains roughly 40,000 pounds) raises the price of the pre-arranged 100-carload sales by two cents a pound, or by $80,000 for each 100 carloads. By the time the meat reaches the dinner table, this two-cent increase can become five or 10 cents a pound. Allegedly, packers will return these favors for each other as needed.

Specific examples of such a scheme, if they exist, would require either a confession from a packer or a thorough examination of the Yellow Sheet's information (and to the extent that the sheet keeps records, they are confidential).

But a former sales employe of one of the country's largest

packers, and a major buyer of meat from the same packing company, both confirmed that the company's sales executives regularly plan to rig the sheet upward in this manner on days for which heavy sales have been contracted in advance.

According to the former sales employe, who is now in another phase of the meat business, the major packing company also tries to rig the sheet down on days when it has contracted to buy cattle. Neither source would allow himself or the company to be identified in print, on the ground that they relied for their livelihood on the continued supply of meat from the company.

Earl Tromberg, in charge of sales for another packing company, Spencer Foods Inc., when asked about any packer-to-packer market-rigging scheme, says, "I guess we've all tried that to some degree." Asked about the same thing, Mr. Tromberg's boss, Spencer president Jerry Kozney, simply observes, "You could go to jail for doing something like that." Both Mr. Tromberg and Mr. Kozney are former employes of Iowa Beef.

Mr. Tromberg insists that Spencer, a relatively small packer, usually gets whip-sawed in the price manipulation. He even complains that some wholesalers (who buy meat from packers, process it and sell it to retailers) use similar tactics to drive down the Yellow Sheet price so that they can buy meat cheaper under prearranged contracts.

"On Monday of this week," Mr. Tromberg recalled on Nov. 13, "I was looking for Yield Grade 3 steers [the government ranks steers in five yield grades] and I couldn't find any. I checked with some competitors and they were looking for them, too. I would have paid up-money for them. Yet he [Mr. Norton] took them off a dollar and a half [1½ cents a pound]" in the Yellow Sheet. Mr. Tromberg said he was suspicious of the lowered price in the sheet, but can't prove tampering.

An executive of another small packing firm in the Midwest says, "My sales people have reported that the sheet has gone up or down without any real reason. It didn't make sense. It was the result of someone rigging the market. Any large packer could go out and buy these cattle cheaper after he pushes the market down, and then push the market back up when he is ready to sell." The executive readily names the packers he suspects but says he can't prove they are guilty of rigging.

Mr. Norton acknowledges that the Yellow Sheet accepts

packer-to-packer sales as a basis for price reporting. "You're suggesting there's something wrong with a packer dealing with another packer, and there isn't," he says. "They're short that day and they need meat."

"It goes on all the time," says Roy Green, a spokesman for giant Swift & Co., a subsidiary of Esmark Inc. "Our sales unit will buy from another packer if it's close and they need meat." As for rigged deals to change the market price, Mr. Green says he has heard rumors about them, but "we know of no such deals —we have never been part of any."

Second Alleged Scheme: the high-low processor split. Hypothetical example: A packer (which slaughters cattle) and a processor (which cuts them up and wholesales the meat, functions that may be performed by the packer itself) want a 15-carload transaction at 60 cents a pound. But the packer, with heavy orders scheduled to be sold that day "at the sheet," is riding a recently highballed price of 62 cents reported to the Yellow Sheet and doesn't want to lower the market just before the close. So the packer sells 10 carloads at 59 cents, then the remaining five carloads at 62 cents. The money exchanged is the same as if all 15 carloads had been sold at 60 cents—but the sheet stays up: The Yellow Sheet can be told that the last price was 62 cents.

Mr. Green of Swift, on the other hand, says that any time a sale is conducted at two different prices, it is because two different yield grades or weights of cattle are involved, so are priced separately. "There are no such transactions if the yield and weight are the same," he says. Many in the industry disagree.

Third Alleged Scheme: the savings on the sly. Actual example: The sales manager for a Chicago processor says that on Nov. 8 he called a Yellow Sheet reporter to learn the current market price for superior yield grade, 500- to 700-pound cattle. He says he was told the price had risen to 62 cents a pound from 61½ cents earlier, on the basis of a six-carload sale for 62 cents a pound by Union Packing Co. of Omaha. The sales manager says that he tried to find out if the sale was packer-to-packer or packer-to-processor but that the Yellow Sheet never gives out that information. Then, he says, Nort Racine, a Chicago broker, offered to sell him some loads of the same cattle from Union Packing for an equivalent price of 60½ cents (that is, not including transportation costs, which the 62-cent price also didn't include) provided he wouldn't report the 1½-cent drop in price to the Yellow Sheet. "The broker [Mr. Racine] told us there was no way if we reported [the sale] he would admit it—he would deny it," the sales manager says—and the sales manager turned the deal down.

Mr. Racine confirms this story, and says, "This doesn't happen just occasionally—it happens innumerable times. If you want a bargain, you have to keep it quiet. Any of the major packers would do it." He says he offered the hush-hush deal because that's the way Union Packing wanted it, and that he has personal knowledge of similar deals made on behalf of Iowa Beef.

Carl Frohm, president of Union Packing, denies this and says his firm hasn't ever offered to sell cattle on condition that the sale not be reported.

The Chicago sales manager's story doesn't stop with the offer from Mr. Racine, however. Later that same afternoon, he says, Jake Matuski, beef department manager of Bookey Packing Co., Des Moines, also offered to sell cattle to the sales manager below the Yellow Sheet price if he wouldn't report it; he says he turned that deal down, too. Mr. Matuski, questioned by a reporter, declines to confirm or deny the story; asked if such secret deals aren't standard practice, he replies, "I couldn't answer that."

Finally, the Chicago sales manager says he did give a promise not to tell the Yellow Sheet, in order to buy four carloads of meat at below the "market" price from Banner Beef Co. of Hospers, Iowa. "We needed the meat," he says with an air of embarrassment.

Mr. Norton of the Yellow Sheet says: "If there's going to be someone who hides the trade, we can't control that. It depends very much on what people are willing to tell us."

Many sources on the buying end of the meat business complained of exactly the opposite—that they tried to get low quotes in the Yellow Sheet and were ignored by the reporters. Mr. Norton says some sources are turned away by his service because they are unreliable, but that most of the rejected quotations are the result of "distress sales" involving a firm that must obtain meat quickly to fill an order or a firm that is glutted with product and must sell quickly. "When brokers or packers say we don't report their transactions, that's undoubtedly a distress sale," Mr. Norton says. "That's the misfortune of one guy and has nothing to do with what others would sell at who weren't under that pressure."

Nevertheless, this reporter saw documents evidencing sales, by such major packers as Wilson & Co. and Flavorland Industries, of such cuts as beef brisket, beef flanks and beef navels, all for at least one cent a pound under the sheet price. The wholesalers who bought these goods said they couldn't get their lower quotes into the Yellow Sheet.

Highballing quotes are especially oppressive to sellers who don't happen to work for a major packer. "I tried to sell meat to everybody in the United States Tuesday (Nov. 5) at the same price that was in the Yellow Sheet, and I couldn't get it," one Chicago broker complained. He said his best bid was two cents a pound under the Yellow Sheet quote. The big packers could get the sheet price because their contracts called for it.

A wholesaler of beef trimmings says he found the market very soft Nov. 4 and 5, and was startled to learn that the Yellow Sheet quotes were up a penny. His broker, who also says he couldn't find a market for trimmings those days, says he called the Yellow Sheet reporter and was told that the rising price was due to some small-quantity sales by Iowa Beef to two other packers, Krey Packing Co. and Oscar Mayer & Co., which also are in the ground-beef business. Says Mr. Smith of Iowa Beef: "That's 100% right. If there's nothing trading, one or two loads of beef, or whatever, is setting the market."

43. THE SUGAR SAGA OF '74

Wall Street Journal

Experts who thought the sugar-price peak would have been reached long ago and who have watched the markets zoom past their wildest predictions now are loath to even guess when the general trend of prices will start to move down. But some think that the decline already has started and that it will be as spectacularly sharp as the run-up. In their view, this year's sugar woes will be just a bitter memory a year from now.

In a way, fathoming the future of sugar prices is easier than determining how the big surge came about in the first place. It's no trick to figure that what goes up so fast eventually will come down. But the reasons for the run-up are complex, and it is difficult to analyze them because a lot of the "experts" have vested interests in keeping prices rising or else forcing them down.

Underlying the run-up are the facts that world sugar production has fallen behind consumption and that this year's sugar-beet crop was hurt by bad weather in Europe, Russia and some other places. But production has fallen a bit short of consumption in each of the past four years and in the 1970–1971 season the shortfall was many times greater than it was in the 1973–1974 season. There was no price surge then as there is now. Why?

For one thing, there was a bigger cushion of reserve stocks then. World reserves now have dropped nearly 25% to about a

---

Excerpts from "The Sugar Saga: Price Surge Is Running Out of Steam as Users Cut Back Consumption," in the *Wall Street Journal* (November 26, 1974).

10-week supply, compared to a supply sufficient for at least 12 to 13 weeks that the industry prefers to have on hand. Some dealers say that this stockpile is "dangerously low," while other analysts say that a two-week difference in supply isn't a big deal. In any case, three years ago there wasn't the combination of such factors as free-spending Arab nations and a world-wide inflationary psychology that has made a sweet tooth into a luxury.

As industry sources tell it, some dealers got the idea late last year that they would get even with the Arabs for their oil embargo and petroleum price rises by charging them considerably more for their sugar. Flush with oil money, the Arabs unblinkingly paid the higher quotes, which dealers gleefully raised almost daily. The Arabs also countered with a move of their own however: Instead of spacing their purchases throughout the year as usual, they bought enough sugar for a whole year within about three months (giving them, as it turned out, a considerable bargain).

This is where the psychology comes in. News of the Arabs' concentrated buying sparked interest in sugar futures markets in New York and London. A flurry of new supply-demand projections came forth from the big sugar dealers (who, of course, were involved in the Arab transactions), each more dire than the last. These were based in part on estimates that the Arabs were buying three million to four million tons of sugar; in fact, the Arabs bought only about two million tons—all they needed for consumption—an authority at an international sugar firm now says.

All this raised the specter of sugar shortages in a world that was primed for such a possibility by the succession of grain shortages, fertilizer shortages and petroleum shortages. This, in turn, triggered repercussions that helped fuel the surging prices. For example, sugar-exporting countries that normally supplied the U.S. with a certain amount at a set price abruptly switched their shipments to the Mideast and other markets where the price was better. This forced the U.S. into the world market— where it hadn't been for years, since it adopted a quota system for sugar imports—to compete for supplies.

Much the same sort of thing happened with Britain and its former colonies; other traditional supply agreements also were disrupted. Prior to this year, about 85% of the global sugar trade was conducted by negotiated trade pacts; whatever was left over from these agreements was dumped into the world market. But this year, the world market became the focal point of the feverish jockeying of sugar buyers and sellers.

Thus sensitized, the markets in New York and London reacted far more strongly than previously to such factors as weather, news of purchases by this country or that, and the incessant forebodings of sugar dealers. The exchanges on which sugar futures are traded have limits on how much the price can rise or fall in a day; the limits were one cent a pound until earlier this month when they were doubled. (A sugar futures contract is a commitment to buy or sell a specified amount of sugar—in New York it's 112,000 pounds—in some future month at an agreed-upon price.) In the 26 trading days from Oct. 11 through last Wednesday, prices of some sugar futures contracts in New York rose the daily limit in 24 sessions.

At the end of a trading session that has closed up the limit, traders normally announce the orders that couldn't be consummated. Something like: "Several hundred contracts were wanted at the limit advance with no sellers." This sets up conditions for another rise the following day, if not another limit advance, which helps give a bullish tone to the market.

"It's like living out the results of the next day's race," one commodities trader complains.

The limit moves in the futures markets also had the effect of temporarily squeezing the flow of real sugar. When sugar dealers acquire an inventory of sugar, they normally hedge against price declines by selling futures for a similar amount; when they sell the real sugar, they lift their hedge by buying back the futures. But when the futures market has advanced the limit and the hedges can't be lifted, the dealers hold off selling the real sugar to refiners and other users. If this is prolonged, as it has been on several occasions this fall, the refiners and other users have to scramble for inventories, which feeds into a vicious circle of causing prices to rise, making it harder to lift hedges, and so on.

Sugar consumption has begun to drop noticeably. "Sure there is less sugar in the world than we had several years ago, and rising population does require larger production," one market analyst says. "But what the bulls seek to hide is the fact that less sugar is used when the price is 50 cents a pound or more than was used when it was 10 cents."

Indeed, for all the apparent indications of great demand for sugar, reserve stocks declined only slightly in the 1973–74 season. F. O. Licht, a respected European sugar statistical firm, estimated the reserve stocks on Aug. 31 at 15.6 million tons, down from 15.7 million the year before.

C. Czarnikow Ltd., a leading London sugar-brokerage house that has been emphasizing tight supplies in its statements, says that production has to increase by 3.8% a year to satisfy consumer demand. But because of a cold, wet autumn in Europe, the firm predicts a decline in world sugar output of nearly 2% in the 1974–75 season, which started Sept. 1, while consumption is expected to keep rising.

Some sugar-industry observers in the U.S. think that such forecasts overstate the supply-demand squeeze. One of them thinks that cubacks by confectioners, bakers and soda-pop makers, not to mention housewives, could reduce annual U.S. sugar consumption by roughly 20% to less than 10 million tons.

As for buying sugar itself, consumers haven't shown any signs of slowing down. Sales are holding steady in some stores and increasing in others. Some hoarding may be going on—some stores limit customers to one bag of sugar at a time to discourage this—but managers of big supermarkets figure that holiday baking is responsible for much of the steady buying pace.

Consumer activists are trying to stir the public's wrath in part by charging that sugar refiners are reaping unconscionable profits. The nation's largest sugar refiner, Amstar Corp., reported that net income for its year ended June 30 soared to $31.4 million, or $7.75 a share, from $14.9 million, or $3.27 a share, a year earlier. If the company hadn't switched to the last-in-first-out method of inventory accounting, its earnings would have jumped by 420%. Profits of Holly Sugar Co. doubled to $3.41 a share for its fiscal year ended March 31.

But these are refiners of beet sugar, not cane sugar, and the distinction is important. Beet refiners contract with beet farmers for their supplies, agreeing to split profits from the sale of refined sugar. Cane-sugar refiners, on the other hand, have to pay the going market price for their raw material.

So cane refiners aren't doing nearly as well as beet refiners.

After switching to the LIFO inventory-accounting method, Su-Crest Corp. reported a $14.4 million net loss for its fiscal year ended June 30. Savannah Foods & Industries Inc., another cane refiner, wound up its latest period, the 39 weeks ended Sept. 29, with a net loss of $127,000. Most cane refiners say their profit margins are improving, but they won't say by how much.

But the beet-sugar refiners' profits are attracting attention to the whole industry. Great Western, which was on the verge of selling its beet-sugar refining subsidiary last fall, now is fending off a takeover attempt by Nelson Bunker Hunt and William Herbert Hunt, sons of Texas oil billionaire H. L. Hunt. Great Western directors contend that the Hunt offering price of $27.60 a share is inadequate in light of expected profit of $32 a share in the year ending next May 31, up from $1.95 in fiscal 1974.

The Justice Department has been investigating the sugar industry for possible antitrust violations, mainly price fixing.

Even if indictments are brought for price rigging, it would take months and perhaps years for trials. If the Justice Department wins, the result probably would be a prohibition against certain pricing practices, not a retroactive lowering of prices legal observers say.

44. EVERYTHING YOU WANTED TO KNOW ABOUT CHIQUITA BANANA
(but were afraid to ask)

by William Robbins

The year was 1960. United Fruit was in trouble. United States consumption of bananas, its principal product, had been declining for nearly ten years. Worse, United Fruit's share of the market had dropped from 66 percent in 1953 to 55.7 percent in 1959, though it edged back up to 57.1 percent in 1960. At the same time, the company's profits had been dropping steadily and at alarming rates. From $44.1-million in 1953 they fell to $2.2-million in 1960.

The heart of the problem was that prices were declining as consumption fell.

More significantly, the company had discovered something that has finally been brought home to most Americans only recently through problems such as those encountered by the giant Lockheed Aircraft and Penn Central Railroad companies: Size does not always—nor even usually—equate with efficiency.

United Fruit was the giant of its field, but its smaller competitors had learned to produce bananas of at least equal quality at a cost that permitted them to sell profitably at cheaper prices than United Fruit.

The company had to find a way to pass its higher costs on to consumers, and it turned to the big advertising firm of Batten,

Excerpts from chapter entitled "A Banana Named Chiquita," in William Robbins, *The American Food Scandal* (New York, Morrow, 1974), pp. 76–80. The author is a reporter and editor for the *New York Times* in Washington, D.C.

Barton, Durstine and Osborn to help find the solution. BBDO was not without an answer and, as might be expected, it found the key in advertising.

It noted that manufacturers of branded products were able to pass along rising costs because, through their advertising, they had built a "consumer franchise" for their products. "The retailer knows this, so he is willing to pay more for a well-known brand," says the company report, which covers the years 1960–67, when United Fruit was building such a "consumer franchise." The report was apparently prepared for the company by BBDO. It said:

"The consumer does not know United Fruit bananas from any other kind of bananas and, therefore, doesn't care whose bananas she buys. Assuming that the quality of the bananas is comparable, the lowest priced bananas get the sale."

United Fruit set out to change that, the report said, observing:

"In order to raise the price of its bananas, United Fruit must first build consumer preference for its own brand of bananas." It added: "The objective of the brand program was to sell United Fruit bananas for a higher price than they would normally get."

Realizing that "our bananas would probably not look any better than the competition's at retail," it decided: "We could not use any product claims that were checkable at retail."

The company, with BBDO's help, fixed on the brand name "Chiquita" because it was one that it had already been using in the wholesale trade, and hit on the claim, "Keeps days longer." Market testing of brand-name promotion and advertising was set to begin.

It had two principal goals: First, it wanted to "build a competitive edge based on a product advantage invisible at the point of sale." And then, by that device, it sought to get 20 cents more a box for its Chiquita bananas than others were selling for. The test seemed successful for, in the test markets, retailers were able to get average prices for Chiquitas of 19.2 cents a pound, against an average of 18.6 cents a pound for others.

Now the company was ready to go ahead full speed. It set an advertising budget for 1964 of $6-million and again it set a goal of a price premium of 20 cents a box over what unbranded first-class fruit would bring.

The first seven months of that year bore out the company's hopes. Its Chiquita bananas were selling for 14 to 23 cents a box higher at wholesale than other first-class bananas and 62 cents a box more than all other, unbranded United Fruit bananas. At retail, for the full year, Chiquita bananas were getting about 30 percent of the market at prices about 10 percent higher than other bananas.

For 1965 the company set a still higher goal: increased volume and 50 cents a box extra for the branded bananas while "maintaining a strong consumer franchise position capable of supporting a premium price structure and withstanding competitive countermeasures."

The results were even better than United Fruit had dared hope. It was getting 84 cents a box more for Chiquitas that year than for its other bananas, compared with 63 cents for the full year of 1964. The reason, of course, was the effectiveness of the device of brand-name promotion, as a consumer survey showed. Of women interviewed, 49 percent said they looked for Chiquitas when shopping for bananas; 27 percent said they would ask for Chiquitas by name, and 25 percent said they would even go to another store looking for Chiquitas if the store in which they were shopping did not have them in stock. Meanwhile, more households were buying bananas and paying more for them.

Some of the results were disquieting. Consumers who were most receptive to the advertising claims were among those who could least afford to pay a premium price for a product that had no essential advantage of quality. Among the most ill-used victims, those who tended most often to buy the Chiquita brand when they bought bananas, were low-income blacks of the inner cities.

In the beginning, the advertising message had some slight basis in fact. The Gros Michel breed being promoted does indeed "keep longer" than most other breeds, but United Fruit's Gros Michels did not keep any longer than anyone else's Gros Michels. But then, of course, United Fruit did not say what keeps longer than what.

For production reasons, United had to shift to the Valery breed and to shift from the "keeps longer" claim because it was demonstrably false. The company switched to the contention that Chiquitas were better packaged and therefore less subject to bruising, but it had to drop that claim because of complaints about bruising.

"Emphasis would be shifted to a less specific, less checkable claim," the company report said, "it being the company's desire to retain the good cooperation and sales support of the trade." Its new claims were to be based on wholesomeness and nutrition, but that did not last long either because, the report said: "Parameters established for campaign development were that copy emphasis be more competitive than the existing campaign, yet less specific and checkable than the boxing/bruising story." The new idea was to spread a message that the company was "fussy about we put our label on" and "to convince the consumer that Chiquita brand bananas achieve a quality level consistently higher than the competition."

It seemed to make little difference what the claim was. Each message persuaded more consumers to pay higher prices for bananas. By 1967 another consumer survey showed that 53 percent of shoppers looked specifically for Chiquitas, and the wholesale price spread had risen to 97 cents for the branded over the unbranded bananas. And most important of all to United Fruit, its profits were up $23-million a year since those depressed days before the Chiquita brand was hatched.

45. THOSE SOARING FOOD PRICES

The New Republic

Rising food prices do more than anything else to shrink the average American's take-home dollar. While the Consumer Price Index was climbing 1.3 percent in August, food prices in grocery

Reprinted from the *New Republic* (October 12, 1974).

stores went up 1.7 percent (wholesale prices rose at an annual rate of 91 percent). Poor families have the worst of it. The US Department of Agriculture's low-cost food budget cost 17 percent more in June 1974 than it did the previous June; the higher-price food budget cost "only" 12 percent more.

Can food prices be held where they are, or lowered? It depends upon how much of the upward surge is artificially created and how much is unavoidable. Almost nothing in our economy is as complex as the pricing of food. The shopper's bill at the checkout counter is affected by weather, commodity speculation, exports and imports, middleman profits, government price supports and a host of other factors, many of which defy control. At the moment they are all pushing upward simultaneously. Production costs on the farm—fuel, fertilizer, machinery, baling wire, credit—are on the rise. So are packaging and transportation costs. Foreigners want more of our grain and soybeans and are willing to pay. The Midwest drought has hurt corn, driving up feed prices for livestock and poultry.

But there are elements of artificiality as well in recent price rises, one of which is the inflationary effects of concentrated market power. In the meat packing, cereal, soup, baby food, and canned fruit and vegetable industries, among others, three or four firms dominate sales. Campbell sells 90 percent of the soup we buy; Kellogg, General Mills, General Foods and Quaker Oats have cornered 90 percent of the breakfast cereal market. Del Monte is king of the fruit and vegetable canners; Gerber reigns over baby food. According to Russell C. Parker of the Federal Trade Commission, 50 food processing companies account for more than 60 percent of food processing profits, and the trend toward concentration—attributable almost entirely to mergers rather than internal expansion—is continuing. These market giants specialize in highly advertised, artfully packaged, over-priced products. In 1972 the FTC says, the cost to consumers of less-than-competitive pricing in 13 food industry lines exceeded two billion dollars. At the retail level 20 large chains made 40 percent of grocery store sales in 1970, up from 30 percent two decades ago. Most cities are at the mercy of two, three or four supermarket chains, which account for the stickiness in retail prices when prices to the farmer go down. When wholesale beef prices in Chicago plummeted 25 percent earlier this year, retail prices dropped 10 percent. A supermarket executive explained the discrepancy by saying the chains were "only trying to make up a little of what we lost—1973 was a bad year." They seem to have succeeded: *Business Week* reports that for the first quarter of 1974, profits of the largest chains were 59 percent higher than a year ago, though sales were up only 14 percent. The largest supermarket chain, Safeway Stores, nearly doubled its net profit in the third quarter of this year ending September 7—$32 million compared to $16.4 million in the same period in 1973.

The growing market power of processors and retailers does as little for farmers as it does for consumers. Middlemen now collect about 60 cents out of every dollar spent on food, up from 50 cents in the early 1950s. A USDA study found that between 1952 and 1971, 94 percent of the rise in consumer food prices resulted from increased marketing costs; six percent of the rise got to the farmers.

The lettuce industry is an example of what happens when conglomerates move into food production and marketing. About a third of our lettuce comes from the Salinas Valley in California. A few years ago United Brands (formerly United Fruit) began leasing lettuce farms in the valley. It joined the Central California Lettuce Producers Cooperative, a marketers' association that thwarts competition and is exempt from the antitrust laws under the Capper-Volstead Act of 1922. (The intent of the Capper-Volstead Act was to permit small farmers to market cooperatively, thereby avoiding middlemen; large integrated food companies now use it to increase profits and victimize consumers.) United Brands also launched an advertising campaign to sell lettuce as an expensive brand-name product, as it does with Chiquita bananas. In a recent decision the FTC refused to order United Brands out of the lettuce business, as a hearing officer had recommended. In a concurring opinion, Commissioner Mayo J. Thompson said that he could find "little in the way of redeeming social value . . . in an advertising program designed to make something out of nothing, or as country folks say, 'a silk purse out of a sow's ear.' "

The government's contribution to rising prices, through price supports, quotas, subsidies, reserves, set-asides and marketing orders, has not had the notice it deserves. Most of these special interest gifts came out of the Depression and had the commendable purpose of helping small farmers stay alive. They now help primarily the bigger farmers and food corporations. Take marketing orders, which are devices permitting growers and distributors of a given commodity to collectively set production quotas and quality standards—in effect government-sanctioned cartels. The marketing board for peaches figures out how many peaches can be grown each year without undermining the desired market price. It then allocates production, requiring peach growers to "green drop" a certain percentage of their crop. The percentage is the same for small and large growers alike, though small growers can't afford to lose a portion of their crop as easily as big growers can. Each year millions of peaches rot in the fields so that the price in the supermarket will stay high. There are similar marketing orders for oranges, lemons, apples, pears, grapefruit, plums, avocados, figs, raisins, wine grapes, strawberries, lettuce, potatoes, almonds and other crops. Only one marketing board—the California Egg Board—has a consumer representative on it—one.

The most regulated commodity of all is fluid milk. As we have been reading in the newspapers, the price of milk is set as much by political as by economic pressures. In California where the retail price of milk has risen 33 percent in the past 18 months (and where the California Milk Producers Association dumped 420,000 gallons of raw skim milk into the sewers of Los Angeles last July because it couldn't sell all that milk at prevailing prices) the state director of agriculture sets minimum prices at the processing, wholesale and retail levels. At the processing level, Class 1 milk—which goes into cartons to be sold fresh—gets a substantially higher price than milk used for butter, ice cream, cheese and other dairy products, and each dairyman is assigned a quota for the higher price milk. According to Roy Alper, a lobbyist for the California Citizen Action Group, these quotas—which can be sold—have become quite valuable in recent years. Any dairyman who wishes to increase his sale of Class 1 milk must pay for the right to do so, and sometimes the quota price is the dairyman's single largest expense. "The quota system has not brought us better milk," says Alper. "It has simply made a few dairymen wealthy and raised the price of milk."

Wholesale prices are fixed in such a way that supermarket chains, such as Safeway, which has its own milk processing operation, make a fatter profit than stores that buy from independent creameries. But even nonintegrated retailers fare well, since the minimum retail price set by the director of agriculture includes a 20 percent mark-up for the store. The state auditor general in California conducted a survey of 92 supermarkets and found that the milk mark-up was higher than the mark-up for 11 basic food products whose retail prices are *not* regulated. Some products, such as coffee and sugar, were sold at a loss by a majority of the supermarkets surveyed. Is coffee more nutritious than milk? Should the state require milk drinkers to subsidize coffee drinkers?

One welcome consequence of double-digit inflation is that consumers are more curious than they were about who's picking their pockets, and how. At "mini-summits" and summits, at regulatory commissions and before congressional committees, in local boycott groups, people are asking what portion of recent price hikes represents unavoidable higher costs, what represents high profits, and what reflects noncompetitive market power or politically secured favors. When they learn that their food bills are bigger because of government misregulation or government-sanctioned combinations in restraint of trade, consumers may get mad enough to do more than plant victory gardens.

46. EXPORTING FOOD: CAUSES AND EFFECTS

by Fred Block and David Plotke

The drastic rise in food prices in the United States during 1973 has caused a sharp deterioration in the living conditions of American working people. Although real wage levels of most workers have not risen since 1965, the food price inflation of 1973 has provided many Americans with their most direct experience of economic austerity. Economic austerity, in all its forms, is a result of the declining international position of the United States (expressed dramatically in the balance-of-payments crisis) and the irrationalities of capitalist production. The food price rises provide a clear example of the interplay of these two factors.

The rise in food prices can be traced directly to the chronic American balance-of-payments problem. The payments problem stems from the large outflow of dollars each year to pay for the American military efforts around the world and for the continuing expansion of American businesses abroad. For many years the outflows from these sources were almost balanced by inflows that came when foreigners bought more goods from Americans than Americans bought from them. But as a result of inflation due to the Vietnam War and long-term factors that diminished the international competitiveness of American goods, the United States began buying more abroad than it sold. This meant that the outflow of dollars each year became significantly greater. Pressure from abroad, including massive speculation

Abridged from "Food Prices," in *Socialist Revolution* (July-August 1973). Fred Block and David Plotke are members of the *Socialist Revolution* collective in San Francisco.

against the dollar, became irresistible, and Nixon responded with two devaluations of the dollar—one in December of 1971 and the other in February of 1973.

Devaluation lowers the value of a national currency, making a country's products cheaper abroad, and foreign goods more expensive at home. The idea is that foreigners will be induced to buy a larger share of the nation's products because of their lower costs, and the nation's citizens will be induced to buy fewer foreign goods because of their increased costs. In that way, the balance of trade will improve, and so will the balance of payments. But if a devaluation is effective, there will be relatively fewer goods left to be distributed among a nation's citizens. In the United States, this has meant shortages of agricultural goods, which in turn has meant rapid increases in food prices.

For years, American agricultural exports have played an important role in maintaining a trade surplus. American agriculture is highly productive and efficient because of its scale and high level of mechanization. In contrast to parts of Western Europe where much agricultural land is still owned by families with small plots and little capital to invest in mechanization, the American system of business agriculture makes possible huge agricultural surpluses. Policy makers attempted to take advantage of this agricultural abundance by selling increasing quantities of American agricultural products abroad. Although American agricultural exports expanded steadily through the 1960s, the increases weren't sufficient to alleviate the balance-of-payments problem. The quantity of agricultural exports was limited by two factors. The hungry nations of the world lacked the foreign exchange—the dollars—to pay for a substantially increased flow of agricultural imports. And the developed countries were generally reluctant to raise their agricultural imports from the United States too rapidly for fear of ruining their own farmers, which could be disastrous socially and politically, since small farmers are often a major source of support for bourgeois political parties in Europe.

Since the possibilities of unloading American agricultural surpluses abroad were limited by these constraints, the United States continued the program of restricting agricultural production begun in the Depression. This program reduced the number of acres under cultivation from 345 million in 1950 to 296 million in 1972. But in 1972, new factors eliminated the old constraints on agricultural exports as soaring foreign demand increased American farm exports by sixty per cent in one year. The major factors involved were the Soviet wheat deal, an increase in demand in other industrial countries, and a series of crop failures, particularly in the underdeveloped world.

The Soviet need for wheat was caused by a particularly bad harvest, the chronic weakness of Soviet agriculture that dates back to the forced collectivization of the twenties, and the fear by the Soviet leadership that reductions in food consumption could contribute to mass political opposition. American officials were eager to supply the Soviet Union with American wheat as part of the long-term campaign to push up agricultural exports to improve the American trade balance. Nixon also used the opportunity to solidify the United States-Soviet détente. Nixon realized that détente would contribute to his own personal prestige and chances for re-election, while simultaneously advancing American purposes globally. A United States-Soviet understanding is of crucial importance in a period in which the United States faces intensified economic competition from our European and Japanese allies. And for some sectors of the American business elite, détente is seen as a means to open up the Soviet market to all kinds of lucrative economic deals. Finally, there is some evidence that the Soviet willingness to look the other way while the United States mined Haiphong harbor in May of 1972 was conditioned by their eagerness to obtain our wheat. If the wheat deal gained Soviet cooperation in American efforts to force a Vietnam peace settlement, then higher domestic bread prices would have been a small price for Nixon to pay.

The Soviet purchases were so large—347.8 million bushels in 1972–73—that they put strong upward pressure on domestic wheat prices. However, only a few wholesale grain dealers with inside information made a killing—most wheat farmers had sold their grain long before Soviet demand had bid the prices up. But the Soviet Union got the wheat at bargain prices because government subsidies—designed to encourage agricultural exports—paid the wholesalers the difference between the world market price and the much higher domestic price. The sheer size of the Soviet purchase created huge problems in the transport system that took the wheat from farmer to purchaser. These transport tie-ups hindered normal agricultural distribution and contributed further to upward pressure on prices.

The Soviet grain deal was only the beginning. Demand from other countries for American farm products, particularly feed grains, pushed American prices higher and higher. Much of this acceleration in foreign demand was the consequence of the American devaluations, which made American farm products relatively cheaper abroad. The devaluations have increased the international purchasing power of European and Japanese currencies, which has meant an increase in the capacity of European and Japanese consumers to command agricultural goods in the world market. For some time, the diet of West European and Japanese consumers has been gradually improving relative to the American diet. Now, the devaluations are making possible a much more rapid improvement in the West European and Japanese diets. Because much of the improvement in diet takes the form of increased consumption of meat, the upgrading of diet leads to a rapid increase in the need for animal feed. Since meat is a biologically inefficient source of protein, the substitution of meat protein for protein from grain sources in a nation's diet requires a far larger increase in that nation's total consumption of grains or other protein sources used for animal feed. The increased purchasing power of the European and Japanese currencies has given those countries the opportunity to buy from the United States the protein-rich feed necessary to increase their meat production and consumption.

Part of the increase in demand for American agricultural goods might prove temporary. Increased imports into the industrial countries have supplemented domestic farm production and made possible higher levels of consumption. However, expansion in agricultural production to meet these higher levels of demand and to decrease dependence on the United States is likely, particularly in Europe. Also, the past few years have seen bad harvests in many different parts of the world—both world wheat and world rice production were five per cent below the previous year's level in the year ending June 30, 1973. Underdeveloped countries that have experienced agricultural disasters —the Philippines, India, Bangladesh, and the six sub-Saharan nations suffering from a prolonged drought—have been forced to prevent mass starvation by increasing their agricultural imports. Despite their limited resources for buying agricultural imports, this increased demand has been a factor in the expansion of United States exports.

47. THE CAPITALIST FOOD SYSTEM: A FRAMEWORK FOR UNDERSTANDING FOOD INFLATION

by the URPE/PEA National Food Collective

Food prices continue to soar. With every passing month it becomes obvious that we are experiencing a world food crisis. Business and the government tell us that the crisis will go away soon enough, but their reassurances seem increasingly meaningless. Orthodox economists tell us that supply adjustments will soon bring prices back into line, but we've been waiting for those adjustments too long already. What's wrong?

The recent explosion of food prices has not been an "accident," the product of some temporary disturbances in the normal balance between supply and demand. We would argue that food inflation has flowed directly from the internal structure and dynamics of our capitalist economic system. The food crisis is not likely to go away within this economic system, and food prices are not likely to return to their former levels. More generally, food crises of the kind we have recently experienced are themselves natural and necessary outgrowths of the normal development of capitalist economies. In short, we cannot reform

---

Unpublished paper. URPE/PEA is identified in Suggested Readings.

our food system to prevent further food crises without fundamentally restructuring the economic system upon which the food economy is based.

In our view, the recent inflation of food prices has been jointly caused by three kinds of developments which interact in complex ways, feeding back upon each other. Nor can the crisis be explained by any one of these developments alone, for the effect of each depends in part on its interaction with the other two. The depth of the roots of these developments and the complexity of their interaction reflects the systemic character of the causes of the crisis and the need for systemic solutions.

These developments are: (a) a series of short-term events, coincidentally acting simultaneously upon supply and demand; (b) the transformation of the food economy in the United States, through which large corporations have been able to achieve an increasingly oligopolistic concentration of power over the production and distribution of food; and (c) a series of economic adjustments flowing from the intensification of the current world economic crisis, itself reflecting the basic instabilities of capitalist economies.

I. Short Term Events

We reject apologetic arguments that food inflation can be explained entirely by a series of "accidents," blaming the soaring prices on bad weather and shifting currents. We would agree that some short-term events have contributed to this inflation and in some cases may have "triggered" the explosion of longer-term forces, providing the occasion for the manifestation of concentrated corporate power to manipulate prices. We must clearly understand the importance of these short-term events in order to avoid illusions about the temporary character of the crisis.

Four short-term events seem clearly to have had some impact: calamities of nature, the unusual coincidence of hog and beef cycles, the Soviet wheat deal and the sudden increase in fuel prices.

Effects. Calamities of nature—drought in Russia and Africa, inadequate rain in South and Southeast Asia, shifts in the Humboldt current, heavy rains in the United States—coincided in 1972 to reduce world grain output by about 3 per cent from the previous year's level. The hog and beef cycle in this country intensified the effects of rising beef prices because pork supplies, at that moment, were at the bottom of their own cycle. The Soviet wheat deal, *only because of the way it was handled,* intensified the shortage of grains. The rise in fuel prices after 1973 placed increasing pressure on the supply prices of farm inputs *and* on our balance of payments problems.

Insufficient Explanations. These short-term factors triggered such a sharp inflation of food prices precisely because they did not operate in isolation. They occurred in a particular economic context, a context dominated by increasing American control of world grain exports, by the longer-term erosion of world grain stocks, by the increasing corporate power of American agribusiness and by the emerging world economic crisis. It was the dominance of these underlying forces which conditioned the intensity of the impact of these short-term events.

Moreover, we argue that we cannot properly interpret all of these short-term factors as "accidents." While the calamities of nature and the coincidence of meat cycles seem random, our vulnerability to their occurrence reflects the anarchy of capitalist production. Further, the Soviet wheat deal and the increase in fuel prices were not accidents at all; they reflected the symptoms of more fundamental underlying developments in the world economy.

Symptoms of the System. The importance of these short-term factors as triggers reflects the character of our economic system. Two aspects of that argument seem most important.

First, as we noted above, our vulnerability to these kinds of events reflects the general "anarchy" of capitalist production. In an unplanned market economy, no matter how its vicissitudes are "moderated" by government management, proportional growth of basic supplies is unlikely to continue for sustained periods. Almost any accident can throw the system out of whack.

More concretely, the mechanisms through which these short-term events "triggered" inflation reflect the specific forms of post–World War II capitalist development: American hegemony, growing corporate concentration and uneven development between advanced and Third World countries. These developments contributed to the long-run erosion of world grain reserves during the 1960's and to the increasing international economic instability of the current period—themselves some of the aspects of the current situation which left us so vulnerable to the short-term events.

II. Concentration of Corporate Power in the American Food Economy

Many of the reassurances offered us by the media, the government and conventional economists rely on the presumptions of competitive economics. For all of us, the food economy has provided the archetype of competitive market economics. Prices could never increase, we're told, because increasing prices would generate, through competitive market adjustments, a rapid increase in food supplies.

This view of the food economy is antiquated. Lagging behind the rest of the economy, the food sector has nonetheless achieved "maturity": that is, it has slowly been transformed over the past fifty years, and particularly since World War II, into a system of production and distribution nearly as concentrated as the rest of the economy. Small farmers remain, but their freedom to adjust "competitively" has been eroded by the squeeze of suppliers of farm inputs on the one hand, and by food processors on the other. Even agriculture itself has fallen more and more under the control of corporate agribusiness. Any analysis which elides this fundamental transformation of the food economy will necessarily obscure some of the major forces effecting the explosion of food prices and the current food crisis.

Effects. The trends toward concentration of the food economy are unmistakable. Corporations now control roughly four fifths of farm output, either through direct control or by control over its distribution. The top twenty food-processing firms made 67 per cent of the profits in food processing in 1972. The twenty-five largest supermarket chains account for half of all retail food sales. This concentration now seems to grow with every year.

Concentrated market power tends to create an upward pressure on prices and we would firmly argue that this transformation of the food economy helps explain the intensity of recent food inflation.

We do not succumb to the simple view that corporations can "fix" prices absolutely. Rather, we argue that corporations create upward pressures by their ability to limit the growth of supplies in response to increasing demand and rising prices on one side, and by their ability to respond to falling demand by contracting production and charging higher prices at the same time. (This latter possibility is illustrated by the auto companies' price hikes when demand for their cars has been collapsing.) Corporations also create upward price pressure through the mechanisms by which they seek to consolidate their concentrated power—through contracting arrangements, through advertising and product differentiation, through increasingly capital-intensive production techniques. The upward pressure on prices results, in short, from an interaction between the means by which corporations increase their power and the consequences of that power.

These effects can be seen at several different levels.

1. In the economy as a whole, concentration has generated increasing prices. During the nineteenth century the wholesale price index, though fluctuating cyclically, revealed no upward tendency over time. During the twentieth century the aggregate wholesale price index, still fluctuating cyclically, reveals a dramatic upward secular rise.

2. Within food itself, the competitive price adjustment becomes less and less evident as corporate power becomes consolidated. After the rapid inflation of farm prices during the Korean War, those prices returned quickly to their previous levels, apparently reflecting the continuing influence of competitive supply adjustments. During the current inflation, even during the recession of 1974–75, there has been no evidence of food prices returning to their previous levels, much less declining at all, and therefore no evidence of that same competitive supply-adjustment effect.

3. The means by which corporations have consolidated their control over the food economy have also held the growth of world food supplies below its potential. Internationally, the American grain companies and the government used foreign-aid programs and surplus commodities to undercut grain production in underdeveloped countries, always keeping the world price of grains low enough—by threatening to dump surplus

grains on the world market—that underdeveloped countries were deterred from investing in the expansion of their own domestic agricultural capacity. (In just thirty years, almost all the underdeveloped countries have changed from being substantial exporters of basic food grains to being substantial net importers of basic grains.) Domestically, price-support and acreage-restriction programs, whose subsidies largely benefited large farmers, were used to keep much productive U.S. farming land *out of* production, artificially limiting potential supplies. (As late as 1973, after the shortages of 1972, the government was still paying over $3 billion to keep roughly 50 million productive acres out of farming use.)

4. In the current situation, at the concrete level, we can see the ways in which corporations can limit the competitive supply adjustment characteristic of the earlier food economy. Large meat processors withheld supplies in their freezers, able by their financial strength to weather the temporary loss in revenues. Sugar refiners can continue to raise prices, given relatively inelastic demand, and forestall supply adjustments by their control over sugar production. The power of farm input suppliers to raise their prices keeps farm margins so low that many small farmers, heavily in debt, are unable to borrow enough to increase current production.

Insufficient Explanations. While these consequences are fundamentally important, they cannot explain the explosion of food prices by themselves. First, at one end, the short-term factors did operate as triggers. Second, at another level, the intensification of the current world economic crisis conditioned some of the forces to which corporations in the food economy were responding. While the government was always helping agribusiness with one hand, for instance, it was also desperately pursuing policies which would help ameliorate the declining trade position of the United States; these policies provided an occasion for agribusiness to manifest its power in ways which might not otherwise have become possible.

Symptoms of the System. Many "neo-populists," clearly aware of the effects of corporate concentration on the food economy, call for "trust-busting." They offer the hope that we could prevent recurrence of these kinds of food crises by returning to the "golden days" of competitive agriculture.

We submit that these arguments miss the essential point. Concentration flows inevitably from the rules of capital accumulation in capitalist economies. It did not happen as a result of government neglect; it happened because it was the only way of resolving the contradictions of overproduction in competitive markets. If we could somehow magically break the power of the current "trusts," the laws of capital accumulation would, in our opinion, produce new and equally powerful corporations rising out of the ashes of the old.

Others maintain that concentration in the food economy is "efficient," allowing us to take advantage of "economies of scale." It may conceivably be true, these apologists hold, that corporations create inflationary pressures, but they also permit higher standards of living and more consumer choice.

In reply, we argue that the evidence does not support these claims. "Economies of scale" do not require the current level of concentration—far from it. Moreover, the means by which corporations develop and use their power waste enormous resources on advertising, packaging and food gimmicks while they simultaneously adulterate the quality of the food we eat. A more rational use of our resources, we suggest, could provide us with just as high a "standard of living" without wasting resources and poisoning our food.

III. World Economic Crisis

The food crisis, finally, has been both triggered and fundamentally exacerbated by the development of the world economic crisis. It has been influenced especially by the kinds of policies which the U.S. government has desperately pursued in trying to salvage the stability and hegemony of the American economy.

Effects. Two main aspects of the developing world crisis underlay the policies which ultimately helped cause the food inflation. First, the American balance of payments continued to deteriorate during the late 1960's as American corporations faced increasing international competition and as the sustained American boom pushed U.S. prices further out of line. Second, the growth of multinational corporations further exacerbated some of the impact of international competition as multinational corporations rapidly transferred credit and currencies around the advanced countries, amplifying the wild gyrations of monetary movements and speculation.

To correct the increasingly persistent deficit in the balance of payments, the U.S. government pursued two policies, both of which simultaneously created the basis for exploding food prices. First, the government sought to push food exports as fast and as fully as possible; food exports more than tripled between 1969 and 1973. These policies tended not only to create a situation of tight supplies in the United States but also to divert American food surpluses from Third World countries without funds to more affluent advanced countries. (The Soviet wheat deal was only one of many packages encouraged by this export drive.) Second, the government was pushed to devalue the dollar twice. This tended to increase American exports in general and American food exports in particular as U.S. prices became relatively cheaper internationally.

The several aspects of the developing world crisis, by 1971, also combined to produce converging business cycles in all the advanced industrial countries. As the United States tried to pay its way out of the short recession of 1969–1970, its expansionist policies tended to exacerbate an unusually amplified world inflation, with every country's prices moving rapidly together. These increasingly *general* price movements obviously reinforced the tendencies in the food sector itself.

The international fuel crisis, finally, also had an important effect on food prices through its effects on food input supply prices and transport costs. This crisis, partly the creature of accident but more fundamentally the product of American oil corporations' strategies and the developing world economic crisis, had causes parallel to those of the food inflation and ended up exacerbating the food crisis itself.

IV. The Significance of This Analysis

This analysis provides an essential corrective and counterpoint to the reigning conventional explanations of the food crisis.

Orthodox economists have often applied simple supply-and-demand analysis, based on competitive models. Their apologies almost always imply—though they manage to hold on to this faith less and less—that food prices will somehow eventually come down as supplies expand. We fundamentally oppose this kind of analysis because we don't believe that competitive forces dominate the food economy any longer or that "equilibria" represent the typical situation in capitalist economies.

The government seeks to turn our attention away from the fundamental character of the food crisis by blaming its various coincidental causes. We should all be patient, President Ford says, and we should all eat a little less, Nixon said, while the market weathers the storm. If we get too piggy, we are told, we will merely make things worse. We fundamentally oppose this orientation as well, because we feel that important forces in the development of the economy have caused the current crisis, not our own piggishness. Government policies have been framed by the effort to force the American people to pay the costs of a crisis created by large corporations and by the instabilities of world capitalism.

Critical opposition to these apologists has been dominated, so far, by the collection of "neo-populists" clustered around Ralph Nader and some public interest groups. In the neo-populist view, monopoly pricing and power have uniquely caused the crisis. If we were able to break monopoly power, we could prevent such crises. We should restore, they say explicitly, the protective blanket of market competition in the food economy. Power to the small farmer! We also oppose this orientation, not because we think monopoly power has had no effect, but rather because we believe that we cannot eliminate monopoly power without changing the basic rules of capital accumulation in capitalist economies. Nor could we eliminate the basic instabilities of capitalist economies, manifested through cycles and crises, by simply busting the power of the trusts.

Our analysis bears much more than this simple critical significance, finally, because it clarifies the very limited options we have for dealing with the present crisis and preventing future crises. If the combined causes of this crisis all flow, directly or indirectly, from the nature of the capitalist system, then we must clearly transform that system itself.

III

CORPORATE-GOVERN-
MENT INTERVENTION
AND THE FUTURE OF
CAPITALISM

Introduction

FOR YEARS we were assured by establishment economists that "it"—the word "depression" was unutterable, even unthinkable —could never happen again. Edition after edition of Paul Samuelson's best-selling authoritative text, a constantly updated gospel, if you will, synthesized the latest nuances in the Keynesian arsenal of counter-cyclical policy.

In short, Keynesian economics, we were told, ensured the perpetuation of prosperity. Knowledge was the key. No government would again raise taxes in the midst of mass unemployment, as happened in 1937, nor would it raise interest rates, as it did in 1931. Keynesian remedies were simple, even pleasurable: interest rates could be reduced and government appropriations expanded for housing, roads, hospitals and schools— this litany of goodies has been updated to include funds for urban mass transit, antipollution projects and neighborhood day-care centers. (The preceding is the *hypothetical* world of Keynesian theory; throughout most of the postwar period *actual* government expenditures were dominated by *military* goods and related items. Arms expenditures in point of fact do not compete with special private interests, while public housing and even mass transit do. The reality, then, is that military expenditures turn out to be one of the principal forms Keynesian economics usually assumes.) Finally, and appealing directly to the most hedonistic impulses of all, taxes could be cut for rich and poor alike. And no one would ever have to pay for this veritable orgy of fiscal and monetary expansion. Any increase in the national debt, we were told, is of no real concern since everyone shares in the wealth it creates (such as the F-111's!). Moreover, we simply owe it to ourselves. At worst, servicing the debt transfers income from poor to rich, a redistribution easily offset by more progressive income taxes. Unfortunately, this never happens.

There was only one possible hitch in the Keynesian scheme of things. Political will might be lacking: conservative moss-backs might object to welfare spending or to budgetary deficits. By the early 1970's, however, the conservative opposition to Keynesian economics had all but melted away and Richard Nixon himself could proudly announce that he, too, was a Keynesian.

So much for antirecessionary ideology. One consequence of Keynesian myopia was a failure to recognize the impending crisis: as late as September 7, 1974, *Business Week* could caption a short summary on business conditions, "A Consensus of Economists: No Recession in '75." Moreover, Geoffrey Moore, a leading business-cycle specialist, in a paper presented December 28, 1973, was quoted as saying the following:

> Business recession—periods of actual decline in economic activity—have become less frequent, shorter, and milder. . . . One of the factors underlying this shift . . . is the trend in the industrial composition of employment. Industries that normally experience larger percentage reductions in employment when recession hits are less important in the overall economic picture nowadays, while industries that often continue to expand right through recession have become more important. . . . One of the implications of the employment trends I have just reviewed is that future recessions are more likely to be in the nature of slowdowns in the rate of growth. (*Monthly Labor Review* [April 1974], p. 11)

Ludicrous and embarrassing, but it illustrates a common failing of bourgeois economics. It assumes that changes are gradual, incremental and cumulative. What underlies today's economy underlies tomorrow's, and on this basis one projects the harmonious growth implicit in the quoted passage. In reality, every capitalist boom sooner or later creates fundamental changes which guarantee that its duration is limited. In the situation at hand, Geoffrey Moore apparently overlooked the fact that building up was an unprecedented situation: runaway inflation, dangerous indebtedness, international financial disorders and increased competition associated with the European and

Japanese recovery from World War II. These factors were more than sufficient to ensure the end of prosperity. The quadrupling of oil prices may have been the straw that broke the camel's back, and a heavy straw at that, but the camel was already buckling under its burden before the straw was added.

Nor is Keynesian economics any better equipped for offering solutions than it is for making predictions. Everyone is aware of the fact that the downturn has been accompanied by rampant inflation. Keynesian economics, however, makes the fundamental assumption that unemployment and inflation are basically separate problems with a set of diametrically opposite solutions. In texts, these are often put side by side for visible contrast. Inflation in a strict Keynesian model is a consequence of too much aggregate demand, while unemployment results from its insufficiency. One doesn't need a degree in logic to realize that you can't have too much aggregate demand at the same time that you have too little. Nor can you implement solutions that call for expanding demand to counteract recession while simultaneously reducing it to stop inflation.

In reality, unemployment and inflation are entwined in complex ways that are not fully understood. In the last analysis, depressions occur because of capitalism's inability to generate enough purchasing power in the right hands to buy back the goods the system is capable of throwing on the market. Military expenditures provide one answer, but at the cost of considerable inflation. A second solution is a banking system willing to extend sufficient credit to business corporations and consumers to enable these goods to be distributed in return for IOU's. The upshot is a progressively shakier debt structure and persistent inflation. The latter inevitably results when monopolistic industries push prices up to avoid an erosion of profits due to high employment-induced wage demands and high rates of interest.

Whatever elaborations or modifications one makes of the preceding account, it is clear that events of this type have permanently eroded the efficacy of fiscal policies based on manipulations of aggregates. Some Keynesians like James Tobin, a former member of President Kennedy's Council of Economic Advisors, have already thrown in the towel and are calling for economic controls. What we can say at this point is that Keynesian economics, as a system of push-button monetary and fiscal policies designed to finely tune the economy and create full or near-full employment with zero or mild inflation, has seen its day. In retrospect, its failures reflect the fact that it never had an integrated theory of full employment without inflation, one that included the key elements of wages, profits, productivity and monopoly.

A second, interrelated failing was its inability to deal with the consequences of overextended debt. It neither anticipated the problem, nor can it offer much of a solution. When sections of the economy become inoperative because of bankruptcies and financial panics, government spending programs are apt to worsen matters by creating inflationary pressures wherever production is actually taking place, while not having much effect on those sections already closed down. In cases like these, *macro*-economic cures are not needed. Necessary are *micro*-economic solutions to what are essentially *macro*-economic problems. That is, to stave off a crisis the government must intervene on an individual basis, for which the Lockheed case with its $250 million government handout is an apt prototype.

The Federal Reserve, to be sure, can pour endless billions into ailing financial institutions, the Franklin National Bank being a case in point. It can also pressure commercial banks into extending loans to financially weak corporations like Chrysler and W. T. Grant. Perhaps it can engineer the bailing-out of Pan Am as well. But as often as not, these are cases of pouring in good money after bad, temporary shore-ups, setting the stage for an even shakier banking system in the future. Operations of this sort, if large-scale, are also highly inflationary.

It is clear that banks have been anything but prudent—the staid guardians of our money have been speculating and losing their stuffed shirts everywhere in the Las Vegas–like world of international currencies! But they will not likely go along with endlessly loaning to credit-unworthy corporations. For this reason, proposals for national planning emanate from the highest capitalist circles (see reading #48 by Felix Rohatyn, a partner in the influential investment house Lazard Frères). Rohatyn recommends the creation of a new government corporation (a reconstituted Reconstruction Finance Corporation) that will make the needed loans. Perhaps a system of "socialism for the rich" can be put together in time to stave off many of the bankruptcies which otherwise would occur. If so, it is direct government planning and not Keynesian economics that saves the day.

A third limitation of Keynesian economics is that it is basically *national* planning, more befitting the situation that existed in 1936 when Keynes published his *magnum opus,* but no longer true today. As Barnet and Müller put it (see reading #19 in Part II), "The Keynesian vision of how to control money transactions assumed a market in which national banks and national corporations transacted their business within the context of national boundaries." That situation no longer exists.

The preceding limitations of orthodox Keynesian economics are not technical shortcomings to be overcome by further refinements in its theoretical apparatus. Keynesian economics has failed because of its politics and not its techniques—in broadest terms, because it attempted to paper over the class conflicts present in a capitalist society.

For these reasons, and more, Keynesian economics will either be supplanted entirely or undergo drastic modifications. Heretical comments are already being heard. Arthur Burns, chairman of the Federal Reserve Board, told a congressional committee in the summer of 1974 that a $10 billion *cut* in the federal budget would *create* jobs (the exact opposite of what Keynesian economics predicts) by reducing federal borrowing. These increases in employment would occur as a result of the reductions in interest rates and the concomitant revival of the stock market.

Another departure from Keynesian economics is provided by the highly respected economist Robert Mundell, who calls for a combination of tax cuts and tight money, a distinct contradiction in Keynesian circles.

In any event, tax reductions, it seems clear, we will certainly get. Nonetheless, it is doubtful that they will play a significant, positive role—not only will they be inflationary but if Burns's arguments have validity, job increases in some sectors of the economy may be offset by others, in particular construction. Because Keynesian economics and its offshoots have so little to offer in a era of double-digit inflation and near-double digit unemployment, the feeling is widespread, and growing, that sooner or later (and probably sooner) the government will resort to a system of wage and price controls.

By no means, though, is planning of this type likely to solve the problems of contemporary American capitalism. In the first place, controls within a market capitalist context are immensely complicated and possibly unworkable. The Justice Department is still (in 1975) prosecuting rent cases arising out of the controlled period of 1972. The 1940's offer us few assurances for the present: compliance was possible then because of patriotic appeals based on war. Vietnam eroded the basis for any contemporary equivalent. In addition, the American economy is now much more dependent on raw materials from abroad whose prices cannot be controlled.

In reading #49, Robert Samuelson examines the technical inadequacies of controls during the Nixon era. He shows how bottlenecks arise when prices are controlled in the United States but not abroad. That is, shortages develop here as goods are exported in response to higher prices elsewhere. The introduction under Nixon of wage and price controls should not be seen, however, as some kind of misguided scheme to stop inflation in the national interest. As readings #50 and #51, by Stephen W. Welch and David M. Gordon, show, their unstated purpose was to increase profits by "zapping" labor.

If off-and-on-again controls are highly disruptive, permanent controls are, from the capitalist point of view, downright dangerous, since they transfer the determination of income from the free market, where events are mystifying, to the political arena, where blame can be placed, creating the possibilities for a working-class political movement.

The final three articles in this book discuss these issues and raise serious questions about the political and economic future of American and world capitalism (reading #52, by William K. Tabb, reading #53, by Richard H. Levy, and reading #54, by Stanley Aronowitz). These authors, like others elsewhere in the book, believe that a new stage of capitalist planning is now in the offing. Unfortunately, Americans erroneously associate the kind of planning we are apt to get with "socialism." They believe that the enormous growth of government has meant that we have journeyed a considerable distance down the socialist path.

No one, however—whether pro-capitalist or pro-socialist—should mistake capitalist planning for socialism. In the past, under crisis conditions such as the Great Depression, capitalists have extended the apparatus of government planning to meet their needs to survive. Individual corporate interests, to be sure, (often those smaller and on the rise) rejected governmental controls as unnecessarily restrictive of individual capitalist prerogatives, though I think it safe to say that nowadays virtually all of big business has fully accommodated itself to big government and enjoys the access to the public treasury and other fringe benefits that accrue. Extending, though, the system of capitalist planning beyond the Keynesian regulatory framework, which is general in nature to *individual* controls on prices, wages and resource allocation, has serious shortcomings from the capitalist point of view. Apart from politicizing income, planning places capitalists in a double bind. If controls work badly, all of the problems of unemployment, inflation and profitlessness continue apace. But if they work well, the working class may begin to reassess its bias against real socialism, so carefully cultivated all these years by the culture of capitalism. After all, if government coordinates the economy and removes all the risks, what do we need the Mellons, Rockefellers and Gettys for, to take all the profits? Why not a workers' government?

Finally, an additional note for those who prefer to believe that the contemporary capitalist system is a mixed economy—part capitalist and part socialist. This I would strongly deny (see also reading #52). Ideologues like Ayn Rand would have us believe that somehow we have departed from "true" capitalism, which is some kind of perfect political state, like the notion of God transferred to politics. I would remind those who approach political issues in this fashion that "true" capitalism is a hypothetical laissez-faire construct, one which never has existed in reality and never will. Eternal, and "existing" only in the mind, this approach is totally ahistorical.

It ignores first of all the brutal origins of capitalism. As Marx put it, "If money, according to Augier, 'comes into the world with a congenital blood-stain on one cheek,' capital comes dripping from head to foot, from every pore with blood and dirt." It also ignores the entire history of its development, one in which the capitalist class itself increasingly made use of state power to increase its profits and ensure its survival. If it is silly to believe that Richard Nixon—a reactionary Republican of long standing, with close ties to big business—became a socialist on August 15, 1971, when he promulgated a wage-price freeze to solve the problems of capitalism, it is absolutely ludicrous to call state planning under Nelson Rockefeller "socialism." We'll know that socialism has arrived when we see Nelson enter a cab and sit down behind the wheel!

On a more serious level, to some people the word "socialism" conjures up unspeakable horrors—slave labor camps, arbitrary arrests and totalitarian rule—while to others it is the source of whatever hope there is for humankind. Those among the latter, like myself, have an obligation to inform others why we believe socialism to be a giant stride forward rather than a leap backward toward a totalitarian society.

On the level of theory, socialism is first of all characterized by public, or state, ownership of the means of production and comprehensive planning to make sure that material and human resources are wisely used. These conditions are *necessary* for the achievement of socialism, but they are not *sufficient*. In the first place, public ownership and planning are not incompatible with the existence of privileged elites, nor do they exclude the arbitrary rule of the few over the many. Secondly, there is no assurance that socialism, defined in this fashion, will not retrogress toward capitalist forms and ultimately to capitalism itself, especially if planning takes the form of emphasizing individual incentives and the use of the market mechanism. Many socialist critics of capitalism believe the Soviet Union is somewhere on this backward path.

The implication, then, is that socialism is more than an economic system of production and distribution but a social system in which social, political and economic privilege has been eradicated (or at least the direction of movement is continuously toward this ideal). In short, the socialist goal is that everyone should be able to live up to his or her potential or at least not be denied it because of an inegalitarian system of power and stratification.

In the light of what has just been said, it is obvious that socialism is not something flipped on like a light switch. It is, to be sure, an alternative to capitalism, its crises, its alienation and its gross inequalities. But it is not one achieved on the day after the taking of power from the capitalist class. That significant milestone is simply a gigantic first step on the road to what socialists believe is a more human and just society.

For those who reject socialism because of its negative features where it already exists (or in countries describing themselves as socialist), I would counter with an old, yet valid argument—that these experiments in socialism have taken place in backward countries where the need was to build a modern industrial economy on an underdeveloped, agricultural base. These were countries lacking traditions of democracy and civil liberties; moreover, they were surrounded by hostile and aggressive capitalist powers.

The United States is hardly economically backward—many would call it *over*developed. We are also a people who cherish our civil liberties and democratic processes, however much they have been eroded. Should America become socialist, no hostile capitalist power of any consequence is apt to threaten our existence.

American socialism, then, when and if it arrives, will necessarily be qualitatively different from what now exists. Its specific features are of course unknown at present, but it will obviously reflect our level of development. Socialism, though, is no more around the corner than Hoover's prosperity. The question is whether or not the economic crisis will be used to reorganize capitalist society along increasingly regimented lines, or alternatively, whether the crisis can be used to build a popular, socialist movement which will in the short run protect the living standard of working people and in the long run prepare the way for the eventual reorganization of our society along socialist lines.

48. A WALL STREET CALL FOR A NEW RFC AND STATE PLANNING

by Felix Rohatyn

With the country sliding rapidly into what appears to be a serious recession, suggestions are being made to revive the Reconstruction Finance Corporation as part of an overall economic program. The Democratic leadership has proposed this step and has introduced the necessary legislation.

Revival of the R.F.C. as part of a plan to get the economy on its feet is desirable without any doubt. In the Depression years of the 1930's, the R.F.C. played an important role in providing liquidity to banks and key industries, thereby preventing failures and a deepening spiral of the economic downturn. However, simply recreating the R.F.C. to provide additional credit to borrowers otherwise unable to obtain it, would be to overlook key aspects of the actual role played by the agency and to ignore basic differences between the financial structure of United States enterprise then and now. If the R.F.C. is to be recreated, let it become a vital instrument of economic growth and not just another lender of last resort.

The R.F.C. itself was a revival, in this case a revival of the War Finance Corporation of World War I. It took place in January, 1932. It was charged with providing emergency facilities for banks and other credit institutions. It was also given broad authority to make loans to agricultural, commercial and industrial enterprises.

Of approximately $4-billion proposed R.F.C. expenditures

Abridged from the *New York Times* (December 1, 1974). Felix Rohatyn is a partner in Lazard Frères & Co., a New York investment house.

for 1934, the largest portion, $1.4-billion, was earmarked for the purchase of bank preferred stocks. Eventually the R.F.C. expanded into other areas through subsidiaries such as the Commodity Credit Corporation, the Electric Home and Farm Authority, the R.F.C. Mortgage Company and the Federal National Mortgage Association. It also financed public works programs, made industrial loans and provided emergency relief.

By 1938, the R.F.C. had disbursed $10-billion, including approximately $4-billion to financial institutions, $1.5-billion to agriculture and $1-billion each to railroads and public works. The fears of many that the R.F.C. would become an instrument of creeping socialism or of state planning were unwarranted: a vast investor of public funds, the R.F.C. nevertheless was operated essentially along the lines of a private banking institution.

This brief review should be kept in mind when consideration is given to the role and the powers of a new R.F.C. in today's economic environment. Certain factors would appear to be the most obviously telling:

· At every level of our economy our institutions are overburdened with debt. In the past 10 years the debt-equity ratio of individual corporations has gone from 25 per cent to 40 per cent. Inflation and the collapse of the equity markets has accelerated this trend.

· The continued decline in the equity markets has resulted in 80 per cent of New York Exchange stocks presently carrying a multiple of less than 10 times earnings. A majority of such companies have market values of less than their book values. Many are unable to sell equity at any reasonable price.

· The Big Board has recently estimated that the equity requirements of American industry for the foreseeable future could approximate $50-billion a year. It would appear that 1974 will produce only about $5-billion.

· The United States banking system, trying to keep pace with the requirements for credit, has itself become dangerously overextended. The requirements for equity by the banking system may, in some ways, be proportionally greater than those of the industrial sector.

· The dangers to the international banking system caused by the deficits of oil importing countries are too well known to require more than a mention.

This environment of fragility in both the industrial and the financial sectors exists at a time of steeply declining production, sharply increasing unemployment and continued inflationary pressures. The downward leverage, under those circumstances, would be vicious.

There exists today no public instrument for providing the only true safety net that a major corporation or bank should avail itself of when in difficulty—a major infusion of equity capital. A massive infusion of credit, such as was undertaken by the Federal Reserve System in the case of the Franklin National Bank, will provide temporary relief to cover withdrawals by depositors. It will not provide capital support to the bank in the case of a major default.

An emergency loan guarantee enabled the Lockheed Aircraft Corporation to obtain necessary short-term credits but it did not resolve the company's long-term requirements; a major re-structuring of its debt and a large infusion of new equity capital will be required to do this.

At a time when loss of confidence is an almost palpable thing, accelerating the downturn of a shaky economy, a major bank-ruptcy either in the industrial or the financial sector is to be avoided at any reasonable cost. The R.F.C. should be the safety net, but the cure should be permanent. From its inception, it should be an instrument, empowered to make significant equity investments, in the form of either common or preferred stock, for the long-term resolution of financial problems.

There will be wide opposition to such a thesis both on ideo-logical and practical grounds. The specter of socialism will be raised by the conservatives and the cry of "big business bail-out" will be heard from the liberals. Serious concerns with respect to the governance of such an enterprise, to its potential political power, to the possible conflicts-of-interest and corruption posed by such a mass of capital, will have to be debated and resolved. But the need for the enterprise would appear to be sufficiently great to outweigh the drawbacks.

In addition to being an investor of last resort empowered to make equity infusions into banks or industrial enterprises deemed to be "in the public interest," the R.F.C. could become a catalyst of stimulation in many areas. If a Manhattan-type project in the area of energy is ever undertaken, as is clearly required, the

R.F.C. could play a major role as an investor, risk-sharer, lender and guarantor in a variety of projects. Although state-regulated concerns such as utilities should perhaps not be eligible investments, the financing of massive generating facilities, the output of which would be shared by various grids, could be considered. Construction of over $20-billion worth of generating capacity has been canceled so far this year, its effect to be felt years from now.

There can be no denying that such an organization, with the type of wide-ranging freedom described above, can be perceived as a first step toward state planning of the economy. Yet the time may have come for a public debate on this subject. Our economy is today subjected to certain traumas which have nothing to do with the result of free market interaction. The oil cartel and the prices of other basic commodities that directly affect our economy such as phosphates and alumina are the result of political rather than economic decisions, and are totally beyond our control.

At a time when the oil producing countries are levying an initial tax of $60-billion a year on the rest of the world, the United States has become capital-poor. The possible impact on this country's welfare, as well as its security, of foreign control of major enterprises has not been evaluated. The premise that, under such circumstances, the country has to husband its resources more carefully, allocate them more prudently and match its financial capabilities with its social priorities would appear to be worth considering. What many will call state planning would, to the average family, be no more than prudent budgeting.

There are many who believe that long-range economic planning, at the Federal level, will become a necessity. A plan without instruments to bring it to reality, however, is simply one more piece of paper. The R.F.C. could be one of the key instruments in this kind of approach. By injecting equity capital where none is available in quantity, it could facilitate major restructuring for the public purpose.

For instance, if a merger of Pan American World Airways and Trans World Airlines appears to be nationally desirable, a $250-million equity investment in the merged company could accomplish much. It could cause the lenders of both corporations to convert some of their debt to equity, or reduce carrying charges or stretch out maturities. It could insure the merged company's ability to ride through the storm, achieve its savings and efficiencies and ultimately be profitable enough to provide a fair return to the investors (including the R.F.C.), a viable employer and pass some savings on in lower fares.

The R.F.C. should, thus, become a permanent part of our economic establishment, not just as a last-ditch creditor but as a vibrant instrument of both rescue as well as stimulus. It need not, and should not, be a permanent investor in any one particular enterprise. It should only remain as an investor, either as a part-owner or creditor, until such time as it can, in the public interest, divest itself of the enterprise in which it invests and this investment is eligible for normal market channels or until the markets are capable of performing their function. The R.F.C., therefore, should, in effect, become a revolving fund— hopefully a profitable one—which steps in where no alternatives are available and which steps out when the public interest has been served and normal market forces can again operate.

An initial capitalization of $5-billion in commonstock subscribed to by the Treasury, and the authority to issue up to $10-billion in United States guaranteed obligations, would provide a major safety factor to the economy in the coming times of peril, as well as simultaneously taking pressure off the banking system. These obligations could provide a logical investment for the surplus dollars of oil-producing countries.

Financing the capital subscription should come from the private sector. It could take the form of a levy of 1 per cent of pretax profits of all enterprises earning over $1-million per annum. This would reimburse the Treasury's subscription in less than five years.

The R.F.C. should combine public purpose with prudent business practice and, with the proper leadership and oversight, should accomplish both to the ultimate benefit of the tax payers.

Its own board of directors should include the secretary of the Treasury, the chairman of the Council of Economic Advisers, the chairman of the Securities and Exchange Commission and the chairman of the Federal Reserve System. With a large audience gazing over its shoulder, its management will have to practice a degree of asceticism and conform to standards of an extraordinarily high order. We should not despair of that possibility, however. Other agencies have been held to such standards. There is no reason for the R.F.C. not to be able to do the same.

49. WHY PRICE CONTROLS STOPPED WORKING . . .

by Robert Samuelson

There are a few essentials to know about fertilizers. Plants need nitrogen. Fertilizer gives them nitrogen. The more fertilizer, generally speaking, the bigger the crop. The bigger the crop, the greater the supply. The greater the supply, the lower the price.

There is a fertilizer shortage in the U.S. now. The process works in reverse, so less fertilizer will probably mean higher food prices. No one disputed this logic. Nor, I found, did many people dispute the fact that economic controls had contributed to the shortage.

The story was simple. In 1972 the world price of key fertilizers rose significantly—50 to 75 per cent—above U.S. prices. A very predictable thing soon happened: with U. S. prices held down by controls, fertilizer firms began shipping their supplies abroad.

There were some complaints, but it wasn't until September, 1973—after the industry, through its trade association, the Fertilizer Institute, officially asked for exemption—that the Cost of Living Council began seriously considering the removal

Extracts from *Washington Monthly* (May 1974).

of controls on U.S. fertilizer prices. Removing the price ceilings, of course, would allow U.S. buyers to bid for the scarce supplies on an equal footing with foreign purchasers.

The time lag was no surprise. Bureaucracies habitually react to problems, rather than anticipating them. Institutional sluggishness. You could blame it on stupidity, or ignorance, but, in the case of government bureaucracies, there was a more fundamental reason: a problem has to exist before it can be solved. You couldn't take the price ceilings off fertilizer to avoid the problem. People would accuse the controllers of sabotaging their own program without any good reason. You had to wait for the reason to develop. You had to wait for the fertilizer to be exported.

Even after the industry's appeal, the Cost of Living Council hesitated. Part of the problem was ignorance: the inevitable absence of the answers to today's questions today. A lot of fertilizer was already tied up in long-term export contracts, but the Council didn't know how much. The prospect was troubling. Prices might rise without producing much additional supply for U.S. farmers. There was another problem. Exempting the fertilizer industry would inevitably stimulate exemption requests from other industries. Not all these could be cavalierly ignored. The explosives industry complained that if it weren't exempted, it wouldn't be able to compete with fertilizer manufacturers for ammonia nitrate, which is used in the manufacturing of both fertilizer and explosives. Then there would be a shortage of explosives for coal mines, which would eventually lead to a scarcity of coal. The world was complicated. Ultimately the Council exempted both the fertilizer and explosives industries.

But fertilizer was no freak breakdown of controls. Copper and scrap steel supplies also had flowed abroad because domestic prices were held artificially low. Lumber had been withheld from the market. A shortage of tomato paste had developed, in part because the price had been held too low and encouraged a depletion of stock. The experiment with direct food controls had failed conspicuously. Farmers, faced with rising feed costs— which hadn't been controlled—smothered baby chicks and sent their breeder chickens off to slaughter; hog farmers, confronting the same cost-price squeeze, limited expansion of output.

There were dozens of stories in dozens of industries about how controls had misfired. One newspaper executive claimed, for example, that controls had aggravated the newsprint shortage: you held down advertising rates and people advertised more; the more they advertised, the more paper you needed.

But the stories were prone to exaggeration. Consider fertilizer. Controls or no controls, there would have been a shortage. Demand had risen spectacularly because the government had freed nearly 60 million acres of land for production. The industry hadn't expanded in the last few years, because it was just emerging from the economic slump in the late sixties. All that could be said was that the controls had made a bad situation worse. If controls hadn't been lifted, more fertilizer would have been sold abroad. It was a frustratingly ambiguous conclusion.

The same thing that happened in fertilizer happened in plastics. World prices of petrochemicals (the essential raw ingredient for plastics processing) soared above domestic prices, tempting major petrochemical manufacturers (about 25 giants, including DuPont, Dow Chemical, and Exxon Chemical, supply about half the country's plastic resins) to export their product. The incentives to do so were powerful. To give but one example: the domestic price of polystyrene was effectively frozen at 18 cents per pound, while the world price was more than three times as high.

While the diversion of fertilizer supplies overseas undoubtedly hurt U.S. food production, the escape of petrochemicals abroad had more curious consequences.

First, business success—indeed survival—became a matter of who you knew, not how well you ran your businesss. Because the petrochemical companies were still selling considerable amounts of supplies in the U.S., you could stay in production if you knew the petrochemical company's marketing vice president better than your competitor did.

Second, competition in the plastics industry became more political and less economic. Many of the small independent companies soon realized that their problems lay in Washington: if they could ease the Phase IV rules, allowing domestic prices to rise to world levels, then some of the chemicals would stay in the U.S., and American firms could bid for supplies. So, the small plastic companies formed a Washington-based trade association. . . .

Finally, people tried to get around the price ceilings. The result was "black markets," "distortions," or whatever label you want to attach to intricate, suspicious transactions designed to beat the government rules.

Consider this situation: a marketing vice president of a large petrochemical firm has a huge supply to sell. He must sell the chemicals at prices fixed by government ceilings. At the free market (world) price, the same stock might be worth three or four times as much. What does he do? The possibilities aren't hard to imagine. Sell to a broker friend and split the profit? (Under Phase IV rules, the broker could probably sell at a free price, because, being a "small businessman," he would have been exempted from price rules.) Take a kickback from a grateful buyer, desperate for petrochemicals to keep his plant running? Act honestly?

All this, of course, undermined competition. The artificiality of prices created enormous gaps between firms. If company A bought its petrochemicals at the fixed price, but company B bought its supply at a free price, three or four times as high, it wasn't hard to figure out which firm would prosper.

But again, I ran into maddening ambiguity. Given the oil shortage, there would have been a scarcity of petrochemicals anyway. Some of the big plastics companies had a natural advantage over the smaller firms because they made their own petrochemicals. Eventually, the Cost of Living Council partially decontrolled petrochemical prices. No one knew quite how many small plastics firms had been forced out of business, whether they had been forced out permanently, or whether they might have gone bust under any circumstances.

The Federal Reserve building is a white-marbled temple on Constitution Avenue that's rarely visited by anyone who doesn't work there. Inside the building is Arthur Burns, chairman of the Federal Reserve Board and also chairman of the Committee on Interest and Dividends. The CID, as it was called, maintained a "voluntary" system of controls over interest rates and dividends. These items hadn't been included in the coverage of the original Economic Stabilization Act, but, to give the appearance of being even-handed with business and labor, the Administration believed it couldn't ignore them. Hence the CID.

The incident which interested me occurred in early 1973. At that time, major commercial banks began to raise their so-called "prime rate"—the rate of interest they charge to their very best business customers (less trustworthy borrowers usually received loans at a fixed level above prime which rose and fell with fluctuations in the prime). Over the years the prime rate had become a media superstar, attracting enormous attention—well beyond its real importance—any time it changed. Its upward movements in early 1973 drew the customary page one stories. All this upset Burns. He decided to stop—or at least slow—the rise of the prime.

As chairman of the CID, he fired off telegrams to big banks, demanding that they justify the higher rates and declaring that the increases threatened the Administration's anti-inflation program.

It was an intriguing picture: Arthur Burns holding the big, greedy banks in line, battling to keep inflation under control, and protecting the interests of the common man. That's the picture the press painted. But it is not, alas, what happened. Burns' primary motivation in standing up to the banks was not so much to hold interest rates down as to head off legislation that might place interest rates under *mandatory* controls.

Worried about rising prices and climbing interest rates, congressmen—particularly Rep. Wright Patman, the formidable chairman of the House Banking and Currency Committee—were agitating to require Burns (or someone) to regulate all rates. Burns apparently thought this impossible to do, disastrous to try. The confrontation with the banks was designed to undercut that campaign by demonstrating that Burns was already fighting to hold down the key rates.

It didn't take much research to turn up a few more examples of politics getting in the way of economics.

Consider rents. Not many economists believed rents could be effectively controlled on a nationwide basis. Housing conditions varied too greatly from city to city. Anyway, housing was generally very competitive; there were lots of landlords and lots of builders. If land costs rose, if labor costs rose, and if local taxes rose, it followed that rents would have to rise. To try to hold them back would, in the long run, probably be self-defeating;

landlords would cut back on service and maintenance, and, ultimately, new construction might decline.

But rent is a highly visible and emotional symbol of inflation. So, in Phase II, the Price Commission tried to control rents. It was not a very satisfactory experience. The rules were monstrously complicated. "Lawyers in the Price Commission and the Internal Revenue Service found them difficult to write," C. Jackson Grayson, chairman of the Price Commission, would recall later. "We found them difficult to explain, and the general public couldn't understand them. . . . We tried revision after revision to clarify and simplify, and each time we seemed to generate more confusion."

And what about Burns' dance with the prime rate? Was that simply a harmless exercise in politics and public relations? Well, maybe not. It did succeed in neutralizing pressure for mandatory interest rate controls, but its economic consequences may have been less benign.

While Burns was busy sitting on the prime rate, big businesses were stumbling all over each other to take out new bank loans. They knew that the cost of money—that is, the interest rate—would be higher later, so why not take advantage of a bargain while it lasted. In the first half of 1973, business loans at commercial banks rose at an astounding annual rate of about 30 per cent.

The explosion of loans occurred precisely when economists recognized that the U.S. economy was in the midst of a demand boom and was desperately in need of some restraint. Burns realized this. The Fed was attempting to tighten credit, which normally would raise interest rates, choke off some borrowing, and help slow down the economy. As chairman of the CID and the Fed, Burns was moving in opposite directions simultaneously.

How much damage did it do? No one will ever really know. But, at best, Burns was fighting inflation with press releases. At worst, he was pouring the proverbial oil onto the fire.

Lesson Number One was about political reality and economic reality. Politics demanded instant and simple solutions. Prices were going up. Stop them. Damn the torpedoes, full speed ahead. Economic reality didn't work quite that way. There were choices —unpleasant choices—to be made. It was like chocolate: you could eat a lot of chocolate, but you might get cavities. Years later, of course. Wage-price controllers were constantly being tugged between the two realities, but, with their eyes glued to the monthly price indexes, they were always tempted to do anything that might give them instant success, minimizing the possible ill aftereffects—which might take years to surface.

. . . [T]he Cost of Living Council had commissioned a number of reputable economists to try to figure out the overall impact of controls on prices. The economists fed the statistics into their computers, ran the numbers forward and backward, subjecting them to all sorts of generally incomprehensible, but respectable, forms of analysis. The results were mixed. One analysis concluded that controls had had no impact at all. Another estimated that without controls prices would be one per cent higher than they are. The final analysis said that controls had generally kept non-food prices down 2.3 per cent.

"So we got [remarks Samuelson's source] a two-percent reduction in the cost of living, at best, for the controls, and we got a lot of trouble in a lot of industries. Maybe we're lucky, though, because we avoided the biggest risk. A political smash-up, caused by a confrontation between big labor and government. Something like what happened in Britain. People forget that wage-price controls are fundamentally aimed at labor, not business. The price controls are added to make wage controls politically palatable and give the impression of impartiality.

"In effect, the government bargains with big unions. The record of government in bargaining situations isn't too good. There's a lot of press coverage. Issues get publicized, and positions gets polarized. We've had enough bitter municipal strikes to prove that. There are a lot of unions that can tie this country up pretty quickly: the Teamsters, the railroad unions, the coal miners. Longshoremen and steelworkers and auto workers can make things pretty messy, too. Controls are a natural target for strike or protest. Look what the independent truckers did to the oil allocations, and they were weak and unorganized. I don't like the idea of a really powerful union trying the same trick.

"If you want to be totally cynical about it, imagine the following scenario. It's 18 months before a national election. Unemployment is high. Inflation is unacceptable. The party in power, though it's skeptical about the lasting value of controls, puts controls on the economy. By the next summer, things are looking fine. Unemployment has come down. Prices have been artificially restrained. The party wins big, but, after the elections, the problems of the controls become increasingly apparent. Prices soar." Of course, that's precisely what had happened in 1972.

The lesson in all of this, he said, is simple: controls involve large risks, but promise small rewards.

50. "ZAPPING" LABOR: A RADICAL PERSPECTIVE ON WAGE-PRICE CONTROLS

by Stephen W. Welch

Announcing that "The time has come for decisive action—action that will break the vicious circle of spiraling prices and costs," President Nixon inaugurated the first peacetime wage and price controls in this country in August of 1971. Although he stated that "We must stop the rise in the cost of living," he more accurately should have revealed that he intended to put a crimp in labor's demand for higher wages in hopes of reversing a significant decline in corporate profits over the previous six years. How do various economists, business and labor leaders view controls? What impact could controls have on corporate profits in the early 1970's? Are controls biased in favor of corporate interests rather than labor? Is there a need for controls in the mid-1970's? If so, how would further controls fit into the overall crisis which the economy now faces?

Economists are far from unanimous in their view of controls: essentially three views may be distinguished. Libertarians from

Especially written for this book. Stephen W. Welch is assistant professor of economics at Kenyon College.

the University of Chicago contend that no form of incomes policies is needed to solve the inflation problem; a decrease in the
rate of growth of the money supply, given sufficient time, will
cure rapidly rising prices. The imposition of controls will only
postpone the inevitable price increases associated with pent-up
demand; worse still, they will cause distortions in the allocation
of goods and services, leading to inefficient use of resources.
Investment will be discouraged, supplies will dry up or shift
abroad, and black markets may spring up. Recent examples of
such distortions and their allocative impact are numerous. For
instance, restricting the price of fertilizer below the world price
encouraged fertilizer exports in 1972 and short supplies here at
home. U.S. farmers consequently realized less output per acre,
with the predictable result to farm prices. Similar movements
abroad were seen for polystyrene (an essential petrochemical
for the plastics industry), tubular goods (tubing, casings and
pipe used in oil drilling), copper and scrap steel. Administration
profit-margin rules led industries to reallocate their production
toward those sectors which returned relatively higher profits in
the best two fiscal years from 1969 through 1972. In the steel
industry the result was a severe shortage of less profitable steel
reinforcing bars in 1973, while in the paper industry heavier-
weight paper was produced at the sacrifice of resources which
could have produced more lightweight substitutable paper products.

Liberal economists, following the lead of Harvard's John
Kenneth Galbraith, maintain that controls on wages and prices
worked adequately during two war periods; hence there is sufficient evidence, they claim, that controls will be able to cope
effectively with rising inflation during peace time. A variant of
this argument holds that short-term controls may be necessary to
break the inflationary psychology of both buyers and labor, enabling them to readjust their expectations to lowered levels of
price increase, which then may slow down their demand for
goods as well as money wage increases.

Radical economists can hardly deny the validity of the distortions argument of the libertarians. Surely controls eventually lead
to shortages because they suppress market forces which, however socially irrational, have their own internal coherence in our
capitalist system. Who cannot recall seeing baby chicks

smothered before TV cameras as irate farmers were caught between frozen sales prices and climbing feed prices in the summer of 1973? Radicals are also quick to point out that Galbraith's harkening back to wartime conditions ignores the realities of today's international trade. The fertilizer and copper examples cited above are evidence not only of allocation problems associated with controls, but also of the impact of international trade. With price controls on copper in World War II, we did not have to contend with copper flights to Germany and Japan, two of the main consumers of our copper in the 1972–74 period. The primary hallmark of the radical analysis is the assertion that controls are aimed at the labor sector to slow down the rate of wage increase in order to enhance the profit position of the corporate sector. Price controls merely are added to make the controls politically palatable and give the impression of impartiality.

The radical contention is supported by the very nature of controls themselves. First, it is easier to control wages than prices, since pricing practices generally are more varied and complex than methods of calculating compensation. Second, prices can be "raised" merely by changing the quantity or quality of the goods or the services associated with the delivery of the goods. Third, price increases usually take place on a continuous basis and may involve differential increases for thousands of individual commodities, while wage changes are often made on a fixed cycle of across-the-board adjustments. Hence wage increases are visible and amendable to control. Fourth, when all employers are under similar restraints and unlikely to compete for a given labor force, built-in cost-reduction incentives guarantee that wage controls will not be evaded.

The views of business and labor leaders help to clarify the substantive issues involved in a critique of wage and price controls. For instance, the business sector strongly supported President Nixon's initiation of controls in 1971. *Fortune* magazine editorialized for controls in the spring of 1970. In October of 1970 the Business Council, composed of top executives of the largest corporations, told Administration representatives that they could not dispel demands for activist intervention by appeals to conservative ideology. These business leaders were obviously concerned about their declining profits, especially evident since 1965. Precedent-setting construction-wage settlements of over 10 per cent in 1970 were also worrisome to business because of the large number of union collective-bargaining contracts coming up for renewal in 1971. As the *Wall Street Journal* expressed it: "Actually, many businessmen never did favor permanent controls. Many just wanted some temporary government intervention to block what they considered to be unreasonable union wage demands" (March 4, 1974, p. 1). Toward the end of the Nixon controls in the spring of 1974, the business community had not experienced the rejuvenation of their profit position as they had expected. Disillusionment with controls was evident. But *Fortune* magazine again editorialized: "The Phase IV fiasco, however, should not be allowed to discredit the idea that restraints on wages and prices can sometimes be useful" (March, 1974, p. 100). The editors noted that in times of slack overall demand for goods and services, controls might be a useful device to apply again to the labor market. The year 1975 certainly qualifies as one of slack demand.

But a contradiction in business attitudes is also apparent. Ideologically, big business maintains a public stance against government intrusion into the market place (unless it is their specific market place and the intrusion is either a subsidy or regulation to restrain aggressive competitors). Business worries that wage and price controls may lead to economic planning and further restraints on independent decision making within the corporate sector. Indeed this might be the case. Thus the contradiction arises between the business community's desire for government help to hold down union wage demands, and so spur declining profits, and the fear of controls leading to unforeseen fetters on the business sector.

The position of the other main protagonist, organized labor, is also ambiguous. Since 1966 the AFL/CIO, actually representing less than one quarter of the labor force but acting as if it were the spokesman for all labor, has publicly stated that it would cooperate with mandatory controls, provided such controls were "even-handed and across-the-board." This position was repeated in a statement issued just two days before the freeze was announced. It is difficult to understand how labor conceived of fair controls emanating from a Republican Administration. Possibly the previous two years' unexpectedly large (by 1960 standards!) price increases of 5½ and 6 per cent were seen as the cause of the decline in real take-home pay during 1969 and 1970. The AFL/CIO may have felt that with a large number of contract renegotiations coming up in 1971, the key to real increased take-home pay would be achieved through controls on prices. But four days after the announced freeze, the AFL/CIO executive council denounced the freeze as "unequitable, unjust, unfair, and unworkable." Besides lambasting the lack of controls over executive compensation, new products, some agricultural products, interest, profits and dividends, the council also pointed out that previously negotiated wage hikes due during the freeze were not permitted while employers could enjoy extra profits, since their price structures would already have reflected the negotiated wage increases. Attempts to close some of the "loopholes" cited by the AFL/CIO after the Phase I freeze did not prove either effective or sufficient to satisfy the labor leaders. The naming of manifestly pro-management "public members" to the tripartite wage-monitoring Pay Board also angered labor. By March 1972, all AFL/CIO members had departed from this board.

The leadership of the AFL/CIO may not appreciate the full significance of the present profit crisis and thus initially may have placed too much faith in controls. Profits are very low and declining; there is no self-adjusting process which business can rely upon to make sure that the free enterprise system will restore profits; and the nation is beset by troubles emanating from the international crisis. The end result of this situation may be government economic planning on a broad scale which may ultimately rely upon controls to help bolster corporate profits.

The use of corporate profits as a key analytical tool is another hallmark of the radical economists. However, profit studies are not their province alone, as is exemplified by the recent comprehensive study of profits by William Nordhaus of Yale. The title of his paper, "The Falling Share of Profits," aptly summarizes his findings. These results lend perspective to the wage-price controls issue.

Once nonfinancial corporate profits have been adjusted for a number of factors, Nordhaus' data clearly indicate a secular decline in corporate profits over the postwar period, expressed in a variety of ways. The after-tax rate of return on corporate capital, for instance, has fallen, though not continuously, from 9.7 to 5.4

per cent between 1948 and 1973. It is instructive to note that the cyclical upswing in the corporate rate of return experienced from 1960 to 1965 was dramatically arrested after 1965 through 1970. The year 1971 saw a slight increase in the rate of return, with the following two years again experiencing a decline. The latest figures indicate that the corporate rate of return is just slightly over half of what it was in 1965. Despite the banner headlines announcing record profits, the adjusted data do not paint such a rosy picture.

Nordhaus contends that the long-run decline in the corporate rate of return is due to a response to decreased risk of corporate ventures as the government has learned how to dampen swings in the business cycle via monetary and fiscal policy. Though the present unemployment rate of over 7 per cent may call this reasoning into question, there is other evidence to buttress the idea that there has been a decline in risks taken by entrepreneurs in this advanced capitalist economy. Consider the risk-aversion implications of the Penn-Central bail-out, the Lockheed loan, the recently passed oil-cargo–hauling act, and the recent discussion of reviving the Reconstruction Finance Corporation to buck up companies in dire financial straits. There are some who think that this does not have the ring of free enterprise; others will point out that the function of the state in a capitalist economy is to support the corporate interests—the absence of adequate benefit-cost ratios and "market failures" notwithstanding.

A quick look at some of the factors underlying the profit erosion experienced in the latter half of the 1960's and the first half of the 1970's may shed some light on what might be called the myth of the self-regulating economy. During the first half of the 1960's, increases in labor productivity and increases in prices more than made up for the increases in wages. But as the expansion continued, bolstered by war expenditures, production bottlenecks were encountered, labor-productivity increases slowed down (and actually declined in 1968), and increases in costs could not be passed on in the form of price increases, in part because of the significant increases in imported products. The result was a continuance of the secular (or long-run) profit decline. Conventional thinking predicted that the recession of 1970 (brought about by a leveling off of defense expenditures and a budget surplus) would restore profits, and hence encourage subsequent expansion as a slack in the labor market would mitigate wage demands and labor productivity would pick up. But the Nordhaus data indicate that profits continued their decline except for the year 1971. Wage demands skyrocketed, spurred on by unanticipated increases in the cost of living; labor productivity increased very little after 1970; and interest payments cut deeply into corporate profits. The interest issue is more important than is generally realized, since the ratio of interest payments to corporate profits rose from 3 per cent in 1948 to 24 per cent in 1973. In part this change reflects the expanded share of debt in corporate securities, and in part the increase of nominal interest rates on corporate debt over the postwar period.

Nor was the magnitude of the 1970 recession sufficient to dampen labor's demands. With the political machinery geared to maintaining full employment, unemployment ceases to play its primary role of disciplining the labor force. Thus there is no automatic regulating mechanism governing the corporate profit rate. The corporate sector currently appears caught in the dilemma of the full employment-profit squeeze and recessionary catch-up wage demands. As the present recession rolls on, further profit erosions are anticipated as debt-ridden corporation find it extremely difficult to meet their fixed-interest obligations. The inability of unemployed workers to maintain payments on personal debts will only exacerbate the situation.

Because of the lack of a self-regulating profit mechanism, new tools may be necessary to deal with our own problems. Major decisions along the lines of energy use and recent talk of a revitalized Reconstruction Finance Corporation are suggestive of economic planning. The planning imperatives for the United States arising from the current crisis only reinforce the existing belief that the superior performance of Japan and West Germany in the 1960's was based in large part on the fact that they relied on planning to a much greater extent than the United States. Wage and price controls would then be one tool in the planner's toolbox. At this point the radical economist is quick to point out that as long as the individuals who are planning are responsive to the interests of the corporate sector, the controls, as well as other programs, will continue to be what they were in the past—in effect, props for corporate profits.

The London *Economist* recently characterized President Ford's new Cost of Living Task Force as "a thin end of a new controls wedge." Recent polls have shown that Americans again want some form of controls. Since incomes policies have never been successfully instituted in situations of excess demand, the recession year 1975 appears ripe for the institution of permanent controls. Radical economists contend that such controls will immediately politicize the income-distribution issue. They point to the following scenario: government determination of the distribution of income between labor and capital; the rationing of final goods, raw materials and credit; the imposition of anti-strike legislation; the eventual allocation of labor; and an increased level of class and political conflict.

Whatever the exact details of the future when controls are reinstituted, let no one mistake the undeniable class interests masked behind the myth of impartial wage and price controls. Those forgetting the lessons of the first peacetime controls of 1971–74 might ponder the words of Arnold Weber, former executive director of the Cost of Living Council:

> Business had been leaning on [Secretary of the Treasury] Shultz and [Chairman of Economic Advisers] McCracken to do something about the economy, especially wages. The idea of the freeze and Phase II was to zap labor, and we did. (*Business Week* [April 27, 1974], p. 108.)

51. CAPITAL VS. LABOR: THE CURRENT CRISIS IN THE SPHERE OF PRODUCTION

by David M. Gordon

Everyone is feeling the pinch of the current economic crisis in one way or another. Consumers face soaring prices. Workers face layoffs. Workers' real wages continue to decline. The poor suffer cutbacks in essential social services. Even corporations—oh, pity their impoverished coffers—fear liquidity crises.

Most economic discussions of the current crisis have focused on the *appearances* of the crisis in the sphere of circulation—dealing almost exclusively with the behavior of monetary variables like prices, wages, profits and interest rates. There is another, equally important dimension to the dynamics of the current crisis, hiding beneath the surface of those economic aggregates, underlying policies and strategies, framing the growing struggle between corporations and working people in this country. The crisis *also* involves the struggle between capital and labor in the sphere of *production*. In order to understand the current situation, in order to discuss strategies for defending our own interests, we must focus clearly on these struggles between capital and labor as well.

Seeds of Struggle in the Late Sixties

Conflict between capital and labor began to sharpen during the sustained boom of the mid-1960's.

From the corporations' perspective, prosperity continued longer than it should have. As the demand for labor tightened

Unpublished paper. David M. Gordon teaches economics at The New School for Social Research and is a member of URPE.

after 1965 and as unions bargained more and more strenuously to keep up with rising inflation, corporate profits got squeezed. Corporate profits as a share of national income began to fall and the ratio of profits to wages plunged.[1]

Ordinarily, corporation would have tried to protect their profits by continuing their practices of mark-up pricing, passing on higher costs in continually higher prices, maintaining their margin of profits over average costs.[2] Partly because of increasing international competition, corporations' freedom to raise prices continually was gradually curtailed. Particularly in such industries as auto and steel which felt the impact of international competition most severely, the limits on continuing price increases were clearly felt.[3] This meant, among other things, that corporations were beginning to find it more and more difficult to salvage retained earnings for continual investment in plants and equipment.

From the traditional Marxian perspective, capitalists will respond to rising wages by trying to substitute capital goods for labor, striving to increase relative surplus value by increasing the productiveness of workers.[4] When profits are squeezed and investment funds begin to dry up, their ability to pursue those strategies is often constrained by the declining investment fund and the high costs of many labor-saving technological innovations.

Many corporations, in the period of continuing boom in the

---

[1] Absolute profits fell by 4.0 per cent per year (in real terms) from 1965 through 1969. The ratio of profits to wages fell from .165 to .09, and the share of profits in gross corporate product fell from roughly 17 per cent to 10 per cent over the same period. See R. Boddy and J. Crotty, "Class Conflict, Keynesian Policies and the Business Cycle," *Monthly Review* (October 1974); and W. Nordhaus, "The Falling Share of Profits," *Brookings Papers on Economic Activity*, No. 1 (1974).

[2] Nordhaus (*ibid.*) provides useful evidence that corporations had been following average cost mark-up pricing throughout the 1950's and the early 1960's.

[3] Nordhaus (*ibid.*) also shows, from his own estimations, that the gap between aggregate prices and aggregate estimated "average total normal cost" fell to its lowest point in 1968–69 since the mid-1950's. See Figure 5, p. 196.

[4] This refers to the analysis originally developed by Marx in Vol. I of *Capital*, part V, on the "Production of Absolute and of Relative Surplus-Value."

late 1960's, tried to compensate for declining retained earnings by increasing their borrowing, hoping to maintain constant levels of investment in structures and equipment. Corporate indebtedness, having grown rapidly throughout the post–World War II period, grew even more rapidly during the mid- and late 1960's.

External financing of investment does not solve the problem of diminished retained earnings quite so simply, however. Borrowing to finance earnings involves heavy interest payments. By 1973, corporate interest payments had reached fully a quarter of total profits, eight times greater than their share immediately after World War II.[5] Those interest payments, as they grew more and more expensive, represented another kind of drain on profits.

As the 1960's wore on, therefore, corporations were faced with the same kind of problem in either of two forms. Profits were declining. Corporations could either lower their investment, slowing their replacement of labor by labor-saving capital goods, or they could try to maintain their rate of investment by borrowing to finance those investments, incurring increasing interest charges. In the one case they had to try to protect profits by finding some other means of compensating for higher labor costs than replacing labor through automation. In the other case they could continue to replace labor but had to find some way of compensating for the drain on profits from higher interest payments.

In either case, then, the drain on profits remained serious. Marxian theory would predict that corporations would seek to maintain and restore profits in those kinds of situations *by seeking to increase relative surplus value through the intensification of labor*—by trying to *speed up* the pace of production in order to get more output from workers in any given hour of the working day. Employer efforts to speed up production always encounter worker resistance, and such efforts are almost always bound to sharpen capital-labor conflict in production itself.

And by a variety of indications, that was precisely what began to happen in the late 1960's. Especially in those industries suffering increasing international competition, evidence of speed-up and worker resistance abounds.

One interesting indication of speed-up involves industrial acci-

[5] Nordhaus, *ibid.*, p. 171.

dents. When corporations are trying to substitute capital for labor, industrial accidents appear to fall.[6] Indeed, the incidence of industrial accidents had been falling in this country since World War I, a period during which corporations had been turning more and more to automation.[7] But during the 1960's, as speed-up began to replace or complement labor-saving investment, the rate of industrial accidents began to rise. The rate of industrial accidents in manufacturing was 27.7 per cent higher in 1970 than it was in 1963.[8]

Workers do not endure such speed-ups and accidents without protest. They feel it in their muscles and they suffer it when they get hurt. Largely in response to speed-up, wildcat strikes began to increase during the late 1960's as well. Workers marched out of the plants protesting working conditions. Reflecting their anger, the index of aggregate strike activity began to climb along

[6] Marx had argued, in Vol. I of *Capital,* that employers' ability to increase relative surplus value through the intensification of labor was indeterminate, in part because workers might get worn out or injured by speed-up too quickly and would have to be replaced. Increasing their productiveness did not suffer that particular indeterminacy.

[7] One consistent series on work injuries in manufacturing extends from 1926 through the early 1960's. The incidence of injuries, measured as hours lost through disabling work accidents over millions of man-hours worked, fell from its peak in 1926, at the beginning of the series, almost continuously to the early 1960's, when it began to level off at exactly half the 1926 peak. See the U.S. Bureau of Census, *Historical Statistics of the United States, Colonial Times to 1957* (Washington, D.C., U.S. Government Printing Office, 1960), p. 100, for data up to 1956; and the *President's Report on Occupational Safety and Health* (Government Printing Office, 1972), Appendix B, Work-Injury Rates by Industry, 1958–1970, pp. 71 ff., for more recent data.

[8] See the *President's Report on Occupational Safety and Health,* Appendix B. There is further evidence from that table that the increases in injury rates came especially in those industries which had previously experienced the most substantial labor displacement through automation. In what Robert Averitt calls "core industries," those concentrated industries in which market power and capital/labor ratios are highest, the average increase in the incidence of industrial accidents between 1963 and 1970 was nearly 50 per cent, or almost twice the overall increase in manufacturing. See Robert Averitt, *The Dual Economy* (New York, Norton, 1968) for the distinction between core and peripheral industries, and David M. Gordon, "Class and Segmentation in the United States: A Methodological and Empirical Review," New School for Social Research (in progress 1975), for the empirical distinction between the two sectors.

with the rate of accidents. By 1968, work time lost through strikes was 2½ times greater than it had been in 1963. After a brief decline during the recession of 1969, work time lost through strikes climbed again in 1970 to 3½ times its 1963 levels.[9]

Corporations began to panic. Their profits were being squeezed and workers were beginning to resist their efforts at intensification. So we began to hear the hue and cry of the famous "productivity crisis." America was losing its position of international economic advantage, we were told, because our workers weren't working hard enough. All those lazy workers, taking off Mondays and Fridays! To save America, we all had to work a little harder. The National Commission on Productivity posted billboards along the highways, urging us to knuckle down.

The workers' struggles at the Vega plant in Lordstown, Ohio, were symptomatic of these developments. The General Motors Assembly Division had taken over management of the Vega plant in 1971. As *Business Week* had reported, "The need for GMAD's belt-tightening role was underscored during the late 1960's when GM's profit margin dropped from 10 per cent to 7 per cent." [10] Among its "modernizing" innovations, GMAD increased the speed of the line from sixty cars per hour to over a hundred. The workers protested and finally struck. The press talked innocently about changes in the workers' attitudes, about some new, mystifying preoccupation with nonmonetary issues. The workers talked quite simply about the speed of the line. As the local union president observed, ". . . people refused to do extra work. The more the company pressured them, the less work they turned out. Cars went down the line without repairs." [11]

[9] Further indication of this effect comes from specific data about the purposes of strikes. The number of workers involved in work stoppages over "speed-up" increased by 350 per cent from 1965 to 1969, and work time lost through stoppages over "speed-up" increased by 240 per cent during the same years. For aggregate strike data, see the U.S. Bureau of Labor Statistics, *Handbook of Labor Statistics, Bulletin* #1925 (1974), Table on Work Stoppages in the United States, 1927–1972. For the data on strikes by objective and grievance, see *ibid.*, pp. 373 ff.

[10] Quoted in Stanley Aronowitz, *False Promises* (New York, McGraw-Hill, 1973), p. 22.

[11] Quoted, *ibid.*, p. 42.

Controls Shift the Terms of Struggle

As the boom continued, as profits eroded, as workers began to resist speed-up, it became more and more obvious to corporations and the government that workers' strength had to be directly attacked. When the Nixon Administration took office in 1969, it moved quickly to cool off workers by trying to cool off the economy, by inducing a recession.

The economy had been booming for so long that a fairly lengthy recession was required to cool it out. The Nixon Administration, beginning to plan the President's re-election campaign in 1971, could not risk continuing unemployment for much longer. Corporations themselves were wary of a lengthy recession; their profits were already very low, and profits normally continue to decline during the first stage of the downswing.

But the Administration could not afford normal expansionary policies, either. The balance-of-payments deficits made normal expansion, with accompanying inflation, much too risky, so controls were the answer. We were told that we needed controls to curb inflation and protect the dollar. However, one of their more fundamental purposes, reflecting the mounting struggle of the late 1960's and the inadequacy of the short-lived recession, was to control wages *and* workers. Their purpose, as the deputy director of the Cost of Living Council later admitted, was to "zap labor."

And they did. Wages were carefully controlled, while prices, more difficult to control, permitted recovery of profits by late 1972. Equally important, wage controls also curbed workers' militance. Strike activity began to fall rapidly as workers recognized the impossibilities of improving their living standard by exercising their right to strike. By the last stage of controls, in early 1974, strike activity had fallen below the levels of the early 1960's. The index of work time lost through work stoppages was less than one-quarter its level during the peak of workers' resistance in 1970.[12]

The timing of controls was important too. Large numbers of major contracts were expiring in late 1971 and early 1972, like the mine workers' contract. By racing to institute controls in

[12] Data on work stoppages since 1972 from Bureau of Labor Statistics, *Current Wage Developments,* Vol. 26, No. 12 (December 1974), p. 32.

August 1971, the government helped corporations forestall a bitter set of bargaining demands at precisely that point when workers' anger was rising most dramatically. For many industries, the timing of the controls bought the corporations a three-year lease on life (most major contracts have three-year terms), a respite during which they were assured of at least wage moderation. It was precisely during this period that the public relations campaign announcing the productivity crisis reached its peak, seeking to convince workers to settle into a more intense pace, to tolerate their loss of bargaining power over wages.

Controls Are Lifted and the Crisis Intensifies

Controls themselves could not last forever, for many shortages and bottlenecks developed in the economy. When they were lifted in March 1974, the economic crisis exploded. Many corporations raced to increase their prices as soon as they were permitted. Workers were beginning to experience the sharp decline in their real earnings by May, as workers' real earnings fell back to the levels of 1966 and 1967.

In protest, workers marched out on strike again. By June the index of work time lost through stoppages had soared to its highest levels since the late 1940's. Almost 800,000 workers were involved in strikes during the month of June alone. The index of work time lost rose to four times its level in 1963, a third higher than the previous peak of 1970.

The Administration faced its most serious test. Prices were still soaring. The economy was beginning to give the first hints of stagnation. The balance-of-payments deficits began to spurt again after price controls were lifted. And workers were beginning to see through the mystifying rhetoric of "productivity crises" and price "controls."

What to do?

Phase I of the Attack: Public Relations and Recession

The Administration was confused. Corporations were confused. Orthodox economists were confused, but there was no time for the luxury of confusion. By early summer, corporations were beginning to face an extraordinary period of contract negotiation. During 1974 and the first half of 1975, contracts covering two thirds of all workers protected by "major contracts" were expiring.[13] Many of these contracts, lasting three years, had been negotiated just after controls had been imposed in August 1971; workers in those unions were bristling for a fight, anxious to try to compensate for the real wage losses they suffered during contracts negotiated under the club of controls.

More specifically, corporations looked ahead in early 1974 to the expiration, among others, of the communications workers' contract in July, the steelworkers' contract in August, scores of aerospace contracts in October, the mine workers' contract in November, the railroad contracts in December, hundreds of construction, utility workers' and food workers' contracts throughout the early part of 1975.

In many of those negotiations, workers were going to be not only struggling to make up for past real wage losses but also demanding cost-of-living escalator clauses which would automatically adjust their contractual wages to rises in the cost-of-living index. (As of October 1974, only 45 per cent of workers covered by major contracts were protected by cost-of-living escalator clauses, and none of these clauses provided for a penny-for-penny full adjustment.[14]) The Administration and the mine companies expected that at least the miners would strike and that an expensive settlement in the mines would set the trend for more expensive settlements later on.

If wage controls could not be continued politically, then it must have seemed fairly clear, in the early months of 1974, that another return to a period of recession was necessary, *if for no other reason* than to curb labor's bargaining power during the negotiations in the months ahead. As a British banker admitted during the same period, in arguing for a recession with somewhat more candor than we Americans are accustomed to, "We've got to get some discipline back into this country's work force, and the only way to do it is to make the blokes damn grateful to

[13] For information on contract expiration, see U.S. Bureau of Labor Statistics, "Wage Calendar, 1974," Bulletin #1810 (1974), p. 2. There were 10.3 million workers in the United States covered by major contracts of 1,000 workers or more in early 1975.

[14] Cost-of-living clause information from "Wage Calendar, 1974," p. 4. Only about 600,000 workers not covered by major contracts have escalator clauses, so that, of all 85 million workers in the United States, only about 4.6 million—or barely more than 5 per cent, receive such protection.

have any sort of job at all." [15] A leader of the International Brotherhood of Electrical Workers admitted recently, reflecting on the same phenomenon from labor's side, "Layoffs take the steam out of members to a certain degree. They take away the urge to strike." [16]

The Administration could hardly talk openly in such terms, however, and its public relations campaigns built during the summer toward Ford's summit conference. Laying the ground for the deepening recession, already in motion, Ford talked more and more about the need to "bite the bullet," to "tighten our belt buckles" for "mutual self-sacrifice." We were all in this together, and we all had to sacrifice together. Significantly, his only definite statement during the period was that he would not tolerate more wage-price controls. Given the imperatives of curbing workers' anger, that left recession—for however long—as the only other alternative.

So, public relations and recession we got. Unemployment climbed rapidly during the second half of 1974, reaching 7.1 per cent by December. Administration spokespeople talked openly of the recession continuing well into 1975, with unemployment rates potentially reaching as high as 8 per cent. As the recession deepened, the public relations campaigns eventually slackened, for it became increasingly clear that people would not easily accept such "sacrifices" for long.

In the short run, however, the combination of public relations and recession was obviously having its direct effects on worker militance and bargaining power. After strike activity reached its post-controls peaks in June and July of 1974, work stoppages began quickly to plummet. The number of workers involved in strikes fell from almost 800,000 in June to less than 200,000 in November and the index of work time lost through stoppages fell back to its levels during the controls of 1972 and 1973.

More important, the combination of propaganda and recession had an impact on some of the crucial bargaining sessions of the period. The United Mine Workers of America did strike, as expected, in November. Demanding substantial wage recovery, they were able to win large wage increases. But in the last stages of their negotiations, despite those successes, the union leadership

[15] Quoted in the *Wall Street Journal* (November 18, 1974), p. 1.
[16] Quoted, *ibid.* (December 18, 1974), p. 27.

began to soften some of its demands. Many rank-and-file mine workers had been demanding a concrete contractual protection of their right to engage in wildcat strikes. The leadership met several times with the Ford Administration, and according to informal reports, began to wear down under the insistent argument that a prolonged strike would irreparably deepen the recession. We were all in this together, the UMWA leaders heard for the six hundredth time, and the litany softened their determination. Much to the dismay of large blocks of the rank-and-file membership, who actually opposed ratification of the contract, the leadership gave in on the wildcat-strike-protection issue.

It would be a mistake to exaggerate the importance of government policy in dealing with the economic crisis. Structural instabilities in the world economy may bring about a deep and protracted depression despite the apparent Administration efforts, announced in January 1975, to begin an expansionary policy, reversing its anti-inflationary tactics of 1974. It is nonetheless important to be clear about the factors which affect the *timing* of changes in government policies.

As the government anticipated the end of controls in late 1973, it knew that the crucial period of major bargaining was approaching. Given that controls and recession represent the only two available strategies for curbing labor militance, and that controls were politically impossible to continue at that time, recession represented a necessary stage in the evolving government arsenal. By now the Administration can move on to other tactics; after June 1975 the bargaining calendar will be virtually empty for more than a year. Major contracts covering only 500,000 workers, or 5 per cent of workers covered by major contracts, will expire in the second half of 1975. In the first half of 1976, only the Teamsters among major unions will be negotiating, and the Republican Administration has had a cozy relationship with the Teamsters for years. After June 1975 the need for a cool economy to cool workers will have diminished. Combining the velvet glove of moral suasion and the iron fist of recession, corporations and the government will have played out their moves during this phase of the crisis.

Fighting Recession

The first phase of the corporate and government strategy has represented a direct attack on working people. Profits have been declining, worker militance had been increasing, and it was clear, from the corporations' perspective, that something had to be done.

This strategy has meant that working people in this country have been asked to provide the basis for restoring profits by sacrificing their jobs, their social services, their livelihood and their standard of living.

Recession has had many causes, some of them complicated, but recession has also been permitted and exacerbated by conscious, calculated *political* decisions made at the top. Those of us attacked by those decisions must take direct *political* action to overcome that strategy. While it seems clear that the Administration has begun to move away from its recessionary strategy, we cannot wait to see whether their policies have the impact we would like.

In order to fight the recessionary strategy, we can and must demand

· no layoffs by corporations unless and until corporations can demonstrate to workers that such layoffs are absolutely required for the continuing solvency of the company;

· open corporate books and accounts, so that workers can decide for themselves whether corporate layoffs are actually justified by the need to maintain corporate solvency;

· full, inclusive and uniform unemployment compensation, covering 100 per cent of all workers' salaries, during the course of this recession;

· the maintenance of (real) social service expenditures at previous levels, with no cutbacks, to guarantee that those who do not work or who need special care do not suffer special hardship during a period of recession and rapid inflation.

Through these demands, we can continue to raise the costs of recessionary strategies. Through support of longer-term efforts to create guaranteed public service employment, we can move steadily toward the day when everyone in this country will be able to work at a decent job.

In the meantime, corporations and the government know that the political costs of a continued recession are too risky. Milton

Friedman, the conservative economist, says that we have no
choice but to continue the recession in order to restore balance
to the economy: "There is no way to avoid living with an abnor-
mally high unemployment rate for the next five to eight years." [17]
More realistic corporate executives and bankers, speaking in
their own journals, know that the political risks of such a policy
would be too great.

But moving out of the recession in the present period would
involve increasingly rapid inflation once again. People will resist
inflation just as strenuously. So what will happen next?

Phase II of the Attack: Public Relations and Planning

It seems clear, from reading the business press, that corporations will begin to press very quickly for a new kind of economic
management in this country. Recession to cool out the economy
will be too costly. Normal expansion, in this time of crisis, will
involve too much inflation and dislocation. Expansion with price
controls will be necessary. But most people admit that the first
stage of wage-price controls, from 1971 to early 1974, fell apart
at least partly because bottlenecks and shortages developed.
This time around, corporations recognize that more extensive
management of the economy will be required. Wage and price
controls will be insufficient. It will also be necessary to exercise
government management over investment policies and credit policies—in short, over the allocation of resources. [18]

It will be important to remember, as we approach that stage
of management, that corporations will be seeking planning for
their own benefit. And such corporate planning will, as always,
have two aspects. One of them will focus on the distribution of
income between profits and wages. If prices and wages are controlled, corporations will obviously seek to manipulate the planning process in order to protect profits at the expense of wages.
Looking ahead, foreseeing this direction, some unions are racing
to negotiate their contracts before phase two begins. Negotiating
during recession is bad enough, but negotiating during controls
may be worse. The West Coast dock workers, for instance, are
requesting early expiration of their contract in order to get a new

[17] Quoted in *Business Week* (December 7, 1974), p. 88.
[18] See reading #52 by William K. Tabb on economic planning.

contract before controls resume. As Harry Bridges, the long-shoremen's union leader, explained recently, "We've got to worry about controls because controls won't be equitable." [19]

Another aspect of the struggle in a period of planning will necessarily involve the sphere of production. If prices, wages and profits are controlled during a period of planning, corporations will be seeking—among other tactics—to deepen their control over the production process in order to get as much surplus value out of workers in production as they can. Their degrees of freedom for protecting and improving their profits in the sphere of exchange will be more limited. Correspondingly, they will seek to reorganize and intensify production in order to make up for whatever they may lose under price controls.

Some of these kinds of developments seem to have occurred during the first, more limited stage of wage-price controls from 1971 to 1974. Facing limited price controls, corporations appear to have tried to change work rules in order to get more work out of their employees. During 1972, the first full year of wage-price controls, workers' wildcat strikes over "work rules" grievances soared, climbing to ten times their levels in 1965 and 1966, and almost four times their levels during 1968 in the peak of speed-up.[20]

If and when these contests in production begin, workers will depend fundamentally on their rights to strike over grievances, on their right to protest attacks in production by withholding their labor power. Significantly, one has some reason for fearing that corporations recognize that probability. Slowly but surely, the first signs of an attack on workers' right to strike have begun to appear. Two recent legal decisions provide the barest hint of that attack.

The first involves the right of workers to strike over outstanding issues in contract negotiations. During negotiations in the steel industry last year, the corporations convinced the steelworkers' union leadership to accept a "no-strike agreement," under the terms of which the union agreed not to strike over outstanding bargaining disagreements but to submit them to compulsory arbitration. Rank-and-file steelworkers challenged that

[19] Quoted in the *Wall Street Journal* (December 18, 1974), p. 27.
[20] The data on "work rules" stoppages come from *Handbook of Labor Statistics* (*op. cit.*), pp. 373 ff.

agreement in court. The no-strike agreement was upheld by the U.S. district court in which the case was heard. In supporting the corporations and the union, the judge argued that "in any system of self-government, in theory and in practice, even the most precious of rights may be waived. . . . In denying plaintiffs the relief they seek, this Court does no more than permit the [no-strike] . . . negotiating procedures to proceed as, at least potentially, an evolutionary step forward in labor relations." [21]

The second precedent involves the right to wildcat strike over specific grievances during the term of contract. A Supreme Court decision of 1962 had ruled that federal district courts could *not* issue injunctions against wildcat strikes, even though such strikes represented breach of a no-strike provision in a contract which guaranteed binding arbitration of the dispute. In a potentially historic decision in 1970, the new Nixon Supreme Court overturned that earlier decision. It argued that district courts could and should issue injunctions halting wildcat strikes in such situations. The intent of the decision was clear. Arbitration must prevail and strikes must not. The majority decision argued that "the very purpose of arbitration procedures is to provide a mechanism for the expeditious settlement of industrial disputes without resort to strikes, lock-outs, or other self-help measures." [22] Since almost all contracts currently provide for arbitration, the decision potentially provides the basis for court injunctions against all wildcat strikes over any issues *unless* the contract explicitly guarantees, in writing, the workers' right to engage in wildcat strikes. It was such protection which many rank-and-file mine workers sought in their 1974 negotiations—explicitly mindful of the 1970 Court decision—and which they were unable to obtain.

In this context, armed with these kinds of court precedents, employers will undoubtedly press ahead with their public relations campaigns during the stage of planning if and when it arrives. Talk of the "productivity crisis" will undoubtedly re-

[21] Huber I. Teitelbaum, "Opinion of Court," Aikens et al. vs. I. W. Abel et al., No. 74–17 Civil Action, in the United States Court for the Western District of Pennsylvania, pp. 22–23.
[22] See Boys Market, Inc. v. Retail Clerks Local 770, 398 U.S. 235, 90 S. Ct. 1583, 26 L. Ed. 2d 199 (1970), opinion reprinted in *Labor Relations Law,* ed. by R. A. Smith et al., 1973 Cumulative Supplement (New York, Bobbs-Merrill, 1973), p. 147.

sume. Workers will once again be asked to pay the costs of economic crises with their muscle and their sweat in production.

In short, if and when planning comes, workers must recognize that as before, the economic crisis will continue to unfold at two levels. In the sphere of circulation, political struggle will take place over the division between profits and wages through the mechanisms of wage and price controls. In the sphere of production, necessarily, political struggle will take place over how hard workers must labor in the service of employers' surplus value. Through every stage, at every moment, workers must maintain their strength and their militance in both these spheres, at both those levels, to protect their own interests.

52. CAPITALIST STATE PLANNING IS NOT SOCIALISM

by William K. Tabb

There is increasing talk in this country about a gradual, relatively painless transition to socialism. This is dangerous and foolish talk, especially when it comes from self-professed socialists who should know better. In its approach it is very close to the "greening of America" notions of the 1960's, which deny the central point of class contradictions and thus presume away the strength of the obdurate forces which preserve the system. The issue is not being faced.

Liberal theorists see the state as above the rest of society, mediating between different interest groups. In the pluralist

Unpublished paper. William K. Tabb teaches economics at Queens College, CUNY, and is a member of URPE.

model, many voices are heard and some compromise which accords with the "public interest" is developed. It is assumed that different views exist, coalitions are built, and while conflicts do arise, it is in everyone's interest to compromise. After hard bargaining each accepts the outcome, at least for that round. In place of the liberal's question, "Given a certain class structure, how will the various classes, with their divergent and often conflicting interests, manage to get along together?," the question might be posed as: "How did a particular class structure come into being, and by what means is its continued existence guaranteed?" Radicals drawing on the Marxist conception might well say: "It is clear that the state exists as the creation of the most powerful class or classes in a given historical epoch and is used in their interests." The assertion that the state stands above individual interests is a weak reed on which to place the burden of a serious argument. While the desires of the dominant group are put forward as if they were in the interest of all of society's members, too much evidence exists to lead to easy acceptance of such a notion. Consider the implications of a situation in which the disadvantaged classes held state power; attempts would surely be made to establish a social order more favorable to their own interests. Why can't the same presumption be made about the rich and powerful who, after all, hold office in government? The dominant class has every interest in seeing that its representatives hold public office, that its ideology be widely accepted and that its preferences appear to be naturally correct. The most important aim of the state under capitalism is to preserve property relationships—the right of some to own the factories, mines and other capital, and the necessity of most people who do not own such assets to work for them. Under the guise of protecting individual rights to own a home, a car, etc. (assets which do not allow further accumulation), capitalists encourage workers to defend the power of banks, large corporations and capitalist relations more generally. But private property and capitalist property are not one and the same thing. The latter requires a relationship of exploitation, the former does not imply class domination.

As Paul Sweezy, a leading Marxist theorist, writes: "Capitalist private property does not consist in things—things independently of their ownership—but in a social relation between people. Property confers upon its owners freedom from labor and the disposal over the labor of others, and this is the essence of all social domination whatever form it may assume."

There is no secret conspiracy involved in the government's protecting of capital. The government is staffed by corporate executives and lawyers who have spent their lives in the service of corporations. The relation between most members of the Cabinet and Congress and our large corporations is an intimate one. There are few production workers in Congress, and consumer advocates are unlikely to be invited to sit in the Cabinet. Yet, who would doubt that a representative chosen from the plant floor in open debate and by free ballot would not serve working people and consumers generally better in government than do the lawyers, corporate officials and other representatives of wealth who now dominate government?

This is not to say that gains cannot and have not been made under capitalism. By winning the right to vote and by struggling to form unions, working people have won important weapons. It is too facile to say that there is no one to vote for who can realistically win, that unions act as agencies to control worker militancy. While both statements may in many, even most instances be true, the working class is better off because it can to a greater extent than previously make its demands effective. Short of seizing state power, it must use whatever weapons it can, no matter how inadequate. The task is to build organizations which genuinely serve working-class interest.

Planning and the State

The difficulty with pushing reformist solutions so far that they break asunder the bounds of the old order is that the way in which the reform is implemented is not decided by the mass movement raising the demand and pressuring for its acceptance, but instead by those controlling the dominant societal institutions. Even control through an electoral upset, enlighted court precedent or the appointment of honorable officials can never be extended to the point of qualitative transformation. Short of socialist victory, such institutional vehicles can never be secure or be expected to be strong enough.

As early as in the nineteenth century Rosa Luxemburg, a

leader of the militant German left, expressed this point in the following manner: "The institutions which are democratic in form are in substance instruments of the dominant class interests. This is most obvious in the fact that as soon as democracy shows a disposition to deny its class character and to become an instrument of the real interests of the people, the democratic forms themselves are sacrificed by the bourgeoisie and their representatives in the state."

From Chile to Greece to South Korea to Brazil, such has actually been the pattern. When advanced capitalist classes are threatened, the same has happened—witness Nazi Germany and Fascist Italy. In the present crisis, such a threat hangs over many of the nominally democratic nations of the world. It is in this light that we must look again at the notion of planning.

Liberal leaders neglect to point out that the question is one of *Who does the planning and in whose interests is the planning done?* If we assume a national unity, then planning is done for everyone, for the general welfare. However, if planning is done *by the powerful, for the powerful*—as it has been and will continue to be if "unity" is allowed to act as a cover for privilege— then we should expect that the dominant class, with the minor participation of "responsible" labor statesmen, will plan in the interests of those very corporations which liberals admit already have too much power. The government will be used by giant corporations to do the kind of colluding (planning) which they can't do as well by themselves. Concretely, this means that the right to strike will be taken away from labor. The logic is clear enough. First, planners' decisions made "in the national interest" will require an uninterrupted flow of goods and services—especially in key sectors such as steel, coal, other basic industries (where, it happens, trade unions are strongest)—and second, unless planners' decisions are legally enforced, the planning system will quickly break down. Strikes then become an impediment to the "public interest."

Simultaneously, capital will be allowed to move freely in order to equalize wage rates as a method of lowering costs. Put differently, it will become part of the logic of planning to encourage corporations to move plants to low-wage nonunionized areas at home and abroad.

By the same logic, it follows that the powers of the government will be used to provide, through forced savings, for the investment needs of the private sector's more risky ventures. Funds will be provided collectively, but profits will continue to be enjoyed privately.

Once the outlines of the planned economy of monopoly capitalism are spelled out, they resemble more and more the *economic* policy of the fascist state. These policies need not be accompanied by the full political manifestations we identify with Hitler's Germany or Fascist Italy. For the polity to move toward fascism, it is necessary for the democratic forces to be discredited to the point of being, for all intents and purposes, dead.

The economic form of fascism has been described by Paul Sweezy in the following terms: "Under fascism, control over the economic system is centralized, conflicts between the different branches of capital are largely suppressed in the interests of capital as a whole, and heavy risks are pooled through the instrumentality of the state. We have here what Nazi economists have appropriately called a 'steered economy.' "

Historically, fascism has also led to war when economic expansion could not be continued on any other basis. National chauvinism, race bigotry, suppression of trade unions, and forced cartelization and state planning may not be preferred by individual capitalists; but as crisis deepens and a left movement develops, fascism may be the preferable choice. The militarization and crude fascism of the Chilean junta may be an evil omen of what is possible elsewhere today.

Maurice Dobb's view is that "If one is to summarize shortly the historical preconditions of Fascism, one can speak, I think, of three factors as preeminent: a despair on the part of Capital of finding a normal solution for the impasse created by the limitations of the investment-field; considerable and depressed 'middle class' or declassé elements, ripe in the absence of an alternative rallying-point, to be recruited to the Fascist creed; and a working class, privileged enough to be resistant to normal pressure on its standard of life, but insufficiently united or non-class-conscious (at least in its political leadership) to be *politically* weak in asserting its power or in resisting attack."

Fascism projects a dream of reconstruction, of glory, mixed

with appeals to racial hatred and national chauvinism. How many of these elements are present in the United States in the mid-1970's?

Those who consider themselves progressives should feel a sense of urgent concern over such possibilities and take a closer look at what national planning would mean in our historical context. People who stress the benign potential of planning and see it as a way toward full employment and the re-establishment of American affluence, and possibly even the greening to a humanitarian socialism, see only one of two possible directions such planning may lead us.

The relation between forms of state planning and the ultimate creation of socialism has a twofold nature. It raises the possibility of a planned economy, but as Ernest Mandel, the Belgian Marxist, notes, it is really in its essence capitalist. Mandel maintains: "Increasing state intervention in the economy, the growth of a 'public' sector, and even nationalization of certain unprofitable branches do not amount to 'socialism.' An economy can no more be a 'little bit socialist' than a woman 'a little bit pregnant.' State intervention, management of the economy, operate within the framework of capitalism in order to consolidate capitalist profits, or at least those of the decisive sections of the capitalist monopolies . . . The idea of planning is accepted and applied by the bourgeoisie; indeed, one can even say that it is of bourgeois origin. But the bourgeoisie accept and adopt it only to the extent that it does not imperil the *profit motive,* does not embrace the whole of economic life, substituting production to meet need for production for profit."

Further, at this point in world capitalist history, the question is not only one of theoretical possibilities. Instead, it is unlikely that the adoption of state planning can in fact overcome the contradictions which are rooted in the very nature of capitalism. Rather like a junkie, capitalism seeks new highs through finding new opiates. It must take higher and higher doses—of militarism, consumerism and credit. The contradiction between the needs of capital and labor, the interclass struggle and the intraclass conflicts among the capitalists themselves cannot be papered over through a disinterested planning. The struggles are simply moved to a higher level. The outcome will depend on two types of developments: the degree to which irreconcilable interests can compromise and temporarily moderate the tendencies toward collapse, and the degree to which an alternative vision of society that seems desirable and possible can be developed in the very act of struggling to actualize itself.

53. THE CRISIS AS TRANSFORMATION

by Richard H. Levy

Introduction

There is little question in most quarters that the American economy is in crisis. The evidence—double-digit inflation coupled with rising unemployment and falling output—has become part of the everyday reality. The questions that emerge as economic activity continues its decline are: What has turned the Keynesian dream of a finely tuned and continually expanding economy into a full-blown depression nightmare? Who is responsible for killing the growth economy that most Americans revere and see as everlasting?

Certainly there is no shortage of scapegoats: the Arabs, the major oil companies, the wheat traders and the Soviet Union, and yes, the federal government. However, the difficulty with the questions is not, as many might argue, that there are no clear or well-grounded answers, but that they assume economic growth to be a continuous and even process when modulated by an appropriate set of fiscal policies. Accordingly, to be taken by surprise by the degree and breadth of the present economic

Especially written for this book. Richard H. Levy teaches economics at John Jay College, CUNY.

downturn only indicates the extent to which we have come to accept the Keynesian perspective.

In this article we shall depart from this perspective in a number of ways. First, we shall argue that capitalism is no more capable of continuing economic growth than any other system or organism is capable of perpetual motion. Second, we shall place the corporate sector rather than the federal government at the center of the economy, thereby bringing into question the central and autonomous role of the government in directing economic activity. Finally, and most significantly, we shall argue that depression is an integral stage of the capitalist dynamic.

The Capitalist Dynamic

Indeed capitalism is expansive. If it is to survive, it must continue to grow. If it is to grow, it must bring its methods of production and organization into new areas, thus creating new markets. However, as it continues to expand it begins to strain existing structures and institutional arrangements ultimately to the breaking point. In other words, like most growth processes, capitalist growth is dialectical; as it expands it creates tensions which threaten the very existence of the system. Invariably, the system reaches a point beyond which it cannot continue to expand as constituted at present. The resumption of economic growth might require the introduction of new technology, the reorganization of existing institutions, and the creation of new organizations, all of which must affect prevailing social and political relationships. Put simply, capitalism historically has demonstrated a tendency to grow in stages, and the process of reorganization involved in the shift or expansion into a new and higher level of development can be called *transformation*.

Transformation is neither mythical nor abstract. Rather, it is the process by which the overextended capitalist business system transcends the impediments to its further expansion. The strategic elements of the system, i.e., the transformers, must reestablish their authority in order to create the conditions and environment necessary for the reorganization. Accordingly, the crises that result from the overextension of the system, if well managed, can provide the environment for the necessary reorganization. It was Henry Kissinger, crisis manager *par excellence,* who recently noted: "If you act creatively you should be able to use crises to move the world toward the structural solutions that are necessary. In fact, very often the crises themselves are a symptom of the need for a structural rearrangement" (*New York Times*, October 13, 1974).

Depression is crisis and change. Accordingly, depression is awesome for those who don't understand the ongoing changes and for those who are adversely affected by the crises. What people see as doomsday and critics see as the failure of the existing order should, nonetheless, be viewed as a managed, though disruptive, reorganization of the capitalist system by those at the center. From this perspective, depression is but one phase, albeit the most striking and possibly most challenging in the process of capitalist development.

Historically, depression has been a time in which the central forces of capitalism have consolidated their energies through a combination of merger, technological innovation and institutional reorganization. In the depression of the 1930's, when most people were fearful that the system was being torn asunder, the largest corporations were self-consciously undergoing changes in structure that were to permit them to expand their area of operation and the degree of their control. The Harvard historian and Du Pont descendant Alfred D. Chandler provides some insight into this dynamic:

> It took the economic pressure created by the slowing down of the economy in the 1920's and its miserable performance in the 1930's to turn these technically sophisticated enterprises to the new strategy of expansion . . . During the depression General Motors (and to a lesser extent other firms in the automobile industry) moved into diesels, appliances, tractors and airplanes. Some makers of primary metals, particularly aluminum and copper, turned to consumer products like kitchenware and household fittings, while rubber firms developed the possibilities of rubber chemistry to compensate for declining tire sales. In the same period food companies employed their existing distribution organizations to market an increasing variety of products.

This strategy of product diversification required the reorganization of the large national corporation into a multidivisional structure. The new structure permitted the corporation to take on a new product or area of production by adding a new division. Likewise, it could shed a division with minimal disruption to the rest of its structure. This increased flexibility enhanced the corporation's ability to plan and implement new strategy and contributed to the growth of a central office or cortex.

American capitalism has gone through several periods of transformation as it developed from a more competitive embryonic mode. These stages are most readily seen in the growth in size and change in nature of the representative firm from the workshop onward to the factory, the national corporation, the multidivisional corporation and now the multinational-turned-global corporation. This growth, as Steven Hymer, the pioneering analyst of multinational corporate strategy, has noted,

> has been qualitative as well as quantitative. With each step business enterprise acquired a more complex administrative structure to coordinate its activities and a larger brain to plan for its survival and growth.

What is more, these changes in strategy and structure of the corporate sector have required changes in most other social and productive institutions, from government and organized labor down to the structure of the family.

It is the business sector, and more specifically the leading or strategic firms within the business sector, which has defined the nature and set the terms of these changes. "Business itself produces more change, probably, than any other institution," the Mobil Oil Corporation claims in a recent advertisement. Mobil proceeds to tell us how and why:

> Through its research and development programs. Through new technology it develops and applies. Through new plants it builds. Through its needs to be a good employer. Because its own long-term self-interest dictates a better life for people everywhere. Because it must face facts and think rationally about what may appear to be unthinkable. . . . Because change is what we're inseparably bound to.

Indeed, the very nature of capitalism is that social and personal needs are secondary to or dependent upon the needs of the business sector. Thus, the material well-being of the people is dependent upon an increase in the productive capacity of the business sector. From this comes the dictum "What is good for American business is good for the American people." But as the dominant American corporation has taken on a global perspective as well as a strategy to internationalize production and consumption, a divergence has developed between the interests of American workers and consumers and the U.S.-based global corporations. Stephen Hymer concludes:

> Right now, we seem to be in the midst of a major revolution in international relationships . . . Multinational corporations are in the vanguard of this revolution because of their great financial and administrative strength and their close contact with the new technology. Governments (outside the military) are far behind, because of their narrower horizons and perspectives, as are labor organizations and most non-business institutions and associations.

The Corporate Sector

The current changes in the American economy must be viewed in context of the evolving structure of the corporate sector. When we survey the economic landscape of the American economy today, we see that major industries such as transportation, communications, electrical equipment, metals, chemicals, petroleum, etc., are all dominated by three or four very large international corporations. These giant corporations encompassed in the *Fortune* top 500 comprise the center of the economy. This has been recognized by Robert Averitt when in *The Dual Economy* he noted that

> within the population of American business firms, a relatively small number of economic giants form an economy apart, creating and reacting to economic forces differing in substance from those impinging on their small rivals. We have named this economy of elite firms "the center economy."

The strategy of the center firm is to extend its area of activity, for continued growth is essential to maintaining its dominance. In the past this has meant vertical and horizontal integration and product diversification. Now it means spatial, or global, integration—the creation of a world market dominated by a few hundred global corporations.

The outer layer of the "dual economy," the periphery, is composed of the majority of corporations which must take institutional arrangements and market conditions as given. These firms compete with center corporations in the domestic economy or operate in wholly competitive industries outside the direct domination of the center. They employ mostly unorganized labor but lack the power to determine wage rates, product prices or relevant government legislation. The quest of the more enterprising periphery firms or entrepreneurs is to create an enterprise (or constellation of enterprises) that can transcend market forces and facilitate entry into the center. This has traditionally been accomplished through the monopolization and exploitation of a new technology (e.g., Xerox, IBM, Polaroid) or through the agglomeration of related or unrelated periphery firms (e.g., LTV, Gulf & Western, Litton, Textron).

This dualism is not simply a structural description of a static reality; it encompasses a dynamic or dialectical interaction between components. During a period of expansion, when the center is developing and producing the technology for extending its area of control, it in turn creates opportunities for growth at the periphery. As the expansion continues, enterprising periphery firms are presented with opportunities for making inroads into the center. Quite often the institutional needs of these pockets of new wealth conflict with the needs of center firms, a conflict which is often played out in struggles over policies of the state. The continuation of this double-edged process begins to strain financial institutions and finds center firms overextended and threatened by the entrepreneurs and speculators of the periphery. Eventually the center is faced with an erosion of its financial and political control, and thus is forced to respond creatively to the developing crisis or accept a diminution of its power. This is the time when the center acts to tighten the reins, compressing economic activity and reorganizing relevant institutions in a way that reinforces its control over the economy and related institutions, a time of consolidation. The eminent establishment economist Oskar Morgenstern cryptically alludes to this tactic when he writes:

> I wish to indicate the fact that . . . some sets of functions performed by a system may be deemed "essential" while others are

less so, and that as a consequence the system can perhaps be "compressed" to those activities without total *collapse* . . . The resources used for the non-essential performances can either be cut off (e.g., lost in a war), or they can, at least in part, be used for enlarging the system's inner core, i.e., for securing more existing or even new basic functions.

Origins of the Present Transformation

The origins of the present period of transformation lie in the late 1950's and early 1960's. This was a time in which the center corporations, which had long been active internationally, were beginning to rationally pursue the integration of the world economy. The necessary technology, which included a global satellite communications network, air supertransport, and information retrieval and control systems, had been developed and awaited implementation.

The structural need was to create regionally integrated economies with a recognizable growth potential in the less-developed regions of the world; areas to which international corporations could begin exporting production to take advantage of the low cost of labor while building up the consumer markets of the future. America's center corporations had the support of the federal government in promoting the reorganization of the most promising of these economies through its massive foreign-aid program. The center could also count on the support of such American-dominated international institutions as the World Bank and newer regional development banks. The technical and capital support provided by such agencies facilitated the building of the infrastructure: local transportation and communications networks, the reorganization of the government apparatus, and the training of bureaucrats and managers of center-initiated enterprises. At the same time, this effort captured the imagination and channeled the energies of American university professors and corporate executives alike.

The transformation of underdeveloped economies did not proceed without resistance and dislocation, nor was it expected to. As an executive of the Chase Manhattan Bank noted, in justifying the bank's investments in the war-torn Nigerian economy at the height of its bloody civil war, "America had its civil war too, and likewise it was essential to our development."

As America's center corporations expanded outward pursuing a new and more sophisticated strategy of internationalism, the domestic economy prospered. Exporting "center-dominated" development generated demands in center-dominated industries at home. No economy was better prepared to supply the capital needs of the developing world. Even as the strategy of global integration met resistance, such as in Southeast Asia, the military effort launched to deter such opposition provided further stimulus to the rapidly growing American economy, at least in the short term. The outward expansion not only contributed to the growth of center industries but also gave birth to new industries at the periphery. The electronics and data processing industries were the most notable. It also gave rise to a new corporate form, the conglomerate.

This period of unprecedented growth was not without its contradictions. As America's workers and consumers began to take the expansionary economy for granted, they began using their growing economic power to make demands on the corporations for higher wages, safer products and serious antipollution measures. An even more important contradiction was the cost of the escalating conflict in Southeast Asia. Vietnamese resistance to the integration of Southeast Asia into the global framework also began to foster another level of resistance in the United States. Large segments of the middle class actively protested the war and attacked corporations for their responsibility. This resulted in a degree of visibility that center corporations did not need and could not tolerate.

As the corporations were being attacked from without, they were also being challenged from within. The growth economy built on the outward expansion of the center and the concomitant growth in the defense sector contributed to new defense industries at the periphery. Entrepreneurs such as James Ling and Charles "Tex" Thornton, with their profitable defense-oriented electronics firms and the strength of the stock market, were able to pyramid their respective corporations into multi-million-dollar concerns with the strength to gobble up larger but vulnerable old-line center corporations such as Jones & Laughlin, Armour and almost, but not quite, the Chemical Bank. At the same time, the massive outflow of American dollars required to finance the transformation of nation-states into regionally integrated economies brought fatal pressures to bear on the international financial system. The Bretton Woods agreements, which reorganized world finance after the collapse of the 1930's, were not flexible enough to facilitate the ongoing global reorganization. After a number of revaluations and devaluations, including a two-phased devaluation of the almighty dollar (the first since the last great depression), the international monetary system is presently propped up by makeshift arrangements, waiting for a new set of agreements and a more appropriate structure.

The Current Crises

The crises of the mid-1970's are the aftermath of this over-extended American economy. By the late 1960's, indicators such as the rising price level and the severe deterioration in the balance of payments signaled the coming storms. Since then the bottom has fallen out of the stock market. The most visible sign of the "creative" manipulation of crisis has been the center corporation's—specifically, the oil company's—compression of economic activity via the energy crisis. While most Americans view the energy crisis with understandable skepticism, the shortages, no matter how manipulated, are real. The global redistribution of basic resources, which is a fundamental if slow-moving element of transformation, puts very real strains on existing supply. Americans now feel vulnerable in a way they haven't since the depression of the 1930's. As the compression of economic activity has dramatically forced the unemployment rate up, Americans have become more concerned about jobs than pollution and are more willing to respect the needs of the corporations because ultimately it is the corporations that provide them with jobs.

And what are the corporations saying? Robert V. Roosa, the former Assistant Secretary of the Treasury, adviser to multinational corporations and partner in the investment house of Brown Brothers Harriman & Co., puts it this way:

Rapidly growing population, more widely distributed income gains and a revolution in expectations have combined to put almost all of the world's resources under very great pressure.

And Roosa's solution:

> We must make a transfer from current consumption to current investment on a fairly massive scale. (*New York Times,* June 30, 1974)

So much for the revolution of rising expectations. Austerity will be the watchword for the 1970's; and for large segments of the world's population unfortunate enough to find themselves in the stagnant backwaters of undeveloped economies (such as southern India), the writing on the wall spells starvation.

Center corporations cannot proceed to internationalize production and consumption while the American people, who comprise only 6 percent of the world's population, account for 35 percent of the world's annual energy consumption. New technologies such as nuclear energy are needed and in turn require massive financing schemes. Given the collapse of the finance markets the only options are through excess profits or government subsidy. Thus the American people must help pay for the technlogy required by the center corporations to extend their domain internationally.

As in past periods of transformation, the corporation is already looking for government assistance. Indeed, such luminaries as Henry Ford II have called for the creation of an agency similar to the Depression-era Reconstruction Finance Corporation

> to make large amounts of capital available to industrial concerns, utilities and banks that cannot raise money now because of the collapse of equity markets and shortages of loan funds. (*New York Times,* December 10, 1974)

Lazard Frères & Co. partner Felix Rohatyn would give the RFC an even broader range of operation, to include the financing of new technology. For example,

> if a Manhattan-type project in the area of energy is ever undertaken, as is clearly required, the R.F.C. could play a major role as an investor, risk-sharer, lender and guarantor in a variety of projects. (*New York Times,* December 1, 1974)

This is just the beginning. The center corporations will rely on the government to help make a broad set of changes encompassing education and organized labor at home to accomplish the stabilization of the international monetary system. Indeed, a variety of agencies, private and public, will be involved in promoting such changes. Nevertheless, at the center of these changes will be the global corporations, for they are, in the words of Pfizer's John J. Powers, "the agents of change, socially, economically and culturally."

It is premature to speculate on how successful the transformers will be in using the current crisis to effect the necessary reorganization of government activities and financial markets and the redistribution of income and consumption. Though the center corporations currently hold most of the power, the situation is unstable, with many battles still to be fought. The major dilemma for the center is that it must convince America's workers, consumers and periphery corporations that the austerity required to effect the desired redistribution and reorganization is also in their interest. This may prove difficult because unlike past transformations, Americans have little to gain (and possibly much to lose) from the center's international strategy. However, for Americans to react to the ongoing transformation, they must first be able to see it as it is rather than in the apocalyptical terms in which it is being portrayed. It is time to remove the Keynesian blinders and to look directly at the activities of the center-cum-global corporations. Only then can we begin to evaluate the consequences of the current crisis on the American people, and for that matter on the people of the world.

54. THE FUTURE OF THE AMERICAN DREAM

by Stanley Aronowitz

The transformation of American capitalism is now becoming manifest. On one hand, the pluralistic myths are no longer capable of sustaining the belief in the overall rationality of the corporate system. The quantum leaps of accumulated international wealth, control and power are now so much a part of our ordinary lives, and permeate the institutions of mass communication so completely, that mass disaffection is almost a "given" of the political world. On the other hand, this judgment implies that, at the core, bourgeois rule is no longer sustained by ideology but by the sheer exercise of power. The tolerance of political opposition that was among the vaunted forms of social legitimation for the corporate order in the 1960s when its economic problems seemed minuscule in the midst of war-induced expansion have all but disappeared. The enemy without is no longer easily identified. It is now located within. The enemy within is not an agent of a foreign power. It is as much generalized terror as it is the organized forms of political opposition. The corporate bourgeoisie desperately seeks assent and senses resistance among the population at the invisible crevices of daily life. Mass surveillance cannot be justified on the basis of the old notions of Communist-inspired subversion. Instead it rests on the pervasiveness of criminality that is said to stalk the cities.

Abridged from "The Future of the American Dream," the last chapter of *Food, Shelter and the American Dream* (New York, Seabury Press, 1974). Stanley Aronowitz is also the author of *False Promises: The Shaping of American Working-Class Consciousness* (New York, McGraw-Hill, 1973).

Mass fear may be said to have gripped large numbers of Americans. The walker in the city at night has become a rare person, scolded by friends and acquaintances for recklessness.

The specter of criminal behavior lurking in every human person has replaced the ideological enemy. Instead of communism we have invented the evil within us all.

Yet dissent is ineradicable despite the proliferations of surveillance activities, firings of dissenters, the end of "radical" themes in film, the difficulty experienced by many left-wing authors getting their work printed by magazines and book publishers.

Popular cynicism was reflected in the attitudes of the news media toward the energy and food crises. Nightly, television newscasts reported the refusal of ordinary people to accept the explanations for shortages and rising prices offered by the large oil corporations and the government. Despite the best efforts of public relations salespersons they suspected that the oil companies were making a giant profit grab at their expense. What is remarkable about these reports is that the statements of doubt were expressed by small-business people and professionals in smaller cities and towns who have been the historical bedrock of American ideology.

The apparent inability of the corporations to tell their story to a sympathetic audience raises some significant questions for the shape of things to come. There are no precedents since the Depression for a massive reduction of living standards in peacetime. Americans have been raised on the belief that economic expansion is a permanent feature of the corporate system.

The 1974 recession portends much more serious consequences. Compounding the chronic inability of the United States economy to sustain economic growth except under wartime conditions, is the realignment of the world system of production. The tendency toward the decentralization of industry on an international scale will affect the material living standards of American workers. Moreover, the days of cheap food and energy may be over so that even if a loose credit system can be maintained, working people may find that their incomes are simply insufficient to make new commitments to houses, cars and appliances. The large corporations in these industries are mostly multinational and have become conglomerates. Their pattern of capital investment overseas and into the most profitable sectors regardless of the impact on the internal and international economic situation has produced a serious imbalance in the American economy. In turn, the tendency toward investment in highly profitable service industries at the expense of the expansion and modernization of productive forces within the United States is narrowing the capital base of the United States economy.

Capital investment in modernization activities within the steel machine-tool industries at home and in consumer goods production overseas has been supplemented by a tremendous quantity of investment in service, retailing and other nonproductive sectors. This means that the classic inflationary situation has been built into the economy. The real basis of economic development, the production of commodities, is deteriorating within the United States, while a great deal of "spurious" capital formation is taking place, that is, capital that rests on the productive sector but is actually invested in services. For example, it is more profitable to invest in rental cars than in automobile production. Retailing is beginning to yield a relatively high rate of profit in comparison to former years when this industry was operating on very narrow profit margins. The point is that unless actual output of goods expands faster than the output of services the inflationary trend will continue and perhaps accelerate. Another example of this trend is that the heavy rate of investment in machinery, fertilizers, processing plants and other expansion of material goods is part of the maintenance of the basic productive forces of society. But, much of the investment is located in "futures"—speculative capital that banks on price increases, the consolidation of marketing and distribution into fewer hands, and other forms of nonproductive investment. This development means that more capital is chasing a highly restricted quantity of output of food because as the degree of concentration within the industry increases, the tendency is for a relative slowdown in production in order to keep prices high, and profits bountiful.

The reversal in the historical belief that profits are the outcome of high volume or mass production spells disruption for the ordinary processes of production and consumption. There will be frequent manipulated shortages of almost everything that is bought and sold. The notion that inflation can be stemmed by government action has one central defect—which is that the government is subject to the political domination of the large corporations. The penetration by corporations of government agencies charged with regulating business activity vitiates the idea that the state is separate from the marketplace and independent of ruling class control.

The transformation of the government into a direct instrument rather than a deterrent of price inflation is no more evident than in the agricultural sector where regulation has had an inflationary impact. Not only are prices kept high by direct government policies in terms of the size of agricultural output; as I have argued, the distribution of existing output between domestic and foreign consumption affects domestic prices.

The shortages in raw materials in the agricultural and the industrial sectors are the outcome of the chronic weakness in the international trade position of the U.S. economy and the reluctance of U.S. corporations to undertake capital investment in primary raw materials development without substantial government subsidies. The problem with securing these subsidies is that federal financing has become the universal instrument for stabilizing economic activity. The private sector, particularly in highly concentrated industries, is simply beyond taking risks. Capital investment must be insured, supplemented and otherwise guaranteed by the state. The high degree of control exercised by the corporate sector over the state has removed the major source of inflation control.

There are no effective mechanisms for controlling inflation within a highly centralized and monopolistic economy. Nor are the American people likely to accept mass unemployment and the progressive decline of real wages without a struggle. The high cost of living has already depressed real wages to their 1965 levels in the past two years. Clearly, corporate and government decision-makers will be constrained to find some solutions to the crisis. I believe that the chance of stemming inflation depends entirely on finding ways to expand production of real goods. This option is foreclosed by the international commitments of United States corporations who hold the reins of power. Their decision has been to expand investments in oil, consumer goods and information-related industries such as computers, in other countries.

The second option for allaying discontent is to expand war industries and other forms of public expenditures. Despite the balanced budget ideology of the Nixon administration, its efforts to maintain relatively high employment levels were concentrated on increasing defense contracts with large corporations and retaining the traditional Republican backing for highway and other transportation projects such as the expansion of the interstate highway program and pipeline construction to aid the flow of oil. A Democratic administration would certainly accelerate the volume of public spending to alleviate the economic crunch. The emergence of the "hawk" forces to a position of hegemony under Senator Henry M. Jackson (D—Washington) after the defeat of the liberal "doves" within the party prefigures the probability that the Democrats will run in the 1976 elections on a platform of guns and butter. The statement by Senator Jackson in spring 1974 that he would be willing to run for President on a ticket that included Alabama governor George Wallace may signal a realignment of the Democratic Party in a rightwing populist direction. Jackson is a candidate with a long New Deal/Fair Deal record, fully supported by the AFL-CIO as well as the representatives of the pro-armament western capitalists. Wallace speaks for the anti-corporate, isolationist wing of the party with a base among rank-and-file workers and agrarians. Neither is considered part of the statist, internationalist wing of the party that has held the reins of control since the 1930s. Yet, both are considered militant fighters against the growing domination of big business and big government over American life.

The liberal wing will be hard pressed to hold back the bid of this powerful coalition, especially if the Jackson-Wallace candidacy is able to retain a commitment to welfare while, at the same time, expressing the anti-statist sentiments of its constituency. McGovern's defeat in 1972 is bound to hurt the chances of any candidate who poses as the logical heir of his program.

The worsening economic situation within the U.S. will probably result in the widening of military influence. There are substantial problems in implementing this option. First, the United

States lacks an available external enemy. Since the détentist policies of the Soviet Union and the emerging rapprochement between the United States and China have occurred, the old standby arguments for military preparedness have not been destroyed but they have certainly suffered erosion. Second, the outcome of the Vietnam war has certainly dampened popular enthusiasm for military action. The most devastating feature of the Southeast Asia adventure was the deep understanding by most Americans that the doctrine of United States invincibility was a myth. In any case, short of the employment of nuclear weapons as an instrument of battle, there seems no chance of victory in a "limited war" against a determined popular enemy even if technical superiority can be maintained by the United States throughout.

Which raises the distinct probability of the emergence of new forms of authoritarian rule at home. The pervasive enemy can no longer be located in the rhetoric of the "red peril" or the "yellow peril." The prospects for a war psychosis cannot be precluded if the détente fails. Yet, it is more likely, at least in the near future, that the preponderance of efforts by government and the corporations will be directed toward the elimination of internal sources of opposition.

The most important of these is crushing worker militancy. The propensity of employers to take advantage of adverse economic conditions by demanding increased productivity through speedup and stretchout will certainly encounter working class opposition. The crucial steps now being undertaken by the steel industry to deprive the workers of their strike weapon through voluntary agreement for the arbitration of all disputes including wage disputes is probably going to become the major corporate strategy in the next few years. There is no reason to believe that union leaders are hostile to the deferment of the strike weapon in favor of some important benefits to older members. However, some industries may not be in an economic position to offer sufficient incentives to get such an agreement. Among the options that cannot be precluded is that laws may be proposed to outlaw strikes under certain circumstances if collective bargaining fails. The disruption of production caused by strikes, particularly those directed against rising living costs, will certainly take on a political coloration in the future. Since the government and the largest corporations are closely inter-twined, the development of a definite national incomes policy in the light of the current situation is more probable than ever. The incomes policy may be directed toward preventing workers from maintaining real wages, much less improving them.

There is mounting evidence of a more repressive corporate policy at the work place as well. The careful, systematic weeding out of militants in the auto industry is not confined to organized radicals. Wildcat strikes are being met by summary discharges in the auto industry. This was particularly evident in the 1973 walkout in the Chrysler stamping plant in Detroit, the discharge of the leader of black militants in the Ford Mahwah, New Jersey, plant and more than 40 workers in the Linden, New Jersey, plant of the General Motors Corporation. In all cases, the corporations were given assistance by the United Auto Workers. Similar collusion to crush discontent within the steel, telephone and trucking industries was in evidence during 1973 and 1974. Within the Teamsters Union, for example, the repression spread beyond the shop to include dissenting union officials. The forced retirement of Harold Gibbons, a leading liberal with the union and a vice president for many years, and the government indictments against several well-known local officials who supported George McGovern in 1972 and have maintained their autonomy from the growing centralized power of the national union, were signs that the labor movement was an important target of both the government and the labor bureaucracy.

We are on the road to what Bertram Gross has called "friendly fascism." Unlike its European predecessors, American fascism may not be marked by an "open terroristic dictatorship." The foundation of fascism has already been laid in the consolidation of political and economic power in incredibly few hands. The strengthening of the executive branch of government to the point of almost dictatorial power has taken place without the traditional symbols of repression. No synagogues have been smashed, radical and workers' organizations remain legally operating, and there has been no mass roundup of the Left. Moreover, trade unions can continue to operate as long as they are useful for the implementation of national policy—as long as they assist in the task of disciplining the labor force.

The vocationalization of education and the concomitant decline of the liberal arts and humanities are other features of the gentle repression.

These tendencies are maturing rapidly. The highly publicized secret study by the RAND Corporation prior to the last Presidential election setting forth the conditions under which a national election may be suspended will probably not have to be implemented as long as the Democratic Party, its working class and middle class constituencies, remain in disarray. Democratic forms are always a more effective method of rule as long as the scale of opposition remains sporadic and uncoordinated.

Countervailing the judgment that fascism is arriving without terror is the possible consequence of the crisis of legitimacy. Under these circumstances, resistance may turn into rebellion since the corporate capitalist class lacks the symbols needed to maintain a high degree of trust in its rule. Pluralism as an ideology has declined in proportion to its eclipse in practice. Only the most authoritarian new ideologies such as those which invest wisdom and power in the hands of a single leader may be adequate to the new corporate priorities. Such a leader would have to attach himself to the coat-tails of protest and resistance. The material conditions exist for such a development since the requirement of austerity has no recent legitimation outside of war preparations.

On the other side, the real basis exists for the new radicalism as well. Against the power of central bureaucracies in government and the corporations, the demand for popular control of social and economic institutions and a socialist alternative to the hortatory direction of national life has greater resonance, at least incipiently, among the population. The question of revolutionary politics is no longer to be regarded as rhetorical, but may be seen as a practical chance to overcome the long-term movement toward regimentation, military discipline in the work place and in the neighborhood and the ultimate danger of war as the only resolution of the crisis.

Resistance to the authoritarian tendencies inherent in the food and energy crises cannot be confined to proposals for the restoration of the balance of government power in the direction of greater legislative autonomy and control, although this step is certainly desirable. Nor would government ownership of energy industries contribute significantly to stemming the assault on living standards as long as the government itself remains structurally tied to the corporate economy.

Certainly the history of government regulation of big industry in the past seventy-five years within the United States reveals that it has consistently operated in the interest of the regulated rather than the public. The greatest beneficiaries of the controls of the last several years were the corporations themselves. Government antitrust policies have never been directed against the most powerful corporations, except in token measures. In the main, antitrust has been a weapon of the largest corporations against the upstarts. The use of government regulation to foster economic concentration rather than competition has been far more significant than its trust busting activities under both Republican and Democratic administrations.

The real alternatives are to be found, not in strengthening central government administration of the economy, but in a radically new technology and mode of social control. On one hand, new forms of energy can be developed to replace the regressive coal and oil industries. The solar, geothermal and fusion sources of energy do not rely on fossils, would not require the devastation of the physical environment and would not be limited in their quantities. To be sure, some of the technologies for the use of such sources are "uneconomical" in relation to the ratio of capital investment to profit, and research is still at a relatively low level, particularly in terms of the practical issues involved. But it is plain that government policy is now directed toward finding new sources of coal and oil rather than using tax money for research in new fields. This is a political, not a technical, question.

On the other hand, the new energy sources would permit new modes of management. Public power need not imply government monopoly. Instead it could be managed by workers and consumers on a local level, and central resources could be confined to research and coordination. Solar, windmill and fusion power, by their very nature, lend themselves to decentralized systems of coordination and administration.

The movement for new social arrangements presupposes more

than an articulate political opposition. In fact it may be argued that a genuine radical alternative to the global policies of the supranationals cannot be generated without a new sense of self-awareness among the population.

The central ingredient of this self awareness is already apparent in the impulse away from the wanton consumption of social waste, the subversive character of the end of patriotism, and the incipient efforts of young Americans to redefine their priorities. The creation of countercultural communities in the late 1960s was a form of political opposition to the material foundations of the United States corporate system to the extent that it represented a rejection of atomistic ways of life. But this counterculture was successfully isolated from the main-stream of American politics and culture and failed to penetrate the consciousness of most Americans.

It remains imperative that we examine how the giant cor-porations were able to impose their priorities on the whole country without encountering effective opposition. The main point of this book has been to argue that the explanation of events of the past two years cannot be confined to the cate-gories of administrative and political manipulation, or repres-sion by force, although these have been marked features of the energy and food coups that were successfully completed in 1972–73.

The capacity of the United States to avoid the most repres-sive forms of rule available to human beings in wartime and economic crisis was always predicated on the privileged position enjoyed by this country in terms of standard of living, produc-tive expansion and being spared from physical destruction. These presuppositions no longer obtain. And herein lies the danger. The advances in military technology make United States destruction as probable in the event of another war as that of any other country. The decline of the United States *national* economy has raised the question of whether the erosion of all democratic forms in this country can be justified in terms of economic superiority over others. This is the real choice now before Americans: *shall we, on the basis of our internalized sense of helplessness to deal with global issues, accept the game plan of the large corporations and its unintended consequences, or shall the means be found to offer more than resistance, that is, concerted efforts to overcome the crisis on the basis of a broad, democratic movement for the transfer of management over our economy and social life?*

Glossary

Automatic stabilizers—Structural features of American capitalism that tend to slow down a decline (or advance) of the economy. These include the progressive income tax and unemployment compensation. They are automatic in the sense that they do not require new legislation.

Cartel—When applied to the international economy, a formal (often secret) agreement between large multinational corporations and/or governments (see OPEC) to fix prices and engage in other practices designed to avoid competition.

Consumer price index—A government-computed, weighted average of prices of several hundred commonly purchased consumer commodities. It is the basis for wage adjustments by unions that have cost-of-living or escalator clauses.

Devaluation—A deliberate step undertaken by governments to reduce the value of their currency in relationship to gold and hence to other foreign currencies. Invariably, an attempt to expand exports (now cheaper) and reduce imports (now more expensive) to correct a deficit in the balance of payments.

Eurodollars—Vast sums of American dollars held by European financial institutions, mainly commercial banks.

Fiscal policy—Government actions designed to curb inflation (by raising taxes or lowering government spending) or prevent recession (by lowering taxes and increasing government spending).

Inflation—Rising prices for goods and service. Economists refer to cost-push inflation, as inflation generated by increases in the costs of production (usually labor), and demand-pull inflation, as increases in spending not matched by increases in the supply of goods and service.

International Monetary Fund—The IMF was established by the Bretton Woods Conference of 1944 to stabilize international trade by making it possible for nations running a deficit in their balance of payments to obtain foreign exchange without deflating their economies into a depression.

Keynesian economics—John Maynard Keynes held that depressions were caused by a lack of aggregate demand—in particular, insufficient private investment. The remedy, according to modern Keynesians, is to counter the drop in private investment by increases in government spending, decreases in taxes or increases in the availability of credit. Since World War II, Keynesian economics has also come to refer to a set of policies designed to stop inflation by doing the opposite of the above. In spite of a growing gap between the theory and reality, Keynesian economics remains the reigning orthodoxy of the day.

Kondratieff cycle—Nikolai D. Kondratieff, a Russian, suggested in 1925 that there are long waves or cycles in capitalist development lasting approximately fifty years. While generally ignored or even ridiculed by most economists (a noted exception being the late Joseph A. Schumpeter of Harvard University), the notion of a Kondratieff cycle has recently enjoyed a mini-revival.

Labor force—The Bureau of Labor Statistics defines the civilian labor force as the civilian, noninstitutional population, sixteen years old and over, who are employed or who are unemployed but are actively looking for work. This definition has been the source of much controversy, since it excludes many unemployed people who are too discouraged to seek work. As a consequence, many economists believe the unemployment rate is highly underestimated.

LIFO-FIFO accounting methods

LIFO: *Last In–First Out*—A method for valuing inventories in which stock on hand is priced at the unit costs of the oldest items. It is based on the assumption that the last items purchased or produced are the first items sold. This method minimizes the effect of inflation on the inventory account in the balance sheet. Many firms are switching to LIFO to reduce reported inventory profits, thereby reducing their tax bill.

FIFO: *First In–First Out*—The more common method of valuing inventories in which stock on hand is priced at the unit cost of the most recent items produced. FIFO is based on the assumption that the first items produced or purchased are the first items sold. Under FIFO a rise in prices will tend to inflate reported profits.

Labor-force participation rate—The percentage of the total noninstitutional population which is in the labor force. Also broken down by race, age and sex.

Liquidity crisis—A situation when the ratio of liquid assets to debts currently falling due is historically low. In such a situation, a decline in sales can result in bankruptcy.

Monetarism—A school of economic thought originating at the University of Chicago, and led by Milton Friedman, which argues that inflation, depression and growth can and should be controlled exclusively through control of the money supply.

Monetary policy—Actions of the Federal Reserve—open-market purchases (or sales), reductions in bank-reserve ratios, etc.—to control the supply of money, interest rates and credit, and thereby regulate the economy.

Money supply—Under the most common definition, the sum of checking accounts and cash (coins and currency). Cash makes up a very small percentage of the total. Under a broader definition, the money supply also includes time deposits such as saving accounts.

"Most favored nation" agreement—A trade agreement between two countries by which they agree to extend to each other the benefit of any concession made to any other country. Currently a bargaining point in the U.S.-Soviet détente.

Multiplier effect—The ratio of the total change in national income to a change in new investment or other spending. The idea of the multiplier is that increased spending—caused, for example, by an increase in military expenditures—brings about an increase in national income greater than the original increase in government spending itself.

OPEC—The Organization of Petroleum Exporting Countries, OPEC is a cartel whose purpose is to maximize oil benefits for its members. It began in 1960 and it includes Abu Dhabi, Algeria, Indonesia, Iran, Iraq, Kuwait, Libya, Nigeria, Qator, Saudi Arabia, Venezuela and Ecuador.

Petrodollars—Enormous accumulation of money, usually dollars, earned from petroleum sales, held by some oil-exporting nations (see OPEC). Viewed by Western powers as a potential source of economic chaos.

Phillips curve—Theory which says that there is a trade-off between unemployment and inflation whereby a rise in the one would be matched by a decline in the other.

Prime interest rate—The interest rate charged by banks to the largest and most creditworthy corporations.

Real wages—A measure of wages that corrects the actual money earnings workers receive for changes (usually rises) in the price level.

Recycling—Petrodollars which oil-producing countries return to the world economy through loans to American and European banks. Unless further reloaned to the weaker oil-consuming countries, such as Italy, recycling is incomplete, jeopardizing the solvency of these countries, and hence the stability of the capitalist world.

Reserve army of labor—A term used by Karl Marx to mean those workers who can be brought into production but who remain unemployed. Marx called them a reserve army because they are held in reserve by the capitalist class for use when new workers are needed.

Revaluation—An increase in a currency's price in relation to gold or another currency. West Germany revalued a number of times during recent years to combat inflation.

Reserve ratio—The percentage of a bank's total deposits which the bank has to keep as a reserve. By manipulating the reserve ratio the Federal Reserve Board can regulate credit.

Special drawing rights—In 1968 the IMF created special drawing rights (SDR's) to supplement gold and dollars as currency reserves. SDR's are sometimes referred to as "paper gold." SDR's are only used in transactions among governments and central banks and are backed by the obligations of IMF members to accept them and pay a convertible currency in return.

Suggested Readings

Business and Government Periodicals

Business Week. Weekly magazine giving business news in readable form.

Economist. British economic weekly magazine known for its informed, pungent and conservative views.

First National City Monthly Economic Letter. Monthly economic analysis put out by First National City Bank.

Fortune. Monthly magazine, with in-depth articles from a business point of view.

Monthly Labor Review. Monthly labor statistics and analysis put out by the Labor Department.

Morgan Guaranty Survey. Similar to the First National City newsletter. Put out by the Morgan Guaranty Trust Co.

Survey of Current Business. Monthly publication of the U.S. Department of Commerce, containing detailed current economic data and some analytical articles.

Wall Street Journal. Well-known and respected business daily newspaper.

Radical Periodicals on the Crisis

Dollars & Sense. A monthly bulletin of economic affairs sponsored by the Union for Radical Political Economics (see below). For information, write to *Dollars & Sense,* 324 Somerville Avenue, Somerville, Mass. 02143. Subscription rate: $5 per year.

Economic Notes. Published monthly by Labor Research Association, 80 East 11th Street, New York, N.Y. 10003. Rates are 30 cents a copy or $3 per year.

Monthly Review. Published monthly except in July and August, when bimonthly. 62 West 14th Street, New York, N.Y. 10011. Subscription rates: regular, one year, $9; student rate, $7 per year.

Socialist Revolution. Published bimonthly. 396 Sanchez Street, San Francisco, Calif. 94114. Subscription rate: $10 per year.

Union for Radical Political Economics. URPE attempts to develop economic analyses that serve the interests of people struggling for progressive change. URPE brings together people who see the need for a drastic re-evaluation of the role of the economist in our society.

The organization publishes a quarterly journal, the *Review of Radical Political Economics* (*RRPE*), resource materials and a newsletter. Membership with subscription to the *RRPE* and Newsletter is $20 (high income), $7.50 to $20 (low income), $30 (institutions). Write to URPE, Office of Organizational Services, Michigan Union, Ann Arbor, Mich. 48104.

URPE-PEA—*Political Education and Action* (PEA) was established by URPE to provide information, analyses and contacts to labor, community and other progressive groups. PEA has produced a "food packet" and an "energy packet" containing studies of specific aspects of the food and energy industries, from which reading #47 was taken. PEA is currently working on other packets, including one on the economic crisis from which readings #11, #17, #18, #25, #51, and #52 were excerpted. PEA also attempts to fill requests for research on economic problems, and produces occasional news releases and reports. Write URPE/PEA, 133 West 14th Street, New York, N.Y. 10011.

Books on the Current Economic Crisis

Aronowitz, Stanley, *Food, Shelter and the American Dream.* New York, Seabury Press, 1974.

Baran, Paul, and Sweezy, Paul, *Monopoly Capital.* New York, Monthly Review Press, 1966.

Braverman, Harry, *Labor and Monopoly Capital: The Degradation of Work in the Twentieth Century.* New York, Monthly Review Press, 1974.

Dowd, Douglas, *The Twisted Dream: Capitalist Development in the U.S. since 1776.* Cambridge, Mass., Winthrop Publishers, 1974.

Kolko, Joyce, *America and the Crisis of World Capitalism.* Boston, Beacon Press, 1974.

Magdoff, Harry, *The Age of Imperialism.* New York, Monthly Review Press, 1969.

O'Connor, James, *The Fiscal Crisis of the State.* New York, St. Martin's Press, 1973.

Perlo, Victor, *The Unstable Economy.* New York, International Publishers, 1973.

Robbins, Harold, *The American Food Scandal.* New York, Morrow, 1974.

Sweezy, Paul, and Magdoff, Harry, *Dynamics of U.S. Capitalism.* New York, Monthly Review Press, 1972.

Tanzer, Michael, *The Energy Crisis: World Struggle for Power and Wealth.* New York, Monthly Review Press, 1975.

————, *Political Economy of International Oil and the Underdeveloped Countries.* Boston, Beacon Press, 1969.

Weisskopf, Thomas E., Edwards, Richard C., and Reich, Michael (eds.), *The Capitalist System.* Englewood Cliffs, N.J., Prentice-Hall, 1972.

About the Editor

DAVID MERMELSTEIN is a native of Baltimore, born in September, 1933. A graduate of Amherst College, he received his Ph.D. in economics from Columbia University. He is the editor of *Economics: Mainstream Readings and Radical Critiques* (New York, Random House, 2d ed., 1973) and co-editor (with Marvin E. Gettleman) of *The Great Society Reader: The Failure of American Liberalism* (New York, Random House, 1967 [2d ed., 1970, entitled *The Failure of American Liberalism: After the Great Society*]). His articles and reviews have appeared in such journals and magazines as *Monthly Review, Science & Society,* the *American Economic Review* and the *Quarterly Review of Economics and Business,* among others.

A member of the New American Movement and the Union for Radical Political Economics, Mr. Mermelstein is an Associate Professor of Economics at the Polytechnic Institute of New York. He lives with his daughter Julie on Manhattan's Upper West Side.

VINTAGE BIOGRAPHY AND AUTOBIOGRAPHY

VINTAGE WORKS OF SCIENCE
AND PSYCHOLOGY